Persistent Inequalities

Persistent Inequalities

Women and World Development

Edited by
IRENE TINKER

New York   Oxford
OXFORD UNIVERSITY PRESS
1990

Oxford University Press

Oxford   New York   Toronto
Delhi   Bombay   Calcutta   Madras   Karachi
Petaling Jaya   Singapore   Hong Kong   Tokyo
Nairobi   Dar es Salaam   Cape Town
Melbourne   Auckland

and associated companies in
Berlin   Ibadan

Library of Congress Cataloging-in-Publication Data
Persistent inequalities: women and world development
edited by Irene Tinker.
p.   cm.   Bibliography: p.   Includes index.
ISBN 0-19-505935-2 ISBN 0-19-506158-6 (pbk.)
1. Women in development.   I. Tinker, Irene.
HQ1240.P48   1990 305.4′2 — dc20   89-32559   CIP

9 8 7 6 5 4

Printed in the United States of America
on acid-free paper

Preface

This book is a celebration of Ester Boserup and her pathbreaking work, *Woman's Role in Economic Development*; of the thousands of activist women who lobbied for and through the United Nations Decade for Women to put women on the world agenda; and of the hundreds of development practitioners and scholars, women and men, who have broadened and deepened our knowledge of the persistent inequalities facing women everywhere.

This book aims to provide an introduction to the field of women in development by offering an overview of the past and current debates in the field that have challenged many earlier assumptions about development and the reality of women's work and lives within and outside the household. In addition, the book shows both the connection between this field and the global women's movement and the impact that these advocates and new scholarship on women have had on the policies and programs of development agencies. It presents material useful for university courses both in mainstream economic development and in women's studies, while offering itself as a basic book for the growing number of courses on women and development.

Authors included in this collection come from both developed and developing countries; among the authors are theoreticians and practitioners, development economists and feminist scholars, men as well as women. Each one has, in remarkably different ways, addressed the question that binds the volume together: why do inequalities persist? Are current assumptions about development and women inaccurate or biased? Have we framed the inquiry around the wrong values or goals? This book is a celebration of opening, but it is a chronicling of an unfair reality that must be addressed.

Purposefully, these writers represent a broad range of ideological persuasions. Thus there is no advocacy in this volume for a particular interpretation of history, or of economic development, or of the future. Throughout the volume, this diversity of proponents and the debates among them are reflected as the authors interweave policy and programmatic issues into their theoretical discussions. The various chapters often contradict or challenge one another, clearly demonstrating the dynamism being released as scholars utilize new insights into male–female relationships in their interpretations of economic development theory. The unifying theme is women; the unifying problem is the persistence of inequities in the face of development; the unifying goal is the identification of approaches that will improve women's condition.

As always along the path from idea to realization, putting together a book of this scope has been the enterprise of many people, all of whom have my deepest thanks. The concept of a book interpreting the field of women in development for the academic community arose from the realization that all the studies and data produced for the U.N. Decade for Women had had remarkably little impact on either development economists or women's studies scholars in the universities. For years the policy papers produced by the Equity Policy Center under my direction had drawn on scholarly research; it seemed timely to reverse that process. A planning seminar for the book held in May 1985 at Cremona Plantation in southern Maryland was preceded by many letters and discussions with both those who participated and others who were unable to attend. Funding for the seminar was provided by the Ford Foundation and the International Development Research Centre. Members of the development and scholarly communities in Washington read and commented on the chapters as they were submitted. Staff of the Equity Policy Center helped plan and run the seminar and assisted in various phases of the book; editors Noelle Beatty and Susan Gibbs ensured that all the chapters were accessible to the nonspecialist.

The bulk of my final editing for the book was undertaken while I was also visiting professor in the International Development Program of The American University; Ann Held rendered much needed logistical support while research assistants JoAnne Yaeger, Lisa Pruegl, and Sara Grusky helped at various stages of the editing process. The authors must be thanked for their dedication in writing and revising their contributions. Most particularly I wish to express my profound gratitude to my colleague Jane Jaquette and my husband Millidge Walker for their critical support throughout.

Chevy Chase, Md.   I.T.
February 1989

Contents

Contributors

SIMI AFONJA is a Reader in the Department of Sociology and Anthropology at the Obafemi Awolowo University in Nigeria. She has contributed chapters to four significant books on women and development, published numerous articles on gender inequality, and is coeditor of *Social Change in Nigeria*. She participated in a United Nations University study on primary health care and was recently appointed project director of the Canadian-Nigerian Linkage Program in Women's Studies.

ESTER BOSERUP began her career as an economist with the Danish government, then worked for ten years for the U.N. Commission for Europe. Her field work in India (1957 to 1959) helped crystallize the theories she presented in her three related books, *Conditions of Agricultural Growth*, *Women's Role in Economic Development*, and *Population and Technological Change*. She is a member of and presides over various research boards and committees in Danish and U.N. organizations.

SUSAN C. BOURQUE is Professor of Government and Director of the Project on Women and Social Change at Smith College. She is the author of *Cholification and the Campesino*, coauthor with Kay Warren of *Women of the Andes: Patriarchy and Social Change in Two Peruvian Towns*, and coeditor of *Women Living Change* and *Learning About Women: Gender, Politics and Power*. Her current research focuses on the state, development, and women's education.

CHARLOTTE BUNCH, a founder of Washington, D.C. Women's Liberation and of *Quest: A Feminist Quarterly*, has edited seven anthologies; her latest book is *Passionate Politics: Feminist Theory in Action*. She has worked extensively on issues of global feminism and now holds the Laurie New Jersey chair in Women's Studies at Douglass College, Rutgers University, where she and Roxanna Carrillo teach a course on feminist theory and strategies for the women's movement internationally.

ROXANNA CARRILLO, Peruvian feminist organizer and journalist, was a founder of Centro de la Mujer Peruana: Flora Tristan and Centro de Documentacion sobre la Mujer in Lima. An organizer of the II Feminist Encuentro for Latin America and of international workshops in Nairobi, she is presently a graduate student in Women and Politics at Rutgers University.

JANE S. JAQUETTE is Professor of Political Science at Occidental College. She edited *Women in Politics*, coedited *Women in Developing Countries: A Policy Focus*, and is currently finishing an edited book on women and democracy in Latin America. She has written extensively on women in development issues and female participation and is currently working on developing a feminist critique of power.

KEN KUSTERER is an economic sociologist at The American University in Washington. He has carried out research on the social impact of capitalist firms, especially agribusiness, in eight countries of the Americas. Married with grown and growing children, he and Faith Petrazualo Kusterer have been dialoguing about domestic production for most of their lives.

LINDA Y. C. LIM is an economist from Singapore who teaches Southeast Asian Studies and International Business at the University of Michigan. A frequent consultant for international development agencies, she has published widely on the economies of Southeast Asia and the Asian nonindustrialized countries, especially on industrialization, trade, foreign investment, labor, and women in development.

JOYCELIN MASSIAH is the Head of the Institute of Social and Economic Research at the University of the West Indies, Barbados. In addition to writing many articles and research reports in demography and women in development, she is the general editor of *Women in the Caribbean Project: Research Papers* and serves on various national, regional, and international boards.

VINA MAZUMDAR is Director of the Centre for Women's Development Studies in New Delhi. She founded the Centre in 1980 to carry out work she had begun as member-secretary of the Centre on the Status of Women in India and as director of the program for women's studies of the Indian Council of Social Science Research. She brings her earlier teaching of political science to her analysis of women's inequalities in India.

CHRISTINE OBBO is Associate Professor of Anthropology at Wayne State University. She is the author of *African Women: Their Struggle for Economic Independence* and a number of articles. Her major research interests are social change, urbanization, and gender.

HANNA PAPANEK is currently Senior Research Associate at the Center for Asian Development Studies and the Department of Anthropology, Boston University. Since 1984 she has also been codirector of a United Nations University project on women in South and Southeast Asia. She has written many articles on women and development, edited several books, and been an active participant in the new scholarship on women.

AMARTYA K. SEN is Lamont University Professor at Harvard University and teaches in the Department of Economics and Philosophy. His publications include *Collective Choice and Social Welfare, On Economic Inequality, Poverty and Famines, Commodities and Capabilities*, and *On Ethics and Economics*. He is a past president of the Econometric Society and currently the president of the International Economics Association.

BENJAMIN SENAUER is a professor in the Department of Agricultural and Applied Economics at the University of Minnesota, where he has been on the faculty since 1974. He spent 1978 to 1979 with the U.S. Department of Agriculture and 1984 to 1985 with the International Food Policy Research Institute in Washington, D.C. His research interests include household behavior, food consumption patterns and trends, and food and nutrition policy both in developing and developed countries.

KUMUD SHARMA is a Senior Fellow at the Centre for Women's Development Studies in New Delhi. She has written a number of articles and served as a research officer on the Committee on the Status of Women and as Assistant Director of the Women's Studies Programme in the Indian Council of Social Science Research.

IRENE TINKER has devoted her professional life to being both an activist and a scholar. As founder-president of the Equity Policy Center (EPOC), the International Center for Research on Women, and the U.S. Council for INSTRAW (the U.N. International Research and Training Institute for the Advancement of Women), she has both conducted research and lobbied. Currently she is a professor at the University of California, Berkeley, where she holds a joint appointment in the Departments of City and Regional Planning and in Women's Studies.

KAY B. WARREN is Professor of Anthropology at Princeton University, where she also served as founding director of the Program in Women's Studies. She wrote *The Symbolism of Subordination: Indian Identity in a Guatemalan Town* and is coauthor with Susan Bourque of *Women of the Andes: Patriarchy and Social Change in Two Peruvian Towns*. She is currently studying ethnicity and cultural constructions of violence in Guatemala and writing on women and international development in Latin America.

INTRODUCTION

1

A Context for the Field and for the Book

IRENE TINKER

Since the mid-1970s, an increasing number of women and men concerned with global equity have become aware that both planned and unplanned development have too often had an adverse impact on women (Tinker & Bo Bramsen 1976). The resurgence of the worldwide women's movement has legitimized the investigation of women as a distinct category; it has also documented how these inequities persist across class, cultural, and ethnic lines and how they vary in form and intensity. The resultant flood of research has washed away many conceptions and assumptions about the worlds of work and power and household which had been based on male perceptions and experience.

It is important to understand at the outset, however, that the field of women in development began as a policy concern focused on changing the priorities and practices of the development assistance agencies. Although anthropological university-based research published before 1970 formed the basis of early advocacy, the more recent studies of the impact of development on women have been stimulated and often funded by development agencies as they sought to carry out the new policy directives issued as a result of this advocacy. Thus the field of women in development now encompasses the thoughts and goals of the advocate, the practitioner, and the scholar.

The tripartite origin of the field of women in development is responsible not only for the considerable impact this field has had on development agencies but also for its near invisibility in university curricula. To explain this apparent paradox, some history is in order.

ORIGIN AND IMPACT OF THE FIELD

The decade of the 1970s was an optimistic one for the international women's movement. The United Nations Decade for Women 1976–85 heralded the acceptance of women's concerns as legitimate issues for national and international policy. How to integrate women in development became the subject of newly created offices in nearly every development agency. The international women's movement itself expanded exponentially. It is no longer a network solely of the urbanized and Westernized educated elite; in both developing and industrialized countries, women's groups can be found in villages or among domestic servants as often as among college graduates.

The study of women also became legitimate as a topic of research on most U.S. university campuses, leading to a phenomenal increase in the number of dissertations written about women. Research centers on women have been established in nearly every state in the United States and in many capitals around the world. Women of the South in developing countries are increasingly challenging the approaches and theories propounded by their colleagues of the industrialized North.[1] Multifold opportunities exist, within the U.N. system and through scholarly organizations, for these women to meet and debate on a frequent basis.

This was not the case in 1975 when we began planning the first major international Seminar on Women in Development at the Office of International Science of the American Association for the Advancement of Science, which was to be held in Mexico City just prior to the International Women's Conference. The objective of this seminar was to bring together scholars, practitioners, and advocates to explore reasons why development programs so often failed to reach and benefit women and to emphasize the waste of human potential that has resulted from ignoring the contribution of women to economic and social growth. Hardly any of the 95 women and men from 55 countries had ever met before! At that seminar, the participants began an

---

[1]Terminology used to group countries at various stages of development is infused with political or economic valuation. The use of North or South to refer to the industrialized countries versus the developing countries is a reflection of debates that characterized the United Nations in the late 1970s when the Group of 77 developing countries, soon to number over 100, demanded new terms of trade with the North. This somewhat inaccurate geographical terminology (Australia and New Zealand are considered part of the North) avoids the equally inaccurate political or economic terminology used previously.

Economically, countries emerging from colonial rule in the 1940s and 1950s, were called "underdeveloped" or "less developed countries" or LDCs. As differences in the stage of development among these countries became evident, the term LDC was restricted to the 30 or so Least Developed Countries. Still, "developing countries" continues to be used as an umbrella term that includes the LDCs, the NICs (newly industrializing countries such as Taiwan and South Korea), the OPEC nations, and the middle-tier countries such as Brazil and Venezuela. Politically, because many newly independent countries joined the Non-Aligned Nations group, they were often referred to as the Third World to distinguish them from the First (West and democratic) or Second (East and communist). Given the political diversity that exists among them today, this terminology is also unsatisfactory but still widely used.

analysis of the problem of persistent inequalities which this book continues to address.[2]

In 1975 we naively assumed that correcting the biases of data concerning women's work and exposing the constraints on women's education and credit would automatically solve many of the inequalities as planners incorporated new data and insights into their programming. Chapters in this book document and evaluate a wide range of such efforts to include women in development programs. These examples illustrate the complexities surrounding social change as power relationships within and without the household and economic priorities of both the formal and informal systems affect microefforts to ameliorate women's lives. However, since most studies of women in development have been undertaken for development agencies, their conclusions have been directed at influencing program directions or policy decisions rather than at questioning the values and goals of the process or challenging the theoretical underpinnings of economic development in general or of the contracting agency in particular. Because these studies avoid theoretical stances, which are the stuff of scholarly debate, and because they tend to exist in fugitive form, which makes them difficult for most university faculty to secure, this research has not yet been widely utilized by the academic community despite its value as real world case studies.

On the other hand, the policies championed by the women in development community have strongly influenced the way development agencies design and implement programs. Planners who scoffed at considering women in any role beyond motherhood now design programs to ensure that women participate in and benefit from development programs. They do so primarily for practical reasons: efforts to improve the lives of the poor work better and are a more efficient use of funding when women are involved. Such interventions have helped thousands of women obtain credit or education or jobs.

Despite the recognition of the importance of including women in the planning and implementation of development programs, much of the early optimism about the ability of practitioners to greatly alter the lives of poor women in developing countries has been moderated. New agricultural crops and new technologies have increased women's work burden as often as they have reduced it. Rapid urbanization and the pressures for two incomes per family have resulted in more women entering both the formal and informal labor force; but the control of this income and the sharing of the increased work burden are still too often hostage to patriarchal control (Dwyer & Bruce 1988). The global economic downturn has pressed most heavily on women-headed households, which are everywhere in the world the poorest of the poor, exemplifying the phrase "the feminization of poverty."

---

[2] Twelve background papers for the seminar, a list of participants, and summaries of the five workshops on food production/technology, urbanization/employment, education, health/population, and women's organizations appear in Tinker and Bo Bramsen (1976).

The need to explore the reasons why development programs that help some women in some places have adverse effects in others has forced advocates and practitioners to look for the root causes of unintended results or failures. In doing so, they have intersected with feminist scholars who have been criticizing mainstream development theories because they view the world through a male lens. Both scholars and practitioners find it essential to examine the structures of the family and to analyze power and work within as well as outside that unit. The authors in this book are representative of the scholars now trying to rethink the assumptions and solutions about development and women.

CONCEPTUALIZING THE BOOK

The working title of this book, *Persistent Inequalities: Rethinking Assumptions About Development and Women*, was a collective choice of those authors who gathered in late May 1985 at a seminar convened by the Equity Policy Center (EPOC) at Cremona Plantation in southern Maryland to present their ideas on the "state of the art" in the field of women in development.[3] Although the subtitle proved too long for the publisher, it is quite descriptive. Essentially we argue that the new scholarship on women not only has challenged the entire spectrum of development theories but has also altered the definitions of such fundamental concepts as household and work. This new understanding is of practical use to those agencies that are in the business of funding development. For example, the predictability of who benefits from food subsidies is increased if intrahousehold distribution of food is factored into program design. Similarly, new insights on control of women's income can assist advocates to frame and propose more equitable development policies.

Participants at the Cremona seminar represented all three viewpoints of the scholar, the practitioner, and the advocate; it is fair to say that some of us have worn all three hats at one time or another. Indeed, the difficulty of separating these views has led to much of the confusion among observers as to the meaning of the term women in development. Chapter 3 of this book analyzes the origins and augmentation of these various views in an attempt to provide a coherent history of the field.

The original idea for this volume came from a desire to honor Ester Boserup for her book *Woman's Role in Economic Development*, which provided a conceptual foundation for the field. However, the unifying theme of the book is not primarily an examination of her profound insights; rather it is an exploration of how the expanding impact of women in development

[3]Participants at the Cremona seminar included authors Simi Afonja, Ester Boserup, Jane Jaquette, Vina Mazumdar, Christine Obbo, Hanna Papanek, Kumud Sharma, and Irene Tinker. Others attending were Neuma Aguiar (Brazil), Rosemary Aquino (Philippines), Rounaq Jahan (Bangladesh), Deniz Kandiyoti (Turkey), Sarah Loza (Egypt), Per Pinstrup-Andersen (Denmark), Vesna Pesic (Yugoslavia), and Millidge Walker (United States).

studies is changing the way scholars, practitioners, and advocates view the world. Since Boserup's ideas stimulated much of this activity, it seems useful to review them here.

Boserup's Thesis

Ester Boserup's 1970 book was part of her trilogy on economic development related to agriculture, women, and population. Her viewpoint then and now, as clearly expounded in her contribution to this volume, is that population density provides the critical mass necessary to develop and sustain technological change in agriculture, and that such technology requires an increase of labor input, which alters the work assignments of women and men. Boserup's book drew extensively on her familiarity with European development gained as a result of her work with the Danish government during World War II and later with the U.N. Economic Commission for Europe in Geneva. The concept for the trilogy, however, was triggered by her experiences in India, where she and her husband went as part of a research team working with Gunnar Myrdal as he geared up to write his extensive study of development, *Asian Drama*.

Returning to Denmark, she published *The Condition of Agricultural Growth* in 1965. In that book Boserup attributes the existence of various types of farming systems as a response to population pressure rather than to soil or climate, the dominant theories of the time. Since the progression from shifting cultivation toward more intensive agricultural systems requires more—not less—labor, Boserup argues that it is a mistake to assume widespread rural unemployment, however seasonally or underemployed rural men might be. In her view, rapid rural–urban migration might delay rural development while adding immeasurably to inequities between women and men.

The changing gender relationships as societies moved from extensive shifting cultivation to more intensive farming systems was a major focus in her 1970 book. She identifies shifting cultivation as a female farming system, typified by Africa, and plow cultivation as a male farming system, typified by South Asia. More intensive cultivation of irrigated fields, such as rice farming in Southeast and East Asia, increases the labor of both women and men. Boserup notes that female farming is found in Latin America among the Indians and the African immigrant communities, but she includes the rest of Latin America in her category of male farming systems. Since the publication of her book, several scholars of Latin America agriculture have documented the ambiguity of women's roles in agricultural production where the Indian culture mixes with the Spanish–Arab influences to produce a composite system that fits uneasily into the male–female dichotomy (Bourque & Warren 1981a; Deere & Leon 1980, 1987; Huntington 1975).

Boscrup's designation of towns in developing countries as male towns and female towns has received much less attention, perhaps because of the general lack of interest in urban studies among the development community as well as the predominance of theoretical debates over the informal sector or the globalization of multinational industry. Female towns, generally located in areas of female farming systems, are characterized by the visibility of women traders. Male towns are of two types: those that actually have a surplus of men caused by higher migration rates for men and those where women are secluded so that visually the town is predominantly male. Employment in bazaar and service occupations provides an intermediary step between agriculture and modern occupations for both women and men. Boserup argues that the recruitment of women into the modern sector helps accelerate economic growth, a view that contradicts assumptions held by many bureaucrats who assume women at work necessarily replace men. She rounds out her book with observations on the need for improved educational opportunities for women.

The scope and clarity of her presentation made *Woman's Role in Economic Development* the fundamental text for the U.N. Decade for Women. Her presentation was theoretically original and, in her mind, noncontroversial. She simply utilized existing studies to illustrate how the division of labor between women and men shifted as economic development proceeded with its gradual change from family production of goods and services to specialized production. Previous books had focused on change in selected countries or documented the impact such change had on lives of individual women (Paulme 1960; Ward 1963). In contrast, Boserup pointed out that the introduction of modern technologies and the expansion of cash cropping benefited men while often increasing women's work burden both as family and casual labor—thus indicting the prevailing assumptions held by economic planners that their efforts benefited everyone.

Feminist scholars cited and contested her work. For those of us immersed in trying to change development policies, her analysis of women's work in agriculture provided a basic justification for arguing that economic assistance should reach rural women as well as men. Clearly, she well deserves her eminence among women concerned with development. Ester Boserup, a consummate independent woman of her age, is nonetheless uncomfortable with the often strident advocacy of militant feminists and has continued to insist that she is a scholar who happens to be a woman, not a feminist who might use scholarship to her purpose. Perhaps it is this very dedication to scholarship that has made her so invaluable to the field.

ORGANIZATION OF THE BOOK

Ester Boserup's ability to crystallize global trends caused by modernization is beautifully illustrated in her contribution to this book. She expands her observations on the impact of economic change on women by analyzing how age, sex, class, and race hierarchies modify changes in women's roles in different types of societies. Thus industrialization can have opposing effects on different groups of women. In conclusion, she reminds us all that Western culture was until recently strongly antifeminist and that "it is only as a result of recent economic and demographic changes in the Western countries that their traditional sex hierarchy is beginning to be undermined."

The Politics of Women in Development

Contributors to this section approach the field of women in development from a variety of perspectives, all of which have advocacy as part of their goal. Chapters 3–5 review the global groundswell of women's organizations and networks as they articulated their particular priorities for ameliorating women's lives in every country around the world. The following two chapters focus on a specific issue and delineate the controversies of translating the issue into one of feminist concern.

The field of women in development is set into its historical and political context as Tinker identifies the distinct goals and approaches of the three groups most involved in the field: advocates, practitioners, and scholars. All were motivated by the compelling belief that work enhanced status. Confronted with the paradox that increasing women's opportunities to work often resulted in longer workdays with no commensurate improvement in status, women in all three groups have begun rethinking their assumptions about development and women.

In Chapter 4 Jane Jaquette suggests that Boserup's book provoked such a strong response among feminists because it provided them with an argument of justice based on efficiency. Data that underscore women's lower productivity than men's due to their nurturant role lead Jaquette to argue that feminists must recast their claims for justice. Toward this goal, Jaquette contrasts three meanings of justice in terms of their institutional contexts: equality is enforced by laws, equity by the marketplace, and need by bureaucracy; she discusses the strengths and inadequacies of each.

Charlotte Bunch and Roxanna Carrillo explore the somewhat stormy interrelationships between supporters of women in development and of global feminism. At the start of the U.N. Decade for Women, feminism was perceived as Western and irrelevant by most women from the Third World who focused on development. The growth of feminist organizations in the South and an increasing global knowledge of feminists in the North have moderated the initial misunderstandings and antagonisms. The authors argue that global feminism provides a framework for examining the failure of many efforts to integrate women in development by providing new insights into a just and equitable society.

Susan C. Bourque and Kay B. Warren are concerned with the policy implications of the increasing importance of technology and the comparative lack of women's involvement in technical/scientific education. They identify and contrast four perspectives both in theoretical terms and with regard to their impact on women. Their focus on technology provides concrete illustrations of the differences in approach to development of liberal or Marxist feminists, proponents of the female sphere, and development practitioners. The authors argue that while access to scientific and technological education is imperative to enhance women's opportunities in these fields, the content and structures of education must also be altered.

Linda Y. C. Lim was one of the first to study the socioeconomic impact of export industries that had been set up by multinationals in Third World countries. In her provocative chapter, Lim explores the reasons why this issue, which in fact involves only a tiny proportion of working women in developing countries, became such a *cause célèbre*. She writes that the vision of multinational greed and exploited young women served ideological stances of Marxists, feminists, and trade unionists. As a result, facts were overwhelmed by symbolism as these various protagonists utilized and interpreted reality to suit their purpose.

Taken together, these five chapters document the interaction between global issues of development and the emerging networks of feminist scholars and development professionals. Issues of justice, global feminism, and the value of work have provided basic concepts for the field while more specific problems relating to multinational expansion and technological transfer have aroused a broader public concern. These debates have not only projected new interpretations of reality into a wide range of discussions; they have created their own dialectic, which requires a rethinking of many basic assumptions.

Intrahousehold Distribution and Control

Chapters in this section focus on intrahousehold dynamics, a topic long ignored by economists. Although new household economics has recently focused attention on this unit in economic theory, most feminists reject its underlying assumption that the household through its patriarch maximizes utility for all its members. Economists Amartya K. Sen and Benjamin Senauer move beyond this economic view of the household in their considerations of resource distribution; sociologist Hanna Papanek delves into psychological and social conditioning which perpetuate gender inequalities.

Searching for a framework within which to analyze the household and noting that conflicts of interest within the family are quite unlike other conflicts — say of class — because cooperation is required to maintain the unit, Sen suggests that household negotiations can best be understood in terms of "cooperative conflicts." He argues that individuals within the household are motivated not only by personal well-being but also by their perceptions of obligations and legitimate behavior which should characterize family members. Applying this interpretation to food entitlements within the family, Sen modifies a strictly economic interpretation to take into account the qualitative as well as quantitative relations that influence intrahousehold divisions.

The issue of internal household food allocation is of vital interest to governmental programs designed to ensure basic nutrition to the poor. These programs range from food stamps to ration shops to job creation. To compare the efficiency of various alternatives, greater understanding of intrahousehold economics is essential. At Cremona, Per Pinstrup-Andersen, then head of the Food Consumption and Nutrition Policy Program at the International Food Policy Research Institute (IFPRI), complained that economists had traditionally viewed the household as a black box. To correct this error, he stressed the need for empirical, methodologically sound studies on resource control and consumption within the family, which, in particular, would differentiate women's use of income. Senauer, who was his colleague at IFPRI, analyzes three such studies conducted in Sri Lanka and the Philippines. Each case study is discussed independently; the combined findings indicate that behavior within the household can be modified by improving women's economic opportunities outside the household.

Papanek explores the methods by which patriarchal perceptions of obligations and behavior are imposed on women in Asia. "Compulsory emotions" and required pain are identified as major elements in conditioning women to expect and accept their subordination within the household with its diminished entitlements and patriarchal control over their labor. She emphasizes that this patriarchal control of women's labor diminishes the importance of work as an indicator of higher status or greater self-worth and stresses that economic work is not the only activity valued when families accord status to women.

As these chapters show, the understanding of intrahousehold dynamics is a central problem for economics and sociology, both theoretical and applied. While efforts to assign an economic value to women's unpaid work may influence development planners, such revaluation has had little effect on the status assigned to such work either in developing or industrialized countries. Rather, as was pointed out at the Cremona seminar, the value as well as the fact of women's work is mediated by patriarchy. Yet increasingly this patriarchy is seen as the organization of patriarchal institutions beyond the family, for data indicate that one of every three women is opting out of patriarchal families to head her own household. At the household level itself contradictory trends may be observed. Increased resources from development programs increase patriarchal control as well as female dependency. On the other hand, pressure by women in development advocates and practitioners for greater employment opportunities for women and for increased resources flowing directly to women and women's groups assists women who have rejected patriarchal family life.

Challenging Patriarchy

The tenacity of patriarchy has confounded many feminists, who anticipated its demise along with modernization. Thelma McCormack writes,

> The shock . . . is that patriarchy was itself modernized. . . . It is legitimated not through references to holy texts or sacred scripts but to scientific studies. . . . Male preference, male privilege, and male norms constituting standards of excellence are the outcome of a process which, in theory, should have given us a gender-free division of labor, a set of gender-free standards of achievement, and gender-free institutions. (1981:28)

At the EPOC's Cremona seminar there was heated discussion over the merits and evils of contemporary patriarchal systems. Sarah Loza portrayed the Egyptian version of patriarchy as a benevolent system that protects women while allowing them a good measure of autonomy; "in a society that accepts separate spheres, equality has no meaning." Loza argued that living in a patriarchal household with extended kin support was a much better situation for most women than coping alone with the anarchy of independent living. Deniz Kandiyoti, who fled patriarchy in Turkey, conceded that women must find something in the concept or they would not continue to accept patriarchal control. She hypothesized that different systems of production and kinship represent distinct kinds of "patriarchal bargains" which not only shape "women's culturally specific sense of sexed subjectivity" but also act "as a powerful determinant of women's potential for adaptation or resistance in the face of change."

The patriarchal bargains described by the next four authors vary considerably, but in their discussions on India, East and West Africa, and the Caribbean, they all indicate that patriarchy has consolidated its traditional dominance and expanded its control as these societies have modernized. The explanations are distressingly familiar: inadequate access of women to resources, devaluing of unpaid work, low wages in insecure jobs, male control of women's sexuality. Because these inequities exist across class, the authors emphasize the predominance of gender hierarchies. The earlier debates among Marxist feminists over the relationship of gender and class are largely ignored in the face of this increasing dependency of women.

Vina Mazumdar and Kumud Sharma draw on their extensive research on Indian women to delineate how new forms of subordination and gender asymmetry have superseded the old, leaving patriarchal control firmly lodged in place. Further, they use the example of the Indian textile industry, once a female preserve, to illustrate how the dominant Hindu legacy may be interpreted to reinforce patriarchy. To resist this use of myth and history to maintain existing hierarchies, the authors call for more studies of women's actual, as contrasted to ideal, roles; they also suggest that women mine history to identify "remnants of matriarchal myths and symbols" that might be used to reconstruct gender equality.

Simi Afonja argues that Western writers have become so "beclouded" by the autonomy of West African women traders that they failed to appreciate the extent to which these same women were subordinate to their husbands. In fact, Yoruba farm women had to engage in alternative income activities such as trading, food-processing, or home crafts, because the food they grew was never sufficient. Drawing on historic and contemporary data, Afonja reinterprets women's roles among the Yoruba by showing that patriarchal control did in fact characterize preclass and precolonial society. Under capitalism, women's lack of access to critical resources prevents capital accumulation and so increases dependence on husbands.

Christine Obbo explores subjective dimensions of women's subordination, showing how songs and stories as well as empirically measured reality reaffirm gender differences in her native Uganda. Women are socialized to believe that work, and how they do it, defines both how they think about themselves and how society perceives them. Obbo investigates three categories of urban women who have fled rural areas hoping to negotiate a redefinition of their personal relationships: elite women; incipient elite women; and unskilled women. She concludes that as long as women's work is easily appropriated and until women have greater access to resources, gender inequality will persist in Africa.

Joycelin Massiah reports on a study of women's work in the Commonwealth Caribbean. Because women in the survey saw no distinction between maternal and economic roles, the definition of work was expanded to include "home services." In these small economies, employment opportunities are limited; most women earn income working for others rather than in self-employment or home production. To ensure economic support for themselves and their children, women in residential family unions rely more on assistance from their male partners than do women in visiting unions or who are unattached. But all women work when necessary and may also seek assistance from other family members.

Although these four authors present gloomy pictures of how women's subjugation has in many ways increased with development, each finds some cracks in patriarchy. In both Nigeria and India ancient myths that endow women with economic and psychological strength could be used as the basis for new concepts of women's possibilities. Obbo implicitly calls for new myths to help urban women reject imposed self-perceptions that maintain their subordination. Massiah finds the Caribbean unique not only for its slave history but for its island economy, which affects how women manipulate the system to survive. The variety of family unions which have been traditional in the Caribbean is becoming more universal. The pleasures and difficulties that women face as sole household heads are issues that need much further exploration.

Ken Kusterer predicts the imminent demise of patriarchy as a necessary part of *human* liberation projected by Marxist theory. Utilizing the reinterpretation of Marxism propounded by dependency theorists, he argues that articulation theory can be used to encompass both class and gender in a single explanatory model. He describes the economy of contemporary society as a system of multiple modes of production, dominated usually by the capitalist mode but based importantly on a patriarchal domestic mode; their interaction is primarily responsible for the perpetuation of both poverty and patriarchy in developing societies. This analysis provides a powerful tool for evaluating women in development projects in terms of their ability to break down patriarchal control.

This book, with its blending of theory and practice, of scholarly pursuit and passionate advocacy, is meant to provide the reader with an understanding of the depth and breadth of the field of women in development.

2

Economic Change and the Roles of Women

ESTER BOSERUP

Women's work, women's fertility, and women's role in the family and in society at large are radically changed by economic development. To understand this it is important to view these changes in women's position not as isolated factors but rather as part of general changes that come about as human societies slowly develop from subsistence economies to high-technology societies. Economic development is a gradual change from family production to specialized production of goods and services. This specialization of production makes it possible to use better technologies, scientific methods, and an increasingly elaborate economic and social infrastructure (Boserup 1981).

As economic development proceeds, family production for its own use diminishes and a larger and larger share of goods for family consumption is produced outside the family in specialized enterprises. Moreover, most of the services that family members in subsistence economies produce for each other (including physical protection, health care, and education) are taken over by public institutions or specialized private enterprises. During this process, the family gradually is stripped of most of its original functions. This causes radical changes both in the relation of family members to the outside world and in the relations between family members. All contemporary societies are in transition between subsistence economies and fully specialized economies. Even in highly industrialized countries, production of goods and services in the family, mainly by women, accounts for a considerable share of total work hours. In developing countries family production is much more important, and in the least developed countries it accounts for the major part of total production of goods and services.

FAMILY ORGANIZATION IN SUBSISTENCE ECONOMIES

Pure subsistence producing families are rare today, but the traditional attitudes in many rural areas of the least developed countries continue to be those typical of subsistence economies. The family head has extensive, if not absolute power over other family members. Older people have power over younger people, adults over children, and men over women of the same age group. The extensive power of the family head, and the whole hierarchical organization by age and sex, may have secured the discipline necessary for family survival in difficult circumstances and situations, but it usually results in discrimination in favor of the dominant groups (Sen 1985c). However, under this system women are not the only subservient group. Although they are subservient to husbands, fathers, and brothers, older women have extensive power over younger women and girls, and sometimes over boys and younger men. Old men constitute the top of the power hierarchy, and girls occupy the bottom position, but other age and sex groups are dominating in some relations and subservient in others.

Privileges and obligations are usually distributed according to this ranking. The members of dominating groups enjoy more leisure, perform the most interesting and pleasurable jobs, and pass onerous and tedious jobs to the persons over whom they have power. Other privileges for groups in power are access to the best food and other consumer goods and to sufficient food in times of scarcity, when members of dominated groups may starve. Groups in power also have the right to control the movements and the sexual relations of the members of subservient groups. Under this system, the prime obligation of young men is to secure the physical protection of the family group, and they are trained in weapon use. Young women must do hard work while delegating lighter tasks to children.

The need for self-protection is a strong incentive for rearing large families. Together with the large work burden carried by women and children, this makes subsistence families pronatalist (Boserup 1985). Thus all women are married off at puberty, and since long periods of breastfeeding are important determinants of fertility, women spend their childbearing period under a permanent stress of hard work, pregnancy, or breastfeeding, except for peoples who impose periods of postpartum abstinence even longer than the periods of breastfeeding. Under these conditions, female morbidity and mortality, spontaneous abortion, and child mortality reach such high levels that few women succeed in rearing large families, although some family heads obtain large families by marrying many women. In this type of society, young women and children serve as family investment and providers of social security for the privileged groups of old people. Children belong to the father, and men and women are usually eager to adopt children.

DISCRIMINATION IN ACCESS TO RESOURCES

Primitive subsistence producers usually live as hunters, herders, or food producers using long-fallow methods in regions of low population density where they have free access to the natural resources of the tribal area. When population density increases in such a region, competition between different tribes over land, water, and other natural resources becomes acute, and warfare persists among pastoral and cultivating tribes. The result may be dominance of one tribe over another. Either the militarily strongest tribe establishes itself as an upper class, imposing tribute or labor services on members of the vanquished tribe, or the latter become servants or slaves in the households of the members of the stronger tribe, excluded from access to natural resources and forced to till the land or perform other services. In both cases, family heads of the weaker tribe lose their autonomy, and both male and female members must work harder than before. But the members of the stronger tribe, including the women and children, are likely to be relieved of a large part of their work burden, which is passed on to the members of the vanquished tribe. Thus the inequality between women (and men) belonging to the same age group but different ethnic groups increases sharply.

Another result of increasing population density is the need to intensify the use of land for food production. With permanent instead of incipient use of the land, the system of tribal ownership of land is usually transformed into a system of peasant production with private ownership of land and with use of animals for cultivation and transport (Boserup 1965). In addition, these changes are accompanied by important changes in women's position (Ahmed 1985; Boserup 1970). The favored male group becomes owner of the land and usurps the use of the new and more efficient equipment. Men are taught to operate the animal-driven equipment while women continue to prepare the land with hand tools. Men use pack animals and wagons for transport while women carry head loads. The discriminatory use of technology continues even when the stage of mechanized equipment is reached. In Asian regions of the Green Revolution, where land preparation for paddy production has been mechanized, men ride tractors while women continue to work with hand tools or without any tools, performing the backbreaking, tedious work of weeding and transplanting. But owing to inequality in landholdings between families of the same or different ethnic groups, some women can escape work in the fields while others must work hard on family land, for wages, or both.

In regions of peasant production marriage systems tend to differ from those typical of tribal areas with common land. In the former, marriages arranged by the parents are used as a means to secure and, if possible, to add to the family landholding, and girls and boys may be married off long before puberty. Women who do not work in the fields are felt to be an economic burden for the husband's family, who insist on payment of a dowry, whereas bride prices are usual in regions and among tribes in which women do most of the work in the fields (Boserup 1970). The attitudes toward childbirth are also different (Schutjer & Stokes 1984). In regions of private land ownership, late marriage and celibacy, as well as precautionary spacing and termination of childbearing by traditional methods, may be applied as means to avoid subdivision of land, and the number of daughters may be limited by discriminatory treatment or infanticide.

FROM FAMILY ENTERPRISES TO LARGE-SCALE ENTERPRISES

In the change from family subsistence production to large capitalist enterprises based on wage labor, small family enterprises producing for the market are often an intermediary step. A family producing only for its own use, and perhaps to pay taxes or tribute, may increase its production of one or more crops, or other products, and offer them for sale to traders or directly in local markets while continuing to be subsistence producers of other items. If the production for sale becomes important, the household is transformed into a family enterprise with specialized production, in which all or some of the family members take part. If the goods or services produced for sale are some traditionally produced by male family members, the oldest male will become the manager with younger family members and servants as assistants; but if women were traditionally producers of the items offered for sale, the housewife may become the manager, assisted by younger women, children, and servants. Often such female-managed enterprises are created by widows and divorced women, who in this way provide for themselves and their children and other dependents (Buvinic, Lycette, & McGreevey 1983; Dauber & Cain 1981).

The creation of such enterprises can be a means to liberate women from family obligations and unhappy marriages, but in most societies there are many obstacles to such a process. Whether the traditional family hierarchy is imposed by custom or is confirmed by formal legislation, men's customary right to dispose of women's labor usually becomes extended into a right to dispose of their income-earning activities (Columbia *HRLR* 1977). Women are now allowed to undertake money transactions or to engage in outside work without permission from their male family guardian, whether he is father, husband, brother, or perhaps son. And even if a woman gets such permission, the guardian remains the master of the woman's activities, with right to the money earned by her, and is thus able to prevent her from investing in and expanding her enterprise. Moreover, women's household obligations, pregnancies, and breastfeeding are powerful obstacles to business activities on any large scale. Usually all or nearly all the family enterprises that succeed in growing into more productive and remunerative capitalist enterprises are those managed by men, with women and other men as assistants. When the transformation of some family enterprises into large-scale capitalist enterprises creates an increasing economic gap between persons belonging to different families, the traditional age–sex–race hierarchy is transformed into an age–sex–race–class hierarchy, with positive results for some women and negative results for some women.

Family enterprises may be located either in rural areas or in towns. Until fairly recently, health conditions in towns were so poor that urban populations did not reproduce themselves by natural growth but had to rely on migration from the countryside to preserve and expand their population base. Townspeople who could afford it might send their children to rural areas to reduce the risk of early death, and married migrants might leave wife and children in the countryside, especially in regions where women were accustomed to doing most of the agricultural work with the help of the children. Often towns had a large surplus of adult men over women, and prostitution flourished. Such circumstances are conducive to attitudes that exalt female chastity and the mother role and seclude women in their homes if it is at all possible for the family to subsist without allowing women to work outside the home. It is no coincidence that regions with the longest urban experience are those where traditional culture is most oppressive to women (Boserup 1970).

In spite of the cultural objections to female participation in the labor market, women from poor families are forced by economic necessity to work in family or large-scale enterprises. But the female-managed enterprises suffer from severe handicaps, partly because of the lack of economic autonomy of their managers, as mentioned, and partly because women from less poor or from well-to-do families (who could better provide the resources needed for business than the poorest ones) may be unavailable for work in such enterprises due to cultural prejudices against female labor market participation, their unwillingness to do double work, and their desire to take good care of their children. Therefore, economic development often results in the gradual disappearance of female-managed enterprises, even in countries where such enterprises are tolerated. The large majority of female labor market participants are working as low-paid or unpaid assistants to male managers and supervisors. In all countries the typical organization, in both private enterprises and public service, mirrors the typical hierarchical organization in subsistence economies, with old men at the top, younger men at middle levels, and women at the bottom. But for women, there is an important difference: old women lose their preferential status and are relegated to the bottom group—if they are not fired before they grow old.

INVESTMENT IN HUMAN CAPITAL

Human capital investment in subsistence economies consists of two elements: training of the young generation in the necessary technical skills and transmission of traditional cultural features, including knowledge of, and respect for, the existing hierarchical order relating to age and sex and to foreigners. From a young age children of both sexes are socialized to accept their present and future roles, not only without protest, but also without resentment. Boys learn to fight, girls to obey.

Since the use of improved techniques is usually monopolized by the men, economic development gradually creates a widening gap between the skill levels of men and women. Boys get systematic training as apprentices in family enterprises, while girls continue to be taught only simple household and agricultural operations by their mothers. When large-scale enterprises appear, male craftsmen and apprentices are recruited for skilled and supervisory jobs while women and foreigners are excluded from learning anything other than routine skills in simple, specialized operations. By denying women access to training, men prevent them from getting better jobs and higher incomes, supervisory work, and management jobs. Much job discrimination in recruitment and advancement is made inevitable by the traditional sex discrimination in training.

The transfer of education of children and youth from the family to private and public schools is another change that has far-reaching effects on the position of women and other disadvantaged groups. School education is a means of supplying the next generation with the superior skills that become necessary as the national economy evolves or that are recognized as necessary to make further development of the economy possible. Educational systems have started everywhere with the education of male children from the most privileged family groups, thus widening the gap in opportunities between dominant and subservient groups. However, development requires that a larger and larger share of the population be provided with more and more knowledge and skills of the types that are taught in schools and higher educational institutions. Education therefore is extended gradually to disadvantaged groups as it becomes obligatory and free. As a result, the gap between men and women in education first widens and later narrows. Similarly, the gap between women belonging to racially and economically disfavored families first widens and then narrows. Nowhere in the world have these gaps completely closed.

The role of school systems is not only to teach intellectual skills and scientific knowledge, but also to indoctrinate pupils with the dominant cultural values. However, cultural education for both girls and boys is usually (whether deliberately or unintentionally) a teaching of traditional prejudices, not only against foreigners, but also against members of the female sex. The early socialization of girls by parents and brothers as well as the later experience in schools contribute to the development of superiority feelings in boys and inferiority feelings in girls.

In developing societies, education will gradually replace physical strength and ability in weapon use as male status symbols. When this change coincides with rapidly increasing education of women, it may be felt as a potential threat to male domination, both in the labor market and within the family. This threat may be reduced by educating women to lower levels or in less prestigious fields than men. Thus middle-level education in some fields may be arranged mainly or exclusively for women, pushing them into positions as assistants to better educated men belonging to the economically and racially dominant groups. The female occupations that require middle-level education are mainly in shops, offices, schools, hospitals, and other social services; for educated women, they provide escapes from the traditional unskilled female jobs.

THE DECLINE OF BIRTH RATES

Until the middle of this century, the societal changes brought about by economic development had gradually increased the differences in the lifestyle of adult men and women. In the industrialized countries virtually all adult men were full-time labor market participants, whereas a large share of the adult women were fully occupied with child care and domestic duties. Nearly all the women who participated in the labor market worked in unskilled, low-wage occupations specially reserved for female labor. It is true that the functions of the family household had been much reduced by gradual specialization of goods and services, but this had been compensated for by transfer of children, adolescents, adult men, and female servants from work within the family household to schools and specialized work in the labor market (Tilly & Scott 1978). This process gradually transformed most housewives from small-scale managers of younger family members and servants to lonely performers of routine manual domestic work, confined to the household by child care.

The reduction of the number of tasks performed in the family is accompanied by a reduction in the autonomy of the family, which becomes dependent not only on the market but on the government and other public institutions. These changes also influence the power of the family head over other family members. Although his exercise of physical power over other family members most often becomes restricted by law, both obligatory schooling and institutionalization of religion may serve either to limit or to reinforce the influence of the family head and the older generation. Moreover, the economic requirements of a developed society induce changes in the legal and factual position of younger family members and of those women who are drawn into the labor market as monetization of the economy proceeds. When the individual household is stripped of more and more functions as the supply of public services and purchase of goods from outside increase, the participation of female family members in money-earning activities serves the economic interest of the male head of household and the tax authorities. Thus in the course of European development adult status in economic affairs was granted to more and more groups of women. It was granted first to widows, who, by entering into market trade and small-scale production, could support themselves and their offspring and thus avoid becoming economic burdens for male family members and public relief systems. Later, for the same reason, adult status in economic affairs was granted to adult unmarried women, while married women continued to be "nonadults" until recently (Columbia *HRLR* 1977).

The transfer of functions from the family to the labor market and the public sector has important effects on birth rates (Boserup 1986). No longer valuable contributors to the family labor force, school-age children become an economic burden. Parents' need to rely on help from adult children in emergencies and old age is reduced when the public sector or private institutions take over functions of physical protection and economic support. The number of surviving children increases when child mortality declines due to public health measures and medical progress, and this provides additional incentive for application of traditional or modern means of birth control within marriage.

The gradual reduction of birth rates to reproduction level or less inaugurates a period of rapid change in marital relations. Married women return to the labor market when their children reach school age, or they continue without interruption in the labor market, leaving preschool children to public or private care outside the home, and modernizing the household by purchase of mechanized household equipment and semiprepared food. Nevertheless, the inequality in access to leisure between male wage earners and wives with child care, domestic duties, and full-time participation in the labor market leads increasing numbers of women to take the initiative to divorce or to avoid formal marriage and further reduce births. As a result, public opinion in the industrialized countries is more and more preoccupied with the prospects for population decline and decay of the traditional authoritarian marriage institution.

DETERMINANTS OF WAGE DIFFERENTIALS

In subsistence economies, the age–sex–race hierarchy is reflected in the type of work a person performs; in monetized societies, the hierarchy is also reflected in the differentials between the wages paid to young and old, indigenous and foreigners, men and women (Boserup 1970). Although age differentials in wages have become less important—in fact, they are sometimes reversed because of increasing education and technical dynamism—wage systems which in effect increase wages by age have by no means disappeared. In multiracial societies, wages for similar work are usually higher for those belonging to the dominant ethnic group. Usually the higher status of men is underlined by paying them higher wages than women for similar work, both in public service and in private enterprise. In periods of acute labor shortages, for instance, during wars or extreme seasonal labor peaks in agriculture, wages paid to women and minorities may temporarily approach those paid to male labor of the dominant ethnic group. As soon as the specific shortage is over, however, the customary wage differentials tend to be reestablished.

Relative prices of products and services adapt to the traditional wage differentials. Products made mainly or exclusively by female labor can be sold more cheaply than products made by male labor. An employer of male labor who has difficulty selling his products may reduce his costs by changing from male to female labor if his workers and their unions allow him to do so, but he will not attempt to eliminate the wage differential of his male workers by paying them female wages. If legislation or public opinion exerts pressure to eliminate traditional wage differentials by sex, the employer is most likely to react by making all operations sex-specific and continue to pay lower wages to women. As a result of such behavior, the trades with the weakest trade unions gradually become female, low-wage trades, while stronger unions are able to preserve a number of occupations as male, high-wage monopolies.

In the period in Europe in which a large share of the female labor force consisted of young, unmarried girls living with their parents, sex discrimination in wages was usually explained not by status considerations but by the need to pay adult male labor a wage on which they could support a family. But permanent female breadwinners, whether single or with dependents, were never paid "breadwinner wages," and single men without dependents were paid more than female wages. Because the female labor market participants were either young or from very poor families and were socialized by family and school education to feel inferior to men, the system was never seriously challenged until recently. Even men who had full-time working wives supported the system because it secured them the status of main breadwinner, which reinforced their marital authority and their general social status. Moreover, since economists taught that wage differences reflected differentials in labor productivity, it was easy to draw the conclusion that their existence everywhere was proof of female inferiority in the labor market. The use of female labor in inferior jobs therefore seemed economically rational (Becker 1981).

Increasing replacement of male by female labor in office trades and other white-collar services changes the traditional wage differences between white-collar and manual work. White-collar work at the higher supervisory stages remains predominantly male and continues to be well paid. At lower levels, however, wage differentials between white-collar and manual work often become reversed. Married women who enter the labor market in large numbers, and in many cases in white-collar jobs with middle-level educational requirements, are often married to manual workers. With increasing numbers of women in white-collar jobs that require middle-level education, manual workers increasingly have wives with more formal education and sometimes with a higher income than the husbands. In such cases, the increase in the wife's prestige and in her earning power strengthens her marital position considerably, and this contributes no doubt to the increasing frequency of divorce, which was mentioned earlier. Women's position in the labor market also improves with entry of more highly educated women belonging to age classes and social classes other than those that had been predominant in the female labor market.

THE CONCEPT OF WESTERNIZATION

It was underlined in the previous sections of this chapter that, at certain stages of economic development, women's position is likely to improve, whereas at other stages it may deteriorate. It was also underlined that development often improves the position of certain groups of women but causes deterioration for other groups of women, and that such changes are likely when there is increasing economic inequality or a shift of power relations between national or ethnic groups. The period of overseas colonization by Western powers and the later shift to national sovereignty are important examples.

During the colonial period, colonial administrators and white settlers recruited indigenous male workers for plantations, mines, and transport, and they taught indigenous male producers to produce cash crops for export to European and North American markets. As a result, the work burden of the women increased. More of the subsistence production was pushed onto women and children when the men got other work to do, and often the women also had to help with the cash crops (Boserup 1970). Because a large share of the additional agricultural work was taken over by women without pay, the costs of agricultural and mining products and the costs of transport investment could be kept low, and the male workers in these activities could be paid wages that covered only the immediate subsistence needs of the worker but not the cost of supporting dependents (Okeyo 1984). In other cases, colonial plantations recruited the whole family, which obtained a subsistence income by full-time work of men, women, and children in the plantation, thus forcing the women to perform the domestic work on top of a full day of hard plantation work.

In the colonial period, married European women, and often unmarried ones too, were denied adult status, and the official ideal of a woman was the faithful, domestic housewife and mother, devoting her work and interest exclusively to husband and children. If administrators and missionaries discovered indigenous women with more sexual and economic freedom than corresponded to this ideal, they did their best to change the customs by legislation and education. This meant that change, from common cultivation rights for both men and women to private property, usually became a change to male property rights, with the result that women's possibility for independent self-support was reduced or eliminated (Boserup 1970). Where she had been an independent producer with free access to land, she became an unpaid family aide on her husband's farm, or she became a wage laborer if local agriculture used female wage labor. If not, and her husband died or left her, her fate might be prostitution or begging. In most colonies, girls' possibility for formal education was limited to attendance in missionary schools, which focused on religious instruction and teaching of domestic skills and elementary literacy.

Independence brought radical changes in the traditional hierarchy for men, but much less change for women. The small elite of young men, who had received Western education in missionary schools and sometimes in schools and universities in Western countries, moved into top jobs in administration and business, bypassing the older, uneducated, or less educated traditional elites. For women, the most important change was the rapid spread of public, female education. Moreover, in countries with rapid industrialization, urban wage employment for unmarried women increased, resulting in later marriages for women and more freedom for women to refuse undesired marriage partners. But these changes were the results of industrialization and related to independence only to the extent that decolonization led to acceleration of the rate of industrialization.

Moreover, for rural women economic changes are more important than political independence. If national governments neglect rural development, women's traditional toil in agriculture continues or becomes worse due to acceleration of male migration from the villages. If independence results in promotion and modernization of agriculture, as has happened in some countries, mainly in Asia, the reduction of the work burden made possible by new equipment and methods benefits mainly the men and the children who are sent to school (Tinker & Cho 1981). Women continue to perform their traditional hand operations unless their families' income is sufficient to allow them to pass all or some of their agricultural work on to women or men from less well-off families (Ahmed 1985).

Industrialization has opposing effects on different groups of women. Whereas young women are drawn into industrial employment and increasing numbers of educated women obtain white-collar jobs in social and other services, the situation of older, uneducated women may deteriorate because the family enterprises in which they work may suffer from competition with the growing modern sector (Buvinic et al. 1983; Dauber & Cain 1987). There are similar opposing changes within the family sphere. Young women, especially those who are educated, achieve a stronger position in relation to both male family members and older women, and the older women lose whatever authority they had in the family, especially if they are the only illiterate family members.

When development is rapid, it is inevitable that these changes create tension between sexes and generations and that pressure groups appear that seek to preserve or reintroduce the traditional, hierarchical cultural pattern. The tension is most acute and the pressure groups become strongest if development is rapid in societies that have long had particularly oppressive age–sex hierarchies. This is the case in oil-rich countries in the Arab world, which have attempted to preserve the family system of domesticated and secluded women by mass importation of foreign male labor, and in which mass movements of Muslim revival pursue the same aim.

Active pressure groups of men and women aiming at preservation or revival of traditional systems of age–sex discrimination are not limited to the Arab world. In most previous colonies, nationalist feeling is accompanied by hostile feelings toward remaining Western influence in the cultural field. Groups that are against changes in the traditional age–sex hierarchy gain strength by describing such changes as results of Western influence, undisturbed by the fact that white rule and, later, Western experts most often strengthened male positions and weakened those of women by their intervention. It is often overlooked in developing countries that "Western culture" was strongly antifeminist in the colonial period, and that it is only as a result of recent economic and demographic changes in the Western countries that their traditional sex hierarchy is beginning to be undermined.

I
THE POLITICS
OF WOMEN IN DEVELOPMENT

3

The Making of a Field: Advocates, Practitioners, and Scholars

IRENE TINKER

Women in development, like any applied field, not only crosses disciplinary boundaries but establishes goals and priorities consonant with the constraints of those systems within which its practitioners work. Scholars commenting on the field too often confuse this art of the possible with their own more abstract view of the world and so criticize development programs from an idealistic, if not ideological, perspective rather than from the realism of the practitioner. This confusion is exacerbated in the case of women in development by the existence of a strong international women's movement which first raised the issue and then continued to monitor its incorporation into development programs. These advocates have their own agenda: equity between women and men. How this ultimate goal translates into action in particular circumstances is the subject of global debate among the advocates themselves and between the advocates and both practitioners and scholars who share the goals but not the perspectives.

One might think of the women's movement as a ray of light passing through a prism. It is essential to understand the constituent colors in order to understand the whole; it is equally essential not to confuse any one-colored refraction with the light ray itself. This chapter outlines the differences among three groups of women and men that have exerted major influence on the gradual evolution of the field of women in development: advocates, practitioners, and scholars. Failure to distinguish among the different goals and activities of these three groups and to appreciate their different audiences has distorted efforts to classify women in development proponents and programs.

ADVOCATES

The impetus for integrating women into development programs arose out of two very different conglomerations of women, the U.N. Commission on the Status of Women and the U.S. women's movement. In the early 1970s, neither the staff and members of the women's commission nor the activists involved in the growing number of new women's organizations in the United States were particularly interested in economic development; rather, they drew on their suffragist heritage in their concern for equality before the law and greater access of women to education. In addition, the U.S. women were increasingly demanding the right to equal employment, which they saw as basic to equal status in a society that measures achievement by income or profession. The objective of both groups of women was to influence governmental policies concerning women.

Women in development advocates emerged from these two arenas quite separately and, conditioned by the different environments in which they operated, brought differing interests and priorities to the field. However, it was the conflation of these two groups of advocates during the U.N. Decade for Women that produced the remarkable expansion of the field.

Origins of Women in Development

The U.N. Commission on the Status of Women had, since its inception in 1946, been proposing a U.N. Women's Conference without success.[1] When, in 1972, the General Assembly agreed to declare 1975 as International Women's Year, no conference was guaranteed. But the women in the United Nations were becoming organized and, echoing the growing demands by American women for affirmative action, had themselves pushed through a second resolution which favored increased employment opportunities for women in the U.N. system. Negative publicity in the press about the lack of women in high-level positions at the United Nations, based on data provided by the U.N. activists, clearly triggered the appointment of the first woman Assistant Secretary General of the United Nations, Finnish lawyer Helvi Sipila. In 1974, Sipila was able to galvanize pressure from women inside and outside the U.N. system and push through the General Assembly a resolution to hold an International Women's Conference. Even then, however, the resolution was burdened with the caveat that no regular U.N. funds be spent on the effort. This meant a concerted effort to seek funding for a conference barely 18 months away.

In keeping with U.N. tradition, themes were proclaimed for the International Women's Year and Conference: Equality, Development, and Peace.

---

[1]The U.N. Commission on the Status of Women was originally formed as a subcommission of the Human Rights Commission at the inaugural meeting of the United Nations in 1945. Fierce lobbying, led by women from the Inter-American Commission of Women, resulted in its upgrading to commission status in June 1946. Its first meeting as a full commission was held in 1947.

Equality had been the predominant interest of the U.N. Commission on the Status of Women. Peace had for some time been viewed as a woman's issue by the Eastern bloc; this theme was added to the resolution by a Romanian delegate.

Development was a more recent issue within the U.N. system, which had begun to shift toward this emphasis as the number of newly independent countries became the majority of U.N. member nations during the 1960s. The First Development Decade 1961–70 declaration did not mention women specifically, but in 1962 the General Assembly instructed the women's commission to prepare a report on the role of women in the social and economic development plans of member governments. At that time most governments and nongovernmental organizations (NGOs) consulted assumed that economic and social development would bring about any desired changes for women, according to Margaret Bruce, who for many years served as head of the secretariat for the women's commission. Commission members feared that too much attention to economic development would divert the commission from its primary goal of women's equal rights; they preferred to emphasize the human element in development and called for greater investment in women as human resources (Tinker 1984).

In 1970 the General Assembly included in the International Development Strategy for the Second Development Decade a phrase — later widely copied — which stated the importance of encouraging "full integration of women in the total development effort." As a first step in implementing that objective, the Commission on the Status of Women, together with the Social Development Commission, convened an Interregional Meeting of Experts on the Integration of Women in June 1972. Ester Boserup attended that meeting and helped prepare its report; but the recommendations by the experts for statistical studies on women's employment and the inclusion of women's work in manpower statistics were not implemented by the Commission on Social Development after the document was issued.[2]

Also in 1972, the Federation of Organizations for Professional Women was formed in Washington, D.C. This umbrella organization was composed of representatives from the many caucuses or committees set up within professional associations to pressure for greater visibility at annual meetings and within the organization itself as part of their effort for enhanced professional employment opportunities. The federation was one of the myriad of newly formed women's groups and newly rejuvenated established women's

---

[2]As the Women's Decade gained momentum, the U.N. Statistical Office issued a report, *Improving Concepts and Methods for Statistics and Indicators on the Situation of Women*; the U.N. International Research and Training Institute for the Advancement of Women (INSTRAW) and the International Labour Organization issued *Women in Economic Activity: A Global Statistical Survey — 1950–2000*; and in 1986 the Expert Group Meeting on Measurement of Women's Income and their Participation in the Informal Sector was convened by INSTRAW (see Tinker 1987b).

organizations that coalesced around such major issues as equal pay for equal work and the Equal Rights Amendment.[3]

These activities encouraged the formation of more women's caucuses, including one called Women in Development, which was set up within the Society for International Development (SID/WID). Like most similar caucuses, SID/WID was formed for both substantive and professional reasons. Professionally, the group wished to increase women's participation in SID meetings and to enhance women's employment opportunities in development agencies. Substantively, its members wished to give visibility to a phenomenon several had observed on recent overseas trips: development seemed to be having an adverse impact on women. The data which these WID advocates were compiling to support this observation dealt primarily with poor women, because in many developing countries elite women actually had greater access to higher education and prestigious jobs than did American women. An early discovery was the growing phenomenon of woman-headed households as the family began to disintegrate under pressures of modernization. These women in particular were neglected by development programs despite the estimates that they comprised one-third of all households worldwide.[4]

In 1974 the SID/WID group produced a bibliography, a mere five pages long, and in the process "discovered" Ester Boserup's *Woman's Role in Economic Development*. Her book was instantly embraced because, as Jane Jaquette suggests in her chapter, Boserup's theory legitimized efforts to influence development policy with a combined argument for justice and efficiency. This utilization of scholarly materials to bolster policy arguments was characteristic of the WID effort during its first decade as women advocates sought to influence and work within the development community at both national and international levels.

In the fall of 1973 the Department of State held a briefing on foreign affairs, including the proposed International Women's Conference. During an unprecedented early morning hearing, State Department officials listened to women's organizations present their ideas about the issues of the conference. The testimony of SID/WID was so persuasive that two State Department staff members, Clara Beyer and Mildred Marcy, determined to promote an amendment to the U.S. Foreign Assistance Act of 1973, then on the floor of the Senate. This amendment required that the U.S. Agency for

---

[3]For the personal stories of organizers of many of the groups that initiated or influenced legislation and monitored the executive branch implementation of these laws, see Irene Tinker, ed. *Women in Washington: Advocates for Public Policy* (Beverly Hills, Calif.: Sage Publications, 1983).

[4]Data on the number of households in which women provide the day-to-day control and management is difficult to collect: men may be casual contributors for the welfare of their children; men who have migrated to the cities may or may not send home remittances; deserted women may keep up the fiction of a husband for status reasons; census collectors may list a son or father as household head. Early estimates that one-third of the households were headed by women (Tinker 1976b) have been substantiated by more recent research (Buvinic, Youssef, with Von Elm 1978; Youssef & Hetler 1983).

International Development administer its programs "so as to give particular attention to those programs, projects, and activities which tend to integrate women into the national economies of foreign countries, thus improving their status and assisting the total development effort."[5] This amendment became known as the Percy Amendment after Senator Charles Percy, who was enlisted to introduce the amendment and who became its champion within the U.S. government and introduced a resolution on women in development in the General Assembly of the United Nations in December 1974 (Tinker 1983).

Three World Conferences on Women

Once the concept of women in development was articulated in economic as opposed to equality terms, it was swiftly incorporated into documents of the General Assembly and the various U.N. specialized agencies even before the World Conference for the International Women's Year, held in Mexico City in July 1975. Unlike many other issues raised in Mexico and repeated at the two other world conferences that punctuated the U.N. Decade for Women 1976–85 — the explosive Mid-Decade Conference in Copenhagen in 1980 and the colossal Nairobi Conference in 1985 — women in development was a popular concept to governments as well as women.[6] Lucille Mathurin Mair, secretary-general of the Copenhagen conference, explains its rapid adoption:

> Early in the Decade the equity principle had been made even more persuasive by its linkage with the utility principle. Women had been a missing link in development, now they were being found; they could actually be a valuable resource, indeed were half, or more, of a nation's human resources, no longer to be wasted. . . . The prospect of steering women from the margin to the mainstream was as exciting to some would-be developers as to female recipients of such policies and programmes. "Women in Development" became the Decade's overnight catchphrase, a seductive one, which for a time, at least, could evade the question of what kind of development women were to be drawn into. (1986:586–87)

The three official United Nations conferences were extremely important symbolically since such international meetings legitimized women's concerns in the eyes of national leaders and required them to address and then

[5]Section 113 of the Foreign Assistance Act of 1973 at first applied only to specific programs initiated under the New Directions mandate to focus more aid on the poor; later the Percy Amendment was extended to cover not only all of USAID programs but those in other agencies using U.S. funds.

[6]The politics of these three world conferences was an explosive combination of the U.N. North-South agenda and international feminism. The most contentious issue at all three meetings related to the equating of zionism with racism, colonialism, and imperialism as causes of underdevelopment. Many women objected to this politicization of the conferences, arguing that such critical international debate belonged in the General Assembly. Others insisted that women had as much right as men to debate the PLO or apartheid and rejected the complaint that discussing subjects unrelated to the conference topic could only deflect whatever impact the conference hoped to make. *Signs* [*1*(1); *6*(3); *6*(4); *7*(3); *8*(2); *11*(3)] includes comments on all conferences.

vote on statements that clearly deplored the devaluation of women's productive and reproductive roles and recorded women's continued inequality and
growing poverty in most countries of the world. Country delegations, although too often headed by men, greatly increased the percentage of women
members from 1975 to 1985, providing experience in U.N. affairs to many
women and proving to governments that women were capable national representatives at international conferences.

The necessary documentation for each conference required member governments to submit sex disaggregated data on a multitude of basic indicators, which forced national planners to confront — often for the first time —
the implications of their own development policies as they were differentially
affecting women. These data have also provided researchers with a surfeit of
macroinformation useful to test against independent surveys and studies on
particular issues such as women's health, education, and employment in
agriculture, industry, and the informal sector. Special studies were also commissioned on such less quantifiable issues as rural women's subsistence
activities and the effects of apartheid on women of South Africa. Utilizing
these data and reports, each conference produced a major document; taken
together, these detail women's roles and status around the globe and recommend a program of action designed to ameliorate women's present and
future condition (Fraser 1987; Tinker & Jaquette 1987).

Perhaps the most far-reaching impact of the conferences was the mobilization of women which they engendered. Although the official conferences
provided the impetus and incentive to investigate global concerns of women,
participation in U.N. conferences is necessarily limited. Official governmental delegates and advisers constituted the majority of the nearly 3000 conference participants; official delegates are not free to discuss their own agendas
but rather are bound to reflect their governments' position on global issues,
which may have only a remote relevance to the subject at hand. Representatives of international agencies and of nongovernmental organizations in
consultative status to the United Nations also attend the conferences, primarily as observers and resource people, though they do have limited rights
to speak.

Thus it was not the official conferences that provided a forum for free-
flowing debates on all matter of issues relating to women. Rather it was the
parallel nongovernmental meetings, open to anyone for a modest registra-
tion fee, that engaged women's hearts and minds and provided a venue for
global interchange. Part fair, part revival meeting, part open university,
these meetings were a marketplace for ideas and handicrafts, a showcase for
songs and movies and debates, a gigantic international party where women
from every country in the world could meet women with similar interests to
form friendships, networks, and organizations. Attendees went from 6000
in Mexico to 14,000 in Nairobi, in addition to the 3000 women and men
accredited to each of the official conferences.

By 1985 women in development had become synonymous with the processes of change that were affecting women in the developing countries.

Instead of being seen as a programmatic concept utilized by development agencies to include women in their activities, its meaning had been enlarged to encompass the much broader goals of the advocates.

Meanings of Women in Development

From this brief history, it becomes clear that there are many strands of women's rights bound up in the term *women in development*. The new concept of ensuring women a fair stake in *economic development* carried with it the earlier ideas of legal *equality, education, employment,* and *empowerment*. During the U.N. Decade for Women, various of these goals predominated at different times; policies and programs were not always clear as to the intended objectives when working with women. It is therefore extremely important to understand the individual strands of women in development as well as the use of the term as shorthand for the broader goal of achieving equity for women.

Equality before the law, as the focus of much of the effort of the U.N. Commission on the Status of Women, resulted in the passage in 1951 by the General Assembly of the Convention on the Political Rights of Women. In subsequent years the scope of such conventions greatly increased until, in 1979, the General Assembly adopted the Convention on the Elimination of All Forms of Discrimination Against Women. This international bill of rights for women has now been ratified by 92 countries; its enforcement is reviewed by a special U.N. committee (Fraser 1987). To monitor the implementation of this convention and to maintain pressure on governments to abide by its provisions, an international consortium of scholars and activists has set up the International Women's Rights Action Watch.

For a time during the Decade legal rights were downplayed. Most governments today have constitutions that grant women equality, but too often these rights are not enforced in the face of custom and patriarchy except among the Westernized middle class. WID advocates have argued that for the poor woman, economic power would have a greater impact on women's rights than unenforceable laws. Yet recent studies, like those presented in Part III of this book, do not necessarily bear out this assumption: significant impact depends on the type of work and a process which empowers. Further, local women's organizations have been able to use legal rights to help protect poor as well as middle-class women who have been abused or divorced. Thus there is renewed interest in improving women's legal rights, particularly in areas traditionally regulated by customary or religious law such as those concerning divorce or inheritance (Schuler 1986).

Education was understood by women both in the U.N. Women's Commission and in the U.S. women's movement to be the prerequisite for improvement in women's status. At the United Nations the Commission repeatedly has urged governments to increase the access of girls and women to formal education; in the United States, which has equal education through college, the focus has been on access to technical education and to professional schools. Yet international development programs for educational assistance were severely cut back during the Decade. One reason for this was the failure of many early literacy campaigns: ironically, this failure could be attributed to the fact that classes held at midday conflicted with rural women's essential economic activities. Constraints on women's time explain not only continued high fertility among subsistence farming families but also the high dropout rates for female students who stay home to help their mothers. As these facts became more widely known, development programs began to stress nonformal rather than formal education and to relate this education directly to income-producing activities. Although such efforts are critical to the helping of poor adult women, they do not address the next generation. As Susan Bourque and Kay Warren write in Chapter 6, advocates today are again emphasizing women's access to formal education, but they are also concerned with enhancing its content and reducing gender biases in the material that is taught.

Employment of women professionals in the United Nations and in development agencies is advocated both as a right in itself and as a more effective way of ensuring that development programs both reach and involve women. Indeed, so pervasive were the demands of women for "affirmative action" in government hiring that many observers equated "women in development" with creating opportunities for women professionals in development agencies. This confusion was evident at the first congressional hearing on women in development called by Congressman Donald Fraser to consider the question of international women's rights. In addition to hearing testimony about U.S. bilateral programs, the congressman, emphasizing the importance of professional opportunities in enabling women to realize their full potential, requested information on the number of professional women in the U.S. Agency for International Development (Committee on Foreign Affairs 1974). Worldwide, there has been a significant increase in the utilization of women in all phases of development work from research to managing to evaluating.

Empowerment is a relatively new term, but the relationship between organization and influence has long been understood. Many international women's organizations were formed during the suffragist period; after World War II they rapidly expanded their membership to the newly independent countries. As NGOs in consultative status to the Economic and Social Council of the United Nations, they worked closely with the Women's Commission and lobbied their own governments to support the International Women's Year. As development issues took on added importance, some of these organizations began to work with grassroots women's groups, funneling information and funds to them. In contrast, most of the women's organizations actively lobbying the U.S. government were newly formed groups representing the new wave of the women's movement. Consciousness-raising was a key element in this feminist organizing approach; when a few of these organizations turned to development work, they drew on this model for training women to recognize and change cultural stereotypes that limited women's leadership roles. But outright efforts at changing attitudes could not be accomplished within the confines of most international development agencies, since they maintained that foreigners had no business tampering with culture. Thus there arose a distinction between global feminism and women in development, which Charlotte Bunch and Roxanna Carrillo discuss in this volume.

Economic development was the original primary focus of WID. In both the United Nations and the U.S. Congress, the motivation to integrate women into development programming arose from the gender bias that had characterized previous attempts at economic development and so had ignored or undercut women's economic activities. The growing number of women who headed households were particularly disadvantaged, a trend encapsulated in the phrase "the feminization of poverty." National planners may have seen women as an unused labor force, but the thrust of the WID argument was that women were overworked and underproductive in their economic activities. Before being available for alternative work, women needed to be relieved of much of the drudgery characterizing their daily struggle to supply basic necessities to their families.

The documentation and valuation of women's work remained the dominant concern throughout the Decade for Women not only for the advocates but for practitioners and scholars as well. Increasingly, however, the other issues became incorporated into programming as practitioners sought to integrate women's programs into mainstream development efforts. Scholars also moved out from work to encompass a broader feminist agenda. The varying implications for the three groups of these issues are presented in Table 3.1.

PRACTITIONERS

Practitioners is the term used to describe those women and men working inside development agencies (or on contract to them) who must, by definition, be constrained by the policies and bureaucratic behavior of those organizations. Failure to distinguish such constraints from the ambitious policy goals of advocates has led to unrealistic expectations of WID programming and consequent disappointment. For practitioners, the central question was *how* to fulfill the mandate to "integrate women into the national economies of foreign countries." The two major approaches used by development agencies in their programming for women since the mid-1970s were *welfare* and *efficiency*. Each approach emphasized only one part of a woman's life: as mother or as worker. Current debates revolve around ways to support women in their dual roles.

Programming for Women's Welfare

Early development programming had ignored women as economic actors and dealt with women only in their reproductive role, and then only as mothers, not as women. Health programs, although called Maternal Child

Table 3.1. Viewpoints of Women in Development Proponents: Issues and Responses

Issues	Advocates	Practitioners	Scholars
		Proponents	
Economic development	Adverse impact Integrate women	Efficiency	Count women's economic activities Class/gender
Equality	Legal rights	Income as liberating	Patriarchy major constraint
Empowerment	Form women's organizations	Women-only projects	Global feminism Distinct values
Education	Access to professional schools	Nonformal education	Scientific and technical Revise content for sex bias
Employment	Affirmative action Basis for status	Microenterprise	Sexual division of labor
Welfare	Seen as dependency creating	Participation in health, population, and housing programs	Dual roles Female sphere
Efficiency	Integration	Sectoral programs	Not feminist

Health (MCH), in reality were child focused; no consideration was given the fact that a healthy mother is the most important indicator for having a healthy child. Population programs discussed women as "targets" of family planning and were surprised that many women did not choose to become "acceptors" of contraceptives. As the economic value of children to subsistence families was recognized, many population proponents began to support programming to reduce women's drudgery and increase their income, drawing the obvious conclusion that an overworked mother will desire many children to help her today and support her tomorrow. This relationship between poverty on the one hand and poor health and nutrition on the other, a central issue for women, is relatively neglected by the health establishment (Blair 1980; Leslie, Lycette, & Buvinic 1986). Only recently has the "Safe Motherhood" initiative of the World Bank put together health and family planning, underscoring the importance of birth spacing for healthy mothers and children.

Welfare was, and continues to be, an integral part of both MCH and family planning programs because these programs are used to distribute foodstuffs through the Food for Peace program. Free food programs have been widely criticized because of the disincentives they create for poor farmers. Practitioners argued that free food distribution was welfare and that such programs merely increase women's dependency. Further, in rural areas food was usually distributed at midday from a center on the main road. Thus rural women had to forgo a day's work to walk to the center to fetch the food. Of course the total programs—free medical care for infants and/or free contraceptives which came along with the food—provide important social services. The problem is the assumption on which the programs are based: women are nonworking dependents who have ample time to walk long distances on a regular basis to attend clinics or receive food.

Food for Peace programs began as a response to famine and remain a critical activity in times of crisis. The confusion arises when such giveaway programs are institutionalized as development efforts and so continue to treat the symptoms, not the causes of poverty. The welfare ethic provides an easy approach for development agencies; it garners support at home, as it continues to do with pictures of famine in Africa; it takes less effort to give something away, such as food, than to organize local groups to earn it; and it does not threaten the status quo.

To the WID advocate, such programs simply reinforce the stereotypes of weak and dependent women and their children. In contrast, WID proponents support income activities to help poor women since they consider economic activity as the key to improving women's status. They are not alone: many NGOs that solicit contributions on a welfare basis—because that is what moves the public—have nonetheless instituted multifaceted community development programs often featuring income activities for women.[7]

The major problem with the welfare approach is not these frankly charitable programs but the tendency of the welfare attitude to "misbehave" by permeating and eventually dominating programs theoretically designed to generate income for poor women (Buvinic 1986). Three programmatic characteristics of these poverty-alleviation programs predict this outcome. The first characteristic is the setting up of women-only programs through intermediary organizations whose primary expertise is in running welfare projects for women. Second, assumptions are made by these organizations about group membership and cooperation; these tend to exclude the poorest women, who were meant to be the beneficiaries of these programs. Finally, a major drawback of early poverty-oriented women-focused programs was that the organizations chosen to implement them were themselves outside the mainstream of development programming.

Women-only projects were the easiest and earliest response of most donor agencies to WID. Women's organizations or church groups were usually selected to implement such programs, although they lacked not only experience in creating viable income activities for the poor but also experience in running their own organizations on a business basis. Because these organizations had run social programs before, they tended to retain stereotypes about women's domestic roles, and they set up income projects based on incorrect assumptions about women's needs, daily activities, or skills. These

---

[7]These include Save the Children and Foster Parents. UNICEF also has sponsored community development programs and income activities for women.

projects assumed that women were predominantly housewives with ample free time who only needed "pin money" for supplementary food or clothing. Further, these new income activities assumed that women had skills in sewing and knitting, middle-class activities quite foreign to most poor women in farm families. As a result, such projects — sewing and knitting clothes for tourists, weaving jute bags, crocheting — seldom resulted in economic returns without constant subsidies.

This concept of teaching poor women middle-class skills to use in earning money is not a recent one; missionaries in India taught low-caste converts to crochet as early as 1860. Recent studies of this enterprise show that as the export of lace increased, upper-caste men took over and expanded the work force to other castes which valued seclusion of women. Maria Mies argues that only the constant reassertion of the value of seclusion for status allows such poor wages to be paid to women, because they could earn more as agricultural laborers if they would violate purdah (1982b).

Gradually projects moved into areas with a greater potential for profit by utilizing skills that women already possessed, which means that these projects remained firmly within the female sphere: drying fruits or making purees for the urban centers, baking crackers, waxing batiks. A major failing of such small-income projects has been insufficient analysis of available markets. Efforts of many Peace Corps volunteers to create income for women, making baskets in Kenya and Nepal or tablecloths in El Salvador, have relied on the volunteer herself to market the products; her access to customers in the capital city can seldom be duplicated when she leaves. But markets alone will not necessarily make a project self-sufficient: a mango-canning project in Honduras which had secured a hospital as a major client was located in a remote valley; breakage of the glass containers destroyed profits until the project was reformulated to produce dried puree "fruit leather" for the city and mango drink for valley consumption (Tinker 1981). Increasingly, however, such projects rectify the problems and begin producing income for the women involved (Yudelman 1987).

Local women's groups were set up by intermediary organizations as a mechanism to deliver information and services. Typically such a group is open to all adult women in the village and income activities are frequently communal. Both these features make it difficult for the poor to participate. Income differentials exist in all villages and leadership of groups generally falls to the better off and better educated, who naturally tend to make decisions that favor their own interests. Such interests may include community betterment such as supporting new schools with income earned from farming, as happens often in Kenya. But the poorest women cannot afford to take time for activities that do not immediately help them support their families (McCormack, Walsh, & Nelson 1986; Muzaale & Leonard 1985). Nor can poor women subsidize others who might work less hard, despite a romantic notion that the poor are less competitive than the middle class.

The importance of the individual receiving a fair return for her own efforts helps explain the recent rapid expansion of *affinity* or *solidarity*

groups as a source of credit for starting microenterprises, a technique pio-
neered by Bangladesh's Grameen Bank. According to this model, individuals in the group, though landless and without other assets, are able to
borrow based on group surety. Before asking the group to guarantee loans to
individual members, it is imperative to foster a sense of group solidarity.
This is done by keeping the groups small, by having as members only persons of similar socioeconomic status and sex, and by encouraging both
individual and community improvement objectives, which range from reducing family size or refusing to pay dowries to improving community water
supplies.[8]

Marginal projects, however successful, seldom have any impact on the
large bureaucracies that characterize national and international development agencies. Since women-only programs have generally been small and
underfunded and were widely perceived of as being welfare oriented by
definition, they have remained outside the mainstream of national economic
planning. Practitioners have documented that only when women's issues
were integrated into regular development programming would such programs have either the prestige or the resources adequate to the task (Carloni
1987). Yet the need to offer help to poor women is so overwhelming, and the
vision of women as mothers so basic, that welfare programs continue to be
the predominant type of programming which reaches women, even in an
egalitarian country such as Sweden (Himmelstrand & Bickham 1985).

Efficiency as the Basis for WID Programming

The original concept of WID was based on the adverse impact of inappropriate economic development programs that undercut women's economic
activities by treating them only as mothers. The solution to this inequity was
to design development programs so that women were integrated into them;
the result would be more successful programming for the poor. Thus efficiency became the primary argument used by practitioners as they tried to
convince the development community that development projects would be
more likely to attain their goals if women were an integral part of both
design and implementation.

Arguing efficiency was an easier task in the 1970s when development
emphasized basic human needs than it would have been under earlier development strategies. Further, the desire of WID practitioners to get out of the
welfare mode reflected the insistence within the development agencies that
basic needs should be provided through self-sufficiency rather than welfare.
The focus on self-sufficiency meant that the poor had to be encouraged to
participate in development programs rather than being passive beneficiaries.
Experience had amply illustrated that top-down programs functioned only
as long as the donor agency continued to provide inputs or funds; self-

[8]Current reports indicate that women account for over 80 percent of all borrowers in the
Grameen Bank. Their repayment rate is over 98 percent (Tinker 1989).

sufficient programs required changes in behavior and attitudes that would occur only if the people understood the reasons for change and also benefited from them. For all the rhetoric about participation, however, most programs, if they reached the village at all, reached the male elite. Yet it was obvious that the behavioral changes needed for self-sufficiency often involved women, so participation also had to involve women. Because the logic of self-sufficiency and participation included women, there was relatively little bureaucratic resistance to this approach; the problem became how to do it.

Integration into sector-focused programs (such as agriculture or energy) that were designed to alleviate poverty seemed a logical programming device. Self-sufficiency involved improved methods of obtaining food, water, fuel, and housing as well as greater opportunities to earn money to pay for improved services. Time budget studies had clearly demonstrated women's dominant role in providing these basic needs in subsistence economies. They consume many hours a day fetching water and fuelwood, but the most time-consuming activities involve the production, processing, and preparation of food for family consumption. All these activities are labor intensive and accomplished using traditional technologies; obviously more efficient methods of securing basic necessities for survival would free women to earn in the marketplace.

The challenge to find technologies for rural poor women and men was taken up by the appropriate technology groups, which began to design grain mills, solar ovens, biogas disgesters, and more efficient cooking stoves (Cecelski 1984; CEPAL 1983; Islam, Morse, & Soesastro 1984; Tinker 1987a). Installing improved wells and pumps for the provision of clean water has become the focus of UNICEF funding and a goal of the U.N. Decade for Water 1981–90. Evaluations of such projects show that greater benefits are derived from new wells if women are consulted about their placement during the planning process and taught how to use and repair spigots and pumps themselves. Yet myths persist about women's abilities to understand and utilize new machineries or methods, and too often women are left with labor-intensive traditional technologies as men modernize their tasks.

Responding to women's agricultural and agroforestry roles took longer. Again this lag was caused by incorrect assumptions about women's roles both by male agricultural experts who saw farming as a male preserve and by female home economists whose training was suited to middle-class housewives, not to women doing subsistence farming. Early efforts to reach women farmers with separate extension programs also "misbehaved." Changes in existing bureaucracies of agricultural ministries, universities, and extension programs have proved exceedingly difficult, particularly in Africa where extension programs themselves were not very strong (Lele 1975). A recent program in Cameroon provides one of the first models for truly integrated extension both of officers and farmers (Walker 1987). Women's roles in utilizing and planting trees were long ignored by foresters, whose training focused on commercial timber; today women's knowledge of local species makes them a vital part of the new efforts at social forestry: the maintainance of forests for social, not commercial use (Fortmann & Rocheleau 1985; Hoskins 1983).

Part of the basic needs strategy was to increase employment opportunities, particularly in small enterprises and microenterprises in both rural and urban areas. Research has documented women's and men's roles in these activities, and programs to support their activities have usually not discriminated by sex. But the fact that women's enterprises tend to cluster at the micro end of the scale and to use profits for improving family nutrition or paying school fees has caused some commentators to dismiss women entrepreneurs as unbusinesslike because they do not reinvest in their enterprise in order to expand.[9] Yet it is these women microentrepreneurs who are borrowing and repaying loans from the Grameen Bank and similar institutions at rates far above male borrowers at any level of enterprise.

Rural development has preoccupied development agencies from the outset. Cities were seen as middle class, and even urban poor were assumed to be better off than their rural cousins. The rapid growth of squatter settlements forced agencies to begin to look at issues of housing and community development. Caroline Moser traces the critical role women play in these urban settlements and complains that the management role of women — which consumes a vast amount of time—remains unrecognized (1987). Housing credit programs tend to discriminate against women borrowers because, as household heads, they had greater time constraints and most had fewer resources than men.

Increasing understanding of WID within the bureaucracies of the donor agencies in order to foster integrated programs became a major effort for the development community.[10] Interagency task forces were set up (e.g., linking FAO, ILO, and WHO) to exchange information and share bureaucratic strategies. A women's committee of European and North American donor members of the Development Assistance Committee was initiated to put pressure on the parent body, the Organization of Economic Cooperation and Development. Both INSTRAW and the U.N. Commission on the Status of Women held experts' meetings and circulated the resulting recommendations within the United Nations. Meetings and conferences were held, guidelines published, and training programs instituted. Particularly noteworthy were the sessions initiated for senior administrators by Gloria Scott, the WID officer at the World Bank. It used materials based on the Harvard

[9]Narrow economic definitions once again are used to exclude women when programmers argue that only enterprises that grow should be given credit. I suggest that the definitions be changed and have called for a Human Economy (1987c) that honors other values besides the profit motive.

[10]The organizational and management decisions concerning mechanisms to ensure that WID issues are incorporated into bureaucratic procedures as well as integrated into program design and implementation are critical. Generally, practitioners argue for a focal point in the agency to monitor the mainstreaming of projects. On USAID see Anderson and Chen (1988), Blair (1983), Blumberg and Hinderstein (1982), and Staudt (1982). On international agricultural research institutes see Jiggins (1986).

case method, which provides data and background to the participants, who must then frame their own solutions. This system has been adopted by other agencies, using their own projects as case studies (Overholt, Anderson, Cloud, & Austin 1985).

Universities also became the focus of educational efforts in the United States because USAID provides significant funds, especially to land grant universities, to supply technical assistance. Arvonne Fraser, as director of the Office of Women in Development at AID from 1977 to 1981, supported a network of women professors and researchers at universities and lobbied within AID to ensure that women's issues were included in development studies and projects; she also supported efforts to increase the understanding of development issues by women's organizations around the world.

Reassessing Women in Development Programs

In the last few years there has been a reassessment of WID programming and a rejection of the easy dichotomy between welfare and efficiency approaches. Such a reassessment was necessary as evaluations indicated that most WID programs had begun to resemble one another—whether the origin of the project was sectoral or separate. These programs have the following characteristics:

> Women from similar socioeconomic backgrounds are organized
> into small groups.
> Credit is available on an individual basis with group guarantee.
> Training and technology are used to enhance current work.
> New types of income activities related to the domestic sphere are
> introduced.[11]

Women's projects, whatever their original conception, are today more likely to recognize women's double responsibility of work and family care. Women-only projects focus more and more on activities that provide a realistic economic return, while sectoral programs have begun to include an understanding of women's family responsibilities in their design. This merging of women's projects into a combined welfare–efficiency mode underscores the fact that women's lives are not compartmentalized between household and work or public and private; their concerns are not either–or; they are both. Women themselves see no dichotomy between their roles as housemaker and as economic actor; rather their work of all sorts is closely intertwined.

---

[11]Efforts to set up nontraditional activities such as interior painting in Korea or electrical repair in Egypt have been quite successful despite the conservatism of the society. In both countries, the women worked in pairs in homes under the direction of the housewife; this was seen by the patriarch as an improvement. Carpentry and housebuilding have been taught to women in squatter settlements in Sri Lanka and Ecuador so they could build their own homes. After initial objection by some male masons, the women in Sri Lanka began to work regularly on house construction.

The challenge for practitioners, then, is to design projects responsive to the multifaceted needs of women while avoiding the most serious drawbacks of earlier programs, particularly their fragmentary nature (ICPEDC 1986). Yet if these projects are to address the problem of women's poverty and powerlessness, they must make women more self-sufficient and self-reliant.

New Program Guidelines

To avoid the isolation and marginalization of women-only programs, current guidelines recommend that new projects for women should be embedded in regular sectoral programs organizationally and should be part of the original design, not added on as a "women's component." At the grassroots level, separate women's groups will still be necessary to facilitate women's ability to participate in the project and to express their own opinions. If local groups exist, it is important that they be consulted first, even if it becomes necessary to set up a new group focusing on new activities. Evaluations suggest that the simple fact of organizing is itself an empowering experience as women begin to share problems and to recognize they are not alone in their struggles to survive. But empowerment ought not stop at the group level. Mechanisms should be invented to allow representatives of women's groups to attend integrated meetings and voice women's opinions. At the lower levels the representatives should be chosen from among the grassroots members; at higher levels female staff should be charged with representing any special concerns of women.

Project designers must remember that poor women, whether rural or urban, are already heavily burdened and so may prefer direct assistance in meeting their survival needs over opportunities to undertake new time-consuming income activities. Simply providing more work or income without considering who controls both labor and income in the family may only increase stress on women rather than giving them a measure of economic independence.[12] In fact, independence may seem neither possible nor desirable to many women who accept homemaking as their primary goal and work to improve the lives of their children. So programmers have a double charge: projects must necessarily respond to women's expressed needs if participation is to be a reality, and projects must change the lives of women if the goal of self-sufficiency is to be met. In other words, the process by which decisions are reached and the method by which projects are implemented can foster either dependency or greater self-confidence and self-sufficiency. Therefore, the impact of proposed new activities on women themselves must be analyzed not simply in terms of the type of work or

---

[12]Patriarchal control of women's labor has been widely discussed and is a central issue in many contributions to this volume; see, for example, Kandiyoti (1985). Women's control of money within the family is less studied; Dwyer & Bruce (1988) is the first major volume on this issue. Senauer's chapter in this volume reports on three studies that show a direct relationship between women's work and improved food distribution/consumption within the family.

activity undertaken but in terms of whether such an effort addresses persistent inequalities.

A cautionary note is necessary. Many women's projects will undoubtedly
continue to appear strongly in a "welfarist" mode, though they may be
mixed with the ideas of participation and self-sufficiency to reduce long-
term costs. Governments do not foster destabilizing programs. Therefore,
even programs that increase a woman's power, such as her right to own land
or a home, will not be so described but rather will be presented as programs
to increase agricultural production or to provide urban housing. Even smaller steps may have important long-term effects: simply attending a meeting
of women outside her own compound may profoundly enlarge a woman's
world view.

Practitioners must operate within bureaucratic constraints and accept limited visions of change by male-dominated governments. In their programmatic responses to global change and to women's needs, there exists an
opportunity to provide space for women to alter their lives and increase their
economic independence. The intermediaries most successful in opening this
space have been led by indigenous charismatic leaders who have the prestige
and contacts to intervene on behalf of their poor constituents and do not
hesitate to use them (Tendler 1987). Since any altering of the status quo will
produce some losers, the provision of political and economic protection for
the poor as they organize or switch credit from moneylenders or challenge
entrenched traders must not be forgotten. Astute maneuvering to avoid win-
lose situations has been proven to be more viable in the long run.

SCHOLARS

Scholars of women in development are a much more diverse group than
either the advocates or the practitioners. Constrained neither by the existing
governmental systems nor by agency bureaucracies, they are free to utilize
ideologies or images of the future to test and judge contemporary issues. All
are grounded in feminism; those writing within the two major economic
persuasions of liberal and Marxist economics have provided valuable critiques of these theories. An increasing number of feminists dismiss both
theories as out of date with regard to both women and global reality; nevertheless, they are uncomfortable with the distinctive feminist approach,
which argues for a female sphere (Jaquette 1982). All these commentators
on modernization and development draw on the rich scholarship concerning
women's lives around the world presented in the more static mode of comparative studies.

Feminist scholars are clearly grounded in the current wave of the women's
movement that has as its uniting principle its attack on the inequities in a
world run by men for men. Elise Boulding (1988), tracing the distinction
between women's movements in the nineteenth and the twentieth centuries,
sees this uniting principle as a major difference between the two movements.
The earlier movement focused on social change utilizing what she terms the

"civic housekeeping rhetoric," that is, women translating to the community level "their sense of traditional responsibility for the wellbeing of their family." A major element in this early movement, like that of today, was the concern for peace, because women saw war as the cause of much social misery. Whereas the suffragists allied with men to reach their objectives, members of the contemporary women's movement see women as victims of patriarchy and are angry with men.

This feminism informs the work of all women in development scholars, drawing them closer together as the flood of research swamps current male paradigms. Two sets of basic issues have dominated the field, one revolving around the counting and valuing of women's work, the other around the efforts of adapting or changing development theories to accommodate feminist thought. Rather than discussing each perspective, an overview of these basic issues is presented.

Documenting Women's Work

Women in development advocates, echoing the U.S. feminists' emphasis on economic independence for women as the key to freeing women from male dominance, had argued that development was having a negative impact on women's traditional economic activities. This position set off a search of the scholarly literature for documentation of women's work that could be utilized in the writing of policy papers. In the late sixties there was a dearth of empirical research on women as independent entities; mostly women were portrayed belonging to kinship or family groupings. A few anthropologists, following Margaret Mead's example, had begun to study women's roles in remote parts of the world; since these were subsistence societies, however, little attention was paid to women's economic activity. An important exception was the study of West African women traders (Afonja, Chapter 12, this volume; Tinker 1987b).

As WID practitioners began to design projects for women, their agencies became not only important consumers of data about women but funders of research as well. Most such studies done under contract have tended to be descriptive or analytical and to remain within the current operating theory of the funding agency, namely, liberal economic theory. These are pragmatic studies of actual conditions of women farmers, or traders, or women's organizations; they deal with what is happening and what might be done within the current structures of authority and power. In contrast, the United Nations has supported research on women from a broad theoretical perspective, as indicated by the studies written for the Rural Development Programme of the ILO and the background documents prepared for the Mid-Decade Conference for the U.N. Decade for Women. Such studies are more likely to perceive of women's problems as emanating from colonialism and the current capitalistic structure of global society.

Counting women's subsistence work as they maintain home and family and sell their surplus in the market was the objective of much of this research. Time budget studies proved a particularly useful mechanism for

identifying the amount and types of women's economic activity and showing that real limits on women's time constitute a major constraint to rural
development. Analyses of the sexual division of labor document women's
increasing work burden as men move into more technologically advanced
activities, leaving women with the labor-intensive work of subsistence living
(Beneria 1982b; Kandiyoti 1985; Tinker 1987a).

Most subsistence economic activity was not included in national employment accounts. The 12–14 hours per day that women worked as farmers,
food processors, providers of water and fuel, house builders, traders, craft-
makers, brewers, weavers, potters—none of this was considered work (Jahan & Papenek 1979; Tinker 1976a). Therefore a major effort of WID
scholars has been to challenge both the definition of work and the method
of data collection (Beneria 1982a). Counting women's agricultural work
illustrates the difficulties of statistics and shows how different statistical
methods produce different results (Dixon-Mueller 1985).

Concern with the growing poverty among women turned many scholars to
studies of the urban area (Buvinic, Lycette, & McGreevey 1983), counting
women's work as prostitutes (Phongpaichit 1982), domestics and vendors
(Bunster & Chaney 1985), street food producers and sellers (Tinker 1987b),
or white-collar employees (Schuster 1979; also see Jones 1984; Obbo 1980).
Reports of self-help housing, waste management, and community kitchens
document the variety of women's work in cities (Schmink, Bruce, & Kohn
1986). But far the greatest interest has been expressed in women's work as
microentrepreneurs.

Women microentrepreneurs were largely invisible in the early informal
sector studies undertaken with the encouragement of the ILO in the 1970s
(Young & Moser 1981). However, the realization that this robust sector was a
major source of employment for the rapidly growing urban populations in
developing countries added to the pressure to revise employment data since
neither men nor women working in this highly diverse sector were generally
counted. Women are found throughout the sector, but most often in work
that is perceived of as an extension of their domestic activity: in urban areas
as street vendors or market sellers, in rural areas dying cloth or processing
food. Self-employed women operate microenterprises characterized by weak
market integration and strong face-to-face customer relations (deTreville
1987). Increasingly, however, women working in the home are not self-
employed but rather are vertically integrated into a larger economic activity:
knitting with hand machines, rolling cigarettes, assembling toys. In fact, this
distinction between self-employed entrepreneurs and women working as
subcontractors at home is murky. But the distinction between microentrepreneurs and home-based industrial workers is important to draw when
designing programs to assist and support them.

The independence of women microentrepreneurs and the extent to which
they utilize family labor or work for their husbands varies widely by region
and culture. Similarly, their income varies: a longitudinal study of markets
indicates that women are the smallest of traders whose very low profit

margins prevent expansion or even stability (Moser 1980). In an eight-country study, the Equity Policy Center found that both male and female street food sellers earn an income equal to or greater than the local minimum wage and the comparative income of men and women varies by country (Tinker 1987b).

Because these activities are family or individual enterprises and so do not offer employment to others, the ILO and scholars interested in employment have tended to dismiss microentrepreneurs as that part of the informal sector which is not worthy of support. They argue that microentrepreneurs, particularly the women among them, lack economic acumen because they seldom reinvest in their enterprise, instead using profits for improving family nutrition or sending the children to school. If expansion occurs, it is more likely to do so in an amoeba fashion, the enterprise replicating itself as a family member sets up her own shop (Tinker 1987b).

Resistance to growth would appear to be a sensible policy, however. As growth occurs, men frequently take over (Bhatt 1987; deTreville 1987). Increase in size from a family enterprise to a firm with employees requires a shift in organization and priorities, with a high rate of failure. Further, investing money in an enterprise instead of in one's children is not an overriding priority for most women entrepreneurs. Although this value orientation dismays economists who celebrate the profit motive, it may indicate the practice of a more human economy (Tinker 1987c). Women should not be penalized for questioning the primacy of the profit motive; rather programs should be redesigned to accommodate this differing world view.

Women in home-based industries in South Asia also "tend to attach values other than purely economic ones to their home-based work" (Singh & Kelles-Viitanen 1987:14), particularly their ability to combine work with domestic chores. Nonetheless, as subcontractors, these women may be more exploited by the vertical integration of their activities. Lourdes Beneria and Martha Roldan (1987), in their recent study of homework in Mexico City, are also ambivalent about this type of employment, which they consider a disguised form of subproletarianization. At the same time they recognize this work as part of women's survival strategies. Therefore they differ with earlier Marxist scholars by neither opposing home work nor arguing for collectives or other policies that might reduce the amount of work available.

Organizing these microentrepreneurs or home-based workers into some sort of group is the first step to assisting them, an approach that is now commonly followed. A critical second step, securing political power to protect these poor women, has too frequently been overlooked. In a review of "better-performing" organizations for enterprise development, Judith Tendler (1987) found that all these successful organizations were headed by powerful, if not charismatic leaders, who were not only from the elite but well-connected politically. To protect their clientele, these leaders alternatively challenged and cooperated with entrenched institutions in their countries such as trade unions, banks, and government ministries. The importance of middle-class women's organizations in protecting the poor women's organizations which they have set up has been increasingly stressed and serves to underscore the growing solidarity of women across class lines.

More studies are needed about women microentrepreneurs and home-based workers both in the traditional self-employment and integrated modes. Programs designed to help them must recognize the values these women hold and not try to undermine their human economy with requirements of growth. Organization is essential for empowerment as well as for efficient distribution of information or services. Finally, organizers must recognize that if the programs are successful, they will necessarily challenge the domestic and economic arrangements that have kept these poor women workers from earning an adequate income. Political protection and visible defenders are essential to diminish overt opposition, but programs which include some benefits for those whose power is being displaced, such as husbands or moneylenders, may be the most sensible and enduring approach.

Women in industry became a highly debated topic within the scholarly community as multinational corporations began to set up factories in developing countries. Linda Lim (Chapter 7, this volume) suggests that the intensity of interest was fostered by theoretical debates relating to global capitalism. The issue of whether such employment offers opportunity to women or exploits them continues to be an emotional one. Yet it is interesting that objections to supporting women in the informal sector (at home or in sweatshops) frequently were based on the assumption of capitalist exploitations of that vulnerable and dependent sector; work in industry was seen as preferable (Youssef, Nieves, & Sebstad 1980). Elizabeth Souza-Lobo (1986), in her study of Brazilian industry, concludes that factories have played a positive role in women's survival but that industrial employment has reproduced the gender subordination of the society as a whole through the continuation of the sexual division of labor. As the theoretical debate fades, more research on women's employment in all types of industry needs to be undertaken.

Adapting Development Theory

Scholarly critiques of the development community in general and of women in development in particular have come primarily from three sources: Marxist feminists, women in the developing countries, and scholars identifying with the female sphere approach. As noted earlier, WID advocates and practitioners, because their objective is to influence the development community, tend not to raise basic theoretical issues but rather seek to adjust current development practices to include and benefit women. This non-ideological stance, which includes scholars documenting the WID process, has both annoyed and confused those scholars who are consumed with theoretical arguments, however far they may be removed from reality. As the field matures, the pragmatic approach of the WID practitioners and advocates and the detail of women's lives coming from WID scholars have begun to influence theorists. Similarly, questions of global structures, power relationships, and values raised by the theorists become more pertinent to practice as the easy optimism of the 1970s begins to fade. These changes in perspective and in the perception of predominant issues are discussed throughout this book, but three critical questions require comment here: Do women constitute a category? How do women's issues relate to macroeconomic policies? How should women's work be valued?

Women as a category has been challenged by Marxist feminists, who argue that biological sex is turned into gender relationships between men and women through cultural, social, economic, and political forces that vary by class; following the logic of class conflict, women across classes have no common interests. Feminists have pointed out that women of all classes, and in all societies including socialist nations, are disadvantaged; for them, patriarchy is the source of subordination. Both Marxist and mainstream feminists would alter the structures of oppression toward equality, but the female sphere theorists would celebrate difference. While the debate continues over the predominant influence, both class and patriarchy have been generally accepted as causes of women's subordination (Hartmann 1981; Maguire 1984).

This two-pronged approach has posed a problem for Marxists, who could be accused of injecting dualism into theory and so diluting the revolutionary message; they have addressed the issue in a variety of ways. Caroline Moser continues to insist on the primacy of class (1987). Ken Kusterer (Chapter 15, this volume) gives a sense of the emotion invested in this debate then proceeds to conflate gender and class within his adaptation of articulation theory. Beneria and Roldan criticize both Marxist concepts that "tend toward economic reductionism, resulting in the subsumption of gender hierarchies under class inequalities" and the radical feminists message "that women's subordination is based on male control of women's sexuality, procreative capacity, and ideology" because of its relative neglect of economic factors; their solution is to look at the intersections of class and gender (1987:9). Avoiding dualism by intersection seems to have been widely accepted in Latin America; a report by the Economic Commission for Latin America concludes its discussion of this issue by suggesting that "groupings based on social stratification cut across a society horizontally while groupings based on sex and age cut across a society vertically" (CEPAL 1983:21).

Devaki Jain, coming from a Gandhian tradition, has tried to avoid the class–patriarchy debate by arguing that women need first to sort out their common interests for a just relationship with men and then join with men in a united effort for revolutionary changes in all of society (1980a). In this manner she subsumes the idea of class since all men will unite with all women; she also avoids the condemnation of women's emancipation voiced by many Third World women at the Mexico City conference that feminism, interpreted as a struggle against men, was "unbecoming and western" (Jain, Singh, & Chand 1979).

Over the decade, several other elements have been identified as significant contributors to women's subordination, especially race in the U.S. Women scholars from developing countries, including those represented in this book, utilize class and gender analyses in their research, but add such Third World issues as dependency, underdevelopment, and colonialism. Discussing gender oppression in India, Kalpana Bardhan (1987) cites the additional complications of caste, ethnicity, and religion. She adds a new dimension to this debate by arguing that women in higher classes are subject to patriarchy to a greater degree than lower class women, who are more economically exploited. This difference, typical of societies that place a premium on seclusion of women, reinforces violence against lower class women: required to go out to make a living, these women have lost their status of women by breaking seclusion. The patriarchy that affects these lower class women is class influenced, a fact that illustrates the interrelationships among the many factors which seem to reinforce women's subordination.

This controversy over the structural causes of women's subordination provides an analytical tool for practitioners. Development assistance programs which respond to women's practical or material interests may help them survive and fulfill their gendered roles, but they do nothing to change women's subordination and may in fact perpetuate it. In contrast, programs that take into account women's *strategic* interests, according to Maxine Molyneux, will include such goals as women's emancipation or gender equality (1985). It does not matter whether programs are classified within the development community as welfare or sectoral; the critical point is whether the process of supplying these basic needs includes "consciousness-raising . . . a change of attitudes, organization and mobilization for social and political participation, structural change and institutional and legal changes" (CEPAL 1983:10). Caroline Moser shows how housing programs for poor women either could supply a practical need for shelter or could fulfill a strategic need for change if the woman could own her house herself (1987). In short, if programs do not address the causes of women's persistent inequalities, they should not be considered feminist.

Feminism, then, provides a political basis for organizing women across societal divisions even as it recognizes differences in women's lives. Ann Whitehead summarizes this view: "One of contemporary feminist theory's main contributions to the study of women was to rediscover shared gender as a basis for solidarity and common interest, and different gender as a basis for division of interest and ideological dissonance" (1981:6).

Relating value and status to women's work has been a goal throughout the decade, but the search has frequently been submerged in development literature with its emphasis on economic activities. Although a perusal of studies on subsistence societies will quickly identify many where women worked long hours but were treated as slaves, the prevailing opinion is that work is a necessary but not sufficient condition of high female status (Bardhan 1987; Blumberg 1988; Sanday 1974). Recent studies of new industry in developing countries show that the women participating in the wage economy are far from liberated (Sacks 1987). Practitioners are exercising greater caution not to increase a woman's work without empowering her as well: attending to strategic as well as practical needs. This requires an exploration of who controls women's labor and moves the question back into the household and the issue of patriarchy.

Two different perspectives, both emanating from the female sphere approach, have questioned the pursuit of equality of work as the basis for an egalitarian society. The first is based on the tradition of women's autonomy within the private world, leaving the public world to men. In such a society, family prestige, and therefore women's status, is enhanced when women are taken out of the visible public labor force even though they become economically more dependent (Mason 1984). In many parts of Africa today, as the middle class grows, there is increasing pressure on urban women to stop their income activities, particularly jobs in the informal sector; some women, used to their own income, are not convinced that dependency is an improvement and are choosing to distance themselves from their husbands to retain control over their own income (Hansen 1987). Despite the danger of recreating separate and unequal divisions between men and women and thus reinforcing women's dependence, the concept of autonomy in the female sphere continues to attract supporters. For example, in contemporary Iran, the regime is insisting that men work to support the family while women stay home, a decree that has been welcomed by many poor and formerly hardworking women.

The second perspective questioning male values comes from scholars such as Elise Boulding who argue that as a result of centuries of autonomy, women have developed a female culture geared to nurturing and survival. This autonomy was bolstered by a series of rights and perquisites based both on informal work and on services related to life–cycle events, illness, house building, and the like. The mechanisms through which this autonomy functions include not only kin but simulated kin in a variety of patron-client relationships. These relationships provide female support networks not only in the neighborhood (Loza-Soliman 1981) but, more recently, at the national and global levels (Boulding 1988). Boulding argues that feminine values are essential if the world is to survive: ecofeminists decry male aspirations of ruling or raping the earth and call for environmentally sound, resource-conserving technologies; peace advocates demand more funds for development and less for armaments and also relate male predilection for wars to violence against women.

Influenced by these arguments and perturbed by evidence that development projects supplying more resources may free women from patriarchal control but not from poverty or child care, more and more feminists are searching for alternative visions. They are concerned that the emphasis on work has produced as one-dimensional a woman as did the earlier emphasis on women as mother, and they fear that destroying patriarchy means discarding permanent female–male relationships. Many are beginning to wonder whether, by asking for equal rights with men *as if they were men*, women are denying their own values and priorities associated with caring, and whether, *by using men as their measure*, women will not always be second class. In concrete terms, would granting land ownership to farming women in Africa only increase their work while enabling fathers to avoid any costs of having children, or would such redistribution of resources move African women toward greater equality?

Visions of the future are unformed and constitute a major challenge to global feminism. In reconstructing a new balance among women, family, and community, it is clear that individual responsibilities as well as rights must be stressed. Outlining her view of ethics in feminism, Gita Sen cautions women against seeking individualized autonomy and running the "risk of splitting off from ourselves the nurturant aspects of human existence. . . . If we view a hierarchized, oppressive interdependence versus a non-hierarchical, alienated individuation as the only two possible alternatives, then we lost indeed" (1988:17–18).

Macroeconomic policies and women has become a critical topic of research. The debt crisis has made obvious the connection between global trends and women's poverty even when exact causality is difficult to establish. DAWN (Development Alternatives with Women for a New Era) chronicles the systemic crises that threaten both environment and economic activity—and hence women—at the local level but which are caused by policies that encourage exploitation of land and natural resources, open global capital markets, and militarism. Sen and Grown predict that the impact on women of the global debt repayments will be mixed, with fewer better paid jobs available and more employment opportunities in the low-paying sector; further, government expenditures in the social sector will be reduced (1987:61–62).

Uma Lele related microprocesses of economic activity to women's participation in the labor force and noted how public policy often distorts factor and product markets to the disadvantage of women (1984). Susan Joekes (1988) made a concerted effort to identify how various macropolicies have differential effects on the distinctive structures of the male and female work force. In particular, she shows in her discussion of the impact of structural adjustment policies how these policies both reflect and perpetuate gender bias already existing in normal market-regulating policies. Agriculture is an area where women's differential involvement results in different impacts of macropolicies such as pricing and subsidies; Rae Blumberg, writing on the African food crisis, argues that "misdirected macro level development policies that are blind to the importance of women's economic power and incentives at the micro level" have contributed to the recent African food crisis (1988:1). Such research establishes the importance of relating macropolicies to microeffects when addressing the impoverishment of women; the fragmentary nature of data indicates a need for further studies.

The three women's conferences for the Decade for Women introduced large numbers of women to the formal U.N. process. Even more, these conferences fostered the internationalization of the women's movement; out of Nairobi emerged a variety of global networks based on Third World women to complement and balance the earlier American and European organizing efforts. There is widespread agreement among them that only through connecting women's views of human priorities to national and global issues can women gain access to meaningful resources. This move to consider the impact of macropolicies on women at the microlevel requires that women's groups bring this perspective into national politics, where little support now exists.

CONCLUSION

This series of commentaries on critical issues of women in development is meant to illustrate two trends. First, there is a growing similarity of ideas being proposed by women coming from various perspectives. Women's roles are multifaceted, women's identities are multilinked. There is strength in gender diversity; there is also strength in women's shared culture and values. New research is needed to explore whether these alternative values are merely an expression of subordination or whether they represent a fundamentally different life force or life view. In doing this research, scholars must remember to differentiate between women's objective and subjective conditions, for though the indicators of income and goods suggest women are worse off than before the Decade began, women's organizations at all levels are giving women a sense of participation and power over their own lives they have never had before (Safa 1987).

The second trend is toward greater awareness of political power and of the need to assess political institutions through a gender-sensitive lens. If two decades ago the emphasis was on economics as a path for women to attain greater equity, today the emphasis is on politics: local, national, and global. If patriarchal institutions at all levels are responsible for the maintenance of persistent inequalities of women, then the next feminist agenda must be the analysis of these institutions in order to abolish or change them. If the emphasis of the Decade was to convince the development bureaucracies to include women as the practitioners have been doing, this new agenda must revitalize the advocates to pursue policy change even more vigorously as this current agenda gives women a stake in the political process.

4

Gender and Justice in Economic Development

JANE S. JAQUETTE

Ester Boserup's *Women's Role in Economic Development*, published in 1970, launched the field of women in development. The book was revolutionary because it changed prevailing concepts about women's economic roles in modernizing agricultural societies. As is the case with most revolutions, Boserup's work built on the ideas and insights of others; its publication in 1970 coincided with the rising wave of feminist consciousness in the United States and Europe. In retrospect, as this chapter will argue, the significance of Boserup's book is not only that it offered a coherent argument backed by a historical and comparative analysis of women's work, but also that it suggested a powerful way to argue the case for redistributing productive resources to women, providing a political as well as an economic rationale for changing development policies.

Boserup argued that women's status in agricultural societies was positively correlated with their roles in food production and that as technologies advanced (and as men monopolized the more advanced technologies), women were increasingly marginalized from agriculture. This in turn reduced women's status and consequently their freedom. Colonial bureaucracies exacerbated this tendency by introducing new farming techniques and cash crops; because of Western notions about the appropriate sexual division of labor in agriculture, men were trained to use these new technologies and women continued to work the least productive land with the poorest inputs. As a result, women lost income and status relative to men. Recognizing that modernization entailed urbanization, Boserup also examined the economic situation of women in cities, noting that women were often excluded from formal sector jobs in modern employment by their low levels of education and by discriminatory practices and arguing that women's access to "bazaar and service" occupations could be the basis for improving women's incomes.

Boserup's thesis challenged the common assumption that women's rights and status automatically improve as modernization proceeds. She also directed attention toward policies that could enhance women's chances. If colonial administrations had undermined women's position by failing to recognize women's productive roles, then enlightened policies on the part of national governments and international agencies could correct the mistakes of the past.

Boserup's pathbreaking work defined a new arena of policymaking and marked out a new area of professional expertise. The United States and other countries that are major donors of development assistance took steps to promote the integration of women into the development process (Tinker 1983). The United Nations declared 1976–85 the Decade for Women and established women's offices within agencies like the Food and Agricultural Organization and the U.N. Development Programme. Resources were mobilized, NGOs were organized around the issue, and a vast effort was made to study women's roles in Third World economies and to improve their access to productive resources.

Boserup's theses have also generated debate and controversy. Scholars and practitioners in the field of women in development are still testing her insights and questioning her conclusions. But why did *Women's Role in Economic Development* have such a powerful impact? One obvious answer is timing: Boserup's work appeared as the feminist movement was gaining political influence in the United States, and women interested in development issues seized on her arguments to inject the women's issue into development debates. This chapter argues that it is not only the timing but the content of Boserup's thesis that made a difference. What made Boserup's somewhat academic study of women in development so politically effective was that it put women's demands in a new context: it linked women's condition to effective claims for justice. One purpose of the analysis that follows is to sort out the kinds of arguments Boserup used and assess why they worked well together.

The success of women in development has created a new set of debates that now divide scholars, practitioners, and advocates in the field. This chapter reviews the main criticisms made of Boserup's work, analyzing them as competing ways of arguing about gender justice. By sorting out the normative arguments in the women in development debates, it may be easier to determine whether competing claims can be reconciled with one another or whether they will continue to divide feminist thought and action in ways that weaken public understanding and support and undermine the commitment of development professionals to taking the gender issue more seriously.

History shows us that the existence of severe inequalities does not in itself ensure that those who are discriminated against will be able to claim that the inequality they are suffering is unjust. Even when an inequality is perceived as unjust, that perception must be translated into political and social action that will change the pattern by which resources are allocated. How did *Women's Role in Economic Development* change the dominant perception that development assistance was being justly allocated between men and women? More specifically, how did Boserup's thesis make longstanding gender differences in resource allocation seem both unjust and capable of being changed? What new arguments for gender justice did Boserup's book introduce? What are the consequences of those arguments for sustaining women's claims in the future?

COMPETING CRITERIA OF JUSTICE: EQUALITY, MERIT, AND NEED

Debates about justice are a recurring and often enlivening aspect of political life. Themes developed by Aristotle and Plato, Hobbes and Locke, Hume and Kant are all present in modern debates about justice, which divide along conservative, liberal, and Marxist lines.

We begin with some basic categories. An important distinction has been made between material justice (arguments about the allocation of "values," be they material goods, prestige, or power) and procedural justice (whether an allocative decision was arrived at by a process that is just). Women in development arguments have largely been based on claims for material (or distributive) justice, but procedural questions are still important, not only because reallocative decisions must be arrived at by a process that is accepted as legitimate but because, as this chapter will argue, value-allocating institutions directly affect the form and quality of justice.

Marxist theorists argue that social structures themselves can be just or unjust. Capitalism is structurally exploitative; socialism would resolve issues that are constantly legislated and litigated in capitalist societies by structuring society according to the principle "From each according to his abilities, to each according to his needs" (Taylor 1986).

In practice, both capitalist and socialist societies reveal a gap between egalitarian rhetoric and distributive reality because, explicitly or implicitly, both accept competing criteria of justice as legitimate bases for making allocative decisions. There are three criteria of justice at the heart of the modern debate. The first is that social goods (including property, power, and prestige) should be distributed equally (the equality principle). The second is that social goods should be distributed in proportion to productive contributions (the "just desert" or merit principle). The third is that social goods should be allocated to the poorest and most powerless members according to relative need (the welfare principle).

Equality

Not all societies have valued equality over other principles of justice, even at the rhetorical level. Aristotle and Plato both recognized that specialization leads to different roles and argued that some roles naturally dominate others, just as the captain must pilot the ship and the manager must manage. Political meritocracy and clear distinctions between "citizens" and "others" — including women and slaves — were seen as legitimate in classical political theory. Feudal society was founded on the acceptance of hierarchy; as the bonds of feudal society were loosened and traditional forms of patrimonial authority began to crumble, theorists resorted to the venerable model of the hierarchical patriarchal family to buttress the flagging legitimacy of the principle of the divine right of kings.

The call for equality and demands for democratic rule are synonymous with modern politics. Revolutions are made in the name of equality, against feudal privilege or colonial domination. The nineteenth-century feminist movement added women to the category of humans to which the equality principle should apply. Socialism expands the scope of the principle, arguing that without economic equality, political and legal equality cannot be achieved.

Given its widespread appeal, the frequency with which the equality principle is violated is striking. The United States may have been "born free," without the burden of class polarization characteristic of Europe or much of the Third World today, yet its black population was enslaved and its female population was politically invisible. And although women's equality has again become a major issue in the last quarter of the twentieth century, norms and practices have proven resistant to change.

In theory, as Thelma McCormack observed, modernization should reinforce equality by establishing "a gender-free division of labor, a set of gender-free standards of achievement, and gender-free institutions" (1981:28). Instead, she argues, patriarchy has modernized itself. Male domination is no longer justified by reference to "holy texts or sacred scripts," but by "scientific studies of the brain, of psychological differences, [and] of personality development" that are called upon to legitimize discriminatory practices (p. 28). Modernization has not eliminated gender distinctions, even though it can be argued that they are no longer economically relevant.

The equality claim is an ethical one, and it can be neutralized by ethical counterclaims. This has been especially true for women, as when the point is made that women's moral qualities must be preserved for the good of society. In an essay on the importance of human rights, for example, John Kleinig argues that women (and other groups seeking liberation) should not be encouraged to think exclusively in terms of rights, that "rights-talk" must not "get out of hand." For Kleinig, rights are an "auxiliary apparatus" to be brought into play "only after the primary moral relations of love, care and concern have been broken down" (1978:46).

It is easy to criticize Kleinig for appearing to leave the responsibility for care in the hands of women and other oppressed groups. And it is common to find distinctions that would appear unacceptable when applied to other groups that are seen as appropriate when applied to women — so that society's moral equilibrium may be preserved. It is more difficult to assess such arguments when they are made by feminists. Carol Gilligan's well-known contrast between the typically "male" ethic of rights and the "female" ethic of care (1982) can be used to argue that public discourse has been too one-sidedly dominated by rights debates. It further highlights the importance of procedures, for moral reasoning, like legal reasoning, is supposed to seek the appropriate principle and apply it, rather than weighing competing principles.[1] Although Gilligan has taken pains to argue that the differences between women's and men's moral reasoning are a social and not a natural distinction, the effect of the discovery of women's "different voice" may ultimately have the same effect as Kleinig's argument: to suppress women's demands for change beneath a new, feminist-imposed norm of difference.

Against a history of domination that has been reinforced by norms which make women's inequality seem appropriate and even desirable, the main task the feminist movement set for itself was to gain standing for women, to make it possible for women to claim the same rights as other groups. In practice, standing requires that three conditions be met. First, the group claiming standing must be included in the relevant rule. "All are equal" in practice requires specifying what "all" includes—all men? all people? all living things? Second, implementing a new allocative rule must appear feasible. We can declare that everyone should receive "equal treatment under the law," but we then must convincingly specify, how that rule will be carried out in practice. The costs must not be so high as to endanger other strongly held values. Finally, equality claims must hold up against moral as well as practical counterarguments. It must be acceptable for women to be motivated by interests as well as mother love; to be active politically as well as domestically; to be seen as legitimate holders of wealth and earners of income without having these activities jeopardize their moral status.

Once an equality claim has achieved standing, then what some have called "boundary issues" must also be taken into consideration. All human beings can be declared equal, but what institution is then responsible for making this rule stick and for what population? The nation-state is the most obvious institution to carry out the charge of making sure that individuals enjoy

---

[1]In a superb discussion of the impact of Carol Gilligan's work, Seyla Benhabib argues that the "justice paradigm" is inadequate, that a "communicative ethic of need interpretations," along lines suggested by Jurgen Habermas, provides a more promising model to address the issues raised in this essay. She criticizes the justice paradigm for assuming a universality that denies the concrete reality of individuals' experiences, perceptions, and suffering (Benhabib 1987:93). This chapter shares that concern but argues that issues of justice can motivate political action in ways that an "ethic of communication" is unlikely to do. The object is to broaden the concept of justice rather than abandon it. By contrast, Judith Shklar strongly defends the notion of rights:

> In fact, there are no evident pegs on which one can hang distributive justice now. To injustice, injury and inequality, case by case, day by day, representative democracy slowly and often quite unsuccessfully does respond. Without the procedures of constitutional government we are utterly helpless, incapable of demanding others' rights and our own. If effective rights require rational empathy, it is because that mental and emotional effort is the only possible psychological equivalent of John Rawls' original position which is historically open to us. It may not be much, but it ought to remind those who are so pleased to denounce rights and indeed liberalism generally as selfish atavisms that one might well reflect on the implications of their actual destruction and to reconsider both liberty and the conditions of liberty before abandoning them in the hope of communitarian harmony and of social arrangements untouched by the historical experiences of our world. (1986:32–33)

equality, but it is not the only one. Non–state institutions, such as markets and systems of social norms, may be as important as laws in allocating (and reallocating) values, even when the nation-state is the "ultimate" (most coercive) arbiter. The boundaries of allocative systems may not fully coincide, as is evident in the discrepancies between the boundaries of markets and states or of ethnic groups and states. The conventional wisdom that "you can't legislate morality" illustrates a different kind of boundary problem, and both are relevant to implementing decisions that change the existing patterns of value allocations.

Women's Role in Economic Development gave a powerful impetus to women's equality claims in the institutions that allocate scarce development resources. If women had only recently enjoyed a position of relative equality with men (e.g., in Africa and in the "female farming systems" Boserup identified as characteristic of slash and burn agriculture), then women could not be denied access to resources on the grounds of their "natural" inferiority. Further, the fact that women bore children did not determine their status. Women's role in production was the critical variable: where women were forced to specialize in reproduction, their status was lower.

> In the type of community where women work hard, it is characteristic that they are valued both as workers and as mothers of the next generation and, therefore, that men keenly desire to have more than one wife. On the other hand, in a rural community where women take little part in field work, they are valued as mothers only and the status of the barren woman is very low in comparison with that of the mother with numerous male children. (Boserup 1970:51)

Boserup explained women's dependence as a consequence of the changing relations of economic production. She further argued that these economic changes did not necessarily marginalize women. Women's role in agriculture had been diminished by their lack of access to new technologies, a trend that was aggravated by colonial administrations which provided men with the training, inputs, credit, and markets to produce and sell cash crops while women continued to produce most of the food without benefit of new inputs. Because the lack of access to training and technology was the primary cause of women's economic marginalization, policies that would allocate development resources to them seemed both appropriate and feasible. There was an urgent need to act because letting modernization take its course could only worsen the situation. Boserup's approach also anticipated the moral counterarguments that would be used against women in development: since African women had recently been equal to African men, the claim that women should have more equal access to resources could not be dismissed as a "Western" or "feminist" import.

Merit and the Market

In modern societies, merit is the criterion that is brought to bear most frequently against arguments for full equality among men as well as to justify persistent inequalities on the basis of sex. Jennifer Hochschild (1981) begins her book on American views of distributive justice with the striking point that although Americans now think it is appropriate for women and minorities to make equality claims, they are unmoved by evidence that the gap between rich and poor in the United States is as great today as it was in the 1920s and they remain undismayed when shown evidence that only France among the industrialized countries has a worse overall pattern of income distribution than the United States.

Americans favor equality only when it does not conflict with another criterion of justice — namely, merit — and they define merit narrowly as efficiency. People who produce more deserve more, and people with higher incomes deserve them, because the market works; it is essentially fair. Equating an individual's merit to his or her productivity also postulates that society has chosen to make the production of material goods a very important — possibly the most important — social goal. The result is a conflict between equality and efficiency. This conflict, with all its attendant contradictions and nuances, is perfectly reflected in the work of philosopher John Rawls, whose book *A Theory of Justice* provokes sharp debates between liberals and both conservatives and Marxists.

A Theory of Justice (1971) has been described as the most ambitious effort to develop a universal philosophy of ethics since that of Immanuel Kant (Wolff 1977). Rawls's intent was to build a deductive theory of a just society. He began by constructing a hypothetical bargaining situation reminiscent of the state of nature, also the starting point for the social contract theories of Locke, Hobbes, and Rousseau. In Rawls's scheme, individuals who are knowledgeable about "how [modern] societies work" but are under a "veil of ignorance" about their own skills, talents, or position in life come together to negotiate the simplest set of rules they can devise for establishing a just society. After debating various alternatives, they emerge with two basic principles.

The First Principle maximizes equality: "Each person is to have an equal right to the most extensive total system of equal basic liberties compatible with a similar system of liberty for all." The Second Principle states that "Social and economic inequalities are to be arranged so that they are both: a) to the greatest benefit of the least advantaged, consistent with the just savings principle, and b) attached to offices open to all under conditions of fair equality of opportunity" (Rawls 1971:350). Inequalities are attached to positions that individuals can hold by competing for them. Competition ensures greater productivity and thus greater benefits for all; redistribution of these benefits (the "inequality surplus," to use Rawls's term) is limited by the need to induce individuals to save and invest.

The principles and the conditions discussed at length by Rawls place the central ethical dilemma of liberal capitalism in sharp relief. Liberalism is torn between its commitment to equality and its desire to maintain the conditions for economic growth. Although Rawls tried to broaden the definition of "productivity" to include nonmaterial goods, including the production of community life and participatory politics, the acceptance of the view that inequality is an important incentive for productivity causes the First Principle to take second place, and the failure to address how the "inequality surplus" should be redistributed leaves the reader to conclude, not incorrectly, that *A Theory of Justice* comes close to justifying the status quo in the developed West. From a Third World standpoint, Rawls's argument is weak because it assumes the existence of a modern economy that is sufficiently developed to produce an "inequality surplus" great enough to bridge the gap between rich and poor.

In developing societies, few share Rawls's confidence in market capitalism; issues of how much inequality is tolerable and debates over whether the market is a legitimate measure of an individual's social productivity have been at the center of political conflict and help explain why democratic institutions cannot easily survive. Recent experiments with privatization in China and with perestroika in the Soviet Union have weakened support for state-managed economies and undermined the appeal of dependency theory. There is greater acceptance of the view that markets are the most promising mechanisms to increase growth and to modernize technology. The worldwide recession of the 1980s has increased the leverage of the International Monetary Fund and the foreign assistance agencies, which share these promarket, productivity-oriented views. Americans add to this economic "realism" the belief that economic choice is an important indicator of individual freedom; this perception, combined with the belief that the state should work to create equality of opportunity but not of results, conditions their support for foreign assistance and guides the policies of U.S. foreign assistance.

Women's Role in Economic Development strengthened women's claims to a share of development assistance by combining arguments based on equality with evidence of women's productivity. The conventional wisdom was that women are less productive than men, and that this is "proven" by the fact that, globally, women's wages are about two-thirds those of men. By the standard logic, since the market is the measure of efficiency, women's productivity must be inferior to men's. Under these conditions it would be poor policy to waste scarce resources on those who are the less productive.

Boserup's argument speaks directly to this market conception of a merit claim for women. In the historical past, women were not only equal in status; they were equally productive. Since women cannot be shown to have evolved differently from men (at least not since the end of the nineteenth century!), they are still potentially equal to men. It is differential access to technology that has deprived women of their claim to equal productivity:

As agriculture becomes less dependent upon human muscular power, the difference in labor productivity between the two sexes might be expected to narrow. In actual fact . . . it is usually the men who learn to operate the new types of equipment while women continue to work with the old hand tools . . . the productivity gap tends to widen because men monopolize the use of the new equipment and the modern agricultural methods. . . . Thus, in the course of agricultural development, men's labour productivity tends to increase while women's remains more or less static. The corollary of the relative decline in women's labour productivity is a decline in their relative status within agriculture, and, as a further result, women will want either to abandon cultivation and retire to domestic life, or to leave for town. (Boserup 1970:53)

Boserup's data portray women as hardworking and productive in agriculture and trade, within the limits of the resources available to them. They are involuntarily excluded from full economic citizenship by a series of factors for which they cannot be blamed. Usufruct rights, which guaranteed women's access to land under subsistence agriculture, were too weak to protect women's claims when Western notions of private property were introduced. Land, training, and credit are necessary to improved productivity, but women are routinely denied access to them. As modernization proceeds, the gap between men and women grows larger:

Economic progress benefits men as wage earners in the modern sector, while the position of women is left unchanged, and even deteriorates when competition from the growing modern sectors eliminates the traditional enterprises carried on by women. (Boserup 1970:139)

Boserup's position accepts the market model but argues that policies based on Western notions of women's roles have hobbled potentially efficient producers. It provided a timely and hard to refute rationale for making the claim that women should be "integrated into development," which was used by WID advocates to create and sustain an Office for Women in Development at the U.S. Agency for International Development and in other bilateral and multilateral donor agencies and NGOs.

Need

Because both classical and feudal norms of justice were hierarchical, charity was an obvious necessity—and widely regarded as a means to individual salvation. In modern societies, hierarchy is denied and salvation has become a private matter, but there is still a broad consensus that claims based on need are legitimate and that a society cannot be just if it treats its weakest and poorest members without compassion. This view has had substantial support despite the "modern" counterclaim that "relief" programs are misguided because they encourage laziness. Hochschild found Americans much more responsive to appeals to care for the needy than to arguments that the gap between rich and poor should be reduced.

There is no need to credit those who support welfare programs with a highly developed sense of compassion, however. Meeting the needs of the "truly disadvantaged" is much less costly to the "haves" than income redistribution would be. And, as many social reformers have pointed out (Hochschild 1981; Piven & Cloward 1971), welfare supports the moral as well as the material position of the wealthy because it compensates for the failures of the market system instead of attacking it, reinforcing the view that those who are on top deserve to be there.

In the United States, where individual need arouses a compassionate response but where welfare programs have historically met with resistance, programs for poor women and children have received the most consistent political support. The vulnerability of women-headed families still provides the rationale for one of the few income transfer programs in the United States today that actually benefits the poor. Similarly, foreign assistance reaches poor women almost entirely through maternal and child health and population programs, another example of the point that women's successful claims to resource allocations have historically been based on need, not on equality or merit.[2]

In a truly egalitarian society, the criterion of need would presumably be redundant. But liberal capitalist (and I would argue socialist) societies are not unequivocally committed to equality; they tolerate a greater or lesser degree of inequality in the name of greater productivity. Further, they face similar problems when they seek to redistribute resources "according to need."

It is significant that Boserup avoids making claims for women on the basis of their neediness or portraying women as any less rational or (potentially) productive than men. An appeal based on women's neediness would certainly be effective — relief agencies routinely use women's vulnerability (footage of starving women and children in full-page magazine ads or on television) to increase donations. It is obvious that people would not send money as readily to help healthy and productive women shown laboring in the fields, however logical the argument that providing resources to enhance women's productivity would be much more effective than donations of food in reducing starvation in the long run.

Boserup consistently rejects the welfare perspective. The women she portrays are dispossessed and disempowered survivors, but they are not supplicants. Boserup's women act rationally, although they labor under severe constraints. They are often mothers, but they do not claim special consideration on those grounds. They are realists, responsible for family survival; their decisions reflect economic rather than emotional considerations.

Boserup's instinct to combine equality and efficiency arguments but to refuse to cast women as "needy" takes the more difficult but ultimately more sustainable path. Charity recipients, as John Stuart Mill observed over a century ago, are always subject to the arbitrary whims of the giver: "We may be bound to practice charity or beneficence, but not towards any definite

---

[2]Rawls's axiom that the surplus derived from inequality should be redistributed to the least advantaged members of the society may be a substitution of need for equality. Rawls's society which is made up of self-regarding individuals capable of making "rational life plans," who postpone gratification and save and invest, requires a "safety net" to salvage those who are irrational, profligate, or incapacitated and some kind of neutral mechanism to reallocate the rest of the "inequality surplus" fairly, without the disempowering effects of a "welfare" program.

person, [and] not at any prescribed time" (R. Cohen 1986:15n). Being "less advantaged" is a sure ticket to second-class citizenship. Those "on the dole" are not perceived, and do not perceive themselves, as full participants; they lose the dignity that is accorded "productive" members of society and sacrifice the ability to claim justice on other grounds. They become the objects of someone else's egalitarian political rhetoric.

Boserup set out to arouse a sense of injustice, but not of compassion. Because welfare and "citizenship" are at odds with each other, helping the needy (under current institutional arrangements) does not empower the poor. Awareness of this distinction explains why women in development advocates have often gone to great lengths to distinguish their programs from those carried out under the rubric of health or family planning, despite the position taken by those who advocate these programs that they, too, reallocate resources to women.

BOSERUP'S CRITICS

Two influential articles strongly critical of *Women's Role in Economic Development* have been published over the last several years. In 1975 Suellen Huntington argued that Boserup's attempt to distinguish between female and male farming systems ignored important factors of male dominance that could not be explained by levels of agricultural technology. She disagreed with Boserup's view that women had achieved more or less equal status with men in precolonial Africa and that they were as independent and self-sufficient as Boserup had described them. She pointed out that women can have a significant role in agricultural production without enjoying equal status or greater power. In female farming systems, Huntington wrote, "Men subjugate women and women subjugate other women and their own female children in a system of thoroughgoing and self-perpetuating exploitation" (p. 1008).

What is at stake here is not only the issue of whether women were or were not "equal" to men in traditional African society. To the degree that women in development claims were given standing because of the acceptance of the point that women had once been equal to men in status and productivity (at least in precolonial Africa and in female farming systems), that standing is jeopardized by a convincing counterargument that women have always been subjugated—a return to the conventional wisdom. Huntington's argument serves as a warning that the failure to base women's equality claims on a firm foundation could backfire; equality should be argued on its own merits, not by creating a history of women's equality that is vulnerable to historical refutation.

Although Boserup's arguments were very useful a decade ago, Boserup's thesis is less essential today. The U.N. Decade for Women gave the WID issue a broader political base among Third World women. The growing number of studies documenting the fact that the failure to include women in development projects reduces their likelihood of success (e.g., Staudt &

Jaquette 1983) has increased the effectiveness of the claim that women are productive. Efficiency has displaced equality as the rationale for claiming new resources.

But in a feminist sense, Huntington's approach is more radical than Boserup's and her concerns may yet prove well founded. Boserup's view that lack of access to technology is a prime cause of women's economic marginalization made it possible to argue that women's integration into development could make a difference. Huntington's insistence that male dominance and discrimination were important factors in women's economic marginalization (documented but not emphasized by Boserup) suggests that women in development programs that focus exclusively on women's economic empowerment are inadequate means to the end of women's full participation (see McCormack 1981).

Further, if future studies "prove" that women's productivity is consistently lower than men's—which is probable, given the very narrow economic measures of productivity which do not even credit reproductive work, much less the labor involved in the creation of community life—then Huntington's critique reminds us that a criterion of merit based on the presumption of women's equal productivity by the standard measures could easily be turned around and used against women: if women turn out to be less productive, they "deserve" fewer resources. Huntington's point is that the equality argument should not be abandoned just because the efficiency argument is currently easier to make.

In a series of articles that became the starting point for the Third World perspective on WID elaborated in *Development, Crises, and Alternative Visions* (Sen & Grown 1985), Lourdes Beneria and Gita Sen (1979, 1981, 1982) launched a very different kind of attack on *Women's Role in Economic Development*. They criticized Boserup for accepting the market model. The economic marginalization of women, they argued, results not from women's exclusion from productive labor but from the exploitation of their labor in the global system of capitalist labor relations. Women are forced by their poverty to participate in "a system that generates and intensifies inequalities" and "makes use of existing gender hierarchies to place women in subordinate positions at each different level of interaction between class and gender" (1981:290). Reforms within the system are inadequate because giving women access to productive resources within capitalism is like "treating cancer with a bandaid" (1981:287).

Beneria and Sen share with Boserup the view that women's work is crucial to their claims to development resources; they also focus on the fact that women's reproductive labor is not defined as "work" in either a socialist or capitalist system. In Marxism, domestic work—and the exploitation of women—is to be eliminated by the socialization of production. But Beneria and Sen emphasize that women's responsibility for reproduction has not diminished in socialist societies, and they question the value of fully socializing domestic life. They emphasize, however, that women will always be disadvantaged if their primary responsibility for reproduction of the family is not either compensated for or shared equally with men. The questions raised by Beneria and Sen underline the point that neither capitalism nor socialism has resolved the "woman problem." The pursuit of women's claims based on equality and efficiency has revealed quite starkly the inadequacies of a strategy that fails to take women's reproductive labor into account.

Boserup's work, like that of many feminists in the early 1970s, denied the relevance of male–female differences. At that time feminists feared that any admission of difference would reverse hard-won gains in the campaign for equal rights. In the 1970s and the 1980s, as the percentage of women in the labor force increased dramatically, the success of the campaign for equality forced feminism to grapple with the competing demands of family and work. Feminist theory has changed its direction, celebrating women's differences from men in their capacity to mother (Elshtain 1983; Friedan 1986; Ruddick 1980), their moral reasoning (Gilligan 1982), and even their marginalization from technology, which it is argued gives women less of a stake in exploiting the environment (Boulding 1976; Dinnerstein 1977; Merchant 1980). Feminists have come to argue that women should not be satisfied with competing with men on male terms or with simply seeking a niche in a "male-defined" (i.e., competitive and ecologically damaging) system.

With this change of perspective, the equality claim, once at the heart of feminist activism, has come under attack. Elizabeth Wolgast criticized egalitarian feminism as too narrow and argued that equality on male terms is nothing more than a "Procrustean bed" that limits women's potential and homogenizes society (1980). In this period of reassessment, in what Friedan calls the "second stage," equality is no longer the overriding goal; women are encouraged to seek empowerment on their own terms and not to abandon their moral perspectives or desert their family and community roles.

In rethinking its single-minded egalitarianism, American feminism has moved closer to European and Third World approaches to gender politics (Y. Cohen 1984; Greer 1984; Jaquette 1985). However, arguing difference has its risks, particularly given the role of the equality principle in the American legal system as well as its importance in mobilizing support for change. The argument that women should be equal yet should receive special treatment as women because of family responsibilities makes it more difficult for the courts to sort out the competing principles at stake (Kirp, Yudof, & Franks 1986; Minow 1987; Olsen 1983) and raises the specter of the return to the bad old days of protective legislation—or worse.

What is needed is a more complex theory of justice that will combine the best elements of equality and merit and make room for difference without forcing everyone to be alike or bringing back a concept of gender "complementarity" that denies women access to economic and political power (Illich 1982). In an expanded concept of justice, egalitarian values must hold an important place but be flexible enough to revalue the private without privatizing the public. Redistribution, now seen as welfare, must be restructured to enhance rather then deny citizenship.

Our cliches about justice have not been subjected to sufficient creative revision of the kind that has made feminist theory such a vital enterprise. At this point, we know that equality and efficiency claims have made a substantial difference in the debate on women in development issues and have given women access to some new resources, including an enhanced view of their own potential. If women retreat to complementarity, they will be classified as "welfare" cases, either as wives or as clients of the state.

These contradictions appear to be difficult to resolve; they may prove less so if considerations of procedural justice are reintroduced into the debate. If the *institutions* of justice can be rethought and restructured, the substance of what they deliver (or create) may also be recast.

THE INSTITUTIONAL CONTEXTS OF JUSTICE

Feminist critiques of women in development scholarship and practice often ignore the policy context in which the WID argument must be made; but women in development theory has also fallen far short of being a theory of empowerment rather than a set of ideas for increasing women's economic participation at the margin.

Feminist theory brings new insights to a range of issues about how we will live our everyday lives in the future; it has changed our views of family and state structures and has argued for decentralization, community, and care to counter the negative effects of modernization: centralization, hierarchy, and "enlightened self-interest."

To apply these insights to the question of how to resolve the conflicts between competing criteria of justice (or to modify them substantially), it may be useful to take note of the fact that each of the criteria is implemented by a specific institution. The equality principle is largely the province of law, that is, of legislation and adjudication by the legal system. By contrast, the merit principle has come to be the almost exclusive terrain of the marketplace, as notions of prestige and status have been reduced to the simpler measure of wealth, and wealth is increasingly accepted as a global, not merely a capitalist, standard. Needs, which used to be met by kinship obligations or community charities, have been turned over to state or private bureaucracies which identify the needy and regulate their behavior to justify extending "benefits."

Thus each kind of justice is delivered, if you will, by a different institutional mechanism. (If complementarity is defined as yet a fourth criterion, it too has its own "value-allocating mechanism" in the authority of kinship systems.) Table 4.1 matches the types of justice with their typical "allocators."

Of course institutions do not always behave as theories would have them. Economists recognize that the "free market" exists because the state enforces contracts, and the state may intervene in the market to serve other goals, such as higher levels of investment or more equal distribution of wealth. A full-employment policy may substitute for a system of social welfare, or the state may refuse to "cross the threshold" when there is conflict within the

Table 4.1. Criterion of Justice/Institutional Context

Criterion	Allocator
Equality	Legal system
Merit (efficiency)	Market*
Need	Welfare bureaucracy
Complementarity	Kinship

*In socialist systems, bureaucratically set prices and wages, queues, and barter arrangements have taken the place of the market, but it is precisely these nonmarket mechanisms to set prices (and to a lesser degree wages) that are being abandoned by the command economies.

family, choosing to let kinship authority (or brute force) rule, as has been the case until recently with domestic abuse in the United States or "crimes of passion" in, say, Brazil. Norms taught and reinforced in the family are critical to the legitimacy of the market system (Fraser 1987). Clearly, there are overlapping boundaries among the mechanisms that allocate values and legitimize existing patterns of value allocation (Walzer 1983).

Yet each of these institutions creates a different set of opportunities and constraints, and these may reinforce or even undermine the principles of justice that the institution was established to serve. For example, because bureaucracies determine need, and they are closed, hierarchical, and self-perpetuating institutions, the needy become clients and the very institution that is supposed to remedy the plight of the poor acquires a stake in their continued powerlessness (Ferguson 1984; Piven & Cloward 1971; Sarvasy 1986). Similarly, it can be seen that foreign assistance creates "dependency" and makes it very difficult for "beneficiaries" to define their own needs. The bureaucratic organization of redistribution helps explain why socialism, which is egalitarian in its goals, remains authoritarian in practice.

Rethinking the criteria of justice in an institutional context offers the possibility of moving feminist theory away from the stalemate between egalitarian and difference feminism, and the conflicts between Marxist and liberal feminists seem less dramatic when the *mechanisms* for producing equality in both kinds of systems become the focus of analysis. The feminist case against bureaucracy must also be a feminist case against the market, against patriarchal kinship, and against a legal structure that has proven incapable of dealing with difference without reinforcing it in its most negative and coercive forms.[3]

Feminists today are arguing with one another over how to anchor their claims for justice and whether both difference and equality can and should

[3]There may be a feminist case against the nation-state that is widely accepted as the basic unit of the contemporary international system. This was not always the case. Many have argued that transnational organizations are creating the possibility of a truly global citizenship. The realist view that we cannot move beyond the nation-state offers an interesting issue for feminists (see Apter 1987; Ashley 1986).

be pursued. These debates often pit rights against care, family life against the sharing of economic or political power, and bureaucracy against community. A quick assessment of each of the institutions offers some grounds for optimism.

The market will neither correct for income inequalities nor reward merit in the broader sense, but it does produce goods and services and it can be structured to create more equality or to produce different "goods." Welfare bureaucracies deprive their "clients" of dignity and disempower them, but they could be restructured to respond to the concrete identities of those with whom they work while experimenting with techniques to reduce internal hierarchy. Similarly, in the conflict between egalitarianism and difference, Martha Minow's view that these can be reconciled only when the legal system begins from the standpoint of the "different" rather than from a systemic demand for consistency seems a promising point of departure (1987). It parallels the position that "welfare" bureaucracies — including foreign assistance agencies — should start from the perspective of those they are ostensibly trying to help rather then imposing the assumptions of the planners (Germain 1987; Staudt & Jaquette 1987). The very process of devising individual and collective goals can change women's perceptions of themselves in empowering ways.

Gender justice, however feminists may define it, will not be achieved by pursuing equality alone, yet we lack alternatives that do not put recent advances in women's empowerment at risk. Women are at risk in the marketplace as well as in their roles as dependents, in the legal system as well as in the family. These problems cannot be remedied by legal fiat, by social spending, or by sending women to business school. The criteria of justice, and the ways in which they complement as well as conflict with each other, must be better understood, and the institutions of distributive justice must be rethought before they can be reformed.

5

Feminist Perspectives on Women in Development

CHARLOTTE BUNCH AND ROXANNA CARRILLO

Since the early 1970s, issues of women and society internationally have been shaped and redefined by two major forces within the women's movement, women in development and global feminism. Sometimes these forces have interacted and often they have proceeded separately, but both have grown enormously since their beginnings. These two trends have come together more in the 1980s in part because feminism has expanded in Third World countries and its leadership has had more impact on the women's movement globally. As two feminist activists–theorists from North and South America, we explore here some feminist perspectives on women in development that are coming out of this interaction in the 1980s.

Much of the formative intersection between the ideas of feminism and women in development took place within the context of the U.N. Decade for Women 1976–85. The initial separation of these trends was symbolized in the slogan for the decade proposed at the International Women's Year Conference in Mexico City in 1975: Equality, Development, and Peace. These terms reflected what was understood as central to the "women's question" in each of the three male-dominated power blocs within the United Nations. Thus Equality was seen primarily as a feminist issue coming from Western industrialized countries; Peace was included at the request of the Eastern Socialist bloc; and Development was perceived as key to the improvement of women's lives in the Third World countries of the South.

At the Mexico City Conference and at the U.N. Mid-Decade World Conference on Women held in Copenhagen in 1980, divisions prevailed and often led to debates over what constituted a "women's issue." Although most divisions were seen as between North and South, neither the women in development nor the global feminist perspective was limited by region. Further, in spite of the highly publicized arguments, women from various regions struggled together to understand one another and to create a more synergistic perspective. For example, at the NGO Forum in Copenhagen, KULU, a women in development group in Denmark, held constructive dialogues about development for women with participants from both industrialized and Third World countries, particularly those in Asia and Africa. In another area organized by ISIS and the International Women's Tribune Centre (IWTC),[1] feminists engaged in international networking and a group of primarily North and South Americans held a forum called "What Is Feminism?" The statement that grew out of this initiative came in response to a controversy over whether feminism was relevant to poor women and sought common ground by viewing feminism not as a list of separate issues but as a political perspective on women's lives and the problem of domination (ISIS 1983).

By the 1985 End of the Decade World Conference on Women in Nairobi, many women had rejected the division of women's concerns into three separate areas, and there was increasing emphasis on the intersection of issues. As military budgets devoured the resources needed for human growth, women had learned that there can be no development without peace. This problem is cultural as well as monetary. As the U.N. Secretary General for the Copenhagen conference, Lucille Mair, noted after Nairobi: "This distress [economic crisis] exists in a climate of mounting violence and militarism . . . violence follows an ideological continuum, starting from the domestic sphere where it is tolerated, if not positively accepted. It then moves to the public political arena where it is glamorized and even celebrated. . . . Women and children are the prime victims of this cult of aggression" (Mair 1987:3). As development plans failed in many areas of the world in part because they ignored women, women had also learned that there can be no successful development without equality. A vivid example is the recognition that "the acute food shortage in Africa, while dramatically and tragically exacerbated by drought and war, may be due in large part to the way women

---

[1]ISIS was born in 1974 as the Women's International Information and Communication Service, with offices in Rome and Geneva, aimed at promoting communications among grassroots activist women's groups. Its main vehicle for communication was the *ISIS Women's International Bulletin*, launched in 1976 with a report on the International Tribunal on Crimes Against Women, a global feminist conference held in Brussels that year. The Tribunal created the International Feminist Network, an alert system for world response to women's crises, which is administered by ISIS. In 1984 ISIS was transformed into two organizations: ISIS-WICCE (Women's International Cross Cultural Exchange), based in Geneva, which organizes an exchange among women activists, and ISIS International, which publishes feminist analysis and information about women's activities around the world and has offices in Rome and Santiago. The International Women's Tribune Centre (IWTC) in New York City grew out of the nongovernmental International Women's Year (IWY) Tribune held in Mexico City in 1975 in conjunction with the IWY United Nations women's conference. It began with a newsletter to channel information about what women were doing worldwide as a result of that conference; this developed into *The Tribune*, a quarterly publication focused on information about and technical assistance to women's groups in the Third World, especially in the areas of appropriate technology, community economic development, and low-cost media.

have been systematically excluded from access to land and from control of modern agriculture in that region" (Taylor 1985:25). And as the reality of women's lives in the Third World and the feminization of poverty in industrialized countries gained more public attention, women in the West had learned that there can be no real sexual equality when economic development is lopsided. Women everywhere had come to see that peace is impossible without the development of economic justice and an end to the everyday threat of gender-based inequality and violence against women worldwide. In short, women learned during the decade that equality, peace, and development are indeed interrelated and that all issues affecting human life are "women's issues."

The convergence of issues that occurred during the decade led women to a "deeper awareness of both the complexities of the goals and the limitations of conventional concepts to capture the reality and needs of women" (Antrobus 1985:1). Feminists found that we must not only link these themes but also redefine the fundamental questions, concepts, and approaches of our societies if we are to realize justice. The editors of the Indian women's journal *Manushi* wrote: "Today we no longer say: 'give us more jobs, more rights, consider us your "equals" or even allow us to compete with you better.' But rather: Let us re-examine the whole question, all the questions. Let us take nothing for granted. Let us not only re-define ourselves, our role, our image — but also the kind of society we want to live in" (Kishwar & Vanita 1984:244–45).

The impulse to redefine basic questions around women in development has come from many directions. Feminists who began by working on other issues — whether legal equality or equality on the Left, violence against women or reproductive rights — saw the necessity of addressing them in relation to economics and development. Some women in development practitioners and scholars who felt the need for another framework for looking at development turned to feminism, particularly as it became more globally defined. When the U.N. Decade began, feminism was seen primarily as Western, although there were some feminist groups in Third World countries at the time and there had been waves of feminism earlier in the century in both Asia and Latin America. During the Decade, however, indigenous movements developed in Third World countries "that addressed the specific regional concerns of women's lives and that expanded the definition of what feminism means and can do in the future." This development of global feminism has led to more dialogue between women of the North and South about both the diversity and the commonality of our lives and about how to "develop a global perspective within each of our movements" on all the issues that affect women (Bunch, 1987:328).

Interest in feminist perspectives on development has been a natural corollary of this emergence of global feminism. Women from various regions have made powerful statements about the need to link feminism with re-thinking women and development. Anita Anand from India was one of the early advocates for this approach. In a 1980 article that became the introduction to the ISIS resource guide on development, she wrote:

For women to become a vital force in their societies, change will have to be based on a new theory of development which embraces feminism. Feminism poses some challenges to development theory and praxis that must be addressed if any effective and inclusive work about bringing about a new order is to be done. It questions the artificial barriers between the political, social and economic aspects of society and how individuals relate to these orders. (ISIS 1983:10)

Marie Angelique Savane of AAWORD (Association of African Women for Research and Development) notes that a convergence of views from the North and South is possible:

Feminism as a theoretical framework of the women's movement has exposed and challenged the socio-political, economic and cultural ideologies which legitimize and sustain the subordination of women. Feminism is a wholistic ideology that embraces the whole spectrum of political, economic and social ideologies. . . . In the final analysis the oppression of women is a universal phenomenon. From this standpoint thus, it is possible not only to introduce feminism into the development process but even more critical to render development more feminist. It is clear that the subordination of women emerges out of a dialectical relationship between culture, the economy and politics. Because of this fundamental reality we cannot separate feminism from development or vice versa. (Savane 1984:3)

Global feminism is the key to new development strategies as seen by Peggy Antrobus of the Caribbean:

Feminism offers the only politics which can transform our world into a more humane place and deal with global issues like equality, development, and peace, because it asks the right questions: about power, about the links between the personal and the political; and because it cuts through race and class. Feminism implies consciousness of all the sources of oppression: race, class, gender, homophobia, and it resists them all. Feminism is a call for action. (As quoted in CCIC 1987:8)

The convergence of thinking about feminism in relation to women in development has taken a different path in Latin America. Discussion of development was central to the women's movement in Africa, Asia, and the English-speaking Caribbean during the Decade, but it was less so in Latin America, which has a different linguistic and colonial experience than other parts of the Third World. Women in this region have seen gender issues more as a question of women's political participation and empowerment and related them to democracy, militarism, and class. For example, at the Second Latin American and Caribbean Feminist Encuentro in Lima in 1983, the development workshop focused on the consciousness-raising and organizing potential of development programs more than on the economic questions (ISIS 1986).

This focus on organizing women for political empowerment has generated lively feminist debates over autonomy for the women's movement and its relationship to other political forces seeking change and an end to military dictatorships. Women linked the personal and political aspects of feminism with the cry for democracy in the region as symbolized in the popular feminist slogan "Democracia en el pais y en la casa" (Democracy in the country and in the home), coined by the Chilean feminist Julieta Kirkwood. Women's struggles against dictatorship, such as that of the Mothers of Plaza de Mayo in Argentina, and the growth of grassroots women's groups seeking empowerment around a wide range of issues have characterized this political development. Many of these projects work on women's survival problems, but they were initially formulated around the need for politicization of women rather than as questions of development. However, as the debt crisis crippled economies in the region during the 1980s, feminists have developed more interest in the analysis and experience of women and development that have come from other Third World countries. Thus Latin American women enter the feminism and development discussion with a strong history of working on women's need for self-determination and political power as a crucial component of any development plans.

CRITIQUE OF DEVELOPMENT

The growing body of feminist literature that examines the effects of development policies on women and challenges the assumptions underlying their formulation is built on the work of both feminists and women in development scholars and practitioners in industrialized as well as Third World countries. The critiques range from questioning the idea of "integrating" women into development, to advocating a new ethical framework in which the development process should be placed, to challenging both the concepts advanced by development researchers and agencies and the methods used by the social sciences in gathering the data from which development programs are designed.

Although we cannot cover the entire scope of this rich dialogue here and there is not complete agreement on one feminist analysis of development, we will highlight some of the important common points in the critiques. Basic to the feminist approach is the questioning of the concept of development itself. Too often the predominant assumption, even of much women in development literature, has been that "women's main problem in the Third World was insufficient participation in an otherwise benevolent process of growth and development" (Sen & Grown 1987:15).[2]

The parameters of the concept of development have been shaped by a

[2]DAWN began in Bangalore, India, in 1984 with a meeting of women activists, researchers, and policymakers from Third World countries. It focused initially on preparing for the 1985 Nairobi conferences by producing an analysis of issues of development from the perspective of Third World women, which resulted in a series of workshops in Nairobi and the book *Development, Crises, and Alternative Visions*, published by DAWN in 1985 and subsequently reissued in Gita Sen and Caren Grown, eds., *Development, Crises, and Alternative Visions* (New York: Monthly Review Press). In 1986 the DAWN office moved from India to São Paulo, and the group created several commissions to develop strategies for advancing the cause of development free of gender, class, race, or national oppression.

Western patriarchal and capitalist notion of economic progress that assumes change is linear. "Policymakers typically define the developmental process in terms of Western rationality and scientific knowledge" (Charlton 1984:8), which are culturally limited and yet have been presented as universally valid. This approach is not only hegemonic but also runs against fundamental values stressed by the women's movement: the need to listen to the disempowered along with a commitment to respect differences. It also puts heavy emphasis on the individual (a Western European tradition) rather than on the community, and it measures progress of human beings and societies only in economic terms, leaving out other human needs whether cultural, social, political, or spiritual.

In debating the idea of integrating women into development, the question of whether it can lead to an overall reappraisal of the development concept remains open. Some see the integration of women as inherently challenging to "social and political structures, the distribution of wealth, and cultural mores. It is, in short, revolutionary in its implications" (Charlton 1984:9). Elise Boulding, on the other hand, speaks for many feminists with her skepticism about the Western industrialized development model:

> This is not a model of development, or of the integration of women into development, that one would care to recommend to other countries. . . . What are women to do? To cooperate with those who wish to integrate them into the present international order is to destroy all their hope for a better future. But even the much heralded "new" international economic order, to the extent that its third world authors have revealed their intentions, does not promise to be very different from the old—not for the poor, least of all for women. It only offers the opportunity for more third world women to become marginalized labor in the modern sectors of their national economies, or continue as landless laborers (which most of them already are) at slightly higher wages. (Boulding 1980:48)

Feminist researchers and practitioners have analyzed various aspects of the negative effects of this Western male-biased approach to development. In *The Domestication of Women*, for example, Barbara Rogers (1980) spoke of "problems of perception," reproducing excerpts of conversations with men at different levels of decision making in development agencies that make clear how blind they were to even considering women active and engaged components in the projects they funded. This lack of perception is reflected in the methods and quantitative techniques of gathering data which planners use to draw the information that forms the basis of development projects. For example, the fact that women's work in reproduction is still not considered crucial work for the maintenance of society and therefore an area that should be a social responsibility poses serious questions about researchers' perceptions of reality as well as about the comprehensiveness of the information upon which development plans are based.

Since women's economic activity is often invisible to those in power, it is difficult to gather accurate information about women. Many governments do not see any point in including gender-differentiated statistics, without realizing that their underlying assumption—"simply look at the world of men and proceed to women as an afterthought"—distorts the reality of women's lives (Seager & Olson 1986:7). Various studies have revealed the depth of male bias embedded in development planning and provided new descriptions of women's realities from which it is possible to begin explaining the differing effects of development on men and women. Looking at such gender analysis, one can see how the lack of improvement in most women's lives during the Decade is due not only to resistance to the inclusion of women in development projects but also to the persistence in looking at women only in their role as mothers, "rather than as active agents, workers, and managers of resources" (Anderson & Chen 1988:14).

The way in which male ignorance of the realities of women's lives defies rational approaches to development was reflected in a rural community in the northern provinces of Peru where water is extremely scarce. The village had an electric water pump donated by an international agency. However, it was not accessible to the women for use in their daily chores because the person in charge of it was a community leader who took the keys with him to the fields where he worked all day. This is a minor though telling example of how development policies that do not deal with the problem of male dominance over community resources work to the detriment of women.

The Peruvian pump example demonstrates another point raised by feminist critiques: most development plans reflect a top-down approach that leaves little room for input from the presumed beneficiaries. This attitude is not only politically undesirable but poses serious problems about who defines the needs of a population, and therefore who is involved in the effort to make projects succeed. If one of the goals of development is self-reliance, it should start with the participation of the target population. When land reform was legislated in Peru in 1969, for example, the government put bureaucrats in charge of implementing the new law. The new management failed to take into account the suggestions of the peasants working in the haciendas, and production suffered serious consequences. Women were particularly affected since they were not considered on equal terms with men in the allocation of land ownership—women were entitled to only half the amount of land that men got, even though they were heads of almost 30 percent of the households.

Feminist criticism of the overemphasis on economic growth in most development plans coincides with other progressive critiques. The predominant view during the first development decade was that economic growth would improve the overall situation of Third World countries through the so-called trickle-down approach.

> The recognition of the growing gap between survival needs and their fulfillment, and the failure of growth to trickle down to the poor, led in the mid-1970's to a significant shift in the stated orientation of multilateral development strategies in favor of basic human needs . . . that emphasized the importance of project lending and granting targeted towards improvement in nutrition, health, water, sanitation, housing, and education. (Sen & Grown 1987:38)

In recent years the global economic and debt crises have led to a shift toward deemphasizing basic needs in favor of "structural adjustment" programs, designed by the International Monetary Fund and the World Bank, which have had a devastating effect on the world's poor, especially women.

There are feminist critiques of the various stages of development planning from the production orientation to the basic needs and project-oriented rural development approaches to the advocacy of structural adjustment. As Peggy Antrobus sums it up:

> The up-shot of these critiques is that development planning could be enormously enhanced if gender differences could be taken into account, and recognition given to the fact that people, especially poor women, are capable of promoting their own development if their own efforts and initiatives are recognized and supported. The first step must be to build the "infrastructures," the context in which women can feel some sense of control over their lives. (Antrobus 1987:112)

VISIONS FOR CHANGE

Feminist perspectives on development are not concerned only with the defects in how programs have been conceived and implemented. Women are also proposing new visions of development. Several international meetings in the late 1970s and 1980s made public declarations about feminist visions of development from a global perspective. One of the early international efforts produced a manifesto often called the Bangkok Paper (APCWD 1979). Sponsored by the U.N. Asian and Pacific Centre for Women and Development, 15 women from both industrialized and developing countries gathered in Bangkok in 1979 to consider "Feminist Ideology and Structures in the First Half of the Decade for Women." The group asserted that "the oppression of women is rooted in both inequities and discrimination based on sex and in poverty and the injustices of the political and economic systems based on race and class." It proposed one of the first global definitions of feminism as an ideology with two long-term goals: (1) the achievement of women's equality, dignity, and freedom of choice through women's power to control their own lives within and outside the home, and (2) the removal of all forms of inequity and oppression through the creation of a more just social and economic order, nationally and internationally. This was seen as leading to "the involvement of women in national liberation strategies, in plans for national development, and in local and global strategies for change" (as quoted in IWTC 1980:27).

To achieve those goals, power for women was seen as essential, not in its traditional patriarchal definition as domination over others but as a sense of internal strength, as the right to determine one's choices in life, and the right to influence the direction of social change. Power is critical for women, and one of the paramount goals of a feminist vision of development is the empowerment of women. Such a vision considers women as subjects or "agents of development" rather than as "development problems" targeted by planners and agencies. The great endurance, courage, and resourcefulness of women, especially poor women, must be acknowledged as "qualities which have enabled them to cope with the harshness of their lives and to survive with dignity," and this strength should be envisioned as a potentially powerful force for change, "both for societal change, as well as for changing the perceptions of the women themselves" (as quoted in IWTC 1980:29).

This vision was elaborated further at the follow-up to Bangkok, an international workshop on "Developing Strategies for the Future: Feminist Perspectives" held in Stony Point, New York, in 1980. This meeting approached development as a political process and stated the participants' dissatisfaction with the restrictive definitions of development "traditionally confined to economic development . . . measured by precise economic indices such as growth in the national product." The development process has not been neutral in how it affects the sexes and different classes, and the "integrationist" approach to development was challenged as unlikely to bring justice for women. The report concluded with a call for the empowerment of women: "Unless women define their own needs, goals and strategies even 'benign' governments won't change the basic structures which keep women in a subordinate position" (as quoted in IWTC 1980:6).

The Bangkok and Stony Point papers were seen as manifestoes for the 1980 Mid-Decade Conference in Copenhagen. They aimed at mobilizing women and calling attention to the global implications of feminism in general as well as in relation to development. The participants in the meetings did not plan to build an ongoing group but met briefly with the hope of breaking new ground that would push people to think more about feminism and development. The strong language and broad scope of these documents reflect these goals and the stage of thinking about these issues at the time.

Another international feminist statement aimed more specifically at the question of development was drawn up in 1982 in Dakar, Senegal. Under the sponsorship of the Association of African Women for Research and Development and the Dag Hammarskjold Foundation, some 40 women and a few men from the South and North elaborated their vision and drew up the "Dakar Declaration on Another Development with Women." The Bangkok and Stony Point initiatives consisted of activists from both the global feminist and women in development trends primarily from countries where English was a dominant language. By contrast, the Dakar meeting drew heavily on continental European and French-speaking African development scholars whose focus was more structural. Its Declaration begins by analyzing "the present crisis of the world system, which has increased inequalities between nations and within nations as well as between women and men at the local level." It outlines how the "crisis of capitalism as well as of existing socialist models of social progress" have increased poverty, nationalism, militarism, and religious fundamentalism — all of which have worked against the interests of women (*Development Dialogue* 1982:11).

Their vision was also structural:

> We believe that the most fundamental and underlying principle of Another Development should be that of structural transformation, a notion which challenges the economic, political and cultural forms of domination mentioned above, which are found at the international, national, and household level. Accordingly, at the international level, Another Development should replace the forms of dependent development and unequal terms of exchange with that of mutually beneficial and negotiated interdependence. . . . Nationally, models of development have to be based on the principle of self-reliance . . . and the building of genuinely democratic institutions and practices. Such a model would ensure wide general participation — including that of women — in the definition and actual provision of the basic needs of all citizens, regardless of their race, creed, gender or age. . . . At the local and household level, the vision of Another Development ought to reject existing structures that create or reinforce a sexual division of labour. (*Development Dialogue* 1982:13–14)

In addressing the changes needed to achieve Another Development, they state that it "will only be possible if patriarchal relations and practices are eliminated . . . [which requires] not only improving the situation of women but also changing it by opposing all ideologies that define women's role as subordinate, dependent or passive. Feminism provides the basis for this new consciousness and for cultural resistance to all forms of domination." Thus the Dakar statement articulates the feminist vision that opposition to gender subordination is both linked to and key to ending other forms of domination. Or as Devaki Jain puts it: "Attempts to redress this [sexual] inequality, the very comprehension of the roots of this inequality . . . could show a path for reducing all other inequalities" (1983:20).

In preparation for the Nairobi End of the U.N. Decade World Conference, a Third World Women's Group was formed to define the issues of development from "the vantage point of women." This was DAWN, Development Alternatives with Women for a New Era. The 22 founding members of DAWN were activists, researchers, and policymakers from all regions of the Third World but with heavy emphasis on South Asia. They were women in positions of some authority in their countries who sought to create a powerful global network that would concretely influence development planning. Unlike previous general manifestoes, DAWN prepared a book that addressed specific issues in economic development as well as presenting an overall feminist vision. The group met before the Nairobi meetings to prepare their book and sessions for the NGO Forum that would voice "a sense of urgency regarding the need to advocate alternative development processes" (Sen & Grown 1987:9).

In outlining their vision of development, members of DAWN stressed their belief in a movement for change that draws its ethical basis from women's daily lives, that rejects the effort to catch up with the competitive, aggressive spirit of the dominant system, and that seeks to "convert men and the system to the sense of responsibility, nurturance, openness, and rejection of hierarchy" essential to the feminist vision. Part of that vision is the acknowledgment of diversity and the differing but equally valid meanings of feminism in each region, society, and time. Due to the political nature of the feminist movement, they believe it should be "diverse in its issues, immediate goals, and methods adopted." Beneath this diversity lies a "commitment to breaking down the structures of gender subordination and a vision of women as full and equal participants with men at all levels of societal life" (Sen & Grown 1987:79). A similar approach to diversity and unity was reflected in the Dakar declaration: "Feminism is international in defining as its aim the liberation of women from all types of oppression and in providing solidarity among women of all countries; it is national in stating its priorities and strategies in accordance with particular cultural and socio-economic conditions" (*Development Dialogue* 1982:15).

All of these global feminist statements assert that development from the vantage point of women requires that women define for themselves their needs, goals, and strategies. These visions emphasize the active involvement of women in structural transformation and a deep commitment to self-reliance, which rests on the indigenous cultures rather than on Western models. Development is about human needs in all areas: material, cultural, political. Basic needs then become basic rights, where poverty and all forms of domination and violence would be eliminated.

Many feminists view such development as dependent on reversing the trend toward militarization with its reinforcement of police states and political repression. The ideology of militarism is a doctrine encouraged in the Third World by industrialized countries, whose economies were rebuilt after World War II in great part through production of armaments. Citing a U.N. report of the Department for Disarmament Affairs, DAWN states the connections between militarization and underdevelopment, both of which tend to have an impact on the increase in violence in society, and particularly in "the mushrooming of a culture of violence against women in which machoness and brutality are dominant; its flip side is contempt for women expressed through reactionary notions of women's proper place in society" (Sen & Grown 1987:67). Militarization accounts for the diversion of critical resources that should be directed to the fulfillment of the basic needs and rights of the world's population, but since many of the world's states have military governments, it is unlikely that they would reduce such expenditures, which are key to their control.

A crucial component for realizing feminist visions of development that is lacking is the political will to bring them into being. This can be created only through the pressure of grassroots movements for social change, and it is here that those working toward social transformation from a feminist perspective locate the role of independent organizing as key to the empowerment of women. This is true even in countries where revolutionary processes carried on in the name of socialism show a lack of concern about gender oppression. In a comparative study of the Soviet Union, China, Cuba, and Tanzania, Elisabeth Croll shows how women's organizations under governmental auspices "have so far been more effective in soliciting women's support for official policies than in getting policies changed to meet women's needs" (1986:251).

The importance of women's organizing and action has been stressed throughout the Decade by ISIS, an international women's information and communication service that published *Women in Development: A Resource Guide for Organization and Action* (1983). This book provides a feminist overview of development issues with an emphasis on their activist implications. It highlights initiatives around these questions undertaken by hundreds of grassroots women's organizations throughout the world. By documenting and analyzing the crucial roles that women are already playing in grassroots development and in women's organizations, ISIS asserts that new approaches to development can come from women themselves. The guide also calls for coordination of organizing and mobilizing at the global level given the powerful international economic and patriarchal forces working against women. ISIS has played a crucial role in linking feminists from the South and North by sharing information and by its recognition that feminists from all parts of the globe should be concerned with development (ISIS 1983:1).

The recognition that development is crucial to the North as well as the South grew during the Decade. The global feminist perspective works toward an integrated vision that does not separate issues but seeks to find their relationship to each other even as their manifestations take diverse forms. Viewed from this perspective, the women in development critique leads to important issues for feminists within industrialized countries. Since the world operates globally, Western policies and corporations play a vital role in the problems of the Third World, which feminists must address first as a question of justice. Further, the development dialogue raises domestic questions about the values of what is called "development" in the North and how this has failed women, especially poor and black women, many of whom are interested in learning from women in development experiences in the Third World.

The feminist vision of North–South interaction is based on mutual learning and respect that seek commonality through recognizing and taking seriously women's diversity. This has seldom been the basis of Western international work. As a Canadian women's group notes,

> Effective overseas work is hampered by the failings of our own systems which have not been created to promote equality and mutuality. We need to see our work with people in the South as building toward a better world for all of us. We need to learn from our partners and seek an active exchange of skills, insights, and support. Examples of how feedback from the South has changed our organizations and work in the North can be found in the histories of our own agencies. New priorities on work with local women's groups is one example. Another is the shift from individual child to community sponsorship programmes. (CCIC 1987:16)

Although women's organizations have a long history, the U.N. Decade provided a favorable context for an increase in the numbers and the sophistication of women's organizations as well as for greater international contact. Such organizing has taken place at every possible level, from women's caucuses within existing male institutions to autonomous groups formed around many issues. Yet although independent organizations are crucial to empowering women, their existence alone is not enough to bring about deep structural transformation in society. Women must also work with other sectors across race and class lines, build strong coalitions, and demand that our perspectives be included in all political platforms. This dual process of maintaining independent power bases and influencing mainstream institutions challenges feminists in every region.

Women's organizing and empowerment are crucial to the feminist vision of development, but women's organizations face many problems internally and externally. Most are underfunded, and women engaged in the tasks of family survival often have little time left for organizing. To be strong and effective, organizations must have some basic requirements including "resources (finance, knowledge, technology), skills training, and leadership formation on the one side; and democratic processes, dialogue, participation in policy and decision making, and techniques for conflict resolution on the other" (Sen & Grown 1987:89). Peggy Antrobus (1987) has argued therefore that international development agencies must allocate funds for the needs of women's organizations if a real effort to integrate women's perspectives and needs into development is to take place. The feminist transformation of development will not happen all of a sudden. It is a long-term process of growth that these organizations represent, as women learn to take control over their lives and to exercise more power and responsibility in the development and directions of their societies.

The feminist perspective calls for faith that in the process of women's organizing, more visions of how to create the new development will unfold. This process is seen as taking place on an unprecedented global scale today, demonstrating "the vitality and breadth of feminism in the myriad of grassroots projects, centers, demonstrations, celebrations, and meetings where women voice their demands for a greater say over their lives. Here, too, they take the time and space to plan together how to develop vision into reality" (Bunch 1987:332). Feminists believe that in the course of such activity women undergo the process of empowerment that enables them to become significant shapers of the direction of development policies locally and globally.

6

Access Is Not Enough: Gender Perspectives on Technology and Education

SUSAN C. BOURQUE AND KAY B. WARREN

Technology and its transfer to the developing world have been difficult and contested subjects for policymakers and scholars alike. For some, technology is a primary mechanism for promoting economic modernization and enhancing standards of living in newly industrializing states. For others, technology transfers from the industrialized nations have been a mistaken path for the developing world, leading these nations to misdirect their limited resources in futile attempts to adopt Western patterns which are inappropriate to their needs (Stewart 1977).

These conflicting strains of thought are also found in current analyses of women and technology. The florescence of scholarship during the U.N. Decade for Women (1976–85) added gender as a category of analysis for understanding the consequences of technological change. Social scientists pursued the following questions: (1) How have technology transfers from industrial to developing countries affected women's lives, sexual divisions of

This is one of a series of articles on gender, technology, and international development commissioned and supported by INSTRAW and the Rockefeller Foundation. An earlier version of this analysis appeared in *Daedalus, 116*(4), Fall 1987. Readers should know that we have expanded this essay to reach the wide audience of general readers in the field of development. Our investigation has been inspired by discussions with colleagues at the Rockefeller Foundation, the International Center for Research on Women (ICRW), and the U.N. Institute for Training and Research on Women (INSTRAW). In particular we thank Alberta Arthurs, Jill Conway, Joyce Moock, Irene Tinker, Shirley Malcom, Micaela di Leonardo, Mayra Buvinic, Susan Joekes, and Joanne Leslie for probing questions. Our thanks to Kathleen Thayer for assisting us with word processing. The authors would like to add that, as always, this joint project has been a thoroughly collaborative effort at all stages, from conception to computer disks.

labor, and gender relationships at home and at work? To what extent has more sophisticated technology improved women's lives, lessened their workloads, increased employment opportunites, and enhanced their authority? (2) How have women contributed to the process of technological change? What are the social and economic obstacles to their acquiring more technological training? How might they gain greater access to new technologies and play a greater role in their development and dissemination?

In this chapter we describe the distinctive perspectives that address the impact of technological change on the status of women. Our definition of technology is broad, ranging from the introduction of small mechanical devices to sophisticated systems and industries. Our goal is to assess the various conceptual contributions of a decade of research on the problem of women's access to technology and to evaluate the policy recommendations that flow from these approaches, paying particular attention to the question of education. We first examine the rationales behind four major schools of thought: the feminization of technology, the appropriate technology, the global economy, and the cultural–political integration perspectives. We then relate these conceptualizations to policy decisions in education to show how feminist analyses complicate our understanding of change. From this analysis we suggest a political and research agenda relating technology and gender.

Doubts about the impact of technology transfer on the Third World began in the 1960s with the reassessment of international development programs and their impact on women. Feminist critiques[1] of such programs started with the observation that women were absent from the calculations of most development planners. As a result, women's economic contributions were ignored or underestimated, and the negative effects of induced change on women's lives were not considered (Boserup 1970; Chaney & Schmink 1976; Rogers 1980).

These critics argued that contemporary patterns were reflections of a long history in which Western technology, particularly agricultural technology, was differentially available to men and women. European colonial administrators, applying their own notions of appropriate gender roles, made men the preferred recipients of training by Western technicians, even in areas where women were the primary agriculturalists. As a result of the differential access of each sex to new technology, women's status declined. Local cultural values reflecting male dominance in community affairs, rather than female involvement in productive activities, were often transferred to the new tools and crops (Boserup 1970:53–54; Etienne & Leacock 1980).

Scholars studying women and development initially defined women's lack of *access* as the major issue. Consequently, the logical solution to inequality was to equalize it. Women needed the ability to use tools and machines, as

---

[1]Our notion of feminist research includes scholarship by women and men who have taken gender as a central category of analysis and are interested in understanding the diversities of experience both within and between genders.

well as literacy and education. The message was explicitly protechnology: women had lost ground because of restricted access. The solution to inequities was to open the restricted channels of education and training.[2]

Early analyses of development and modernization also assumed that the process was positive and unproblematic. Like wider access, development might be difficult to achieve, but it was unquestionably the goal. Development, however, was to come under closer scrutiny. In the late 1960s and early 1970s critics of development theories pointed out that industrialization and modernization policies were not producing the expected social and economic improvement in Third World countries. They argued that conditions in the Third World were deteriorating due to the dependence of these economies on the capital, credits, technology, training, and markets of the developed nations. This troubled dependency led many scholars to the conclusion that the wide-ranging adoption of Western models and technologies might not be the solution to the problems of developing nations.[3]

Women and development, as a field of inquiry, and technology transfer to developing societies, as a strategy for change, have also been criticized for reflecting the ethnocentrism of Western feminism. Many Third World feminist scholars argue that the concept of development is an invention of the industrialized states, intended to serve their own interests. Similarly, they argue that Western feminism as a political movement and a scholarly tradition has paid too little attention to imperialism, colonialism, and racism. Moreover, they contend that Western priorities are very different from those appropriate to the Third World (D'Onofrio-Flores 1982; Srinivasan 1982; Tadesse 1982). Specifically they find that Western feminist strategies have been insensitive to cross-cultural differences in the significance of the family and kinship groups, the value of children, and the economic realities of impoverished dependent economies. Because technology transfer touches on these issues, debates between feminists about potential strategies and policies are likely to be affected by these concerns and charges.

The 1980s witnessed the recognition of women's economic contributions to urban and rural households in developing countries, growing concerns about the feminization of poverty, and questions about the costs, in terms of productivity, of discrimination against them (Charlton 1984:63). At the same time as Third World women's productive roles have been acknowledged and patterns of change that reinforce gender inequality studied, femi-

---

[2]Boserup's pioneering work sparked insightful critiques by Beneria and Sen (1981) and Huntington (1975).

[3]See Bourque and Warren's *Women of the Andes* (1981a: Chapter 8) for a fuller discussion of the relation between the critique of "development" and the reconsideration of development's impact on women. Ahooja-Patel (1979:1550) makes the point that the mid-1970s marked an important historical conjunction "when almost simultaneously women and the developing countries made new demands for restructuring economies and societies. Both the Declaration and the Plans of Action of the New International Economic Order and the Mexico Conference emphasized somewhat similar goals, the core of which was the urgent need to create new equitable relationships between the industrialised and developing countries in international economic relationships and between men and women in internal relationships."

nist assessments have been characterized by a strategic retreat from the wholesale embrace of technology.

ALTERNATIVE PERSPECTIVES ON TECHNOLOGY

Distinctive lines of argument have been developed to conceptualize the impact of international development on women during the U.N. Decade, and these diverse approaches have coalesced into major schools of thought (see Bourque & Warren 1987). Each approach elaborates a social critique and appropriate strategies and policies to enhance women's position in the face of technological change. We call these approaches (1) the feminization of technology perspective; (2) the appropriate technology perspective; (3) the global economy perspective; and (4) the cultural–political integration perspective.

The Feminization of Technology

Advocates of the feminization of technology perspective argue that special female values should play a central role in international development. As technological innovation is now organized, according to these thinkers, masculinist values determine its development and application. The result is the continual reinforcement of values emphasizing hierarchy, competition, immediate measurable results, material accumulation, depersonalization, and economic and political expansionism. It is not that bearers of masculinist views are ignorant of other values; rather, they have been forced by the economic order to suppress their "needs for subjectivity, feelings, intimacy, and humanity" and project them "onto the private life and women" (Bergom-Larsson 1982:35).

Adherents of the feminization of technology position hold that technology must be redirected to serve new values, including human growth (rather than economic growth), conservation, decentralization, self-reliance, self-sufficiency, and caring. This view postulates a distinctive women's culture and sees it as a critical tool for transforming the social order toward a more humanistic, egalitarian one, concerned with relationships and welfare rather than individual success and profit. The primary source of this utopian vision is women's involvement in the family, where (this perspective idealistically holds) hierarchy is deemphasized, nonviolent persuasion is stressed, and investment is directed toward the nurturance of future generations. Women learn a wider lesson from their familial vantage point: hierarchy, whatever its form, inevitably subordinates the weaker (Bergom-Larsson 1982; Boulding 1981).[4]

A common theme in this literature is the connection between technological innovation and military objectives. Those arguing for the feminization

---

[4]Much of this discussion is reminiscent of psychoanalytic claims that women engage in a gender-distinctive form of maternal thinking (see Chodorow 1978; Dinnerstein 1976; Gilligan 1982).

of technology voice the belief that women will be less violent than men and will offer an alternative to what many of these writers feel is the imminent danger of war (Bryceson 1985).

Unfortunately, according to these authors, women's values are currently imprisoned by the separation of spheres of home and work. Effective change requires an expansion of women's sphere and a new political procedure for evaluating technology, one that involves women in policymaking roles and includes questions about the impact of new technologies on women and women's culture. According to these authors, as female values successfully inform the public world, hierarchical distinctions between "productive paid work" and "nonproductive unpaid work" will be challenged; women and men will share a personal commitment to responding to the needs of the community; and unnecessary divisions of labor will be rejected (Bergom-Larsson 1982; H. Scott 1984).

Proponents of this perspective argue that women should not necessarily pursue integration into Western-directed development efforts; if they do so, they are likely to lose the decentralized, relatively egalitarian social order of traditional society which Western women ill-advisedly gave up long ago. For those with the option of experimenting outside Western patriarchies, the best strategy would be to strengthen women's networks and expand women's spheres as a source of new economic and political organizations (Boulding 1981).

It is most useful to regard the feminization of technology as a utopian vision rather than an accurate analysis of international development problems or realities. Its roots and values are clearly Western and Freudian, and its elaboration of an ahistorical and universal set of characteristics for women's nature is naive and inaccurate. This perspective dangerously romanticizes women's values, the family, and the nature of Third World societies. One has only to look at the rich and varied constructions of gender in contemporary societies to challenge these images of male and female.[5] Furthermore, by distancing men from the "natural" concerns of women, this perspective limits, by definition, those with whom women might ally themselves, those whose vested interests are to question current arrangements, to articulate options, and to promote change to more humanistic and egalitarian social orders. In contrast to the utopianism of the feminization of technology school, the appropriate technology perspective focuses on concrete development problems and strategies for change.

Appropriate Technology

Appropriate technology directly attacks Third World poverty and underdevelopment by attempting to increase local production without reinforcing patterns of dependence on the industrial nations. The strategy has been to move away from capital-intensive solutions toward a less costly intermediate technology emphasizing local resources. For women, appropriate technology would increase their productivity and give them more time for other

[5]See, for examples, MacCormack and Strathern (1980) and Ortner and Whitehead (1981).

obligations and community development efforts. For example, in rural societies where women spend hours every day gathering fuel for their kitchen fires, women in development planners worked on new designs for low-tech mud-brick stoves that would significantly cut fuel consumption. In the very common cases where rodents, insects, or rot destroys more than a third of family harvests during the early months of storage, design projects concentrated on low-cost storage practices that would increase available food. Hand-operated grinding machines for corn, wheat, and millet, as well as rice hullers and palm oil presses, can free women from hours of daily drudgery without displacing workers. Solar energy, wind power, and biogas are forms of energy that would cut dependence on expensive commercial fuels (Carr 1981, 1984; Tinker 1981).

Although appropriate technology makes sense in conception, in practice it has brought new dilemmas. Foremost is the fear of increased unemployment with new technologies. For women, the cost of innovation is often too high, and they find themselves caught in a circular trap. Limited resources and cash generally restrict women's use of technologies that might increase their productivity and give them access to credit, education, and land (Ahmed 1985). Furthermore, women's economically marginal position makes it very difficult to experiment with their family's welfare. For new technologies to break through women's realistic skepticism, they must substantially increase women's productivity in order to pay for the new technology and to compensate women for the time lost from other work to learn and experiment with new techniques (Tinker 1981:58).

Leading proponents of appropriate technology self-consciously criticize top-down decision making in the development of new technologies, noting that although they may appear to be obviously appropriate in the eyes of engineers and development workers, the people who expect to use the new techniques may not find them at all appropriate (Carr 1981:193). Certainly, African women who experimented with solar cookers found cooking during the heat of the day, continually having to move the stove to collect the sun's rays, and being unable to fit their family-sized pots on the undersized stoves serious drawbacks in a fuel-saving technology (Carr 1981).

Even if full consultation with the "end users" takes place and designs are consistent with local needs and use patterns, the concept of "appropriate" technology to lighten women's work may have fundamental pitfalls. A sexual division of technology may be created in which women gain appropriate technology for domestic work while men become the focus of wider technology training, which generates new employment opportunities (Leet 1981). The issue is of particular significance in societies in which women are expected to be the financers of the traditional domestic economy with their own earnings as well as in cases where social change has multiplied the number of women-headed households.

Moreover, there are potential political drawbacks when policymakers focus their concerns about women on domestic work and the family. Men are seldom viewed as members of households unless they are seen as "heads" or "breadwinners." The focus on women's domestic and reproductive roles has tended to limit policymakers' concerns to those roles. Of course, the family and household are central elements in both men's and women's lives; food preparation, reproduction, and childcare responsibilities necessarily affect women's labor force and political participation. The history of policy in this area, however, has shown that if concern is directed at domestic and reproductive roles, these issues are likely to set limits on national policy directed to women (Beneria & Sen 1982; Buvinic 1983, 1986; Evans 1985; Jaquette and Staudt 1985). As a result, women become the targets of population programs and welfare projects or they are integrated into the lowest levels of production as part-time workers. Little thought is given to providing women access to the full range of skills that would allow them to control and direct development activities.[6] As long as women are conceived of primarily as domestic workers and members of households, there is little tendency to question their absence from society's significant political, social, and economic institutions.

Critical advocates of appropriate technology call for women to be involved in high-tech policy planning in order to influence the use of technology, the agenda of research priorities, the choice of government subsidies, and the discussion of needs (Leet 1982). They conclude it is not the form of technology that determines which gender uses it, but rather who controls its development, dissemination, and products. These issues parallel those found in the global economy approach, which attempts to integrate examinations of the household with wider concerns about the state and the international division of labor.

The Global Economy

Those who hold the global economy perspective would question "technology" in the narrow sense as the focus of investigation, arguing that in an interdependent world system the primary issues are economic and power relations. This view is generally phrased as a neo-Marxist critique which stresses the importance of the historical forces that shape national economies and developing countries' capacities to compete in international markets. Of central concern is the way that capitalist economies have shaped an international division of labor in which developing countries are sources of cheap labor and raw materials for technologically sophisticated industrialized countries where capital is accumulated.[7] From the global economy

---

[6]Buvinic (1986) provides an illuminating discussion of the practical consequences of this process in development projects specifically directed at women. See, as well, G. Sen's wide-ranging discussion (1985).

[7]Beneria and Sen summarize these interrelations in the following terms:

> The capital-accumulation approach analyzes the growth of interconnected processes of production—both quantitative and qualitative—motivated by profits, extension of the market, growing social divisions of labor and modes of production, and the proletarianization of the labor force. Private ownership of resources, and hence of the surplus generated in production (profits, rent, and interest), leads to class differentiation between owners and nonowners of the means of production. Private ownership also signals the private appropriation of productive wealth, and growing inequalities in the distribution of income and power. (1981:157)

perspective, one cannot consider technology without studying the issues of its production and consumption in the context of changing class relations, state policy, and international economics. Feminist scholars have made major contributions to this materialist analysis by pursuing the study of class relations, sexual divisions of labor, and the reproduction of the labor force in the household (Stolcke 1981).

Proponents of this perspective have been very influential in women in development circles. For many it links a needed critique of capitalism and imperialism with gender stratification (Etienne & Leacock 1980; Kuhn & Wolpe 1978; Leacock & Safa 1986; Nash & Fernandez-Kelly 1983; Nash & Safa 1985; Reiter 1975; Young, Wolkowitz, & McCullagh 1981). As Beneria and Sen conclude:

> The problem for women is not only the lack of participation in this process [of development] with men; it is a system [of international capital accumulation] that generates and intensifies inequalities, making use of existing gender hierarchies to place women in subordinate positions at each different level of interaction between class and gender. This is not to deny the possibility that capitalist development might break down certain social rigidities oppressive to women. But these liberating tendencies are accompanied by new forms of subordination. (1981:150)

Stolcke, representing another current of neo-Marxist thought, stresses the function of women's forced subordination in the household in perpetuating wider inequalities:

> The perpetuation of class relations and domination—mediated directly by the institutions of marriage, the family and inheritance . . . determines both women's primary assignment to domestic labour and the undervaluation of this function. In class society, in other words, the sexual division of labour—women's domestication—is ultimately the product of man's control over women's reproductive capacity in the interests of perpetuating unequal access to the means of production. (1981:34)

Both socialists who seek redistributive alternatives to free market economies and nationalists who resent Western influence in their politics and economics find these perspectives useful. While other researchers do not share the utopian socialist vision, it is clear that Marxist analyses have influenced their thinking about the importance of an international perspective that sees various forms of inequality as interactive and central to explanations for current patterns of development even if not historically inevitable.

The insights from the global economy perspective also allow us to focus on a neglected element in many feminist analyses of technology: the interplay of national governments and international markets in shaping national planning, policy development, and the allocation of resources. Of particular concern is the state's creation of labor force policy in areas such as employment, migration, education, housing, agriculture, and industrial development. How does the state formulate priorities for its own development? For the agrarian sector, how does it balance the need to produce food crops for domestic consumption with the need to encourage the production of commodities for export? What alternatives does it see for increasing domestic production, for dealing with shifts in subsistence agriculture and wage labor, and for reducing dependency on the international market for basic food supplies? This renewed focus on national policy also indicates an important shift in development theory from seeing relations between the North and South as fixed to a more flexible view that takes into account the wide range of economies existing today and the influence of policymakers' choices on development.[8]

For the industrial sector, does the state encourage multinational production, and how does it respond to the resulting patterns of centralized and decentralized production? For instance, as workers are pulled toward export-processing zones and assembly work, it is common for new patterns of decentralized outputting assembly, information processing, and service work to emerge. This spinoff work from multinational plants is often organized outside government regulation as part of the informal sector, where work is done in the home or in unregulated sweatshops.

From our point of view, the global economy perspective gives the issue of decentralized, small-scale work a much more complex shape than does the feminization of technology analysis. The latter analysts place a positive value on decentralization and tend to see it as an absolute contrast to hierarchical, centralized systems. The global economy perspective helps us see that decentralization is neither inherently positive or negative nor always an exclusive alternative to centralized modes of production. As in the case of multinational assembly plants, contemporary industrialization can foster decentralized modes, such as subcontracting to domestic outworkers, to produce at a lower cost. The issues are how these work patterns influence the household, whether women will be able to gain greater control of work processes in the smaller units, and whether companies will exploit a fragmented labor force by raising production quotas for constant wages (Beneria & Roldan 1987; Nash & Fernandez-Kelly 1983).

Adherents of the global economy perspective question the common tendency to treat women as individuals without other competing identities and to see women as a category with uniform interests and concerns. To overcome the conceptual simplification of other feminist frameworks, advocates of this view argue that, rather than studying individual women, we should instead examine household units by their class position in mixed subsistence, cash crop, and urban economies. Women's domestic responsibilities vary by class and involve intricate balances of monetized and nonmonetized activities, rapidly responding to changing market conditions (Agarwal 1985;

---

[8]For an insightful discussion of this type of analysis (which lacks an analysis of gender), see Merilee S. Grindle, *State and Countryside: Development Policy and Agrarian Politics in Latin America* (Baltimore: Johns Hopkins University Press, 1986).

Ahmed 1985; Bourque & Warren 1981a, 1981b; Bryceson 1985). However socially valued or devalued, women's privatized household roles are critical for the physical and social reproduction of the labor force. The central analytic project is to study women's reproductive and productive roles as they are mediated by their class position in the wider economy. Thus another important contribution of this perspective is to help restore concrete social contexts to women's work and perceptions.

Yet even as the global economy thinkers have restored concrete contexts to the variability of women's lives, they have left several vital questions unaddressed. When they use the household as the unit of analysis, they downplay the conflicting and competitive interests in the family. As a result, they assume that internal tensions and compromises result from new patterns of employment and fail to scrutinize the impact of local culture and power relations on women's access to technology, training, income, and education.

Cultural–Political Integration

Thus far missing from our discussion of the array of perspectives on women and technology is a position that is neither neo-Marxist nor dependent on the premises of the feminization of technology. The cultural–political integrationist framework is such a perspective. Its adherents are concerned about the limited number of women trained as scientists and engineers and the absence of women from positions of scientific leadership. They share a belief in the possible benefits of technology and a desire to see women participate in its development. Proponents of this perspective argue that the "integration" of women will result in the transformation of basic institutions because comprehensive female participation would challenge existing sexual divisions of labor and authority as well as differential male–female earnings. While this view does not assume that wider female participation would result in a political feminization of technology and industry, it does hold that women would introduce distinctive values and concerns to the work world (Jahan 1985; Malcom 1985).

If one's faith does not reside in a socialist government's ending the inequities of capitalism or in a burst of technological invention following the replacement of men by women who advocate a feminization of technology, what are the possible avenues for change? Women's expanded participation in nontraditional jobs and professions resulting from higher levels of scientific education is one answer, and clearing away the obstacles to that education and subsequent employment is an essential part of the solution (Anderson 1985; Hall 1979). Thus the cultural–political integrationist perspective seeks to account for women's low enrollment in fields directly related to technology, to identify obstacles to women's educational and employment achievements, and to devise programs to reverse gender asymmetries (Briscoe & Pfafflin 1979).

Researchers holding this position have focused attention on the ideologies that surround the acquisition of technical competence and the structural arrangements that reinforce stereotypes marking scientific fields and expertise as male. Not surprisingly they see the key to change in the culture and politics of education and the workplace (Namboze 1985; A. Sen 1985c). To change gender stereotypes and widen opportunities, they argue, we must understand the processes that reproduce existing patterns. This implies that we must (1) understand sexual hierarchy as a product of culturally created social ideologies and the material conditions of women's and men's lives and (2) appreciate that sexual divisions of learning and work are not immutable behavioral specializations to be justified as functional or as vestiges of early human evolution. Rather, the school and the workplace are cultural and political environments where rules and norms are perpetuated and legitimated by contemporary ideologies of exclusion, segregation, and avoidance. Fundamental to this perspective is an understanding of how institutions shape meaning and values as well as how individuals can both internalize and challenge social norms (Bourque & Warren 1981a; Keller 1985). With respect to technology, these analyses extend to the fields in which women have been poorly represented, exploring ways to increase women's enrollment in science and engineering, or developing methods to deal with math anxiety and stereotypes of women that place them in the category of non-scientist (Briscoe & Pfafflin 1979).

At its best this viewpoint does not make the mistake of assuming that individuals are autonomous decision makers who choose to participate or not in technological development. Nor does it reduce education to the status of a "variable" which mechanically accounts for higher rates of technology adoption. Rather, these analysts see education as a process of structural and ideological tracking. As a result, they have had to readdress the question of wider *access* as a solution to gender inequality and to take on institutional change as necessary for structures that have constrained choice and equity.

The challenge for the cultural–political integration perspective is that the arenas that need to be transformed have been remarkably resistant to change. Substantial reform in education or the workplace requires the intervention of political forces that must be convinced of reason and reward for pursuing substantial reform (cf. Buvinic 1983). Moreover, transformation must take place at a variety of levels: in the highest reaches of the national political system and in the political relations within the household. Since many of the changes sought can be affected by executive or bureaucratic action, it is possible to imagine a political plan of action to influence ministers of education and labor, as opposed to the broad electorate. Yet for the types of change envisioned it is often individuals—mothers, fathers, teachers, co-workers, and employers—who will be the primary instruments for effecting meaningful change. Effective policies must appeal at all levels.

Amartya Sen's (1985c) insightful analysis of the intrahousehold power dimensions of gender relations makes an important contribution to this perspective. Sen's work emphasizes the perceptual elements in women's contributions to the household. He notes the generalized reluctance to face the powerful conflicts of interest that exist within households and, for the Indian case, identifies a pattern of "adapted perception" which involves "systematic failures to see intrafamily inequalities and perceiving extraordinary asymmetries as normal and legitimate." Sen notes that

> problems of conflict within the family tend to get hidden by adapted perceptions both of "mutuality" of interests (going well beyond the actual elements of congruence that do, of course, importantly exist) and of "legitimacy" of inequalities of treatment. As a result no policy analysis in this area can be complete without taking up the question of political education and understanding. . . . This is an area in which social illusions nestle closely to reality, and terrible.inequities are cloaked firmly in perceived legitimacy. The importance of information and analysis in breaking the grip of traditional arrangements is hard to exaggerate. The technology of mass communication offers great opportunities as well as powerful resistance. (p. 44)

In addition to family perceptual and political issues, there are at the national level staggering difficulties to the reforms proposed by the cultural–political integration perspective. In many developing countries it is increasingly difficult to make a case for expanded educational opportunity, let alone to plead the special case of women. Since the early 1970s experience has demonstrated that the rapid expansion of education does not solve and may not even lessen development problems. Although most leaders must publicly declare themselves in favor of greater educational opportunity, privately they may fear that expanded education is creating problems. Policymakers in the developing world find themselves unable to meet the demand for jobs from those currently educated; thus the desire to expand these numbers by special attention to women, particularly in the face of potential opposition, limited funds, and overwhelming debt burdens, makes this an unattractive policy option (Jahan 1985).

Moreover, employment opportunities appear to be shrinking in much of the developing world, due, to some degree, to technology transfer and the mechanization of labor-intensive processes. As a result, one of the catalysts for the nineteenth-century expansion of public education in the United States, the desire for a well-trained and docile work force (Katz 1968), may not be as compelling an argument for leaders in the developing world.[9] Constructing a political agenda to expand women's employment opportunities will be even more difficult where employment opportunities are limited. Given this, recent research on the impact of women's education in developing countries takes on special importance because it is from such material that a political agenda supporting change must be constructed.

---

[9]For an excellent review of the literature on women's education in nineteenth-century America, see Conway (1982:82–90).

EDUCATIONAL TRANSFORMATION

Echoes of the concerns of the radical feminists, appropriate technologists, neo-Marxists, and integrationists can be found in the discussions of educational transformation. One finds great cynicism and penetrating critiques of existing educational institutions expressed by the range of feminist analysts. Although inequities in women's educational access and achievement precede current debates over technology transfer, the dominance of technology today and its relationship to formal education have sharpened the significance of this controversy.

Among the critics' most serious charges is that schools perpetuate gender inequalities and class differences by regulating access to knowledge and by teaching world views that justify the status quo. Critics observe that the expansion of educational opportunity for women in the developed world has not eroded unemployment or closed the earnings gap between men and women. Nor have expanded educational opportunities ended the underrepresentation of women in science and technology, though there have been important changes in these fields (Hacker 1986). Significantly, they note that as women have entered the science-based professions two-tiered systems have often emerged, with the less prestigious and less remunerated tier having the highest proportion of women. This pattern is reported for both capitalist and socialist societies (Carter & Carter 1981; Lapidus 1978; Rudolph 1985; Scott 1974; Zimmerman 1982). In addition, some feminist scholars have serious doubts about the integration of women into established scientific fields. They argue that the problem is the structure and ideology of science as currently shaped by the priorities of competitive capitalism rather than by wider social needs. From this point of view the process of training women scientists calls for the wider agenda of critiquing biases — such as the uncritical extension of biological explanations to social and political phenomena — in existing science as well as creating a new and better science (Bleier 1984, 1986; Fausto-Sterling 1985; Keller 1985).

These critiques have led some scholars to conclude that conventional education is a mistaken focus for changing women's relation to technology because educational systems are bound to reflect the cultural biases and values of the societies that establish and support them. Consequently, they are unlikely to be the locus of a radical restructuring of gender roles or power relations. Thus the proponents of the feminization of technology would extend the implications of their analysis to argue that a new curriculum is needed, one not dependent on "male science" or "male values" but one that would reflect a "female" construction of the world. Proponents of appropriate technology would criticize highly centralized educational systems based on an urban Western model and far removed from the needs of substantial parts of the population. Moreover, those concerned with appropriate technology have been eager to recover women's "traditional" knowledge and make it the basis for rethinking policies toward the environment.

From the point of view of both perspectives, educational institutions must be transformed, and new curricula and modes of teaching must be developed for the system to carry another message.

While there is great validity to these critiques, it is clear that Third World women will have very little impact on national development priorities, political ideologies, and development planning until they are literate and have the basic arithmetic skills with which to analyze their political and economic systems. Thus it is to the proponents of the global economy and, even more pointedly, to the proponents of cultural and political integration that the task of thinking about educational reform has fallen. Scholars from both perspectives continue to address the question of access and how to increase women's opportunities at all levels of the educational system while eliminating sexism. Comparative rates of literacy, school attendance, educational achievement, and faculty composition continue to measure gender gaps in areas where improvements have been made.

After a period of relative neglect by the development community, women's education is now receiving renewed scholarly attention. This occurs at an auspicious moment, when it may be possible to integrate the impressive array of research on women produced since the mid-1970s with the theoretical contributions of feminist scholarship, in particular the insight into the cultural construction of gender (Conway, Bourque, & Scott 1987). The key link between the new scholarship on gender and the issues surrounding educational reform is the recognition of the systemic nature of gender relations (a premise shared by the proponents of cultural and political integration). Understanding the systemic implications of gender makes it apparent that policies directed at closing the educational gap between boys and girls or increasing girls' years of education would *not*, in and of themselves, adequately resolve the problem of gender inequity. Differentials in education reflect system-wide patterns of gender relations that must be taken into account when thinking about policy responses.

There are three areas in which research has shed new light on the complex interplay of factors affecting women's education: constraints on getting women into schools; changing the learning environment to provide educational equity; and identifying the basis for a political agenda in support of women's education.[10] Let us briefly examine each.

Constraints on Women's Education

Schooling does not necessarily offer the same direct economic payoff for women as it does for men, partly because of cultural and family expecta-

---

[10]There is a great deal of sophisticated work under way internationally on women's education, as evidenced by the Mount Holyoke Conference on Worldwide Education for Women (November 1987) and reflected in the papers commissioned for that meeting. See as well the work on women's education being undertaken by T. Paul Schultz at the Yale Center for Economic Growth.

tions that domestic and reproductive work will be undertaken by women. Parental and familial assessments about short- and long-term returns on their children's education help explain continuing gaps in school attendance, achievement, and literacy between men and women. Cultural patterns that take girls out of the house at marriage while tying sons to extended households may weaken parental investment in daughters. But the wider economy is also influential. For instance, in the case of urban industrial employment, there are conflicting signals from the market which both promote female education and limit its duration so daughters can contribute to the family economy before marriage.

These findings have implications for development policy: if women's time invested in education leads to remuneration in the cash economy, then it would appear to justify a reevaluation of their other contributions to the family. This conclusion echoes Sen's findings on the importance of cash earnings in the evaluation of women's work and family perceptions of their contribution to its welfare (1985c). Both factors affect the family's decisions about who is "entitled" to investments in such resources as education and nutrition. In this, as in so many areas, the issues of education and employment are linked to one another and to the larger questions of how gender hierarchies are constructed and perceived within a society.

An Economic Commission for Latin America (CEPAL 1983) study found that women in Latin America have higher rates of illiteracy and are less likely than men to complete primary school. This gender difference is greatest in the rural areas and most notable in Peru, Mexico, Paraguay, El Salvador, Guatemala, Bolivia, and Ecuador, all countries in which gender intersects with marked class and ethnic disparities. The authors of the study argue that gender disparities will persist and become greater without special programs focused on women. The problem is exacerbated by the tendency of governments to put more financial resources into secondary and higher education, thus leaving the initial imbalance between men and women unaddressed (CEPAL 1983). Recent findings on literacy suggest that although women show considerable interest in such programs, there is little governmental effort to direct programs toward them (Stromquist 1985). Would a new sex-blind policy change this situation? Probably not, as Elliot and Kelly conclude:

> It is difficult to equalize opportunity once some groups have established an initial lead, and even more so with current constraints on increasing educational investment and government employment. After actively discriminatory policies have set inequalities in motion, sex-neutral policies are sufficient to maintain established patterns. Thus the educational gap continues, as does the clustering of women in low-paid service occupations. (1982:336)

Moreover, literacy and the completion of primary school no longer assure a place in the labor force as in the past. Ironically, equality of opportunity is not necessarily fostered by similar levels of education, because as large numbers of students complete primary school, employers begin to require still higher levels of attainment for the same jobs. This points to an important function of educational systems: they can be used as flexible sorters of the national labor force responding to changing national and international market conditions (CEPAL 1983; ILO 1985).

Changing the Learning Environment

What are the chances of altering educational systems to provide educational equity for women? The changes that feminists identify as necessary require substantial overhauls: new curricular materials, nonsexist textbooks, science laboratories, and mathematics instruction for girls in situations where the limited facilities and instruction have previously been provided for males. Most of the research on education singles out the importance of teachers and the learning environment to widen the horizons of young girls. But a strategy based on such people may require new personnel, new values, and a rethinking of the reasons for educating the young. Extraordinary political skill and commitment will be a prerequisite to garnering support for such a program. Expenditures for this course of action are not among the priorities of hard-pressed government economies, and there is a reluctance among development agencies to press for such changes (Stromquist 1985).

The consequences of sex stereotyping become most apparent when the traditional responsibilities of women are in conflict with the enrollments in the specialized schools of study. Here the case of India is instructive:

> In higher education, India has a relatively strong ratio of girls to boys and a good stock of well-educated women. . . . However, the sex stereotyping of fields is marked, with consequences both for individual career choices and for development programs. Women's enrollment for an agricultural degree are still minuscule, and nonexistent in forestry. This means that development programs in critical areas of women's work — agriculture, fuel and fodder — are designed, directed and evaluated by male experts who, because of customary practices prevalent in most of India, can have no direct access to village women. (Elliott 1982:342)

If development planners can be convinced that scarce training resources are being squandered on the wrong population, or that investment in training women would garner a better return, then one essential component in a viable agenda for change would be secured. But for policymakers to accept such propositions they would have to be convinced that women are technologically capable and educable. This means renewed attention to learning environments.

Constructing an Agenda for Change

How can programs of political support be developed to promote expanded opportunity for women given the economic, political, and cultural obstacles to their education? New findings on fertility, child welfare, and infant mortality may provide grounds to capture the attention of national development experts. The impact of women's education on fertility has been examined in a variety of contexts and the results appear mixed, and at times contradictory. While more research needs to be done to clarify these patterns, Leslie, Lycette, and Buvinic (1986) conclude from their review of the literature that in general increased female education is associated with lower fertility. This finding is also related to the positive effect of maternal education on child health and survival.

> Research done in the late 1970's in developing countries found a surprisingly consistent positive effect of maternal education on infant and child mortality rates and on child nutritional status in all regions. . . . Although higher levels of maternal education are usually associated with both higher levels of paternal education and higher levels of household income, most research has found a positive effect of maternal education on child survival and health separate from its association with other socioeconomic variables. (Leslie et al. 1986:8)

These results are encouraging and can serve as the basis for additional research and policy planning, but it is clear that studies of correlations and associations need to be complemented by research on institutional arrangements and social ideologies to explain how systems perpetuate the status quo and how they might be transformed. Furthermore, the use of the traditional sexual division of child care and nurturance to mobilize political support for change must be recognized as a problematic strategy. Reliance on this strategy — while politically appealing — could ultimately limit women's opportunities in other areas where their work is just as important for family welfare.

One of the central messages from the U.N. Decade is the importance of the construction of viable political agendas for the changes that reformers seek in education, employment, and women's relation to technology. The research of the 1980s has begun to identify potential sources for such an agenda, which can be found in careful assessments of the changing relationship between (1) educational opportunity and perceived return on that opportunity, (2) the link between education and increased child welfare and lower fertility, and (3) the costs of failures to introduce women to technological innovations in agriculture and other areas of the economy.

CONCLUSION

The U.N. Decade has yielded not just one feminist voice but a range of positions, politics, and policies. The conflicts among perspectives — the feminization of technology, appropriate technology, global economy, and cultural–political integrationist perspectives — are important and unlikely to result in a grand conceptual synthesis for Third World and Western feminists. But this is not the point: the debates fostered by these perspectives reveal important contours of reality.

It is clear that these frameworks have grown more sophisticated over time. The feminization of technology viewpoint has taken on the major task of critiquing social ideologies implicit in Western science and the tremendous gaps between scientific practice and these fields' self-perceptions. The appropriate technology perspective has become increasingly attuned to the power relations inscribed in the transfer of tools and skills to solve concrete development problems. The global economy framework has moved beyond economic reductionism with attempts to integrate the cultural issues, including diverse understandings of gender, into its materialist analysis. The cultural–political integrationists have taken their work past an emphasis on individual achievement toward the consideration of institutional and cultural constraints to more comprehensive change. As researchers from these perspectives contemplate the policy implications of their analyses, each is faced with the challenge of showing the greater cost of failing to incorporate gender as a major dimension for national development programs.

However, research has uncovered a series of dilemmas for those concerned with acting to change policy. Just as appropriate technology may be a solution to important problems for women, it has drawbacks as a dominant strategy for change. Overreliance on it may ghettoize women in the midst of wider technological changes involving the use of advanced technologies. Similarly, a truly "appropriate education" might involve women in developing concepts they could use to analyze their own workplace and family situations. Such focus should not deflect women from pressing for access to "higher education" in order to participate in the formulation of national policy in economics, health, and technological development.[11]

As a result of a decade of cross-national research, we now know much more about the questions initially posed in this overview: about the impact of technology transfer on women's lives, sexual divisions of labor, gender relations, employment, and patterns of authority. We also know more about the obstacles to women's wider participation in technology development, dissemination, and use; and we know more about the dilemmas of educational transformation.

Clearly, neither technology nor education is an independent force for modernization. Rather, both are better understood as clusters of economic, institutional, and ideological relations that shape and are shaped by power relations in national and international spheres. Thus neither technology nor education is a unilateral solution to the problems of underdevelopment or of women's continued marginalization in processes of change. In both cases — as attention is paid to the contexts of the production of ideas, skills, tools, and commodities — one realizes how much technology and education are bearers of social relations marked by gender. Access is not enough to change these gendered asymmetries, though it is clearly crucial to the process of change in the forms of education and in the uses of technology.

---

[11]For parallel case studies on the West, see di Leonardo (n.d.), Morgen and Bookman (1988), and Nash and Fernandez-Kelly (1983). J. Scott (1982) charts important conceptual issues in her historical case study of early Western industrialization.

7

Women's Work in Export Factories: The Politics of a Cause

LINDA Y. C. LIM

One of the most popular new areas of research on women in development since the mid-1970s has been research on women factory workers in export industries in the Third World, especially those women employed by multinational corporations. The extensive literature on this subject needs to be explained, since it is disproportionate to the relative importance of such employment for Third World women, the vast majority of whom are employed in agriculture, services, and nonexport, nonmultinational manufacturing activities. In the mid-1980s no more than half a million women worldwide were employed in export-oriented multinational factories in developing countries (ILO 1985:27–28). If nonmultinational export factories were included, this number would at most triple to 1.5 million women, a total that is still minute compared to the several hundred million working women in the Third World. Yet this handful of women have captured the disproportionate attention and imagination not only of scholars and students, but also of journalists, filmmakers, religious groups, feminist organizations, and the labor movement, especially in the Western industrial countries.

The reason for the widespread interest in this subject is the historical coincidence of growing interest in women's changing roles worldwide with the expansion of export manufacturing in Third World countries. Both of these trends were new in the early 1970s. The then newly popular dependency theory seemed to explain the scattered data available, producing a widely accepted stereotype of poverty-stricken Third World women suffering low wages, wretched working conditions, and ruthless exploitation by multinationals located in export-processing free trade zones in Asia and Latin America.

The prominence of this stereotype was enhanced by the proclivity of many scholars and political activists to blame multinational corporations for the world's economic problems. Manufactured exports from the developing countries challenge powerful protectionist vested interests in the industrial countries. They are equally condemned by vested interests in developing countries, which oppose the accompanying trade liberalization and modern factory employment for women. Longstanding nationalist critics of multinationals thus broadened their coalition to include both feminists and patriarchs.

This chapter will examine the empirical validity of this negative stereotype in the light of more recently accumulated data on the life and work of women workers in both national and multinational export factories in the Third World. It will then consider the methodological and political reasons behind the persistence of the stereotype in popular opinion and much of the current literature.

WOMEN AND EXPORT MANUFACTURING

Manufacturing employment for women, even in multinationals, is not new in the Third World (e.g., Chincilla 1977), but manufacturing for export began only in the late 1950s, first in local and then in multinational firms. It has been concentrated in labor-intensive industries, which tend to be female-intensive in all countries, since these industries are sensitive to wage costs and female labor is typically cheaper than equivalent male labor. The job characteristics of these industries also fit well with the needs and characteristics of female labor constrained by the sexual division of labor. Readily learned skills requiring manual dexterity and patience with tedious tasks make women appropriate workers, conditioned as they are by culture and extensive experience with sewing, food processing, and other household tasks. The difficulty of combining factory labor with rearing children also ensures a labor force that is largely unmarried, and therefore young and healthy, with high turnover and a low average wage, without jeopardizing productivity because of the short learning curve. Since labor-intensive industries tend to have low capital requirements, relatively simple technologies, and low skill content, barriers to entry are low. Even in developed countries they are highly competitive industries with low profit margins which exert continuous pressure on production costs and especially on wages, reinforcing the necessity of employing cheap female labor.

Labor-intensive, female-intensive industries in the developed countries thus were the most vulnerable to low-wage competition from newly industrialized developing countries. In the 1950s Hong Kong became the first developing country to export manufactures because of the small size of its domestic economy and disproportionate industrial capacity.[1] By the 1960s,

---

[1] The 1949 Communist revolution in China cut the British colony off from its natural hinterland, sending capitalist industrialists from cities such as Shanghai fleeing with their capital and expertise to Hong Kong.

Taiwan (also endowed with refugee Chinese capitalists) and South Korea had established locally owned import-substituting industries for their somewhat larger domestic markets and were looking for export outlets to expand volumes and lower costs through economies of scale. Local firms in these countries could penetrate developed country markets because the low wages characteristic of preindustrial and newly industrializing economies made them competitive in labor-intensive, female-intensive industries such as textiles, garments, footwear, and toys. This competition from emerging private capital in developing countries and from Japan eventually forced developed country firms in these industries to relocate in Third World countries to take advantage of cheaper labor, becoming "multinational" in the process.

Across the Pacific, Mexico in the mid-1960s was also already embarked on import-substituting industrialization for its domestic market. It then established a new industrialization program along its border with the United States hoping to generate much-needed employment and foreign exchange, as Puerto Rico had done earlier by exporting manufactures to the mainland. This attracted many relocating U.S. firms, some of whom soon joined other firms in migrating to Asia as well.

Most of the early export-manufacturing countries set up special industrial estates for their new industries, which, like established domestic market-oriented industries, were heavily dependent on imported inputs. But unlike the tariff-protected domestic industries, which could raise their output prices to pay for import costs, export industries faced a competitive world market and so needed free trade (i.e., inputs imported at world prices) to succeed. Thus was born the "free-trade zone" or "export-processing zone," where export industries are exempt from import and export duties, often also eligible for tax holidays, and permitted to have 100 percent foreign ownership (Lee 1984). The zones thus allow developing country governments to promote export manufacturing and foreign investment without dismantling tariff-protected, nationally owned domestic industries. In socialist countries like China (and, reportedly, soon Vietnam as well), they allow segregated capitalist sectors to develop without disrupting the rest of the economy.

Today, about a third of all export factory workers in the Third World, male and female, work in these zones. This proportion would rise if "bonded factories," not located in zones but enjoying the same privileges, were included; it may also be somewhat higher for female workers alone, since many male-intensive export industries (e.g., steel, shipbuilding, automobiles) are heavy industries also producing for the domestic market. Analytically, there is little to distinguish export industries located in export-processing zones from the majority not located in these zones; my analysis will therefore not distinguish between them, concentrating instead on export-manufacturing industries in general.

Once the success of export manufacturing became evident, developing country governments began aggressively to promote this development strategy. They did so to generate income and employment and earn foreign exchange required to service import-dependent domestic market industries, which for most governments remained their priority in industrial development. Some, but not all of these governments promoted export manufacturing under the persuasion and even pressure of international development lending agencies like the World Bank and International Monetary Fund, which wanted them to earn foreign exchange in part to repay the debts they had earlier incurred to establish import-substituting industries. Exporting manufactures was considered more desirable than exporting commodities, as developing countries had traditionally done, because of better market prospects and higher productivity, skills, and income. Encouraging multinationals also provided an inflow of foreign capital, which could support broader industrial development efforts.

The success of developed country firms that relocated production in lower cost developing countries to enhance their competitiveness and preserve market share inspired imitation from other firms. Traditional labor-intensive industries with relatively simple technologies, such as textiles, garments, footwear, toys, sporting goods, and accessories, were soon followed by electrical household products and consumer electronics, often manufactured by large multinationals such as Philips from the Netherlands and General Electric and RCA from the United States. American firms in particular were encouraged to engage in offshore production by Items 806.30 and 807.00 of the U.S. Tariff Schedule, which imposed tariffs only on the foreign value added of imports containing duty-exempt U.S.-made inputs.

Beginning in the late 1960s the semiconductor industry expanded rapidly; though high-tech and capital-intensive, it was also highly competitive and included very labor-intensive processes employing female labor. Because of the advanced technology involved, it was not competition from Third World producers which forced the semiconductor manufacturers to locate in the Third World, but rather competition among themselves. Heavy research and development expenditures and short product life cycles made it important to produce the largest volumes at the lowest possible costs to forestall competition and recoup investment before imitation or obsolescence of new products set in. This peculiar characteristic of high-tech industry—now including computers—remains an incentive for selecting developing countries today (Lim 1987a), despite the rapid progress of automation.

European and American multinationals were soon joined by Japanese competitors, as rapid development raised wages in Japan, protectionist trade policies in Western countries restricted imports of goods from Japan, and other developed countries offered trade preferences for manufactured exports from developing countries.[2] By manufacturing for export in developing countries, Japanese multinationals could thus enjoy both lower labor costs and freer and even privileged trade access to Western markets. In recent years the strong yen has encouraged even more production in Third

---

[2]This is mainly the generalized system of preferences (GSP), which allows for the duty-free import into developed country markets of manufactures from developing countries, subject to annual country and product quotas and a minimum local content requirement.

World countries by Japanese firms exporting back to their home market as well as to third-country markets.

These factors explain the demand-side causes of women's employment in export factories in developing countries. It is women who are predominantly employed in these factories because female-intensive industries, being labor-intensive and sensitive to wage costs, are the first to lose their international competitiveness in high-wage developed countries when low-wage developing countries industrialize. This shift of manufacturing capacity from developed to developing countries, initiated by market forces and Third World firms, soon becomes encouraged by Third World government development policies and the corporate strategy of First World multinationals.

WOMEN WORKERS IN EXPORT INDUSTRIES

The supply-side cause of women's employment in export factories in developing countries is more simple and universal: like men, they need and want to work. This is shown by the fact that even women not previously in the labor force flock to the export factories when they are established. Their reasons for wanting to work are primarily economic—to enhance individual and family income—but there are also social and cultural factors involved (e.g., Foo & Lim 1987). In most developing countries, the structure of the economy does not provide many modern wage jobs for women, most of whom are concentrated in inferior employment in farming, domestic service, and the informal sector. Modern factory jobs, whether in the export or domestic sector, are thus much desired.

Altogether there are probably about 1.5 million women directly employed in export manufacturing in developing countries, between a third and half of them in wholly or partly foreign-owned enterprises, which include not only multinationals from industrialized countries but also firms from other Third World nations. There is considerable variation by country; for example, in South Korea, Taiwan, and Hong Kong most employers are local, whereas in Singapore and Malaysia most are foreign. Third World multinationals are more common in the less developed countries such as China, Bangladesh, Sri Lanka, and the Philippines. In each country, the number of women working in export factories is small relative to the total female labor force, with the important exception of small, heavily industrialized, heavily export-oriented countries like Hong Kong and Singapore.

In Asia, where the bulk of the women are employed, most of them are young and unmarried, although this varies by country and industry and over time, according to economic and cultural factors. For example, in the four Confucianist Asian NICs (newly industrialized countries) which enjoy full employment and relatively high incomes, married women's income is not essential for working-class family survival, though it enhances standards of living. Cultural pressures as well as the limited availability of child care discourage mothers from working outside the home. There is also age discrimination by employers against women reentering the labor force after spending some years bearing and rearing children. In Malaysia, similar factors operate, with Islam being the dominant cultural influence. In neighboring Thailand and the Philippines, however, women's income is much more important for family survival because of low male incomes and high unemployment. In these countries local traditions have always accorded women a strong and independent economic role, and child care is more readily available because of an existing rural labor surplus and the persistence of the extended family. Thus many more older married women enter or stay in the labor force, including export factory jobs. By industry, the textile and garment industry has more older and married women than the electrical and electronics industry, while over time, the proportion of older married women workers increases in all countries and industries.

In Latin America and the Caribbean, export industries include more older and ever-married (including separated and divorced) women than in Asia. Locally specific economic and cultural factors appear to be at work here, including a tradition of female breadwinners in the Caribbean and a high proportion of female-headed households along the Mexican border, where many men are absent because they are working illegally in the United States. One may also speculate that the difficulty of remarriage in Catholic societies which forbid divorce produces many older separated women who must work outside the home to support themselves and their children.[3]

Besides age and marital status, the educational levels of women export factory workers also differ by country, industry, and over time. Average educational levels tend to be lower in the textile/garment, and probably also toy and footwear industries, and higher in the electrical/electronics, computer, and other high-tech industries. In part this is simply a function of vintage: the textile/garment industry is longer established than the electrical/ electronics industry, thus employing older women who tend to have had less formal education than younger women, given the relative recentness of the spread of mass modern education for girls in developing countries. Textile/ garment and similar industries utilizing relatively simple technologies and manual processes do not require a high level of education, or even literacy. In the electrical and especially electronics and computer industries, on the other hand, literacy and numeracy are important, especially for operation of sophisticated machines. Education has become more important over time as more advanced technologies have been transferred, especially to the Asian NICs; short product life cycles in high-tech industries also require constant retraining, which is easier for more highly educated workers.

The educational differences by country are more complex. On the one hand, average educational levels and technological and skill levels are higher in the more advanced NICs than in less advanced developing countries. On the other hand, the NICs also have tight labor markets, so that workers with

---

[3]This is not as much of a problem in East Asia, where the divorce rate is very low, or Southeast Asia, where the divorce rate is high but so is the remarriage rate.

more education have access to better jobs than factory work, which tends to attract only lowly educated workers. In contrast, the less advanced developing countries tend to have labor surpluses, and factory work attracts more highly educated workers who do not have better job alternatives. Thus, for example, I have seen similar tasks in multinational electronics factories being performed by primary school dropouts in Singapore, where labor is scarce, and by high school graduates and even part-time college students in the Philippines, where unemployment rates are high. This makes it difficult to predict changes in factory workers' educational status over time. As development and industrialization proceed, production workers in a given export industry may become more highly educated, due to improved public education and technological upgrading requiring more highly skilled workers; or they may become less well-educated, as the more highly educated move into better (e.g., white-collar) occupations, vacating production jobs, which then go to the lowly educated.

In general, women workers in export industries in the Third World tend to be better educated than the average worker in their countries, especially in the less developed countries. Workers in multinational electronics factories in Thailand, Malaysia, the Philippines, and Mexico, for example, usually have at least a mid-secondary school education, several years more than the average worker. Workers in local textile and garment factories, however, tend to have average or lower levels of education. In the NICs, on the other hand, women export factory workers tend to be among the least educated in the urban labor force, though they are still better educated than most rural workers.

The social origins of women export factory workers are similarly diverse. In poor countries with high unemployment and low wage rates, these factory jobs are highly desirable. Especially in multinational electronics factories requiring higher levels of education, the jobs tend to be occupied mainly by urban residents or established rural–urban migrants, who have both the qualifications and the contacts to obtain these jobs, and who reside in the urban locations where most factories are found. They belong to the more fortunate upper strata of the urban working class. The poorest, least educated rural women usually would not be competitive for these jobs, except in the Asian NICs, especially South Korea and Taiwan with their substantial rural populations, where better qualified urban workers can afford to shun these low-level production jobs in favor of better paid, higher skilled occupations. Malaysia is another important exception where government political priorities, specifically the imposition of ethnic employment quotas, ensure the employment in export factories of rural women who are required to fill the quotas, and who therefore migrate to the city to work in these jobs. Ethnically oriented development policies have also ensured that rural women in Malaysia have higher levels of educational attainment than is the case for rural women in most other developing countries (Lim 1989a).

Overall, then, there is considerable diversity among women export factory workers in developing countries in terms of their age, marital status, education, and social origins. But this diversity is readily explained, being determined primarily by local labor market conditions in each country and by the varying needs of employers in different industries. Occasionally labor market forces may change the sex composition of the labor force. In high-tech industry in both California and Massachusetts, for example, previously predominantly female production work forces have been partially supplanted by nonwhite immigrant males, particularly from Latin America and Southeast Asia, who are willing to work for the same low wages as native women. And in more geographically remote locations along the Mexican border, more and more men are being employed by newly established *maquiladoras* (export-oriented factories), which are unable to recruit sufficient women due to the export industry boom and resultant tightening labor market in this region.

WOMEN'S WORK IN EXPORT INDUSTRIES

The existing literature on women's work in export industries is full of complaints about low wages, poor working conditions, frequent layoffs, and lack of union protection. This section draws on recent empirical studies (e.g., Addison & Demery 1987; Foo & Lim 1987; ILO 185; Lim 1987b) to examine these complaints.

The wages earned by women workers in these industries are typically lower than average wages for the manufacturing sector as a whole. There are many reasons for this. Export industries are typically of more recent vintage than the import-substituting industries that dominate most Third World manufacturing sectors; thus their workers are younger, have less seniority, and receive lower wages. Export industries are also usually labor-intensive and must be competitive on the world market; they consequently can afford to pay less than tariff-protected, monopolistic, often capital-intensive and high-profit (if inefficient) industries supplying the domestic market, which can always raise prices to cover higher wages. The preponderance of female workers in export industries also means a lower average wage in these industries than in the predominantly male-intensive domestic market industries; this is because domestic role conflicts mean that women usually have a much shorter working life and thus less experience, less training, less seniority, and lower productivity and wages than male workers. Sex and age discrimination by employers, which affects women who seek to reenter the labor force after rearing children, and a sometimes lower rate of unionization due to higher turnover and weaker commitment to the labor force, also contribute to a lower wage for female workers.

Lower wages in export industries than in manufacturing as a whole do not, however, mean that these workers are poorly paid relative to all others in the economy. Manufacturing wages in general are typically higher than incomes earned in the much larger agricultural, service, and informal sectors. In Mexico, for example, women working in the *maquiladoras* along the U.S. border typically earn at least the legal minimum wage; in a country where unemployment runs as high as 40 percent and barely half of those who have jobs earn the minimum wage, this puts them in the top quartile of the national income distribution. The same is true in Bangkok and Manila, where some estimates are that no more than 10 percent of the urban labor force earn the minimum wage, which is, however, paid by virtually all multinational export factories.

Wages earned by women in export factories are also usually higher than what they could earn as wage laborers in alternative low-skilled female occupations, such as farm labor, domestic service, most informal sector and other service sector activities, small-scale local industry, and, in some countries, even white-collar and so-called pink-collar jobs such as a hairdresser, beautician, or sales clerk.[4] The disparities are sometimes great. One multinational electronics factory in Indonesia paid its workers four times the local manufacturing wage (already higher than the prevailing agricultural wage), while wages in China's export-oriented special economic zones are two and a half times higher than wages outside these zones. Though it may be inferior by developed country standards, work in modern export factories also generates more income, with shorter working hours and better working conditions, than traditional housework, home-based work, and unpaid family labor. This is partly because factory employment is more heavily and readily regulated by governments than, for example, agricultural labor or domestic service, where 16-hour workdays seven days a week are common.

The local purchasing power of women's export factory wages is not inconsiderable. Although these wages, like wages in most urban working-class occupations — including male occupations — in the Third World, are often inadequate to support typically large extended families, they are almost always more than adequate to support the individual worker herself. Especially in poorer countries with high male unemployment and low wages, the woman factory worker may even be the largest income earner in her family, earning more than her husband, father, or brother. When added to other incomes in multiple-income households, which are the norm in the Third World, these wages are often sufficient to raise women factory workers' family living standards to comfortable and even middle-class levels. For example, in Singapore, where women export factory workers are among the lowest paid workers in the economy, usually earning less than the men in their families, their total family income puts them in an income bracket where, in 1983, "96.2% of the households had a refrigerator, 95.9% a television set, 23.1% a video cassette recorder, 12.8% a motor-car, 17.5% a motorcycle, 44.7% a washing-machine, 3.6% an airconditioner, and 3.8% a piano/organ" (Lim 1987c). Singapore, like Hong Kong, may be an exceptional case because of high average wages, publicly provided housing, and low consumer prices due to free trade. But in many if not most countries — especially the NICs and near-NICs like Malaysia — women export factory workers earn

[4]In some countries prostitution is a high-paying exception. See, for example, Phongpaichit (1982).

enough to save for themselves and/or contribute a large proportion of their incomes to family expenses, even where they are rural–urban migrants who live on their own and not with their families.

It also cannot be assumed that the working conditions and living standards of women export factory workers in the Third World are inferior in every case to those of similar workers in the developed countries. This is certainly true in the majority of cases, and in absolute as well as relative terms, wages, working conditions, and living standards leave much to be desired, especially in very poor countries. Working conditions in small locally owned garment factories in Bangladesh, for example, are abysmal even if they are marginally better than the poor conditions prevailing throughout that economy, which has the second lowest per capita income in the world. At the other end of the spectrum, however, workers in large modern garment factories in Singapore and Hong Kong probably enjoy better working conditions and higher living standards than immigrant sweatshop and home workers in the U.S. garment industry, who toil long hours in unprotected conditions yet are not as well off or secure as the Singapore and Hong Kong workers, who earn half their wages in dollar terms.

Beyond the obvious economic benefits of working in export factories, especially those owned by multinationals where wages and working conditions are better, women in developing countries often cite various noneconomic benefits to explain why they work and appreciate, without necessarily enjoying, their work in these factories. These include the ability to earn independent income and spend it on desired consumer purchases or save for marriage or a further education; the ability to help support their families and "repay" their debt to parents; the opportunity to delay marriage and childbearing and to exercise personal choice of a marriage partner; the opportunity to enjoy some personal freedom and the companionship of other women and to experience more of what life has to offer, such as a "widening of horizons" (Foo & Lim 1987; Lin 1986). For example, in Malaysia, a relatively rich country where low status and a strong social stigma attach to factory women, they still consider themselves better off than they would be had they not chosen to work outside the home, and especially better off than their mothers (Foo 1987).

Export factory employment is often considered to be insecure because of frequent layoffs resulting from vulnerability to the world market. But vulnerability to layoffs varies considerably by country, industry, and firm and is determined by both world market and host country factors. Export industries are not necessarily more vulnerable to layoffs than other sectors of the economy, such as export-oriented mining and agriculture and manufacturing for the domestic market. In fact, workers in multinational export factories may be more insulated from economic problems than workers in small local firms, because of the greater strength and resilience of their employers in a recession. Workers in large modern enterprises, whatever their market orientation, are usually also better protected by labor legislation and unions than workers in the traditional sector or unorganized enterprises and are more likely to receive retrenchment benefits. When women are laid off in a recession, this is not necessarily due to their being women but rather to their being employed in industries or firms adversely affected by the recession. (For further elaboration see Lim 1987b.)

Whether women workers in export industries are more or less likely to be unionized than workers in other industries varies considerably by country. On the one hand, employment in the formal sector, especially in large industrial enterprises, provides a better opportunity for organization than most other forms of employment, and in many countries female-intensive export industries are more heavily unionized than other sectors of the ur-ban-industrial as well as rural economy. This is true, for example, of the electronics industry in Singapore and the textile industry in South Korea. On the other hand, the shorter working life and higher turnover rate of women workers makes them more difficult to unionize than comparable male indus-tries. This is true in developed as well as developing countries; in fact the female-intensive electronics industry is more heavily unionized in the Third World than it is in the United States. Some developing countries do restrict union organization in new industries, but export industries are not necessar-ily singled out for more restrictive treatment than domestic market-oriented industries (Lim 1987b).

WOMEN EXPORT FACTORY WORKERS: STEREOTYPE VERSUS REALITY

We have seen that the empirical reality of women export factory workers in developing countries is varied and complex, with significant differences in their situation by country, industry, and period of time. Yet the stereotypical view of these women presented in the feminist literature and popular media is remarkably homogeneous—and generally negative. The predominant stereotype is that First World multinational factories located in Third World export-processing zones employ mostly young, single, female rural–urban migrants, who are ruthlessly exploited in harsh factory environments where they suffer long hours, poor working conditions, insecure, unhealthy, and unsafe jobs, and wages so low that they are not even sufficient to cover individual subsistence (Frobel, Heinrichs, & Kreye 1977/80; Ong 1983). This, together with discriminatory practices by employers and disruptive world market forces, results in a high turnover rate, as women are "ex-hausted" by their employment, or are forced to resign when they marry, or are laid off in frequent recessions. They face constant harassment by em-ployers, supervisors, and even the government, especially if they attempt to unionize or take any labor action. The women are forced to work by poverty and are exploited by their families, who claim a disproportionate share of their wages yet do not accord them more power or status within the family. They thus suffer a double oppression—that of imperialist/capitalist exploi-tation on the one hand and of gender subordination on the other—and benefit little if at all from their employment (Elson & Pearson 1981a, 1981b).

The foregoing discussion suggests that while there may be *some* situations characterized by this stereotype in some or all of its details, it is by no means the norm in *all* or even *most* situations where women are employed in export factories in the Third World. A majority of these women are employed not by multinationals but by local firms, and most are not located in export-processing zones; they include a significant and growing proportion of older married women. Although in most, but not all cases wages, working conditions, and job security in the export factories are inferior to those in the developed countries, they are comparable if not superior to those found in women's (and even men's) jobs in most other sectors of these still poor, underdeveloped local economies. The length of time that women work in these factories varies by country, individual, and over time, and is usually truncated by the mounting domestic responsibilities women face when they marry and have children, rather than by employer compulsion or market disruption. The women working in these large modern factories are better able to organize in unions than are women in most other sectors of the economy and forms of employment, and despite obstacles they have in many cases become more unionized than sections of the male labor force in their countries or than the female labor force in similar industries in the developed countries. They have also not hesitated to undertake sometimes militant labor actions, such as strikes and work slowdowns, and in countries like the Philippines and South Korea, they have even been involved in wider political actions. Women textile workers are considered to be among the most militant workers in South Korea's labor unions.

Women export factory workers typically do not come from the poorest segments of society, who are usually found in the rural areas, but from families located in or near more prosperous urban areas, or those who had the resources to educate them more than the average male or female in their societies and/or to finance their migration to cities from rural locations. Although some women do work because they would otherwise be destitute, most do so in order to improve their own living standards and those of their families, even where families object to their working or have no pressing need for their income. They are motivated by social and cultural as well as economic factors, and they typically are accorded more respect and more say in their families and households because of their employment and contribution to family income, though this is insufficient to completely undermine the traditional sexual division of labor and its cultural constructs (Foo & Lim 1987).

This is not to say that women export factory workers form the elite of the working class in Third World countries, though in some cases (e.g., Mexico) this may be close to the truth. But they are unambiguously better off than they would have been without these jobs. In absolute terms they are best off in the Asian NICs, the countries most heavily involved in export manufacturing for the longest time. Conditions are worst in very poor countries where there are few export factories and where high unemployment and low wages mean that employers do not have to compete for labor. But where there are so many export factories that they dramatically increase the demand for female labor, and full employment exists — as in some of the Asian NICs — workers' market bargaining power is greater, skill levels increase with capital investments and capital/labor ratios, and wages and working conditions are higher as employers have to compete for increasingly scarce but productive workers.

METHODOLOGICAL PROBLEMS IN THE LITERATURE

The great discrepancy between the stereotype and the reality of women export factory workers' work and lives in the Third World needs to be explained. Much of the literature on the subject is methodologically flawed in a number of ways. There is a tendency to employ a static, ahistorical approach to the subject despite the dynamism of developing economies. Authors tend to generalize from their observations in one particular location at one time. This is usually in the earliest stages of the establishment of export factories, when they attract the greatest attention, especially from journalists, and when wages and workers' tolerance of their new working conditions are lowest and labor turnover is highest. This is because the labor market is still slack, workers lack job experience and skills, have unrealistic expectations and problems adjusting to the regimentation of modern factory employment,[5] and often are still earning low "probationary" wages since they have not yet reached minimum productivity. Foreign employers, in particular, may have problems adjusting to a culturally different work force, so that many frictions and tensions arise. Over time, many of these problems are smoothed out, wages rise, conditions of work and employer–worker relations improve, and workers themselves adjust to their jobs. Thus labor turnover rates are always highest for newly hired workers in newly established factories and lowest for experienced workers in long-established factories, even in the same location. A particularly dramatic example of adjustment over time is the sharply declining incidence of mass hysteria among women export factory workers in Singapore and Malaysia as this form of employment has become more widespread and entrenched.[6]

Lack of a dynamic historical approach seriously distorts perspectives on this subject. For example, dated information from the mid-1970s is still quoted today as if it were current, despite enormous changes since then, particularly in the rapidly changing electronics industry (e.g., Fuentes &

[5]This is found in all factories, regardless of their market orientation, the sex composition of their labor force, and operation by capitalist or socialist principles.

[6]Mass hysteria outbreaks have traditionally been fairly common among young Malay (Muslim) girls in all-female environments such as girls' schools, dormitories, and more recently, factories. Such outbreaks do not affect young women of other ethnic groups in the same situations. Though traditionally attributed to spirit possession, a more likely cause of the hysteria is conflict between traditional and modern gender identities. See Lim 1989a.

Ehrenreich 1983; Mies 1986; Ward, 1986). And information from an "abnormal" period is often presented as if it were a typical or representative situation. Thus, for example, large layoffs in female-intensive export industries in Malaysia and Singapore during the post-OPEC recession of 1974–75 are still cited today as "evidence" of the instability of export factory employment (e.g., Heyzer 1986:108–9), despite the fact that recovery was achieved in less than a year. The next round of widespread layoffs in these two countries did not occur until 1985–86, when recovery was also relatively swift. This is a record much superior to that of most agricultural employment in developing countries, where, for example, women harvesters lose their jobs after each harvest or are permanently displaced by machinery.

A second common methodological problem in the literature is the frequent absence of a comparative standard by which to judge conditions in female-intensive export factories. Very few studies evaluate the circumstances of women workers in export factories in direct comparison with control groups of women, or even men, working in other industries or occupations, or who do not work at all. Where comparison is made, it is implicitly or even explicitly made with prevailing conditions in developed countries, which is not helpful in evaluating the developmental impacts of export manufacturing in the developing countries.

For example, to know that women export factory workers in a Third World country earn $2 an hour or $2 a day tells us nothing about the "worth" of this employment to the workers themselves or to their country. To assess this, we need to know how $2 a day or $2 an hour compares with the average wage in the country, with wages earned in other female occupations, and with what the women were earning before they took up their factory jobs or would earn without these jobs. We also need to know the standard of living that this wage will purchase in that country; for example, it may well be that $2 an hour in Singapore buys a better standard of living than $5 an hour in Boston or Los Angeles. The same comparative standard goes for hours of work and other working conditions; for example, 10 hours a day for 6 days a week is an improvement if the local norm is 12 hours a day for 7 days a week. The impacts of their employment on women workers' lives and their position in and relations with their families must all also be assessed in comparison with what these would be in the absence of employment. For example, for a young woman in a developing country, how does living on her own, earning an independent wage in an export factory, and marrying when and whom she chooses compare with the alternative of staying at home with her parents, performing unpaid labor in a family farm or shop or working as a domestic servant, then being married off while still in her teens to a man of her parents' choice?

A third methodological problem with much of the literature on this subject is the absence of a normal multivariate approach to causality. For example, there is the tendency to attribute all the observed impacts of women's export factory employment in developing countries to the designs and practices of multinationals, which do not even constitute the majority of employers. It is frequently asserted that these employers grossly exploit their workers by paying them low wages and extracting intensive labor effort in order to earn maximum profits for themselves. In fact, wages and working conditions are set primarily by the prevailing norms and regulations of the host country, which multinational employers especially tend to match if not better. Women's typically high turnover and short working life is due less to employers' exploitative tactics than to the traditional sexual division of labor, which makes it difficult for women who have primary responsibility for housework and child care to work outside the home, forcing many of them to "voluntarily" leave their jobs when they marry or have children.

These and other methodological weaknesses in the literature on women export factory workers in the Third World are explained by several factors. First, many if not most of the writers on this subject are inadequately informed about the facts of the situation, frequently basing their analyses on only a handful of outdated, empirically inadequate studies. These studies are rarely the product of serious and systematic scholarly research; most consist of anecdotal accounts prepared by journalists and activist groups which are often deliberately selective, focusing on extreme rather than representative situations (e.g., *Asian Women Workers Newsletter*, various years; Christian Conference of Asia, various years; Fuentes & Ehrenreich 1983; Grossman 1979; ISIS 1985; Karl 1983). Even writers who attempt to be scholarly use these limited sources almost exclusively (e.g., Mies 1986). It is true that much of the more serious and recent empirical research done by Third World scholars is relatively inaccessible in the West, being mostly locally published or unpublished and only rarely finding its way into international academic journals. But these sources need not elude the committed researcher. In recent years more comprehensive, systematic, balanced, and up-to-date studies have also appeared in the West (e.g., Fawcett, Khoo, & Smith 1984; ILO 1985: Ch. 5; Jones 1984; North–South Institute 1985), but they have so far been either ignored or only selectively cited by writers attempting "theoretical overviews" of the subject (e.g., Ward 1986).

Second, many writers lack sufficient knowledge and understanding of export manufacturing, the world economy, the workings of labor markets, and simple economics. In particular, the field is dominated by anthropologists, who are used to working intensively with, and generalizing from a single case. They lack the data, the analytical tools, and the macro perspective with which to accurately locate individual cases in their national or international context, yet they frequently aspire to do so (e.g., Mies 1986; Nash 1983; Ong 1983). Errors of fact, omission, and analysis consequently abound.

A third cause of methodological weaknesses is the willingness of many writers, anthropologists in particular, to embrace global political–economic theories that they cannot accurately evaluate, yet they allow to determine their gathering and interpretation of data. The flawed and dated work of Frobel, Heinrichs, and Kreye (1977/80) on the new international division of labor, which I have criticized elsewhere (Lim 1987b), has been particularly influential here. The feminist analysis of Elson and Pearson (1981a, 1981b), linking this new international division of labor with gender subordination, has also become widely accepted despite its many flaws (Lim 1987b). Besides inadequate information and analytical tools, political and ideological predilections appear to be responsible for this uncritical acceptance of questionable theories, which in almost any other field would stimulate many challenges and much theoretical discussion.

IDEOLOGY AND POLITICS

On the ideological level, anti-imperialists committed to a view of the Third World as being relentlessly dominated and exploited by the First World reject any suggestion that at least some developing countries and their workers could benefit and have benefited from export manufacturing, especially where undertaken by multinationals.[7] The work of Frobel, Heinrichs, and Kreye (1977/80) and other sympathizers of world-system analysis supports this view.

Also on the ideological level, feminists who see patriarchy and gender subordination as crucial underpinnings and inevitable consequences of all capitalism refuse to recognize any benefits to women in the Third World from employment in export factories, insisting that such employment intensifies rather than alleviates their gender subordination. The works of Elson and Pearson (1981a, 1981b) are popular with this group.

Ironically, these anti-imperialists and feminists both frequently consider themselves to be Marxist, yet their beliefs conflict with the theoretical predictions of Marx and Engels. Marx clearly considered capitalism to be a historically progressive mode of production, superior to precapitalist modes in its technological and economic achievements and liberating for workers previously subject to feudal bondage. Engels, his close colleague, saw women's participation in factory wage labor as emancipating them from domestic slavery. Both incorporated the concepts of dialecticism and contradiction into their thought, predicting the simultaneous existence of positive and negative, exploitative and liberating features and consequences of capitalist development, as are found in the situation of women export factory workers in the Third World (Lim 1983). In contrast, some feminists have stood Marx and Engels on their heads by claiming that instead of the proletarianization of women, export factories in the Third World contribute to the "feminization" (Fernandez-Kelly 1983d) and "housewifization" (Mies 1986) of industrial production, with negative consequences for women.

On this subject, ideology is given a powerful boost by politics. In the industrial countries, there exists a strong political constituency, a coalition

---

[7]The larger picture of export manufacturing in general has been especially inadequately considered in studies of women workers, though it has been treated in other areas of development studies, especially development economics.

of industry, labor, and local communities, which is opposed to export manufacturing in the Third World because it threatens its own economic and political interests. In the United States, for example, anti-import protectionist fervor is strongest in the textile states of the South, under the leadership of some of the most conservative Republican political leaders (such as Strom Thurmond and Jesse Helms). Yet liberal and even radical social activists in the labor, feminist, and church movements often support protectionism, feeling that it is necessary to support the women who work in labor-intensive import-competing industries in industrial countries. Disparaging the effects of export industries in the developing countries is important to this protectionist effort because it minimizes the negative impact of the resultant loss of women's jobs in the Third World.

In fact this narrow nationalism ultimately undermines not only poor Third World workers, but also industrial country consumers, particularly poorer consumers, who are forced by import restrictions to pay much higher prices to support the monopolistic profits of inefficient domestic manufacturers. This is the "new imperialism," where capital and labor in the First World combine to protect their common interests and industrial domination of the Third World by preventing both capitalist and socialist Third World economies from industrializing for export and thereby providing better jobs and incomes for their workers, especially women.

Feeding this political self-interest is a simple ethnocentrism that values jobs in the developed countries much more highly than the same jobs in the Third World, defending them in the former while devaluing them in the latter, an ethnocentrism that does not oppose the centuries-old export of manufactures from developed to developing countries but does oppose the recent export of manufactures from developing to developed countries. Ethnocentrism also causes writers and activists in the West to judge conditions in the Third World by their own Western standards rather than from the Third World worker's perspective. It leads to the stereotyping of developing countries, resulting in failure to discern their considerable differences from one another in women's indigenous position and the consequences of their export factory employment.

Feminist ethnocentrism is revealed in the common assumption that Third World women workers are introduced to concepts of "bourgeois femininity" by multinational employers' factory cultural practices, which, for example, encourage Western dress, beauty and fashion consciousness, dating and romance among women workers (Grossman 1979; Lim 1978). In fact such feminine values, habits, and practices are already common elsewhere in contemporary developing country societies, where concern about beauty and sexual attractiveness is long-established in traditional society and culture. At the same time, many Western and Western-oriented feminists assume, often incorrectly, that Third World cultures are more oppressive of women than Western culture. This leads them to ignore, for example, the traditionally strong economic and even entrepreneurial role of women in some societies where they seek out wage work in order to fulfill traditional obligations of family support, and consequently appreciate the opportunity to work in export factories.

Political opposition to women's work in export factories also exists in the developing countries themselves. Domestic industrialists dependent on pro- tected home markets and a cheap labor force for their monopoly profits frequently oppose both the trade liberalization that accompanies manufac- turing for export and the participation of multinationals, which compete with them for labor and other productive resources, thereby raising costs (e.g., Lim 1989a). Opposition based on such vested self-interest is readily cloaked in nationalist rhetoric. Never popular in developing countries, multinationals also provide a convenient target for political oppositionists and even labor activists, who find it easier to mobilize nationalist rather than class sentiment in support of their struggles against employers. Large, wealthy multinational enterprises also afford a more promising target for union organization than myriad small, marginal local enterprises, which employ substantially more workers under much worse conditions. Even so, unlike domestic capitalists, few labor leaders in the Third World aim to eliminate multinationals from their home economy, since workers would suffer the most from this; their goal is rather to enlarge union membership by organizing export factories and to obtain employment-based benefits for workers.

Finally, traditionalists and religious and cultural conservatives in some Third World countries — for example, Catholics in Latin America and Islam- ic fundamentalists in the Middle East and Asia — object to women working in export factories, particularly multinationals, because it gives them greater personal freedom and removes them from patriarchal control (often dis- guised as "protection"), including control of their previously home-based, often unpaid labor (Lim 1989a). Because of this opposition, in some coun- tries women do manufacture for export, not in modern, much less multina- tional factories, but from the "protection" (or confinement?) of their own homes, subcontracting to male middlemen (as in Turkey), or in cottage industries and small factories run by local male elites (as in parts of Indone- sia). Needless to say, under such circumstances labor organization is impos- sible, and wages are lower and hours of work longer than they would be in modern multinational factories, confirming Marx's belief in the progressiv- ity of capitalist over precapitalist production.

CONCLUSION

In studies of women in development, it has become commonplace to note that women tend to gain disproportionately less, and lose disproportionately more, from most forms of economic development, which, it is argued, destroy more jobs than they create for women. Export manufacturing, which still accounts for only a small part of most Third World economies, and an even smaller proportion of developed countries' manufactured imports, is one exception that creates employment disproportionately for women. Despite a decade of pessimistic forecasts that have not come true, it has continued to grow, and market prospects are good, or at least better than prospects for most other sectors of developing countries' economies (Lim 1989b).

Yet this form of development, despite or perhaps because of its benefit to women, continues to be disparaged by most writers on the subject, who ignore its diversity and complexity to focus on negative aspects that will validate their theories. The policy implication of this negativity is that export manufacturing and the employment it creates for women should not be encouraged, and perhaps should even be actively discouraged. A powerful coalition of political interests — especially patriarchal, capitalist, and nationalist interests — in both the developed and developing countries advances this position, which regrettably is directly or indirectly supported by many feminists and radicals.

In this chapter I have pointed out the methodological weaknesses of the literature, which feed and sustain this opposition to women's employment in export factories in the Third World. These weaknesses result primarily from biases introduced by ideology, ethnocentrism, and vested political interests. Obviously, my own past and present work is not immune from these and other criticisms. But feminist solidarity should not preclude diversity, disagreement, and mutual criticism, the processes by which scholarly and political advances are made. My hope is that this chapter and works like it will contribute to more careful and objective scholarship and more open and balanced debate, especially by and within the feminist scholarly community, on what is still a very important, if often exaggerated, topic of research in the field of women in development.

II

INTRAHOUSEHOLD
DISTRIBUTION AND CONTROL

8

Gender and Cooperative Conflicts

AMARTYA K. SEN

In the standard literature on economic development there is frequently a noticeable reluctance to consider the position of women as a separate problem of importance of its own. Gender-based analysis is often seen as being unnecessarily divisive. Poverty, undernourishment, escapable morbidity, or avoidable mortality strikes men as well as women, and the lives of all members — male and female — of households at the bottom of the pile are plagued by severe deprivations. It is therefore not surprising that many writers insist on seeing the deprivation of entire families as the right focus for studying misery and for seeking remedies, concentrating on the placing of families in the class structure and in the economic and social hierarchy (and also on the overall prosperity of the community).

That nongender view has much plausibility in some contexts. However, for some problems income and class categories are overaggregative and even misleading, and there is a need for gender classification. In fact, the importance of gender as a crucial parameter in social and economic analysis is complementary to, rather than competitive with, the variables of class, ownership, occupations, incomes, and family status.

The systematically inferior position of women inside and outside the household in many societies points to the necessity of treating gender as a force of its own in development analysis. The economic hardship of *woman-*

This essay draws heavily on two previous attempts to address this set of issues: "Cooperative Conflicts: Technology and the Position of Women," All Souls College, Oxford, 1983 (mimeographed), and "Women, Technology and Sexual Divisions," *Trade and Development* (UN-CTAD) 6 (1985). For helpful comments I am most grateful to Jocelyn Kynch and Irene Tinker. My thinking on this question has been deeply influenced by discussions with my late wife, Eva Colorni, over a number of years, until her tragic death on July 3, 1985, and it is to her memory that I dedicate this essay.

headed households is a problem *both* of female deprivation and of family poverty. Furthermore, females and males in the same family may well have quite divergent predicaments, and this can make the position of women in the poorer families particularly precarious. To concentrate on family poverty irrespective of gender can be misleading in terms of both causation and consequences.

The fact that the relative deprivation of women vis-à-vis men is by no means uniform across the world does not reduce the importance of gender as a parameter of analysis. In fact, this variability is an important reason for giving serious attention to the causal antecedents of the contrasting deprivations. To take an extremely simple and crude example, it is clear that despite the evident biological advantages that women seem to have over men in survival and longevity (when there is some symmetry in the attention they receive on basic matters of life and death, such as nutrition, health care, and medical attention), there is nevertheless a remarkable preponderance of surviving men over surviving women in the population of less developed countries (the LDCs) taken as a whole, in sharp contrast with the position of the more developed countries. Whereas there are about 106 women per 100 men in Europe and North America, there are only 97 women per 100 men in the LDCs as a whole. Since mortality and survival are not independent of care and neglect, and are influenced by social action and public policy, even this extremely crude perspective cannot fail to isolate gender as an important parameter in development studies.

There are also systematic differences among the LDCs in the survival rates of females vis-à-vis males. Asia has a sex ratio (females per male) of only 0.95, but Africa comes closer to Europe and North America with a sex ratio of 1.02 — indeed considerably higher than that in sub-Saharan Africa. Even within Asia the sex ratio is higher than unity in some regions, such as Southeast Asia (1.01), but much lower in China, India, Bangladesh, and West Asia (0.94) and in Pakistan (0.90). There are substantial variations even *within* a given country; for example, in India the sex ratio varies from 0.87 and 0.88 in Haryana and Punjab to 1.03 in Kerala. It is clear that had the average African sex ratio obtained in India, then given the number of men, there would have been about 30 million more women in India today (see Sen 1988). The corresponding number of "missing women" in China is about 38 million. The cumulative contrasts of sex-specific mortality rates — not unrelated to social and economic inequalities between men and women — find expression in these simple statistics, which form something like the tip of an iceberg much of which is hard to observe.

Development analysis cannot really be divorced from gender categories and sex-specific observations. It is, however, difficult to translate this elementary recognition into practice and to find an adequate framework for the use of gender categories and sex-specific information in social analysis. This essay is addressed to some of the issues in this difficult field. The problem is far too complex and basic to be "resolved" by any kind of a simple model, but we can go some distance toward a better understanding of the problem by broadening the conceptual structure and the informational base of gender analysis in economic and social relations.

First, some of the basic notions in the proposed conceptual structure are briefly examined, including "functionings," "capabilities," "well-being," and "agency" (these concepts have been more extensively discussed in Sen 1985a, 1985b). The role of *perceptions* in the informational base of the conceptual structure is also discussed. The identification of well-being with the fulfillment of *perceived* interests is disputed, and the possible causal influence of perceptions on ideas of propriety and legitimacy of different institutional arrangements and through that on the respective well-beings of men and women is noted. Next, the notion of "social technology" is presented, broadening the traditional view of technology. Explicit note is taken of the role of household arrangements in sustaining commodity production.

Different theories of household economics are examined, suggesting that "bargaining models" have an advantage over others (such as standard models of "household production," "family allocation," or "equivalence scales") in capturing the coexistence of extensive conflicts *and* pervasive cooperation in household arrangements. But it is argued that they too have an inadequate informational base and are particularly negligent of the influence of perceived interests and perceived contributions.

An alternative approach to "cooperative conflicts" is then sketched, identifying certain qualitative relations in the form of directional responses of the outcome to certain determining variables in the informational base. These relations are translated into a format of "extended entitlements," based on sharpening the concept of "entitlements" (already used in studying famines and deprivation of households) by incorporating notions of perceived legitimacy in intrahousehold divisions.[1]

The directional responses are examined in the light of empirical information presented in microstudies as well as in aggregative interregional comparisons. Some concluding remarks are made in the final section.

CAPABILITIES, WELL-BEING, AGENCY, AND PERCEPTION

Everyone has many identities. Being a man or a woman is one of them. Being a member of a family is another. Membership of a class, an occupation group, a nation, or a community can be the basis of particular links. One's individuality coexists with a variety of such identities. Our understanding of our interests, well-being, obligations, objectives, and legitimate behavior is influenced by the various—and sometimes conflicting—effects of these diverse identities.

In some contexts the family identity may exert such a strong influence on our perceptions that we may not find it easy to formulate any clear notion of

[1]The notion of "entitlements" was used, primarily for famine analysis, in Sen (1976, 1981). That of "extended entitlements" is discussed in Sen (1985c). See also Tilly (1985, 1986), Vaughan (1985), and Wilson (1987).

our own individual welfare. Based on empirical observations of family-centered perceptions in some traditional societies (such as India), some authors have disputed the viability of the notion of personal welfare in those societies (for a particularly forceful and cogent statement, see Das & Nicholas 1981). It has often been observed that if a typical Indian rural woman was asked about her personal "welfare," she would find the question unintelligible, and if she was able to reply, she might answer the question in terms of her reading of the welfare of her family. The idea of personal welfare may not be viable in such a context, it has been argued.

This empirical problem of perception and communication is indeed important. On the other hand, it is far from obvious that the right conclusion to draw from this is the nonviability of the notion of personal welfare. This is so for several distinct reasons. First, there are considerable variations in the perception of individuality even within such a traditional society, and the lack of a perception of personal welfare, where that holds, is neither immutable nor particularly resistant to social development. Indeed, the process of politicization — including a political recognition of the gender issue — can itself bring about sharp changes in these perceptions, as can processes of economic change, such as women's involvement in so-called gainful employment and outside work, which will be discussed later (see P. Bardhan 1974, 1982; Boserup 1970; Mazumdar 1985a; Miller 1981; Sen 1982b, 1985c, 1986).

Second, insofar as intrafamily divisions involve significant inequalities in the allotment of food, medical attention, health care, and the like (often unfavorable to the well-being — even survival — of women), the lack of perception of personal interest combined with a great concern for family welfare is, of course, just the kind of attitude that helps to sustain the traditional inequalities. There is much evidence in history that acute inequalities often survive precisely by making allies out of the deprived. The underdog comes to accept the legitimacy of the unequal order and becomes an implicit accomplice (see Sen 1985a, 1985b; also Papanek, Chapter 10, this volume). It can be a serious error to take the absence of protests and questioning of inequality as evidence of the absence of that inequality (or of the nonviability of that question).

Third, personal interest and welfare are not just matters of perception; there are objective aspects of these concepts that command attention even when the corresponding self-perception does not exist. For example, the "illfare" associated with morbidity or undernourishment has an immediacy that does not await the person's inclination or willingness to answer detailed questions regarding his or her welfare. Indeed, the well-being of a person may plausibly be seen in terms of a person's functionings and capabilities: what he or she is able to do or be (e.g., the ability to be well nourished, to avoid escapable morbidity or mortality, to read and write and communicate, to take part in the life of the community, to appear in public without shame; see Sen 1985a, 1985b, 1987). While the functionings and the capability to function have to be evaluated (since they are diverse and not *directly* commensurable), the contingent absence of explicit discussion on this evaluative question does not make these functionings and capabilities valueless. There is a need to go *beyond* the primitive feelings that a person may have on these matters, based perhaps on unquestioning acceptance of certain traditional priorities. Social change and politicization may well take precisely the form of making people face those evaluative questions.

Finally, it is also possible to distinguish between a person's "well-being" and "agency." A person may have various goals and objectives other than the pursuit of his or her well-being. Although there are obvious links between a person's well-being and the fulfillment of his or her other objectives, the overall success as an agent may not be closely connected—and certainly may not be identified—with that person's own well-being.[2] It is the agency aspect that is most influenced by a person's sense of obligation and perception of legitimate behavior. These perceptions—while influencible by politics and education—may have relevance of their own (even in their contingent existence), but they must not be confused with the person's well-being or, alternatively, taken as evidence of the nonviability of any personal notion of well-being.

It is, of course, possible to assert the importance of actual mental states as reflections of individual well-being, and in fact, in the utilitarian tradition, the metrics of happiness and desire do occupy a commanding position in the evaluation of individual welfare and through that on the goodness of states of affairs and the rightness of actions. But that approach to welfare and ethics can be—and has been—extensively challenged.[3] Deprived groups may be habituated to inequality, may be unaware of possibilities of social change, may be hopeless about upliftment of objective circumstances of misery, may be resigned to fate, and may well be willing to accept the legitimacy of the established order. The tendency to take pleasure in small mercies would make good sense given these perceptions, and cutting desires to shape (in line with perceived feasibility) can help to save one from serious disappointment and frustration. The deprivations may thus be muted in the metric of happiness or desire fulfillment. But the real deprivations are not just washed away by the mere fact that in the particular utilitarian metrics of happiness and desire fulfillment such a deprived person may not seem particularly disadvantaged. The embarrassment, if there is one here, is for utilitarianism (and for welfarism in general),[4] and not for those who insist

---

[2]The distinction between well-being and agency, their interconnections, and their different realms of relevance are discussed in my Dewey Lectures (Sen 1985b).

[3]For critiques of the utilitarian measures, see Dworkin (1981), Nozick (1974), Parfit (1984), Rawls (1971), Scanlon (1975), Sen (1970), and Williams (1973), among others. See Gosling (1969) for an exposition of the two perspectives of desire and pleasure in the utilitarian tradition. For sophisticated—and illuminating—defenses of the utilitarian calculus, see particularly Griffin (1987), Hare (1981), and Harsanyi (1976).

[4]On the distinction between the particular approach of utilitarianism (involving the *summation of utilities*) and "welfarism" in general (judging of a state of affairs as a function of individual utility information—not necessarily in the form of the *sum total*), see Sen (1970) and Sen and Williams (1982).

that the underfed, underclothed, undercared, or overworked person is in some real sense deeply deprived no matter what the utility metrics say.[5]

The point of arguing this way is not, in fact, to claim that a person's perceptions are not important. Indeed, they may be extremely important in understanding what social and familial arrangements emerge and survive. In fact, later in this chapter considerable use is made of the nature of actual perceptions in understanding the outcomes of cooperative conflicts. But the contingent perceptions are important not because they are definitive guides to individual interests and well-being (this they are not), but because the perceptions (including illusions) have an influence — often a major impact — on actual states and outcomes.

SOCIAL TECHNOLOGY, COOPERATION, AND CONFLICTS

Technology is often seen in highly limited terms, for example, as particular mechanical or chemical or biological processes used in making one good or another. The extremely narrow view of technology that emerges from such a limited outlook does little justice to the "social" content of technology — what Marx called "the combining together of various processes into a social whole" (1867/1967:515).[6] The making of things involves not merely the relationship between, say, raw materials and final products, but also the social organization that permits the use of specific techniques of production in factories or workshops or on land.

The so-called "productive" activities may be parasitic on other work being done, such as housework and food preparation, the care of children, or bringing food to the field where cultivators are working. Technology is not only about equipment and its operational characteristics but also about social arrangements that permit the equipment to be used and the so-called productive processes to be carried on.

Household activities have been viewed in many contradictory ways in assessing production and technology. On the one hand, it is not denied that the sustenance, survival, and reproduction of workers are obviously essential for the workers being available for outside work. On the other hand, the activities that produce or support that sustenance, survival, or reproduction are typically not regarded as *contributing* to output and are often classified as "unproductive" labor.

There has been a good deal of recent interest in the problem of valuation of these activities and also in reflecting them in the estimates of national

---

[5] I have discussed these issues more extensively (Sen 1985b). Welfarism is the approach that takes the value of state of affairs to be a function exclusively of utility information regarding that state. Utilitarianism involving the *summing* of utilities is a special case of welfarism.

[6] Marx is discussing here the nature of "capitalist production" and how it developed technology into a social whole, "sapping the original sources of all wealth — the soil and the labourer."

income and national consumption.[7] However, for the present purpose, these accounting questions are not really central (even though they are, in general, important in seeking a better understanding of the social position of women). What is important here is to take an integrated view of the pattern of activities outside *and* inside the home that together make up the production processes in traditional as well as modern societies.[8] The relations between the sexes are obviously much conditioned by the way these different activities sustain and support each other, and the respective positions depend inter alia on the particular pattern of integration that is used.

The prosperity of the household depends on the totality of various activities — getting money incomes, purchasing or directly producing (in the case of, say, peasants) food materials and other goods, producing edible food out of food materials, and so on. But in addition to aggregate prosperity, even the divisions between sexes in general, and specifically those within the household, may also be deeply influenced by the pattern of gender division of work. In particular, the members of the household face two different types of problems simultaneously, one involving *cooperation* (adding to total availabilities) and the other *conflict* (dividing the total availabilities among the members of the household). Social arrangements regarding who does what, who gets to consume what, and who takes what decisions can be seen as responses to this combined problem of cooperation and conflict. The sexual division of labor is one part of such a social arrangement, and it is important to see it in the context of the entire arrangement.

Seeing social arrangements in terms of a broader view of technology and production has some far-reaching effects. First, it points to the necessity of examining the productive aspects of what are often treated as purely "cultural" phenomena. It also brings out the productive contributions that are in effect made by labor expended in activities that are not directly involved in "production" narrowly defined. A deeper probing is especially important in trying to clear the fog of ambiguity in which the roles of different types of laboring activities are hidden by stereotyped social perceptions, and this is

[7]See particularly Goldschmidt-Clermont (1982) and the rather large literature surveyed there. There is also the related issue of properly valuing nonhousehold work of women, on which see Banerjee (1985), Beneria (1982a), Bryceson (1985), Jain (1985), Jain and Chand (1982), Mukherjee (1985).

[8]A particular pattern — that of capitalist production arrangements with family wages being used for household production — is appropriately characterized by Jane Humphries thus: "The working-class family constitutes an arena of production, the inputs being the commodities purchased with family wages, and one of the outputs being the renewed labour-power sold for wages in the market" (1977:142). On the interrelations between problems of class divisions and gender division, see — among other contributions — Benston (1969), Dalla Costa (1972), Gardiner (1975), Harrison (1974), Himmelweit and Mohun (1977), Humphries (1977), Mackintosh (1979), McIntosh (1978), Meillassoux (1972), Mies (1982b), Milkman (1976), Molyneux (1979), Rowbotham (1973), Secombe (1974), Young (1978), Young, Wolkowitz, and McCullagh (1981). See also the studies of experiences in socialist countries, e.g., Croll (1979, 1986), Molyneux (1981, 1982, 1985), and Wolf (1985).

of obvious importance in assessing the nature and implications of particular patterns of gender divisions.

Second, it throws light on the stability and survival of unequal patterns of social arrangements in general, and deeply asymmetric sexual divisions in particular. An example is the resilient social division of labor in most societies by which women do the cooking and are able to take on outside work only insofar as that can be combined with persisting as the cook.[9]

Third, the division between paid and unpaid work in the context of general productive arrangements (and "the combining together of various processes into a social whole") can be seen as bringing in systematic biases in the perception of who is "producing" what and "earning" what — biases that are central to understanding the inferior economic position of women in traditional (and even in modern) societies.

Fourth, specific patterns of sexual divisions (and female specialization in particular economic activities) even *outside* the household can be seen as being partly reflective of the traditional *within-household* divisions related to established arrangements, which differentially bias the cultivation of skill and tend to sustain asymmetry of opportunities offered for acquiring "untraditional" skills. In understanding the inferior economic position of women inside and outside the household in most societies, the hold of these social arrangements has to be clearly identified and analyzed.[10]

The nature of "social technology" has a profound effect on relating production and earnings to the distribution of that earning between men and women and to gender divisions of work and resources. The divisional arrangements that, on the one hand, may help in the economic survival and the overall opulence of families and societies may also impose, through the same process, a typically unequal division of job opportunities and work freedoms. They influence the division of fruits of joint activities — sometimes sustaining inequalities in the commodities consumed in relation to needs (e.g., of food in poorer economies). The nature of the cooperative arrangements implicitly influences the distributional parameters and the household's response to conflicts of interest.

---

[9]This pattern also influences the type of outside work for which women are typically thought to be "suited." One of the consequences of being offered relatively mechanical jobs involving repetitive activities is greater vulnerability, in many cases, to job loss as a result of mechanization (on this see Sen 1985c). On the nature of women's job opportunities, see Ahooja-Patel (1980), Amsden (1980), Banerjee (1979, 1983, 1985), Boserup (1970), Burman (1979), Deere and Leon de Leal (1982), Jain (1980b), Palmer (1980), Standing and Sheehan (1978). On the nature of threatened job losses through mechanization and technical change, see Agarwal (1981), Ahmed (1978, 1983), Ahmed and Loutfi (1982), Beneria (1982a), Carr (1978), Date-Bah and Stevens (1981), Harriss (1977), ILO (1982a, 1982b), Loutfi (1980), Palmer (1978), Ventura-Dias (1982), Whitehead (1981).

[10]Even in the United States the average woman worker seems to earn only a fraction of the average male worker's earning (62 percent, to be exact, as reported in "Female Sacrifice," *New York Times*, 14 April 1984). These differences arise not so much from different payments to men and women in the same job categories, but from women being more confined to particular types of jobs that are typically less remunerative. On this see Larwood, Stromberg, and Gutek (1986), particularly the paper by June O'Neill. See also Hacker (1986).

HOUSEHOLD ECONOMICS, BARGAINING MODELS, AND INFORMATIONAL BASES

The simultaneity of cooperation and conflict in gender divisions has often been trivialized in the formal economic literature by making particular — often far-fetched — assumptions. One approach is to see household arrangements as resulting from implicit markets with transactions at "as-if" market prices (see Becker 1973–74, 1981), even though it may be hard to see how such implicit markets can operate without the institutional support that sustains actual market transactions.

Sometimes, the same basic model can be substantially varied by postulating that the transactions take the form of falling in line with the objectives of an altruistic family head. As Becker (1981) puts it: "In my approach the 'optimal reallocation' results from altruism and voluntary contributions, and the 'group preference function' is identical to that of the altruistic head, even when he does not have sovereign power" (p. 192). (On the peculiar nature of this solution, see Mansur & Brown 1980; McElroy & Horney 1981; Pollack 1983; see also Berk & Berk 1978, 1979). Others have assumed that somehow or other — in ways unspecified — an "optimal" distribution of commodities and provisions takes place within the family, permitting us to see families as if they are individuals (see Samuelson 1956). The central issues of cooperative conflicts are avoided in all these models by one device or another.

Helpful insights can be obtained by seeing divisions as "bargaining problems," which form a class of cooperative conflicts.[11] The technological interdependences make it fruitful for the different parties to cooperate, but the particular pattern of division of fruits that emerges from such cooperation reflects the "bargaining powers" of the respective parties. This format certainly has many advantages over the models of "as-if markets," or "an altruistic leader's dominance," or "harmonious optimal divisions." A number of recent contributions have brought out these advantages clearly enough (Brown & Chuang 1980; Clemhout & Wan 1977; Folbre 1984a; Manser & Brown 1980; McElroy & Horney 1981; Pollak 1983; Rochford 1981).

Nevertheless, the informational base of the bargaining problem is limited by focusing exclusively on individual interests (typically taken to be cardinally representable), and by the assumption of clear and unambiguous perceptions of these individual interests. The latter assumption misses crucial aspects of the nature of gender divisions inside and outside the family. The sense of appropriateness goes hand in hand with ambiguities of perception of interests and with certain perceived notions of legitimacy regarding what is "deserved" and what is not. These perceptions are also closely related to the nature of the social technology establishing specificity of roles and

---

[11]"Bargaining problems" were first formulated by Nash (1950, 1953), and have been extensively discussed by Luce and Raiffa (1957), Harsanyi (1977), Roth (1979), and Binmore and Dasgupta (1987), among many others. On the *normative* features of bargaining problems, see Braithwaite (1955), Kaneko (1980), Kaneko and Nakamura (1979), Rawls (1971), Sen (1970), among others.

sustaining a presumption of "naturalness" of the established order. Also, they have a role in explaining particular *production* arrangements that are seen as forming the basis of economic survival and success. The informational base needs to be widened to include perceptions of legitimacy and desert, and the specification of felt individual interests must take note of perception problems.

These issues would have to be faced, but we may begin with the neat format of the bargaining problem as a starting point.[12] In the simplest case, there are two people with well-defined and clearly perceived interests in the form of two cardinal utility functions respectively. They can cooperate altogether. The outcome when they fail to cooperate has been variously denoted, and may be called "the status quo position" or "the breakdown position." What happens if the cooperative proposals should break down is of obvious relevance to the choice of the collusive outcome, since the breakdown position affects the two people's respective bargaining powers. Since each person's interests are reflected by an exact (and cardinal) utility function, the breakdown position in a two-person bargaining problem is a pair of utility numbers, and the various cooperative outcomes form also a set of pairs of utility numbers (all with cardinal properties).

If there were only one collusive possibility that is better for both than the breakdown position, then there would, of course, be no real bargaining problem, since the unique collusive solution would be the only one to choose. The bargaining problem arises from the existence of many choosable collusive arrangements—each such arrangement being better for both persons than the breakdown position. If there is a collusive arrangement which—while better for both than the breakdown position—is worse for both (or worse for one and no better for the other) than some *other* feasible collusive arrangement, then the first collusive arrangement—"dominated" as it is—is taken to be rejected straightaway.

Once the dominated arrangements have been weeded out, there remain possible collusive solutions that are ranked by the two in exactly opposite ways. If for person 1, arrangement x is better than y, then for person 2, arrangement y must be better than x. (If not, then x would have dominated y as an arrangement.) At this stage of the exercise the aspect of cooperation is all gone and there is only conflict. The choice *between any two undominated collusive arrangements* is therefore one of pure adversity. But at the same time each person knows that the choice *between any such collusive arrangement and the breakdown position* is a matter of cooperation since the former is better for *both*. It is this mixture of cooperation and conflicting aspects in the bargaining problem that makes the analysis of that problem

12While the classic contributions to formulating the bargaining problem were those of Nash (1950, 1953), some interesting and important variations can be found in Binmore (1980), Binmore and Dasgupta (1987), Braithwaite (1955), Dasgupta (1986), Harsanyi (1977), Kalai and Smordinsky (1975), Kaneko (1980), Luce and Raiffa (1957), Roth (1979), Schelling (1960), Shubik (1983), among others.

potentially valuable in understanding household arrangements, which also involve a mixture of this kind.[13]

What solution would emerge in the "bargaining problem"? That depends on a variety of possible influences, including the bargaining power of the two sides. The problem can be resolved in many different ways. Nash confines the informational base of the solution to (1) the pairs of alternative feasible individual welfare levels, and (2) the welfare levels at the breakdown point. Specifically, he suggests a particular solution that would maximize the *product* of the two people's welfare gains compared with the breakdown position.[14] Others have suggested other solutions.[15]

The main drawback of the "bargaining problem" format applied to gender divisions arise not so much from the nature of any particular "solution," but from the formulation of the "problem" itself. As was discussed earlier, the perception of interest is likely to be neither precise nor unambiguous. There are two distinct issues here.

The first is the need to distinguish between the *perception* of interest (of the different parties) and some more *objective* notion of their respective well-being. Focusing on the "capabilities" of a person—what he or she can *do* or can *be*—provides a direct approach to a person's well-being. Although that format also has many problems (especially dealing with indexing of capabilities; see Sen 1985a), it has important theoretical advantages as well as much practical convenience (for some applications of this format in the specific context of women's relative disadvantage, see Kynch & Sen 1983; Sen 1984; Sen & Sengupta 1983). Especially in dealing with poor economies, there are great advantages in concentrating on such parameters as longevity, nutrition, health and avoidance of morbidity, and educational achievements rather than focusing purely on subjective utility in the form of pleasure, satisfaction, and desire fulfillment, which can be molded by social conditioning and a resigned acceptance of misfortune.[16] The analyses of cooperative conflicts, in this view, must go beyond perceived interests, and we have to distinguish between perceptions and well-being.

[13]The advantages and limitations of the "bargaining problem" format in analyzing household arrangements are discussed in Sen (1985c).

[14]Nash did not see his solution of the bargaining problem as a predictive exercise and seems to have characterized it as a normative solution of this conflict. His method of choosing a solution took the form of postulating some axioms of reasonableness of a cooperative outcome, and these axioms together uniquely identified the product-maximization formula. But, interestingly enough, exactly the same solution as Nash's would be arrived at if the bargaining procedure followed a method analyzed earlier by Zeuthen (1930), whereby the two parties would move from one proposed arrangement to another if and only if the *percentage gain* of the gainer from the move would be greater than the *percentage loss* of the loser.

[15]See footnotes 11 and 12 above. Manser and Brown (1980) used the outcome specified by Kalai and Smordinsky (1975).

[16]The capability to be happy can, of course, be sensibly *included* among the relevant capabilities, but this is quite different from using utility (or happiness) as the *measure* of all types of benefits, or (even more ambitiously) as the ultimate *source* of all value (as in different versions of the utilitarian approach).

The second limitation arises from the informational base of bargaining models being confined to individual *interests* (or *welfare*) only, without letting the solution respond explicitly to other variables such as conceptions of desert and legitimacy (e.g., those related to perceived "productive contributions" of each party to family opulence).[17] The nature of "social technology" makes these ideas particularly influential in the determination of gender divisions. We need, on both these grounds, a wider informational base for studying cooperative conflicts.

COOPERATIVE CONFLICTS: INTERESTS, CONTRIBUTIONS, AND PERCEPTIONS

The informational base of cooperative conflicts must distinguish between interest perceptions and measures of the well-being of the persons involved. Further, the base must include information regarding perceptions of who is "contributing" how much to the overall family prosperity.[18] This greater plurality of the informational structure makes the modeling of cooperative outcomes that much more complex than in the simple special case of the bargaining problem in the tradition of Nash. But the simplicity of the Nash model and the related structures is achieved at considerable sacrifice of informational sensitivity.[19] In this presentation, I shall not try to develop a fully worked out solution function for the cooperative conflict problems. Indeed, a variety of solutions can be suggested, and all that will be done here is to specify a set of *directional* features, related respectively to (1) well-being levels at the breakdown points, (2) perceived interests, and (3) perceived contributions. For our present purpose this is adequate, though—obviously—any attempt at specifying an exact outcome would be impossible without presenting a more complete solution structure.

One particular feature of the Nash bargaining problem has justifiably attracted a good deal of attention. This makes the outcome respond firmly to the nature of the breakdown position. (This is, in fact, obvious from the

[17]The Nash bargaining models are, in his sense, "welfarist," without being utilitarian.

[18]The "bargaining solution function" presented in Sen (1970:126–27) can be readily extended for this purpose. In that characterization of the Nash bargaining model, the solution $\bar{x}$ depended on the breakdown position $\tilde{x}$ and on the welfare combination W, with specified "invariance conditions" corresponding to cardinal noncomparability of individual well-being. To these informational inputs (possibly with changed invariance conditions), we can add the perceived-interest combination I and perceived-contribution combination P, the latter unique (since the units will be so many units of, say, incomes generated by each) in the respective points of collusive solutions. The informational base for the solution will then be $(\tilde{x}, W, I, P)$. In this elementary exposition, we are concerned only with some *directional* responses of $\bar{x}$, the solution, to the determining variables.

[19]Schelling (1960) pointed to the fact that the Nash solution pays no attention to the "salience" of some outcomes vis-à-vis others. Schelling's alternative approach also enriches the informational base of the Nash model but takes us in a different direction, which I shall not pursue here.

method—already described—of identifying the solution.) Indeed, a more favorable placing in the breakdown position would tend to help in securing a more favorable bargaining outcome. Nash had seen his solution as a normative one, and it has been argued in criticism of Nash that in that context this responsiveness to the breakdown position may not perhaps be so easy to defend.[20] But predictively it is, of course, entirely plausible that the fear of the breakdown position would tend to govern the bargaining process and strongly influence its outcome.

With a little more structure in the characterization of the bargaining problem than we have introduced so far, it is easy to get a directional relation of the following form:

1. *Breakdown well-being response:* Given other things, if the breakdown position of one person were worse in terms of well-being, then the collusive solution, if different, would be less favorable to his or her well-being.

The breakdown position indicates the person vulnerability or strength in the "bargaining." If, in the case of a breakdown, one person is going to end up in more of a mess than it appeared previously, that is going to weaken that person's ability to secure a favorable outcome.

The "breakdown response" is a general qualitative property of cooperative conflicts entirely in line with the rationale of Nash's approach to bargaining. Others have extended the idea of bargaining power by bringing in the idea of "threat," that is, a person threatening the other with some harmful action if the bargaining were to fail. This can make the actual result of breakdown *worse* for the threatened person than the previously identified breakdown position, if the threat is carried out (see Binmore & Dasgupta 1987; Braithwaite 1955; Harsanyi 1977; Luce & Raiffa 1957; Roth 1979; Schelling 1960).

This is a plausible direction of extension, though there are some very basic difficulties with any theory of threats, since it has to deal with situations *after* the bargaining has failed.[21] But in the context of a bargaining arrangement that continues over time, there are possibilities of going on making "side threats" (and through them, trying to make the outcome more favor-

[20]Punishing the more vulnerable is not implausible from a predictive point of view, but it is odd to think of this as being "just," or otherwise normatively attractive, though that interpretation has been taken (see particularly Braithwaite 1955). To say "I see you are going to be even worse off (than we first thought) if you do not join up with me, so you better agree to these worsened terms of joining" may not ring untrue (if a little explicit and crude), but it is hardly overflowing with anything that can plausibly be called justice. On the relation between the predictive and normative issues in the context of Nash's bargaining problem, see Rawls (1971) and Sen (1970).

[21]See Sen (1970:120–21). The person who "threatens" to harm the other if the bargaining should fail does it at no direct advantage to himself (otherwise it won't be a "threat" but something he may do anyway, and will be thus reflected in the breakdown position). While it is plausible to try to get bargaining advantage out of a threat *during* the process of bargaining, once the bargaining has failed, the threatener has no obvious interest in carrying out the threat. But that recognition on the part of the threatened person would call into question the credibility of the threat itself.

able in the process of living through it). The nature of "repeated games" gives credibility to threats (on these and related issues, see Sen 1985c).

The influence of perceived interest on the bargaining outcome may take the form of choosing a solution in the space not of individual well-being levels but in that of perceived interests. In fact, a simple translation of the Nash model would be to redefine the solution in terms of these interest perceptions rather than well-being measures. If the breakdown point too is defined in terms of perceived interests rather than actual well-being levels (not as in the "breakdown well-being response"), then this will amount to a simple interpretational shift of the Nash model without necessarily changing the mathematical properties of the solution (but making a substantive difference to the actual solution since the perceived-interest relations may well be much less favorable to one party than the well-being relations, for reasons discussed earlier). In the plural informational format proposed here, both perceived interests and well-being measures may have influence, the latter especially through breakdown response.

The motivation underlying the directional response to be specified here relates to the fact that a person may get a worse deal in the collusive solution if his or her perceived interest takes little note of his or her own well-being. As was discussed earlier, such perception bias in the direction of the interests of the others in the family may apply particularly to women in traditional societies.

2. *Perceived interest response:* Given other things, if the self-interest perception of one of the persons were to attach less value to his or her own well-being, then the collusive solution, if different, would be less favorable to that person, in terms of well-being.

A different type of issue is raised by the influence of a perceived sense of greater "contribution" (and of the "legitimacy" of enjoying a correspondingly bigger share of the fruits of cooperation). This question has already been discussed earlier. "*Perceived* contributions" have to be distinguished from *actual* contributions. Indeed, the idea of who is *actually* producing precisely what in an *integrated* system may not be at all clear. Nevertheless, the *perceived* contribution of people can be important in tilting the cooperative outcomes in favor of the perceived contributor.

3. *Perceived contribution response:* Given other things, if in the accounting of the respective outcomes, a person was perceived as making a larger contribution to the overall opulence of the group, then the collusive solution, if different, would be more favorable to that person.

The three "responses," related respectively to breakdown, perceived interest, and perceived contribution, may throw some light on the way the deal tends to be biased between the sexes. This can be seen both in terms of a stylized reference point of a "primitive" situation as well as a more realistically portrayed "current" one, and the relation between the two situations is itself of some interest. Some disadvantages of women would apply in both types of situations. For example, frequent pregnancy and persistent child rearing (as happens in many present communities and has happened in most of the past ones) must make the outcome of cooperative conflicts less favorable to women through worse breakdown position and a lower ability to make a perceived contribution to the economic fortunes of the family.[22] Other disadvantages are much more specific to the nature of the community, for example, greater illiteracy and less higher education of women in most developing — and some developed — countries today, and these too would tend to make the breakdown positions worse for women.

The perception biases unfavorable to women, both in terms of distancing perceived interests from well-being and recording productive contributions inadequately, will also vary from one society to another. The "perceived interest response" and the "perceived contribution response" can be tremendously more regressive for women in some societies (Sen 1984: Essays 15 and 16).

The relation between the cooperative conflicts in one period and those in the next is of the greatest importance even though it may be hard to formalize this properly. The "winners" in one round get a satisfactory outcome that would typically include not only more immediate benefit but also a better placing (and greater bargaining power) in the future. This need not be the result of a conscious exercise of taking note of future placing or bargaining power (though it can also be that), but the effect may be brought about by the fact that "more satisfactory work" from the point of view of immediate benefit tends incidentally to enhance the power bases of the deal a person can expect to get in the future. For example, getting better education, being free to work outside the home, finding more "productive" employment, and so on, may all contribute not only to immediate well-being but also to acquired skill and a better breakdown position for the future.[23] Also, job training improves the quality of labor and improves one's breakdown position, threat advantages, and perceived contributions within the family, even when these may not have been conscious objectives.

The transmission can also work from one generation to the next, indeed from one historical epoch to the next, as the "typical" patterns of employment and education for men get solidified vis-à-vis those for women. The asymmetries of immediate benefits sustain future asymmetries of future bases of sexual divisions, which in turn sustain asymmetries of immediate benefits. The process can feed on itself, and I shall refer to this process as "feedback transmission."

---

[22]On the importance of the "reproductive" role of women in influencing gender bias, see Bryceson (1985). Leela Gulati (1981) presents an interesting case study of astonishingly rapid impact of an extension of family planning in some fishing villages in Kerala on the health and survival of women and on their earning power.

[23]Consider Becker, Landes, and Michael's (1977) characterization of "working exclusively in the non-market sector" as a form of marriage-specific investment. As Pollak (1983) remarks, "A decision to work exclusively in the non-market sector, however, is also a decision not to acquire additional human capital by working in the market sector" (p. 35).

In the stylized "primitive" situation, the disadvantages of women in terms of "breakdown response" would relate greatly to purely physical factors, even though the role of physical factors is governed by social conditions. For example, at an advanced stage of pregnancy, securing food on one's own in a *hunting* community must be no mean task. The breakdown positions can be asymmetrically worse for women in various types of "primitive" societies, and this can make the gender visions go relatively against women in line with "breakdown response."[24]

In a less primitive situation — a stylized "current" one — the primitive asymmetries, if any, are supplemented by socially generated further asymmetries, for example, of ownership, education, and training,[25] and also a nurtured view of the "fragility" of women (seen as unsuitable for some types of jobs). These all contribute to a worse breakdown position and worse ability to make a "perceived contribution" to the family's economic status. The bargaining disadvantages will feed on themselves through "feedback transmission." It may not be terribly important to know how all this got started, that is, whether *because* of the physical asymmetries relevant in the "primitive" situation or through some other process (e.g., as Engels, 1884, had argued, through the emergence of private property). In the present context, the important point is that such asymmetries — however developed — are stable and sustained, and the relative weakness of women in cooperative conflict in one period tends to sustain relative weakness in the next.[26]

[24]Strictly speaking, "breakdown response" is not concerned with the relative positions of two parties but with the different positions of the same person in two situations with different breakdown features. Indeed, in Nash's own formulation, the position of one person being worse than that of another is not a meaningful statement, since Nash had no provision for interpersonal comparison (on this see Sen 1970:118–25). However, when such comparisons are admitted and a condition of symmetry is used regarding the relation between circumstances and outcomes for the two parties, the property of breakdown response can be easily translated from *intrapersonal* to *interpersonal* relations. The same translation has to be done for the other two "responses" as well, to move from *intrapersonal* formulation to *interpersonal* application. I desist from pursuing the formalities here.

[25]There is, in fact, some substantial common ground here with those neoclassical analyses of women's employment which have emphasized the differences in "human capital" investment in women's working background to explain their lower wages, inferior jobs, and worse unemployment risks (see, e.g., Becker 1981; Mincer & Polachek 1974; see also Apps 1981). That neoclassical literature has done a substantial service in emphasizing these differences related to sex. However, the nature of the analysis suffers from certain fundamental limitations, in particular (1) taking the existence and realization of competitive market equilibrium for granted (with or without market institutions and competitive conditions), (2) ignoring the role of social prejudices and preconceptions operating in the labor market (going *beyond* the "stochastically rational" employer behavior pointed out by Phelps 1972), (3) dealing trivially with "cooperative conflicts" implicit in household arrangements by concentrating either on an as-if market solution or on the assumed dominance of an altruistic head, and ignoring in particular the role of perception biases and bargaining powers in explaining family decisions regarding human capital investment and the gender division of labor, and (4) related to the last point, ignoring the role of "feedback transmission" in sustaining gender asymmetry.

[26]Regarding the role of "threats," the physical asymmetry would be more important in the primitive situation, though it remains important enough even today, judging by the frequency of wife battering, even in the richer countries. But physical asymmetries in the ability to threaten are also supplemented by nurtured asymmetries of social power. It is easy to underesti-

The impact of *"perceived* contribution response" may have been prim-
itively associated with acquiring food from *outside*. The fact that the division of labor within the household *permits* some members to play this role
while others take care of other activities (including preparation of food and
care of children) may not weaken the perception of special importance of
"bringing the food home." Ester Boserup (1970) has rightly taken Margaret
Mead (1949) to task for the following overgeneralization: "The home shared
by a man or men and female partners, into which men bring the food and
women prepare it, is the basic common picture the world over" (Mead
1949:190; Boserup 1970:16; see also Dasgupta 1977 and Slocum 1975, who
go further into "the male bias in anthropology"). But it is nevertheless a
common enough picture in many primitive (and modern) societies, and it
may well have contributed a further force in the direction of gender asymmetry of consumption and sustenance.

Ester Boserup (1970; Chapter 2, this volume) has noted that women
appear to fare relatively better in those societies in which women play the
major role in acquiring food from outside, for example, some African
regions with shifting cultivation. The role of outside earning does seem to be
a strong one in creating a difference within the family. It has been noted that
in India in the regions in which women have little outside earning (e.g.,
Punjab and Haryana) sex disparities are sharper—visible even in the discriminated treatment of female children—than in regions where they have a
bigger role in earning from outside (e.g., in Southern India).[27] As was noted
earlier, even the crude indicator of sex ratio (female/male) is as low as 0.87
and 0.88 in Haryana and Punjab respectively in contrast with the Southern
Indian states (0.96 in Karnataka, 0.98 in Andhra Pradesh and Tamil Nadu,
and 1.03 in Kerala).

The nature of "perceived contribution" to family opulence has to be
distinguished from the amount of *time* expended in working inside and
outside the home. Indeed, in terms of "time allocation studies," women
often seem to do astonishingly large amounts of work even when the so-
called "economic" contribution is *perceived* to be relatively modest (see,

---

mate the importance of threat in the social arrangements (including those within the household) since much of it may be implicit rather than explicit and liberally mixed with other
features of household relations, including love, affection, and concern. But threat can in some
cases be explicit enough, both as a phenomenon in itself and in the transparent role it can play
in maintaining a particularly inequitous household arrangement. (See, for example, Kurian,
1982, dealing with the role of violence and social power asymmetries in the plantation sector of
Sri Lanka, helping to sustain a particularly inequitous situation for women workers.) It becomes, of course, the subject of much discussion when the violence or threat is associated with
other features that arouse social interest, such as the peculiar relationship between pimps and
prostitutes in which threat often plays an important part in securing a regular payoff for the
former from the earnings of the latter (see, for example, Phongpaichit 1982).

[27]See K. Bardhan (1985), P. Bardhan (1974, 1984, 1987), Dyson and Moore (1983), Kynch and
Sen (1983), Miller (1981), Sen and Sengupta (1983), G. Sen (1985). The contrast between
Eastern and Southeast Asia *and* South Asia may also relate to greater female participation in
outside work in the former region (Dixon 1983; Sen 1984). On some more general but related
issues, see also Chakravarty (1986) and Tilly (1986).

e.g., Batliwala 1985; Jain & Banerjee 1985; Jain & Chand 1982; Mukho-padhyay 1982). The perception bias tends to relate to the size of the direct money earning rather than to the amount of time and effort expended (or to the role of nonmarket activities by other members of the family, who *indirectly* support such earnings).

EXTENDED ENTITLEMENTS AND PERCEIVED LEGITIMACY

In a series of earlier studies dealing specifically with starvation and famines, I have tried to analyze the problem of command over goods and services (including food) in terms of "entitlement systems" (Sen 1976, 1977, 1981). The analysis concentrated on the command that the household can exercise over goods and services, and it did not take on the issue of distribution *within* the household. Entitlement is essentially a legal concept, dealing with rules that govern who can have the use of what. Since the distribution within the household is not typically controlled by law (as property ownership and market transactions are), there are obvious difficulties in extending the entitlement analysis to the problem of *intrahousehold* distribution.

But the distributions of food, health care, education, and the like, are of obvious importance in determining each person's actual command over necessities, and this is often a source of inequality. In some empirical studies relating to India and Bangladesh (e.g., Chen, Haq, & D'Souza 1981; Chen 1982; Kynch & Sen 1983; Sen 1982b, 1984; Sen & Sengupta, 1983), patterns of sex bias in nutritional achievements, health care, and medical attention (and in morbidity and mortality rates) have come through strikingly.[28] Some systematic differences have also been observed in other parts of the developing world (e.g., den Hartog 1973; Schofield 1975; see also Vaughan 1985, 1987; Whitehead forthcoming).

There is also some evidence that deep-seated notions of "legitimacy" operate in the distribution *within* the family (Sen 1982b, 1983a), supplementing the operations of entitlement relations at the levels of households, occupation groups, and classes. There is thus a good case for extending the entitlement analysis to intrahousehold distribution as well, taking a broad view of accepted legitimacy (rather than only "laws," in the strict sense). Such an extension will closely relate to the structure of gender divisions with which the earlier parts of this essay have been concerned.

In a private ownership economy, the two basic parameters of entitlement analysis are "endowment" (roughly, what is initially owned) and "exchange entitlement mapping" (reflecting the exchange possibilities that exist

---

[28]See also Bhuiya et al. (1986), Chen (1982), Chen, Haq, and D'Souza (1981), Das Gupta (1987), Hassan and Ahmad (1984), Mitra (1980), Natarajan (n.d.), Wyon and Gordon (1971). However, for some contrary considerations, see also Basu (1988), Behrman (1987), Dyson (1987), Kakwani (1986), Wheeler (1984). Barbara Harriss (1987) has presented an extensive and illuminating survey of the available evidence on different sides. See also Sen (1989).

[29]For a fuller presentation of the entitlement approach and its application, see Sen (1981). See

through production and trade).[29] The person (or the household) can establish command over any bundle of commodities that can be obtained by using the endowment and the exchange entitlement mapping, reflecting both *possibilities* and the *terms* of trade and production. The set of all commodity bundles over any one of which the person (or the household) can establish command is his or her (or its) "entitlement set." If the entitlement set does not include any bundle with enough food, then the person (or the household) must starve. With this very general structure much of the analysis was devoted to studying patterns of endowment and exchange entitlement mappings, paying particular attention to modes of production, class structure, roles of occupation groups, and market forces.

The analysis was also used to study a number of modern famines, in some of which (e.g., the Bengal famine of 1943, the Ethiopian famines of 1973, the Bangladesh famine of 1974) the total availability of food per head turned out to have been no less (sometimes more) than in previous years. The famines were shown to be the results of entitlement failures related to endowment decline (e.g., alienation of land or loss of grazing rights) or to exchange entitlement decline (e.g., loss of employment, failure of money wages to keep up with food prices, failure of prices of animal products or craft products or services to keep up with the prices of basic food), or to both. The famines decimated specific occupation groups while leaving other occupation groups and classes unaffected, sometimes enriched (see Sen 1976, 1977, 1981; see also Alamgir 1980; Ghosh 1979; Griffin 1978; Khan 1985; Oughton 1982; Ravallion 1985, 1987; Snowdon 1985; Vaughan 1985).

For the most of humanity, virtually the only significant endowment is labor power. Much of the analysis thus turned on the conditions governing the exchange of labor power (e.g., employment, wages and prices, and social security, if any). It was also found that the right to the *use* of land, even without ownership — by secured sharecropping rights, for instance — makes a big difference in vulnerability to famine. In fact, in the South Asian context, although landless rural laborers constitute the occupation group most vulnerable to famine, sharecroppers (who are, in normal circumstances, not much richer than laborers) turn out to be often much less vulnerable to famines than are laborers (Sen 1981). The difference relates largely to the fact that the sharecropper gets a share of the food crop directly (without having to depend on the market), whereas the rural laborer faces the dual threat of unemployment *and* possible inadequacy of wages to buy enough food at the relative prices that would happen to emerge. The fact that daily wage laborers often form a much higher proportion of female agricultural workers than of males (see Agarwal 1986; Dixon 1983; G. Sen 1985, among others) is thus of some importance.

Turning now to the intrahousehold distribution of food in famine situations, the empirical evidence seems to suggest conflicting stories. The fam-

also Alamgir (1980), Appadurai (1984), Arrow (1982), Desai (1984), Devereux and Hay (1986), Kamsler (1986), Khan (1985), Oughton (1982), Ravallion (1985, 1987), Snowdon (1985), Solow (1984), Tilly (1985, 1986), Vaughan (1985, 1987), Wilson (1987).

ine experts of the British Raj in India were on the whole persuaded that men died in much larger numbers than women in Indian famines, but the evidence might possibly have been based on biases in data collection.[30] There has been no serious famine in India since independence, but there have been many situations of hardship in acquiring food, not altogether relieved (though typically much reduced) by government intervention. There is considerable evidence of bias against the female, especially the female child vis-à-vis the male child, in such situations of hardship (Sen 1984). And in normal mortality, too, there is clear evidence of female disadvantage in age groups below 35. This is especially striking for children.[31]

One remarkable feature of Indian demography is a significant decline in the sex ratio (female/male) in the Indian population, from 0.972 in 1901 (quite low even then) to 0.935 in 1981. This feature relates to many other ways in which the continued — and in some ways increasing — relative deprivation of Indian women comes through (Kynch & Sen 1983). The problem is present in many other countries as well, and as was mentioned earlier, the female/male ratio is very substantially lower than unity in Asia as a whole.

In extending the entitlement analysis to include intrahousehold distribution, attention must be paid to the fact that the relationships *within* the household in the distribution of food and other goods cannot sensibly be seen in the same way as the relationships of persons and households to others *outside* the household, such as an employer, a trader, a landowner, a retailer, a speculator. That is why a straightforward translation of the entitlement analysis presented earlier would be a mistake, tempting though it might be. To indulge in technicalities for a moment, in this context it is best to see entitlements not as a set of *vectors* (bundles of commodities going to the household as a whole) but as a set of *matrices* (bundles of commodities for each members of the household), with each person's share being given by a column of the matrix. Similarly, endowments are best seen as *matrices* (bundles of ownership for each member), even though the children may

[30]See *Census of India 1911*, Vol. 1, Part 1, Appendix to Chapter 6, surveying the nineteenth-century famine inquiry reports, well reflected by Sir Charles Elliot's summary: "All the authorities seem agreed that women succumb to famine less easily then men." An excess of male deaths was reported also in the Bengal famine of 1943 by Das (1949), based on a survey asking people receiving cooked food relief which of their relations had died. However, more complete data do not entirely support Das's survey finding and indicate that the sex ratio of *famine mortality* in 1943 was similar to the sex ratio of *normal mortality* in Bengal (see Sen, 1981:211–13). Among the relief receivers (the population that was questioned), there seems to have been a higher proportion of women (famine relief policy was more suspicious of supporting able-bodied men), and this bias in favor of *women* in the questioned population would have acted as a bias in favor of *men* being reported as dead in the survey. A woman has typically more male relatives in the nuclear family (including her husband) than female relatives, and thus she has a higher probability of having a *dead* male relative. Similar biases in sampling could have affected the nineteenth-century belief in greater famine deaths among men. But the evidence requires a more thorough examination than it has received so far. See also Drèze and Sen (1989) and Greenough (1982).

[31]See K. Bardhan (1985), P. Bardhan (1974, 1984, 1987), Dyson (1982, 1987), Kynch and Sen (1983), Miller (1981), Mitra (1980), Natarajan (n.d.), Padmanabha (1982), Sopher (1980). On related observations regarding Bangladesh, see Chen (1982), Chen, Haq, and D'Souza (1981), Mahmud and Mahmud (1985).

typically enter with zeroes everywhere, and, more important, most of the adults too would have nothing other than their labor power to adorn the household endowment matrix. Women in particular tend frequently to fall in that category (outside a small class). The exchange entitlement mapping will then specify for each endowment matrix the set of possible commodity matrices. Starvation will occur if — given the endowment matrix — none of the possible commodity matrices includes adequate food for each person. It can also occur even if there is a feasible matrix with adequate food for all, if that feasible matrix does not emerge in the choice process.

This is not the occasion to launch into the technical analysis that will clearly be needed for some purposes to go into detail in the way ownership patterns, production possibilities, and market arrangements (including that for labor power) interact to *constrain* the exchange entitlement mappings. Some of that analysis can draw heavily on the entitlement relations explored earlier at the interhousehold level (Sen 1981), but the supplementation needed must capture the essentials of the sexual division, including intrahousehold distributions. If the intrahousehold distribution patterns are taken as completely flexible, then the possible matrices would reflect that freedom through listing all possible intrahousehold distributions of the same household bundle. At the other extreme, if the head of the household has very fixed ideas of how the bundle must be distributed and has the power to carry out his (patriarchal) decisions, then each household commodity bundle would translate into exactly one household matrix of who would have which good.[32] The actual situation would vary between these limits.

The general issues underlying the formulation of the household arrangement problem as a "bargaining problem" can now be used to characterize some features of the extended exchange entitlement mapping. For example, "breakdown response" will be reflected in the individual consumption of the person (his or her "column") being more favorable in the possible entitlement matrices, given other things, as the person's breakdown position improves. Similarly, the column of each person would be influenced by perceived interests and perceived contributions in the ways specified by the respective "responses."[33]

---

[32]The approach of "equivalence scales" based on the assumption of maximization of a unique utility function for the family as a whole, which is technically perhaps the most impressive part of the literature in intrafamily allocation (see Deaton & Muellbauer 1980), is implicitly based on some assumption of this kind, e.g., the "head" of the family imposing a benevolent preference ordering in making decisions about everyone's consumption in the family. When the "head" has a strictly convex preference map, each household entitlement vector would be translated into a unique household entitlement matrix. There are, however, other ways of interpreting the outcome of intrafamily divisions (see Deaton 1987; Muellbauer 1987).

[33]It is not difficult to extend the mathematical formulation of the vector–vector "exchange entitlement mapping" (Sen 1981:Appendix A) into this expanded format of matrix–matrix "*extended* exchange entitlement mapping," and to specify the "responses" in question as a set of "monotonicity conditions." To be exact, the "extended" exchange entitlement mapping relates a matrix of family endowment to a *set* of matrices of family entitlements, just as the standard exchange entitlement mapping relates a vector of family endowment to a *set* of vectors of family entitlements. The monotonicity conditions would be defined in that format.

PRODUCTION, EARNINGS, AND PERCEIVED CONTRIBUTIONS

A woman's opportunity to get "gainful" work outside is one of the crucial variables affecting the extended exchange entitlement mapping. This can happen in two distinct ways, corresponding respectively to the "cooperative" and "conflicting" features discussed earlier in "cooperative conflict" formulation of sexual divisions. First, such employment would enhance the *overall* command of the household, that is, the family entitlement. Second, for a given family entitlement, the woman's *relative* share may also respond positively to her outside earnings. This latter influence corresponds, of course, to the element of pure conflict in "cooperative conflicts," and the directional link described here would reflect some combination of the three responses discussed earlier. Outside earnings can give the woman in question (1) a better breakdown position, (2) possibly a clearer perception of her individuality and well-being, and (3) a higher "perceived contribution" to the family's economic position.

The empirical basis of the directional link has been supported in a number of studies dealing with women's work, following the pioneering contribution of Ester Boserup (1970). To quote just one example, in her definitive study of the women workers in the *beedi* (crude cigarette) industry in Allahabad, India, Zarina Bhatty (1980) found the following:

> A greater economic role for women definitely improves their status within the family. A majority of them have more money to spend, and even more importantly, have a greater say in the decisions to spend money. Most women claim to be better treated as a result of their contribution to household income. . . . A substantial proportion of women feel that they should have a recognized economic role and an independent source of income. . . . Their attitudes evidence a clear perception of the significance of their work to family welfare and their own status within the family. (p. 41)[34]

The impact of outside earnings of women depends also on the *form* of that earning. In her well-known study of the lacemakers of Narsapur in India, Maria Mies (1982b) notes that these women workers do not get much benefit from their work, because despite the fact that the products are sold in the world market, the women "are recruited as *housewives* to produce lace as a so-called spare-time activity, in their own homes" (p. 172). "As she herself is not able to see her work as a value-producing work, she subscribes to the devaluation of this work as non-work, as purely supplementary to her husband's work, and she is not able to bargain for a just wage. This mystification is the basis of her over-exploitation as housewife and as worker" (pp.

---

[34]See also Beneria (1982a), Croll (1979), Deere and Leon de Leal (1982), ILO (1982a), Jain and Banerjee (1985), Loutfi (1980), Mahmud and Mahmud (1985), Mies (1982b), Phongpaichit (1982), Standing and Sheehan (1978). Lloyd and Niemi (1979) deal with a related problem in the context of rich and economically advanced countries.

173–74). The lower bargaining power of the women workers *vis-à-vis the employers* depresses the exchange entitlement of the household *as a whole*. Further, the weakness of the three "responses" for women workers *vis-à-vis the rest of the family* further affects the *extended* exchange entitlement by depressing their status and the share of benefits that go to them *within* the household.

The extension of entitlement analysis to divisions within the family brings in notions of legitimacy that go well beyond the system of state-enforced laws on which property relations, market transactions, wage employment, and the like, operate and on which the standard entitlement analysis depends. But these notions of legitimacy have a firm social basis and may be hard to displace. What would have looked, in the format of the "bargaining problem," like a might-is-right bargaining outcome (e.g., giving a worse deal to the person with a weaker breakdown position) may actually take the form of appearing to be the "natural" and "legitimate" outcome in the perception of all the parties involved. The idea of entitlement in the *extended* form can be influenced by a shared sense of legitimacy (however inequitous it might be) and adapted perceptions that relate to it.

The care that female children receive vis-à-vis male children (in terms of nutrition, medical attention, etc.) may also be positively influenced by the size of outside employment and earnings of women vis-à-vis men. The neglect of female children and the preference for having male children in India, especially in the North and especially of second and later daughters (Das Gupta 1987; Miller 1981), may well be related to lower earning powers of women. This can be seen in terms of lower "returns" in rearing girls vis-à-vis boys (on this, see Behrman 1986; Rosenzweig & Schultz 1982), but the low level of outside work and earning may also generally harm women's social status and perceived entitlements (see Sen 1984, 1989).

The influence of outside earnings and the so-called productive activities of women for their extended entitlements can also be studied in terms of interregional contrasts. In her pioneering study of women's issues in economic development, Ester Boserup drew attention to the contrast between Africa and Asia in terms of women's outside employment and its effects (1970:24–25). The greater female participation of rural women in Africa than in Asia is brought out also by some intercountry statistics presented by Ruth Dixon (1983). In fact, as Boserup noted, there are considerable contrasts *within* Africa itself in terms of female participation.

The big regional contrast *within* Africa relates in fact to the participation rates in *Northern* Africa vis-à-vis those in the rest of the continent. An aggregative picture of interregional contrasts within Africa and Asia is presented in Table 8.1 with comparative data for five major regions: North Africa, Non-North Africa, West Asia, South Asia, and East and Southeast Asia. "Activity rate ratios" (females to males) for each of these regions have been calculated by aggregating data for all countries covered by the ILO (1986) in the respective regions. The female/male life expectancy ratios for the same regions are also given in the same table, calculated from the coun-

Table 8.1

	Activity rate ratios 1980 (female/male)		Life expectancy ratios 1980 (female/male)	
Region	Value	Rank	Value	Rank
Non-North Africa	0.645	1	1.071	1
East and Southeast Asia	0.610	2	1.066	2
West Asia	0.373	3	1.052	3
South Asia	0.336	4	0.989	5
North Africa	0.158	5	1.050	4

Source: Sen (1986) calculated from country data given in ILO (1986) and United Nations' tapes. I am grateful to Jocelyn Kynch for her research assistance in preparing this aggregative table. The activity rate ratios represent the proportions of total population of each sex engaged in so-called "economic" (or "gainful") activities.

try statistics presented in the United Nations' tapes on "Estimates and Projections of Population".[35] As was discussed earlier, the regional contrasts within India, such as that between South and North India, also seem to suggest a similar influence of female "activity" rate ratios on the deal that rural women receive vis-à-vis men (see particularly P. Bardhan 1974, 1984, 1987; Miller 1981, 1982). The possible *routes* of influence (though breakdown response, perceived interest response, and perceived contribution response) have already been discussed in the analysis presented earlier.

It is interesting that the ranking of life expectancy ratios (female/male) is very similar to that of activity rate ratios (female/male). Although no definitive conclusion can be drawn from these data alone, insofar as anything does emerge from them, it would seem to support and corroborate the conclusions drawn from microstudies and general economic reasoning, which also point in the direction of positively relating female "productive" activity to a better deal (and enhanced extended entitlement for women). The contrasts between South Asia and Non-North Africa, and those between South Asia and East and Southeast Asia, and between North and Non-North Africa, are particularly striking in view of the variety of evidence on greater female involvement in outside work in North Africa and East and Southeast Asia vis-à-vis North Africa and South Asia.

[35]Note that China has not been included in this comparative picture. The role of rural Chinese women in work outside the household expanded quite rapidly after the revolution (along with a rise in the female/male life expectancy ratio), but there is some evidence of a shrinkage of that role since the reforms of 1979, with a return to family-based cultivation (the "responsibility system"). In recent years, the female life expectancy has fallen vis-à-vis the male (Banister 1987; see also Aslanbeigui & Summerfield 1989; Drèze & Sen 1989: Chapter 11; Sen 1989; Wolf 1985). However, China's recent experiences are made more complicated by the presence of special features, in particular the "one-child family" policy and the general financial crisis of communal health services in the rural areas (see Drèze & Sen 1989).

WELL-BEING, AGENCY, AND COOPERATIVE CONFLICTS

In this chapter I have tried to present some elementary relations that might be of relevance in discussing women's issues in economic development. Conflicts of interest between men and women are unlike other conflicts, such as class conflicts. A worker and a capitalist do not typically live together under the same roof—sharing concerns and experiences and acting jointly. This aspect of "togetherness" gives the gender conflict some very special characteristics.

One of these characteristics is that many aspects of the conflict of interest between men and women have to be viewed against the background of pervasive cooperative behavior. Not only do the different parties have much to gain from cooperation; their individual activities have to take the form of being overtly cooperative, even when substantial conflicts exist. This is seen most clearly in the parts of the gender divisions that relate to household arrangements, in particular who does what type of work in the household and enjoys what benefits. Although serious conflicts of interests may be involved in the choice of "social technology," the nature of the family organization requires that these conflicts be molded in a general format of cooperation, with conflicts treated as aberrations or deviant behavior.

The cooperative format makes it particularly important to pay attention to perception problems about respective interests, contributions, and claims. In analyzing cooperative conflicts, we had difficulty in following the leads provided by seeing household economics in terms of harmonious "optimal" divisions (Samuelson 1956), or in terms of "as-if" competitive markets (Becker 1973–74), or in terms of "altruism and voluntary contributions" in line with "a group preference function," which is "identical to that of the altruistic head" (Becker 1981). Even though formulations of household economics in terms of "bargaining problems" (Manser & Brown 1980; McElroy & Horney 1981) succeed in catching one aspect of cooperative conflicts well, they miss many other aspects because of the limited informational base of that game structure, neglecting issues of perception in assessing interests and well-being and in evaluating contributions and claims.

The alternative line of analysis pursued in this chapter takes the form of specifying important parts of the relevant informational base rather than that of pinpointing one exact "solution" of the divisional problem. The analysis presented has focused on a few "responses" of outcomes to the identified informational base, dealing specifically with the influences of (1) the respective well-being levels in the case of breakdown of cooperation (a feature taken over from the Nash, 1950, formulation of "bargaining problem"), (2) the perception (including illusions) about personal interests in a family setting, and (3) the perception of "contributions" made respectively by different members and the "claims" arising from these contributions. These qualitative, rather than quantitative, relations help to establish some directional structure in relating social and personal parameters to divisional outcomes and to notions of "extended entitlements" including *intrahouse-*

hold divisions. The correspondence of these directional structures to empirical observations of variations in gender divisions was discussed in terms of microstudies as well as aggregative regional contrasts.

One of the parameters that seemed particularly important to pursue is the involvement of women in so-called "productive" activities and in earning from outside. These activities are of obvious importance for female-headed households without adult men (Buvinic & Youssef 1978; Visaria & Visaria 1985), but they are of importance also when there are both adult men and women in the family. In addition to contributing to the *overall* affluence of the family, these activities also influence the *relative* shares by affecting the "breakdown positions" of women and also the perceptions of women's "contributions" and "claims." The relative "returns" from rearing boys vis-à-vis girls, which have been found to be of some importance in the neglect of female children in some developing countries (see particularly Behrman 1986; Rosenzweig & Schultz 1982), are also correspondingly influenced by variations in female "activity rates" and "outside earnings." The explanation of the observed relations may involve not merely hardheaded individual calculations of relative returns from rearing boys vis-à-vis girls, but also the social influence of the general prevalence of female activity and earnings on the common perception of "contributions" made by women and of women's entitlements to a better share of the household's joint benefits.

Even the perception of individual interests of women, which—it has been observed—tends to be merged with the notion of family well-being in some traditional cultures, may be sharpened by greater involvement of women with the outside world, and this may have important implications for household divisions. An examination of interregional variations of relative activity rates (female/male) and life expectancy ratios (female/male) provided some corroboration of what was expected on general theoretical grounds in terms of the directional responses of cooperative conflicts, but the empirical picture is far too complex to be summarized in the form of a simple model of quantified cause-and-effect relationships.

One of the central issues that need more examination is the question of women's "agency" as opposed to their "well-being." Neither the well-being nor the agency of women coincides with the utilitarian (or welfarist) mental metrics of happiness or desire fulfillment (though there are obvious connections). Well-being may be best analyzed in terms of a person's "functionings" and the "capability" to achieve these functionings (i.e., what the person can do or can be), involving evaluation of the different capabilities in terms of the person's ability to live well and to achieve well-being. But a person is not necessarily concerned only with his or her own well-being and there are other objectives a person may pursue (or value pursuing if he or she had the opportunity to think freely and act freely). Our actual agency role is often overshadowed by social rules and by conventional perceptions of legitimacy. In the case of gender divisions, these conventions often act as barriers to seeking a more equitable deal, and sometimes militate even against recognizing the spectacular lack of equity in the ruling arrangements.

In the analysis presented in this essay, the importance of perception and agency emerges as being central to achieving a better basis for female well-being in many parts of the world. In the recent development literature there is a growing awareness of inequities in gender divisions and of the neglect of women's well-being. But there is also a danger in seeing a woman, in this context, as a "patient" rather than as an "agent." The political agency of women may be particularly important in encountering the pervasive perception biases that contribute to the neglect of women's needs and claims (see Jayawardena 1986). In addition, even the economic agency of women has an important role in enhancing visibility of women's contributions to social living — a view that is obscured by the conventional form of "social technology." Even the particular influence of women's activity rates and outside earnings, which was discussed in terms of interregional correspondences in Africa and Asia, is an example of the instrumental role of agency in influencing gender division, and through that the well-being — and survival — of women.

The importance of the links between perceptions, well-being, and agency is among the central themes of this essay. The analysis of cooperative conflicts in gender divisions calls for a better understanding of these links. The narrow informational bases of traditional household economics can do with some substantial broadening. The study of women's issues in development can also benefit from informational diversification. The broad coverage of the needed informational base is not really surprising. After all, the subject matter includes some of the central issues of contemporary human existence.

9

The Impact of the Value of Women's Time on Food and Nutrition

BENJAMIN SENAUER

Boserup's (1970) classic study examined the economic role of women in different cultures and stages of development. This chapter focuses on the implications of the economic status of women, particularly as reflected in their value of time, for behavior within the household. Research done within the framework of rigorously defined economic models of the household provides important insights into the crucial role of women in the household economy. The value of time of household members plays a key role in the empirical analyses carried out in the context of these household economic models. Three recent studies were conducted by my colleagues and me at the International Food Policy Research Institute. Our work found some very interesting empirical results, especially concerning the impact of the value of women's time on food consumption patterns, intrahousehold food allocations, and children's nutritional status.

The next section in this chapter provides a brief overview of the economic approaches to modeling the household. The following sections discuss the three empirical studies. Each is discussed in terms of related work on the topic and the broader implications of the research results. The first study examines the impact of the value of women's time on urban food consumption patterns in Sri Lanka (Senauer, Sahn, & Alderman 1986). This analysis focuses on the household consumption of rice and commercially baked bread. The former requires more time-intensive preparation in the household than the latter. The second study analyzes the intrahousehold allocation of food in the rural Philippines (Senauer, Garcia, & Jacinto 1988). This analysis utilizes individual food consumption data and examines the factors influencing the distribution of calories among household members in relation to their caloric requirements. The third study looks at the factors influencing the nutritional status of preschool children, also in the rural Philippines (Senauer & Garcia 1988). This analysis focuses on the children's height for age and weight for height as measures of their nutritional status.

In each of these studies, the wife's and/or mother's value of time is found to have a major impact. The opportunity cost of time is a significant factor influencing the role of women and behavior within the household. The value of time is measured by an individual's estimated wage rate, which is the standard approach used by economists. The final section of this chapter draws together some overall conclusions from these studies and discusses the policy implications of the empirical results. The central policy-related conclusion is that behavior within the household can be modified by improving women's economic opportunities outside the household.

ECONOMIC MODELS OF THE HOUSEHOLD

Considerable controversy currently exists between two schools of thought concerning the conceptual modeling of the household by economists. One school assumes the existence of a single household utility function, which reflects the household's tastes and preferences (Pitt & Rosenzweig 1985, 1986; Strauss 1986). Becker (1981) analyzes the assumptions necessary for this approach, which would allow a multiperson household to be treated as a single utility maximizer. An obvious situation occurs if all household members have the exact same preferences; another occurs if one individual imposes his or her preferences on the other household members. Becker coined the term "altruistic dictator" in referring to the situation where the household head, typically the patriarch, is the ultimate authority in the household. He is supposedly a benign master, who considers the welfare of other family members in his decisions.

The other school of thought challenges this view of the household. It assumes preferences vary among family members and sees a bargaining process as reconciling those differences (Folbre 1984b; Jones 1983; Manser & Brown 1980; McElroy & Horney 1981). The bargaining model approach draws on the work on cooperative game theory by Nash (1953). An individual's bargaining power in reconciling differences in preferences with other household members is determined by how well that person would do if a bargained solution was not achieved. If household cooperation breaks down completely, income is no longer pooled and a common food supply is no longer shared. In terms of the Nash bargaining model, how well an individual would do in the absence of a bargained solution would be largely determined by the person's wage rate or potential wage rate if he or she entered the labor force. Hence the economic status of women outside the home affects their influence on household decisions.

Although many do not agree with all its premises, the theoretical model proposed by Gary Becker (1965) did much to awaken the interest of economists in the analysis of the household. In his model, Becker specifically visualized a single set of household preferences. His conceptual framework, which has been extended and refined by other economists, has been referred to as the "New Household Economics" (Evenson 1976; Gronau 1974, 1977; Michael & Becker 1973; Nerlove 1974; Pollack & Wachter 1975). The major contributions of Becker's model are twofold. First, time is limited and hence has a value, as does any scarce factor. Second, households engage in production, not just consumption activity. In the Becker model the actual consumables that satisfy human wants and needs are produced in the household in a production process, which combines goods purchased in the marketplace with household members' time and household capital. The final consumables can conceivably include anything from meals ready for consumption to good health or the quantity and quality of children. The majority of household production activities are typically carried out by women (Boserup 1986:163).

In addition to the traditional monetary budget constraint imposed by economists, which states that a household's expenditures cannot exceed its income, Becker imposed a time constraint. The time constraint states that allocations of household members' time to various activities cannot exceed their total available time. The most basic allocations of time typically considered are work in the labor force, household production activity, and leisure. Money income is generated by employment in the labor force or from nonlabor income, such as rent. The budget constraint and time constraint can be combined into a single "full-income" constraint. The household's full income equals the sum of any nonlabor income and the total time allotment of each household member valued at his or her opportunity cost of time. This full income is allocated to leisure, household production activities, and through the budget constraint, to expenditures on goods and services in the marketplace.

Economists utilize demand functions to empirically analyze how much of a particular good a household will consume. With the Becker model, a household's demand for a particular good is dependent on the market price of itself and other goods, the value of time of household members, and the household's full income (Deaton & Muellbauer 1980:245–50; Pollack & Wachter 1975:267; Senauer et al. 1986:921).

In the current economic modeling of the household, regardless of the approach, the value of individuals' time plays a key role. There are conceptual, technical, and pragmatic questions concerning the calculation of a value of time, particularly for women (Smith 1980). A major conceptual issue relates to whether time spent by an individual in different activities should be valued at the same rate. Because of constraints, productivity might vary by activity and some work may be more enjoyable, or at least less onerous than another. Nevertheless, an individual's wage rate is the best empirically derivable measurement of that person's value of time. If not employed in the formal labor force, the individual's estimated or potential wage, if employed, is utilized.

Derivation of estimated wage rates is a technically complex undertaking, especially for women, since only a small proportion earn a wage or salary in most developing countries (Heckman 1974, 1979; Senauer et al. 1986; Smith 1980). Boserup (1986:106–18) discusses both why so few women are employed in the formal labor force in developing countries and why whose employed are typically restricted to low-wage jobs. A basic practical problem also exists. The calculation of wage rates as a measure of the value of time requires the necessary data on employment and earnings by individual, which are rarely available.

The distribution of food and other resources among household members can be modeled either in the context of a bargaining model or a single household utility function model, in which an individual's labor output is affected by his or her food consumption. In either model, the value of an individual's time, as measured by his or her estimated wage rate, is a crucial factor. In the bargaining model, individuals with a higher value of time might be favored in the intrahousehold distribution of food because of their increased bargaining power. In the latter model, reallocating food to household members with a higher value of time could increase their ability to work and hence augment the total goods and services available to the household. Within the approach of either school it can be assumed that household members care about one another's welfare and are not simply motivated by maximizing their own personal consumption.

Altruism undoubtedly influences the distribution of household resources to children, since parents typically care deeply about the welfare of their children. Additionally, though, expectations of future intergenerational transfers may affect the allocation of resources to and among their children. In developing countries, parents frequently look to their children, especially their sons, for old-age security (Folbre 1984b:308). Current investment in a child's human capital, which would include food consumption, will influence that child's future economic earning potential. Finally, children can start making a significant economic contribution to their families at remarkably early ages in poor households in developing countries, which could affect within-household allocations (Evenson, Popkin, & Quizon 1980:335–43; Pernia 1979:30).

THE VALUE OF WOMEN'S TIME AND FOOD CONSUMPTION PATTERNS

One of the major changes in the food consumption patterns in many developing countries is a shift away from the traditional grains and root crops and the increased consumption of wheat products, particularly in the form of commercially supplied bread. Wheat consumption increased at an average annual rate of 2.3 percent per capita between 1961–65 and 1975–77 in developing countries, whereas rice consumption increased by only 0.4 percent annually and coarse grain consumption, other than maize, declined by

1.3 percent per year (CIMMYT 1983). Many factors contributed to this shift, including rising incomes, relative price changes, urbanization, food aid, and the Westernization of tastes.

However, one potential factor that has been overlooked are increases in the value of women's time. As Boserup (1986:164) noted, the preparation of many of the traditional foods is very time-consuming for women, who are the primary food preparers for their households. Many wheat products, particularly commercially baked bread, offer significant time savings in comparison to many traditional foods.

The Becker model of the household provides a conceptual framework within which to analyze the potential impact of the value of women's time on food consumption patterns. Previous studies have utilized the Becker model and the rising value of women's time to explain the increasing consumption of food away from home in the United States (Fletcher 1981; Kinsey 1983; Prochaska & Schrimper 1973). The possible effect of the opportunity cost of women's time on food consumption in developing countries had not previously been empirically analyzed, though. Our research tested the specific hypothesis that the bread consumption of urban Sri Lankan households increases and rice consumption decreases as the estimated wage rate of the primary woman in the household increases, ceteris paribus (Senauer et al. 1986). The primary woman was defined as the female household head, either with or without a spouse present.

The data used in the empirical analysis were from the 1980–81 Sri Lankan Labor Force and Socioeconomic Survey, conducted by the Sri Lankan Department of Census and Statistics. This nationally representative survey collected data on labor force participation and earnings for individuals, as well as on household food consumption. Only the subsample representing urban households was utilized. Rice is the major staple in Sri Lanka. However, bread consumption has become increasingly important in the urban areas. Average annual per capita consumption was 203 pounds of rice and 77 pounds of bread in 1980–81 in urban areas.

Wages were estimated for women 15–65 years of age in the urban sector. Below age 15 and above age 65, labor force participation declines sharply. The Sri Lankan survey contained the necessary data on earnings and employment to calculate hourly wage rates for those women who were employed in the labor force. However, only 15 percent of the women were employed in formal labor force jobs. For this reason, a woman's value of time was predicted from a wage determination equation that was estimated for those who were formally employed. The key explanatory variables in the wage regression for employed women were the woman's age, education, and ethnic group. The results from that regression were then used to estimate a value of time for each primary woman based on her age, education, and ethnic group. The wage rate of women increased with their age and years of schooling. Furthermore, the relationship between the wage rate and age was nonlinear. In terms of ethnic groups, European women received a higher wage than Sinhalese or Tamil women.

Because a woman's employment is partially self-determined, the subsample of women in the labor force does not represent a random subsample. The Heckman procedure was used to correct for any possible sample selection bias introduced by the nonrandom nature of the subsample of employed women (Heckman 1974, 1979; Senauer et al. 1986:923–24; Smith 1980). Heckman's approach first requires the estimation of an equation to explain the probability of whether a woman will be employed in the formal labor force.

The factors used to explain a woman's employment status were her age, education, ethnic group, number of children younger than age six, the relation of the woman in the household, the household's nonlabor income, and the wage rate of her husband if one was present. Middle-aged women and more educated women were more likely to be formally employed. Tamils and women with more young children were less likely. The wife or mother of a male household head was less likely to be employed, whereas daughters were more likely. The higher the husband's wage, the greater the probability the woman was in the formal labor force.

The estimated wage rate of the female household head was then introduced as a variable in the household demand equations, which sought to explain the amount of rice and bread a household consumed. In addition to the woman's value of time, the other explanatory factors were the household's income, the number of persons in the household and their age and gender, the ethnic group, and the prices of rice, bread, and flour. The demand equations were estimated separately with both "full income," in accordance with the Becker model, and "observed money income."

In terms of the central hypothesis, the value of time of the primary woman had the expected positive impact on bread consumption and negative effect on rice consumption. With the other explanatory factors held constant, households in which the female household head had a higher estimated wage rate consumed more bread and less rice. On average, a 10 percent rise in the woman's estimated wage led to a 1.3 percent increase in the household's bread consumption and a 0.7 percent decrease in rice consumption (Senauer et al. 1986:926).

More generally, as the employment opportunities for women expand and their education levels rise, the value of women's time is likely to play an increasingly important role in the determination of worldwide food consumption patterns. It will be economically rational for households to shift away from traditional foods which require time-intensive preparation to less time-intensive foods. In some situations this shift could have unfortunate nutritional consequences. The more processed, time-saving foods are likely to be more expensive than the traditional foods. Unless food expenditures increase sufficiently, the nutritional quality of the diet may suffer. In the specific Sri Lankan case analyzed here, the relative nutrient content and price of bread and rice, at least in 1980–81, were such that the observed shift would not be a major nutritional concern.

THE INTRAHOUSEHOLD ALLOCATION OF FOOD

Increasing attention is being given to the intrahousehold allocation of food in developing countries (Haaga & Mason 1987; Lipton 1983; Piwoz & Viteri 1984; Rogers 1983; USDA 1983). Many previous studies found considerable inequality in the distribution of food among household members in relation to their nutritional needs. When the food available to a household is inadequate to meet nutritional needs, an inappropriate intrahousehold allocation can worsen the situation for certain household members. Even when household food availability is adequate, at least to fulfill caloric requirements, some household members may still be malnourished because of the pattern of food distribution within the household. At least in some cultures, the intrahousehold allocation of food exacerbates the incidence of malnutrition among women and children (Haaga & Mason 1987; Piwoz & Viteri 1984; USDA 1983).

Much of the previous research on this topic has been conducted by nutritionists and anthropologists and has focused on the effect of age and gender on intrahousehold allocation (Piwoz & Viteri 1984; USDA 1983). In South Asia, the pattern of intrahousehold food distribution typically discriminates against females, both women and girls (Carloni 1981; USDA 1983:55–61). An age-related distribution pattern found in other studies favors the household adults (Abdullah & Wheeler 1985; Chaudury 1983; Hassan & Ahmad 1984; USDA 1983:29–41). Both an age and gender bias have been found in some cases, with the male household head the most favored individual and young female children receiving the lowest proportion of their nutritional needs (Evenson et al. 1980:307).

In the past, food consumption studies by economists "have stopped at the door of the household" and not examined the intrahousehold allocation of food (Piwoz & Viteri 1984:1). Much remains to be learned about the factors that influence the pattern of food distribution within the household. Haaga and Mason (1987) conclude their excellent review of previous work in this area with a call for further research on the topic. Our study examined the determinants of the relative allocation of food among household members using individual food consumption data from three rural provinces in the Philippines (Senauer et al. 1988). The household, in our study, was defined as a group of individuals who reside together, pool all or most of their incomes, and basically share the same food supply. In the rural Philippines, households are typically nuclear families composed of a husband and wife and their children.

The data used in our analysis were from household surveys conducted in three rural provinces of the Philippines in 1983–84 by the National Nutrition Council and the Ministry of Agriculture of the Philippines, with the assistance of the International Food Policy Research Institute. The three provinces surveyed were Abra, an upland subsistence corn and tobacco area on Luzon; Antique, a coastal rice farming and fishing area in the middle of the archipelago; and South Cotabato, a river basin corn-producing region on Mindanao. The data were collected in four separate survey rounds and the same households (approximately 800) were surveyed in each round. The data are not strictly cross-sectional but are longitudinal.

For a subsample of households, individual 24-hour food consumption data were collected for all household members utilizing a food-weighing method. Information on food eaten outside the household was collected by recall. Philippine food composition tables were used to calculate the calorie and protein content of each individual's diet. Calorie and protein adequacy ratios were then obtained by dividing the individual's calorie or protein intake by his or her recommended daily allowance (RDA) for that nutrient and multiplying by 100 to put them in percentage terms. The RDAs specified for Filipinos were used (Claudio, DeGuzman, Oliveros & Dimaama 1982:283). There is some controversy concerning the use of RDAs as a measure of individuals' nutrient needs (Lipson 1983). The RDAs apply to age and gender categories; they do not reflect possible differences in metabolic rates or physical activity levels among individuals in an age–gender group. However, the RDAs are typically the only practical measure of nutrient needs available.

The average calorie adequacy ratio for the individuals in our study was only 70 percent. In comparison, the national average for the Philippines was 89 percent, which indicates the seriousness of malnutrition in the survey areas. The adults (age 18–65) in our sample received 78 percent of their RDAs for calories. The husbands received 81 percent and wives 78 percent. However, children (age 1–17) received only 64 percent of their calorie RDAs. The overall protein adequacy ratio was 91 percent. The average protein adequacy ratio for adults was 89 percent, for husbands 101 percent, for wives 82 percent, and for children 92 percent. The allocation of food appears to favor adults and especially the male household heads (husbands). The calorie adequacy ratio was substantially higher for adults than children and the protein adequacy ratio was significantly higher for husbands than for wives or children. The protein adequacy ratio was higher than the calorie adequacy ratio for each group, which indicates that overall, energy intake is a more serious constraint in the diet than protein is. For this reason, our empirical analysis focused on calories.

The quantitative measurement of intrahousehold food distribution used in our analysis was obtained by dividing an individual's calorie adequacy ratio by the calorie adequacy ratio for the entire household. This variable is the same as that suggested by Haaga and Mason (1987) and reflects the allocation of the available household calories in relation to each individual's calorie recommendations. A value greater than 1 indicates that the individual's calorie adequacy ratio is above the average for the entire household, and vice versa. In other words, individuals who are discriminated against in the distribution would have a value below 1 and those who are favored a value above 1. A value of 1 for every member of a household would suggest an equitable allocation of the available food in relation to the individuals' RDAs. In our Philippine study, the mean value of this variable for husbands was 1.14, for wives 1.10, and for children 0.90 (Senauer et al. 1988:1974).

The empirical question estimated in our analysis could be generated from either a bargaining model or household utility function model in which an individual's labor output depended on his or her food consumption. The purpose of the study was not to determine which model was more appropriate. The husband's and wife's values of time were hypothesized to key explanatory factors. Wage rates for husbands and wives were estimated using the Heckman technique, as in the Sri Lankan study. In this case, only 14 percent of the wives and 55 percent of the husbands were employed in the formal labor force.

The empirical results showed that as the wife's value of time (estimated wage rate) rose, both she and her children did relatively better in terms of the intrahousehold allocation of calories. Correspondingly, as the wife's estimated wage increased, the husband's relative calorie share declined. On the other hand, as the husband's wage rose, both he and his wife did relatively better, whereas the relative intrahousehold allocation of calories to the children declined. The wage rates reflected the value of the husband's and wife's time and not just employment status, since a wage rate was estimated for every husband and wife regardless of whether they were employed, as in the Sri Lankan study. Considerable similarities exist between this empirical analysis and that done by Fabella (1982) on the relative nutrient shares of household members with a different Philippine data set from Laguna province. Fabella found fewer strong explanatory relationships, however, particularly concerning the impact of wage rates, perhaps because of certain methodological and data limitations.

Other key findings from our study were that boys and children born earlier in the birth order received a higher allocation of calories relative to their RDAs than did girls and children born later. A bias toward boys was also found in several previous studies (Carloni 1981; Evenson et al. 1980; USDA 1983). The relative intrahousehold allocation of calories to women declined during pregnancy. The energy RDA for Filipino women increases by 430 calories per day during the second and third trimester of pregnancy, whereas their consumption increased by an average of only 130 calories per day. Previous studies also noted a decline in the calorie adequacy ratio of women during pregnancy (Chaudury 1983:22; USDA 1983:69–79). This pattern may result from a lack of understanding concerning the additional nutrient needs of women during pregnancy.

THE NUTRITIONAL STATUS OF PRESCHOOL CHILDREN

Preschool children, infants, and pregnant and lactating women are usually found to be the groups with the most serious malnutrition problems in developing countries. Malnutrition has particularly severe consequences for the young. Both their rates of morbidity and mortality are affected, as are their rates of physical and mental development. Preschool children account for a disproportionate number of deaths in developing countries and malnutrition is associated either directly or indirectly with most of those deaths. In addition, children have only a limited capacity for recovering the growth lost due to earlier nutritional deprivation (Austin 1980; Martorell 1982).

This study analyzed the determinants of the nutritional status of preschool children (13–83 months of age). A child's health or nutritional status can be viewed as the outcome of a household production process (Senauer & Garcia 1988; Strauss 1987). If the child's nutritional status is the output, the major inputs into this production process are the child's food consumption, the observable characteristics of the child, such as age and gender, the child's genetic endowment, the time inputs of other family members to child care and other activities which affect the child's well-being, and goods and services other than food which affect the child's health, such as safe drinking water, adequate sanitary facilities, basic immunizations, and available medical care. A key point which this approach makes clear is that a child's nutritional status depends only in part on his or her food consumption. In many cases food (nutrient) intake may not be the most crucial factor affecting the child's nutritional status.

The anthropometric measurements of nutritional status analyzed were the child's height for age and weight for height. The first, referred to as stunting, indicates the child's long-run or chronic nutritional status. The second, referred to as wasting, indicates the child's short-run nutritional status.

The same survey data for the Philippines that were used for the intrahousehold food allocation analysis were utilized in this study. The heights and weights of all children younger than seven years old in the survey households were collected. The analysis revealed a population in which malnutrition among preschool children was a very serious problem, especially in terms of stunting. Some 24 percent of the preschoolers suffered severe stunting, 27 percent moderate stunting, 23 percent mild stunting, and 26 percent had normal height for age. The figures for wasting were 10 percent severe, 9 percent moderate, 20 percent mild, and 60 percent were normal in terms of weight for height (Senauer & Garcia 1988).

Estimated wage rates of the mother and father, as a measure of their value of time, were expected to be important determinants of the nutritional status of their preschool children. Wage rates were estimated in the same way as in the two previous studies. Three avenues exist through which the wage rates of the parents could affect the nutritional status of their children. The first is the impact of the value of time on its allocation among activities. In particular, as the mother's estimated wage rises, she might be expected to devote less time to child care and cooking and more time to labor force activity. However, the possible decrease in the quantity of the mother's time devoted to child care and cooking might be at least partially offset by increases in the quality of that time and the increased participation of other family members in those activities. Second, a rise in wage rates increases the full income, and possibly the money income, available to the household. Some of the increased household income could be allocated to food and other goods and services, which could raise the nutritional status of preschoolers. Third, changes in the mother's or father's value of time might affect the intrahousehold distribution of food and other resources, as discussed in the previous section.

A major finding from our analysis of the Philippine data is that the estimated wage rates of the parents do have a significant impact on the nutritional status of their preschool children (Senauer & Garcia 1988). The father's wage had a negative impact on his children's long-run nutritional status. Stunting was more prevalent among children whose fathers had a higher estimated wage, most likely because of an adverse effect on the intrahousehold allocation of food and other goods and services. In general, increases in the mother's value of time tended to improve the nutritional status of her preschool children. This result implies that if mothers with a higher value of time reduced their time input to child care and cooking, that effect was offset by the enhanced quality of the time input, the increase in the household's full and perhaps money income, and the improved intrahousehold allocation of resources. As indicated in the previous section, the mother and children received a higher relative share of the household's available food when the mother's estimated wage increased.

Additionally, both the mother's and father's education level had a positive impact on their children's long-run nutritional status. The children whose mothers and fathers had more years of schooling suffered less stunting. Previous studies also found that increases in the educational level of the parents had a significant beneficial effect on their children's nutritional status (Strauss 1987). Behrman and Wolfe (1984) emphasized the importance of the mother's schooling, in particular, as a determinant of child nutritional wellbeing. The overall results from both studies with the Philippine data are consistent with the previous findings of Rosenzweig and Schultz (1982) concerning the importance of women's economic opportunities. In their study using data from India, they found that the survival rate of female infants in relation to male babies was higher in areas where there were better employment opportunities for adult women.

CONCLUSION

A major conclusion that can be drawn from these three studies is that the opportunity cost of women's time has significant implications for behavior within households. This finding has important policy implications. The woman's estimated wage rate was found to affect the pattern of household food consumption, the intrahousehold distribution of food, and the nutritional status of children. As economic development progresses in Third World countries, the increased value of women's time must be considered one of the factors underlying the shift from time-intensive traditional foods to time-saving foods, with the possibility of detrimental implications for nutrition.

In addition, the estimated wage rate of the wife and mother was found to have a significant positive impact on both the relative calorie allocation of herself and her children and on her preschool children's nutritional status. Furthermore, an increase in the mother's education level improved the children's long-run nutritional status. An understanding of such underlying causal relationships is essential if the ultimate objective is to intervene to alter behavior within the household in order to reduce the incidence of malnutrition among certain individuals.

The household functions as an intermediary between many policies, programs, and economic changes and their impact on individuals. We must go beyond the doorstep of the household to analyze and influence the welfare of individuals. Governments, however, will find it difficult to directly modify the behavior of individuals within the household. The value of women's time can be utilized as a means to indirectly change behavior and resource flows within the household and thus improve the well-being of women and children in particular.

The value of women's time can be raised by improving the economic opportunities and investment in human capital of women. A woman's human capital or potential productivity primarily reflects her education, training, and health, all of which can be influenced by government policy. The findings of these three studies provide strong additional reasons to make improved education and employment opportunities for women a major policy goal in developing countries. The economic status of women in society and their role and position in the household are formally linked by the value of time. Boserup (1970) in both her preface and concluding section emphasized the importance of education and job opportunities for women for the rate of economic development. Recent research has revealed their significance for the welfare of individuals within the household. Reducing inequalities faced by women in the economy can reduce inequities inside the household.

10

To Each Less Than She Needs, From Each More Than She Can Do: Allocations, Entitlements, and Value

HANNA PAPANEK

Differential morbidity and mortality rates between males and females in southern Asia indicate starkly how inequalities in resource allocation affect women's survival chances. The purpose of this chapter is to bring together two areas of scholarship that are beginning to show signs of convergence: (1) studies by demographers, economists, nutritionists, and health specialists that provide concrete data to document these inequalities and (2) explorations into women's sense of self-worth, their feelings about their place in family and society, and the social learning of gender differences and gender relations. Using Asia as the focus in this chapter, I will relate ideas about socially and culturally formed "entitlements" to resource shares to ideas about the process of socialization for inequality.

This chapter was written in conjunction with my work on the Comparative Study of Women's Work and Family Strategies in South and Southeast Asia sponsored by the United Nations University (UNU), Tokyo, and was presented in draft form at the Third Workshop of the project in Kathmandu (Nepal), December 16–21, 1987.

I owe many thanks to the colleagues participating in the Comparative Study for what I have learned while working with them. Special thanks go to Vina Mazumdar, M. N. Srinivas, Leela Dube, Rafiqul Huda Chaudhury, Alice Thorner, Nevin Scrimshaw, Irene Tinker, and Soedjatmoko for their comments and encouragement. As always, I am grateful for the supportive and stimulating comments given by Gustav Papanek.

I gratefully acknowledge the support of the United Nations University, the Smithsonian Institution, and the American Institute of Indian Studies.

GENDER AND INEQUALITY

Gender differences, based on the social construction of biological sex distinctions, are one of the great "fault lines" of societies—those marks of difference among categories of persons that govern the allocation of power, authority, and resources. But gender differences are not the only such fault line; they operate within a larger matrix of other socially constructed distinctions, such as class, race, ethnicity, religion, and nationality, which give them their specific dynamics in a given time and place.

Gender differences, unlike other social fault lines, also cut across these other distinctions because all other groupings contain both males and females, except under very unusual circumstances. As a result, gender relations—the interaction between males and females—both reflect and reinforce gender differences as allocational principles. Both gender differences and gender relations are of special importance within domestic groups, and it is within the household that children first learn their significance. The adults and older children who consciously and unconsciously teach them also reinforce their own learning in the process.

How a group or society distributes available resources among members reflects not only power and authority relations but also the moral basis of the group, its consensus about distributive justice, and its implicit priorities. Uncovering these implicit priorities is especially important in the case of gender-based inequalities for, having been learned from a very early age, they are unusually resistant to change later on. The relations between males and females are also so full of ambivalences and contradictions that change can be resisted at every turn. For example, cultural ideals in many societies prescribe high respect for women, especially mothers, yet in the same society, social norms accord women little power and authority and smaller shares of available resources. In addition, if the process of socialization for inequality has been successful, most people will not perceive inequalities for what they are—or, if they do, will argue for their moral rightness.

Children are taught very early in life about distributive justice in terms of differences in gender and age. When some get more food on their plate and others less, when some are sent to school and others not, children can see, in dramatic ways, what the differences are between boys and girls in their societies. These are lessons that they will remember, even those rebels who carry their anger over unjust treatment into adult activism for a cause. The way children are taught about shares and inequalities based on gender and age is a crucial part of the way they learn their place in family and society. The "compulsory emotions"—the way one is supposed to feel—play an important role in this learning.

Resource allocation processes within groups are, of course, closely linked to power and authority relations, but the linkage is not always obvious. Bigger shares of resources may signal a difference in power or status, rewarding those who are singled out for "the lion's share." Being able to look forward to getting bigger shares when one is older or more successful may be a goad for getting ahead or a solace while one waits, as in the stereotypical notion of the South Asian daughter-in-law in a patrilineal household who waits resentfully, doing the hard work of the house, until she can unload it on her successor. But age can also bring responsibilities, as in the equally stereotypical case of elder brothers in South Asia who forgo their privileges in favor of younger siblings for whom they are newly responsible. The expectation that mothers will sacrifice themselves for their children is another stereotype—and not only in South Asia.

In this chapter I emphasize resource allocations within households from the perspective of sociocultural *entitlements* to resource shares. These entitlements are based on social consensus and form an important process of childhood socialization. As noted in more detail in the sections that follow, the didactic function of entitlements has much to do with learning how one is valued by others and how one values oneself. Power and authority are also closely related to entitlements—both as a means for obtaining consensus on larger entitlements and as a reward.

A focus on social learning of inequalities is crucial to the process of change—whether this change comes about through major reorganizations of societies or by way of individuals and groups changing their ideas and behavior. One of the tasks of research on inequality is also to explain its persistence so that active attempts toward change can be more effective.

A perspective on resource entitlements and social learning, finally, helps to uncover some of the processes of women's complicity in their own inequality. The "secondary" socialization of adult women that I discuss later in this essay indicates how and why women often teach their children inequality, even if this involves their own remembered pain.

Conscious and unconscious life experiences shape the way one thinks the world works. For some of us, these experiences include residence and research in countries other than those in which we were born; we often face the problem of integrating the experiences of "ordinary life" and "life in the field." Most of the examples offered in this chapter are drawn from my own research and observations as well as many other sources on societies in South and Southeast Asia but also reflect long residence in the United States and Western Europe. This variety of societies and cultures affects my conclusions in ways of which I am not always aware but that will at once be obvious to those grounded in different times and places. As much as possible, therefore, I have tried to locate each example in a specific context.

Finally, a note on the need for commitment rather than detachment in research on persistent inequalities, of whatever sort: given the persistence of gender-based inequalities in power, authority, and access to resources, one must conclude that socialization for gender inequality is by and large very successful. In effect, "the non-perception of disadvantages of a deprived group helps to perpetuate those disadvantages" (Kynch & Sen 1983:364–65). Rebels within a deprived group are among those who perceive these disadvantages more clearly; outsiders to the group who hold different ideas about equality may also do so. The clear perception of disadvantages therefore requires conscious rejection of the social norms and cultural ideals that perpetuate inequalities and the use of different criteria—perhaps from another actual or idealized society—in order to assess inequality as a prelude for action. Inequalities are poorly studied from a detached point of view; the task of the committed researcher is to make arguments persuasive enough to convince the uncommitted and mobilize those prepared for action.

Empirically measurable indicators of inequality are the first step in developing such criteria. The last two decades have seen an unprecedented accumulation of evidence about gender-based inequalities in resource allocations and access to opportunities in countries around the world. In South Asia, researchers often began by focusing on the very distorted sex ratio (proportion of males and females in a population), largely due to the excess of female over male mortality. In the most basic sense—survival—females are disadvantaged (Bardhan 1974, 1982; Clark 1987; Kynch & Sen 1983; Miller 1981; Mitra 1980; Sen 1983b, 1987, Chapter 8, this volume; Sen & Sengupta 1983). These studies mainly deal with India, but the problem of gender inequality is not confined to one country in South Asia. In Bangladesh, for example, detailed observations have shown that females receive less food than males in intrahousehold resource allocations (Chaudhury 1986, 1987) and less medical care (Chen, Haq, & D'Souza 1981).

Other studies have focused on women's employment. In the case of India, declining employment opportunities for poor women were found to be so serious that even the increased employment for educated women in urban technical and professional jobs did not offset the decline, and female labor force participation figures steadily dropped (Government of India 1974). Indeed, research on women's work became a preeminent concern throughout the region and is by now such a well-documented subject that it cannot be readily summarized.

In literacy and education, females are disadvantaged throughout South Asia, except in Sri Lanka and parts of southern India, but are being educated in much larger numbers in Southeast Asian countries. In South Asia, girls attend school in smaller numbers and for shorter periods than boys, with the differences most marked in Pakistan (*World Development Report* 1986). Literacy rates are heavily skewed as a result. There are sharp differences between urban and rural areas throughout the region, in this respect, and these differences reflect not only class distinctions but also differences in family strategies of survival and mobility. Where there are no acceptable job opportunities for educated women, families must think twice before investing scarce resources in educating daughters.

In short, social scientists (both within these societies and outside them) have invoked criteria of equality that may run counter to the conventional wisdom in these societies to document inequalities between males and females in the allocation of the most basic resources. These include inequalities in food intake, medical care, and education. Studies have also demonstrated that the size of the male–female differential varies not only between rural and urban areas of the same country but also among regions of the same country. In many studies, observed differentials are also linked with outcomes, as measured in terms of mortality and morbidity; in others, emphasis is placed on differential outcomes.

The size of the differential between males and females in any particular resource allocation is a crucial measure of the extent of gender inequality. This differential usually varies not only between rural and urban areas of the same country but also between regions within a country, as in the case of the Indian sex ratio where studies show greater inequality in northwestern India and lesser differences in the southern part of the country (Miller 1981).

Gender-based inequalities in resource allocation—and the differential outcomes associated with them—are also key factors in other kinds of social and economic inequalities. For example, male–female differentials in educational participation in several countries in southern Asia and northern Africa vary not only in terms of rural–urban differences but also in terms of class and income distinctions (Papanek 1985a). In these instances, households with few resources to allocate to education and great need for the labor power of children strongly prefer to educate sons rather than daughters. Later employment opportunities for males are seen, realistically, as much better than for daughters; moreover, daughters are needed at home to free mothers for wage work or self-employment. In families with more resources, the direct costs of education can be more readily borne, the indirect costs (from earnings forgone) are more affordable, and the chances of finding education-dependent employment are more easily perceived. Demand for educated women has also increased in many countries as the modern sector has expanded, primarily in urban areas.

As a result of these class and gender differentials in educational participation, the income gap between rural poor and urban middle-class households may widen further in rapidly developing economies. Typically, earning opportunities for uneducated women decline as a result of changes in agricultural and industrial production using new technologies. At the same time, expanding modern-sector demand in education-dependent occupations and rising aspirations in urban middle-class families result in rising labor force participation by educated middle-class women, even from families where women's work outside the home was previously unacceptable. Declining income contributions from uneducated women combined with rising contributions from educated women widen the gap in household incomes between the rural poor and the urban middle class (Papanek 1985a). Differences between the two, in terms of the size of the male—female differential in educational participation, are clearly part of the explanation but are generally not included in conventional examinations of the income gap.

VALUE, SELF-WORTH, AND EMPOWERMENT

Explanations of allocational inequalities in recent studies often focus on the presumed value of women in terms of the anticipated returns to female labor. In the case of excess female mortality in India, there has been a tendency to find causal connections between levels of female participation in remunerated labor (especially in agriculture) and female survival chances. For example, Barbara D. Miller argued that "where FLP [female labor force participation] is high, there will *always* be high preservation of female life, but where FLP is low, female children may *or* may not be preserved" (1981:117). Miller based her conclusions on extensive comparisons of ethnographic and statistical sources, but problems of interpretation remain.

Similarly, Pranab Bardhan pointed to regional disparities in excess female mortality in India and linked them to the level of female participation in the cultivation of major crops. In South India, where female survival chances are greater than in North India, paddy agriculture involves female workers at many stages, either in exclusively or largely female-specialized tasks. Bardhan suggests that "it is possible that in areas with paddy agriculture, the economic value of women is more than in other areas" (1982:1448).

Although a regional interpretation is tempting, it cannot be supported on the basis of a direct material link between economic value and survival. Most of the women who do the actual work in paddy agriculture, for example, are day laborers who work for wages and are mostly drawn from the poorest and lowest status sector of the population (see, e.g., Mencher 1988). They form the "rural proletariat" (K. Bardhan 1986:90). It is hard to imagine, therefore, that a concept of high female value would be generalized *upward* from the bottom of the status hierarchy rather than based on the widespread tendency of imitating the beliefs and practices of a group at its top. Indeed, Miller notes differences among propertied and unpropertied groups in different parts of India in terms of female survival chances, but her findings are inconclusive (1981:132).

Other problems in linking women's value to labor force participation arise with respect to women's indispensable—indeed "priceless"—work in household maintenance and home production. Even if a particular woman can be dispensed with, women's labor in food preparation, water and fuel collection, house maintenance, and care of children and the sick or elderly remains crucial in the absence of institutional substitutes. Many societies allow widowers to remarry quickly but often frown on the remarriage of widows and divorced women. If the value of women was measured in terms of their indispensability to the household, therefore, it might be set very high. Something else is clearly involved here.

On the borderline between strictly material and what might be called "symbolic" work lies a range of activities in the social, political, and economic realms. This kind of work must also be considered relevant to judgments of women's value. To highlight the *outcomes* of these activities rather than their *content*, I have called them "family status-production work" (Ganesh 1985; Karim 1987; Papanek 1979, 1984, 1985a, 1985b; Sharma 1986). They include unpaid assistance in the work of an earning member of the household, as in the "two-person careers" of men in professional occupations (Papanek 1973); participation in children's schooling that directly assists the efforts of teachers or is linked to upward social mobility efforts;

direct "status politics" in the community; and performance of religious rituals tied to family status in the community.

Usually, but not necessarily, status-production work is done by women not doing remunerated work and can act as a multiplier of the efforts of earning members. This can widen the income gap between households that can afford to devote some members' time to status-production and those that cannot. This process shows "women's withdrawal from paid work as not so much the end-product of mobility as a strategy for further mobility" (Ganesh 1985; 687) and stresses the importance of seeing women's activities as "a causal factor, as an instrument — not just a symbol — of stratification" (K. Bardhan 1986:91).

When women enter paid work, they do not give up their concern for family status but may pursue it by different means. In some areas of Malaysia, for example, many rural women have taken jobs in newly established light industries. Wazir-Jahan Karim (1987) documented how these women devote part of their earnings to the purchase of specific consumer items, often displayed rather than used, in order to compete for family status in the home village.

Given the great variation in women's contributions to the survival, well-being, and social mobility of their households and families, it is surely very difficult to assess a unitary "value" of women even within a single group in a single society. But in spite of these variations, the cultural ideals and social norms of societies show some uniformities, for example, in terms of legal and customary rights and in standards of desirable behavior. Even allowing for the inability of some households and groups to live up to these ideals, it is hard to accept an explanation of women's "value" — and survival chances based on this value — that depends entirely on material causes.

Material paradigms are nevertheless very common and have generally dominated the discussion of this set of issues in feminist scholarship. Instead of summarizing this considerable body of argument here, however, I note only some of the short-term strategies for change compatible both with a stress on the material aspects of gender inequality and the importance of women's feelings of value and power.

Efforts are being made in many places to mobilize women — especially very poor women — so that they can more effectively act in their own interests vis-à-vis employers, landowners, moneylenders, and other powerful interests. In South Asia, this has been done mainly through voluntary groups and nongovernmental organizations, although some efforts have also been fostered by international development agencies (see, e.g., Banerjee, Ray, & Sengupta, 1987; Chen 1983; Jetley 1987; Sebstad 1982). Implicitly and explicitly, these efforts stress the importance of women's "empowerment" — that is, learning through collective action that they can successfully challenge individuals and institutions opposed to their self-interests. In a detailed study of several women's groups sponsored by nongovernmental organizations in Bangladesh, Monawar Sultana (1988) explored how differently "weak" and "strong" groups affect women's ability to act on their own behalf. It is clear from Sultana's work (and that of others) that successful collective action deeply affects the participant's sense of self-worth and increases their efficacy in bringing about changes in their environment.

If adult women, through successful mobilization efforts (in "strong" groups), can learn a new sense of self-worth in a short span of time, it becomes even more important to understand how socialization for inequality begins and why it is so effective. An emphasis on socialization can shift the focus of inquiry from looking at women's "value" to others—their households and families—to their sense of value to themselves—their sense of self-worth. These ideas are crucial to understanding the persistence of inequality and basic to strategies for change.

SOCIAL AND CULTURAL ENTITLEMENTS TO RESOURCE SHARES

Women, like men, get a sense of their value to others from the way they are treated by them—a process that begins in early childhood and continues throughout life. Explicitly, as well as covertly, people get messages from those around them on which to base a sense of their value to others; in turn, their sense of self-worth is, at least in part, a reflection of the value they feel they have for others. These messages may be concrete—say, receiving smaller shares of household resources than others—but they may also be interpreted in such positively compensatory ways that some household members can still *feel* valued in spite of being shortchanged (according to outside assessments). More likely, both women and men get ambiguous messages about their value to others from their material shares and the sociocultural interpretations of the rightness of these shares.

Assessing these contradictions and their effects requires a look at both elements, the material aspects of how resources are shared and the interpretations offered to explain them. This must ultimately be done on the basis of empirical evidence collected in specific groups and societies; for the moment, this evidence is scanty and scattered in many sources, so that efforts to address these issues must remain somewhat speculative, using the best evidence at hand.

The links between resource shares and feelings of self-worth are particularly important if one is interested in changing persistent inequalities. People who are consistently shortchanged may be feeling so powerless in their situations that specific attention must be paid to mobilizing solidarity among people in similar situations. Enhanced feelings of self-worth can result from efforts to mobilize a group and from experiencing—often for the first time—that even the powerless can sometimes succeed in changing their situations.

One way of conceptualizing these linkages with a view to changing inequalities is to focus on the concept of entitlements, both in their objective, material form and in the social norms and cultural values that perpetuate differential entitlements. In this second sense, these entitlements represent the social consensus about the value of specific categories of persons as expressed in the norms governing "who gets what and why." As used here, the term "entitlement" refers to the socially and culturally recognized rights of specific categories of persons to particular resource shares. These rights are expressed in common statements, such as "a man needs more food than a woman because . . . "or "a girl does not have to be as well educated as a boy because. . . . " The resources available to be shared include material resources, such as food, clothing, and shelter, as well as the resources devoted to the development of individual capacities, which result from adequate health care, education, and other ways of developing necessary skills.

The concept of entitlement to resource shares embodies the ideas of distributional justice shared by members of a group or society and can therefore be seen as a central part of its moral basis. How this consensus is developed is a process that begins in childhood as a critical feature of the process of socialization. Socialization for inequality is a major focus of this chapter, as developed in the sections that follow. Power relations are obviously crucial in the enforcement and perpetuation of these inequalities, but I touch on them only briefly. Given a focus on socialization for inequality, power relations within the household — as a central theme in examining the dynamics of households — deserve special attention. Domestic groups in which age and gender differences confer power on some over others are poor environments in which to unlearn the norms of inequality. In some societies, including those of South Asia, unlearning is also made harder by the existence of "escalator hierarchies" in domestic groups where the young and powerless must await their turn to enjoy control over others as they age. Until they do, they cannot rebel, for rebellion endangers the possibility of achieving a higher position on the escalator hierarchy (see Papanek forthcoming).

To return to the concept of entitlement, the consensus of a group or society about entitlements can be studied directly through the responses of individuals to specific questions and through the study of existing evidence in social structure, economy, history, and myth. But at present, given the relative scarcity of direct studies of *expressed consensus* about entitlements, notions of entitlement must usually be inferred from the differential outcomes of resource allocations — on the assumption that these outcomes are not accidental but represent the results of systematic differences in resource allocation. Gender-based differences in mortality and morbidity, for instance, must be seen as representing systematic differences in health care and nutritional intake (see, e.g., Kynch & Sen 1983; McKee 1984; Sen & Sengupta 1983). Evidence for ideas of differential entitlement should then be pursued through direct empirical research so that attempts to change inequalities can also directly confront beliefs and practices in socialization for inequality.

The process of allocating resources within the household can be examined from a number of perspectives, depending on the extent to which the internal workings of the household are the specific focus of inquiry. Since this intrahousehold allocation process is of major importance in socialization for inequality and reflects the internal power relations within the household, I will stress three distinct aspects: (1) the objective consequences of an allocational pattern in terms of differences among household members in nutritional status, morbidity, mortality, and skill acquisition; (2) the psychosocial consequences for individuals in terms of how they feel about themselves and how they relate to others; and (3) the moral basis of the group of society that is reflected in the norms that govern sharing of resources. Except for the first aspect, on which there is considerable empirical evidence (especially from parts of South Asia), the discussion I present here emphasizes issues for research on the basis of their relevance to potential change in persistent inequalities.

In the sense in which I use the concept of entitlements, social consensus and implementation within the household are the main focus rather than the legal aspects emphasized in earlier studies or the economic approach developed by Amartya Sen and others for the analysis of famines (Sen 1981, 1983b, 1987). Sen recently expanded his approach to entitlement relations to include the analysis of intrahousehold allocations (Sen, Chapter 8, this volume). The concept of sociocultural entitlements to resource shares developed here is generally consistent with Sen's approach. I share his conviction that conflict and cooperation coexist in domestic groups and that individual self-interests are not necessarily submerged by concern for the domestic group as a whole.

My emphasis on social and cultural elements in the consensus about entitlements leads directly to consideration of the way gender differences are learned (and taught) in a particular group. For example, when children are told that "girls need less food than boys," they are learning something important about the value of persons and not only about feeling hungry.

For the most part, allocational inequalities have been studied largely through their objective outcomes or in terms of material differences in resource shares. The "explanations" offered to justify them are equally important, especially for those who seek to change persistent inequalities. For example, in the Indian Punjab, boys customarily get curds, the richer and more valued food, while girls get buttermilk. This is said to be based on Punjabi beliefs that rich foods are needed to withstand cold winter weather (L. Dube, personal communication, December 23, 1987). What does this explanation imply about the effect of cold on females and about women's capacity for suffering? Similarly, in Meerut District (Uttar Pradesh, India), men and women from different castes told researchers that girls and boys got different kinds of food because rich, "heat-producing" foods like butter, milk, and meat hasten the onset of puberty in girls (Jetley 1987:35). Parents are, in any case, anxious about protecting the sexuality of their daughters and find this reason persuasive. The implications for physical growth are clear, but what about the psychological messages carried by these food restrictions?

The mother who follows these precepts acts according to group norms and is not simply expressing a personal preference. Of course, preference for sons is in the self-interest of all mothers in a society that measures the status of women by their reproductive performance. Sons are supposed to support parents in their old age, whereas daughters have gone to another patrilineage. But a third reason, never mentioned by researchers on son-preference, is the fact that a woman can gain the household assistance of a daughter-in-law *only* by having a son; her own daughters will marry out. The mother need not explain or justify her actions in giving better food to sons but would most likely have a lot of explaining to do in the community if she acted otherwise.

Ideas about entitlements are also part of a larger cultural repertoire containing many other ideas about the relative value of categories of persons. Entitlement ideas, in short, constitute part of a system of beliefs about distributional justice. Unequal allocations of resources not only have objective effects but also fulfill a crucial didactic function. They teach children about their rights and privileges in concrete ways that are understandable even to the very young.

Later on in a child's life, these ideas and actions are elaborated into more complex statements that fulfill multiple goals. For example, telling a child that "men work harder than women and that's why they need more (or better) food" not only justifies unequal resource allocations but also says something about the value of a task and of the person carrying it out. Children know that their mothers are always busy and that their work is often arduous. Women's work is also more salient to children because it is always visible, whereas that of men may not be. But differential entitlements put another face on the reality that children see. The work of men is socially defined as more valuable, not only in words but also in terms of the concrete reward that is explicitly linked to the value of the work and of the worker.

Girls may also receive another message from adults, however, when unequal resource allocations are explained to them in *compensatory* terms that reflect an underlying cultural ambivalence about the value of people and tasks. For example, an elderly Javanese woman recalled from her own childhood that girls were taught to restrain themselves not only with respect to food but also in the enjoyment of other pleasures in life. Her mother told her that girls needed to develop more inhibitions — also in self-expression — because "women set the norms for civilization because men cannot control themselves." Women's role in educating children, for instance, was defined as having more spiritual value than men's role in making a living (S. Suryochondro, personal communication, December 19, 1987). These ideas are consonant with other aspects of Javanese culture, especially with regard to self-deprivation deliberately sought for religious reasons (*tirakat*). This is "rooted in the idea that these efforts will make a person mentally strong and . . . that suffering will be compensated by happiness" (Koentjaraningrat 1985:372). Ideas about entitlements, as in this instance, are not only culturally sanctioned but also sanctified in spiritual terms, a frequent occurrence in other societies where women are charged with greater responsibilities for maintaining a family's social and religious status.

Unequal entitlements are often based on *imputed needs* that differ for categories of persons. The anthropologist Leela Dube (personal communication, December 23, 1987) linked these imputed needs to the anticipated life trajectories of different categories of individuals; these are, in turn, reflected in the care and respect given by others. Dube also notes that the greater entitlement of one person often becomes the increased responsibility for care given by another. A male infant's entitlement to more food and more careful nurturance (as in parts of India and Bangladesh) becomes the responsibility of his caretaker, usually a female adult or child. The importance of differential entitlements to nurturance is dramatically illustrated in the many studies of neglect of female children in parts of India (Bardhan 1974, 1982; Clark 1987; Kynch & Sen 1983; Miller 1981; Sen 1987; Sen & Sengupta 1983; Venkatramani 1986) and differences in dietary adequacy and health care for male and female children in Bangladesh (Chaudhury 1986, 1987; Chen, Haq, & D'Souza 1981; see also McKee 1984).

In its turn, the care relationship is linked to ideas of female self-sacrifice and abnegation as a necessary part of nurturance in some cultures. In her discussion of high mortality among female infants in some parts of India, anthropologist Barbara Miller speaks about a "culture against females" (1981:15), but I think it might be more accurate to speak of a "culture of female sacrifice" (Papanek 1984:143). This might encourage researchers to look more closely at the socialization patterns that ennoble the idea of female self-sacrifice in some cultures and link it with preferential treatment of male children.

Differences in imputed needs can also come to include a broad spectrum of ideas about physiological and psychological processes in women and men. The presumed inability of men to control their sexual impulses is coupled in many societies with restrictions on women's behavior and an emphasis on female self-restraint in sexual matters (for added discussion of this point see Papanek 1988 and references cited there). In addition, notions of women's greater ability in self-restraint are found with reference to other physiological processes (e.g., excretion) and women's presumed greater ability to tolerate pain. These imputed needs — or lack thereof — have obvious implications for personal and public health in addition to their clear relevance to systems of strict sex segregation. But all of these ideas about imputed needs coupled with differences in entitlements are also another kind of social construction of physical realities that plays a role in the perpetuation of inequality.

The didactic importance of entitlements — in the sociocultural sense used here — is especially clear in situations of competition for household resources. Siblings, for example, may be particularly strongly affected by differential resource allocations, as when girls and boys in the same household receive different amounts and kinds of food, health care, and education, and when these differences are explained to them in terms of their entitlements. Much other learning about their society is the likely outcome. Another type of learning (and teaching) occurs when the differences between members of the natal family and newcomers (such as in-marrying brides in strongly patrilineal and patrilocal families) are stressed. These distinctions stress individual differences among people who may be of the same age but different genders or the same gender but different marital status. While such differences may be expressed in terms of ascribed characteristics rather than individual personality, their existence nevertheless suggests that there is ample reason to recognize the existence of individual self-interests even in strongly family-centered societies. They may well be rationalized and explained in terms of the overriding interests of the family as a whole, but this does not preclude the simultaneous recognition of differing individual self-interests. Efforts to reduce persistent inequalities therefore may need to recognize this coexistence of family and individual interests in order to strengthen the awareness of everyone concerned that inequalities must be reduced.

These efforts are especially important in times of rapid change. For example, cultural ideals may prescribe that widowed or deserted women should be taken in by their natal families and supported because they cannot adequately support themselves on their own. But increasing landlessness and poverty may mean that people can no longer live according to the ideals they may (or may not) continue to hold. Inequalities in resource allocation then are more important in signaling inequalities in the worth and power of certain individuals as traditional supports weaken. A weak sense of self-confidence, because they do not feel valued, then makes it harder for women to act on their own behalf to protect newly challenged self-interests. As some successful organizational efforts at the grassroots level have shown, women in these threatening circumstances are best able to protect their own interests when they are mobilized into self-help groups together with other women.

A focus on entitlements to resource shares as part of an approach to the study of inequality is important for the researcher for several other reasons. It requires exploration of beliefs and practices in two specific areas: (1) the belief systems associated with the particular resources being allocated, such as ideas about food, education, medical care, and (2) the process of allocation itself (i.e., power relations and household structures) discussed in more detail later.

Researchers may find these two aspects closely interwoven, often unexpectedly. For example, ideas about purity and pollution associated with food that are held by many Hindu groups in India, especially in upper castes, may not at first seem linked to distributional justice. But it is common throughout South Asia (and not only among Hindus) that women of the household wait to eat until men have had their fill. Men are also offered the choicest portions of the food. This is clearly related to the patriarchal system and shows the more general hierarchies in the society that affect entitlements. Prevailing ideas about self-sacrifice and self-restraint by women also play an important role.

But food entitlements are also affected by other ideas and practices in the cultural repertoire of a society and may be expressed in both ritual and secular domains. When these ideas are linked with notions of deference and hierarchy, they can further limit women's access to food and prevent any attempt to compensate for dietary deficiencies by snacking in the kitchen. In South Asia, many Hindus (in both India and Nepal) hold ideas that are especially important in preventing women from eating — or even tasting — food before a meal. In practical terms, ideas about the polluting power of saliva, expressed in the concept of *jutha*, underlie many practices in preparing, serving, and consuming food (see Bennett 1983:4, 174 for Nepal), but the fact that they are also linked to religious rituals gives them particular power. For example, "among the upper castes, the morning meal is first offered to the domestic gods before it is eaten. . . . Among Brahmins, the morning meal is a sacrament [and] food is prepared while in a ritual condition of purity" (N. M. Srinivas, personal communication, January 4, 1988). Polluting such a meal by tasting it beforehand would be unthinkable. Hindu housewives, at least in the upper castes, must learn to cook without tasting the food; in fact, "the test of a good cook is whether she can judge from the smell alone if there is enough salt" (L. Dube, personal communication, December 23, 1987).

The subject of food is especially important to Hindus, in both material and symbolic terms, for it "ties together ideas of impurity, of exchange and of rank" and has begun to be an important issue for scholarly inquiry (Appadurai 1985). This is another reason for focusing special attention on questions of entitlements to resource shares within the household in explorations of gender-based inequalities.

Finally, the entitlement approach to empirical research suggests some new methodological emphases. In the collection of women's life histories, for example, special attention should be paid to the very concrete aspects of resource allocation — why they are the way they are and whether people accept them readily or resist — and to the recall of explanations offered by adults. Perhaps people will speak more willingly about these concrete details, which are often more clearly remembered, than about abstract ideas like discrimination or status. Perhaps they will also express their feelings more readily about specific inequalities than about any broad sense of being less valued than others. Using the entitlement concept as a starting point, researchers can then proceed to considerations of "value" on the assumption that unequal outcomes of resource allocations are not accidental but reflect underlying concepts in a society's moral order.

SOCIALIZATION FOR INEQUALITY

The concept of sociocultural entitlements to resource shares helps focus attention on the learning component of allocational behavior, which both accounts for the persistence of inequalities and gives some hope of change. Inequality is both learned and taught. In many cases, inequality is also cloaked in the veil of rational self-interest, as in women's preferences for sons in those societies where few women can survive alone but must depend on the support of men. In other instances, inequality is presented in terms of women's superior spiritual qualities, which surpass the material interests of men in ultimate importance.

A persistent puzzle in the perpetuation of inequalities based on gender differences is the complicity of adult women — often in spite of their own remembered pain — in inflicting similar pain on their daughters and, perhaps, their daughters-in-law. Many must still remember how they felt when socialization for inequality began in their own childhood, yet they continue the process with their own children, usually "for their own good." Why don't they rebel? Some, of course, do, thus breaking the cycle of inequality for their own children. Others (and their numbers are growing) engage in the lifetime task of breaking the grip of inequality on behalf of women like themselves.

Why do others perpetuate inequality? Some may feel — in the words of an Egyptian woman — "My people do this, and so I must do like they do" (Atiya 1982:11). This woman had just described her own "circumcision" (a euphemism for painful genital mutilation) and those of her daughters, which she had watched being done, and added: "A girl's and a woman's lives are a trial whatever happens. I don't know why" (p. 18).

Looking at parts of this puzzle, I focus here on two closely related aspects of socialization for inequality: the perpetuation of painful practices to "produce" female bodies suitable for marriage and the role of normative emotions associated with family life. Although they occur in many societies besides those mentioned, perhaps in somewhat different forms, the examples presented here are drawn from several Asian societies, now and in the past.

The Foot-Binding Paradigm

Painful practices mark the passage to adulthood for both males and females in many societies. Some have been explored by demographers and others concerned with their implications for reproduction, morbidity, and mortality (see McKee 1984 for short summary). Many of these practices involve genital mutilation of males or females and are linked to erotic appeal, but some practices mutilate other parts of the body to achieve erotic and sexual goals.

The best known case of the second type of mutilation is the extinct Chinese practice of binding the feet of young girls to achieve a crippled shape that men found beautiful. Foot-binding was customary in many parts of China until its final abolition in the middle of the twentieth century. Evidence suggests that it was not confined to the upper classes but was also practiced by at least part of the rural population. Because it was very painful and disabling, it is an important example of extreme inequality. But it is also important because it was decisively stopped in conjunction with major political, social, and economic changes in the society. It is evidence of the possibility of changing even the most grievous inequality through appropriate actions.

"Pain and binding of the feet were synonymous terms" wrote a scholar greatly interested in documenting an extinct practice (Levy 1966:35). He described it as "a curious erotic custom," which is also how it was seen by other male scholars of Chinese society and history. It has attracted relatively little attention among feminist scholars, perhaps because it has passed from the scene.

In a famous life history of a Chinese woman who grew up in Peking in the 1870s, the daughter of a gardener, the process is described in detail:

> They did not begin to bind my feet until I was seven because I loved so much to run and play. . . . My feet hurt so much that for two years I had to crawl on my hands and knees. Sometimes at night they hurt so much I could not sleep. I stuck my feet under my mother and she lay on them so they hurt less and I could sleep. But by the time I was eleven my feet did not hurt and by the time I was thirteen they were finished. (Pruitt 1967:22)

This woman, who told her life story when she was very old, came from a family that had once been well-to-do but continued the practice even when they were poor.

Social class was a major determinant of adherence to strict forms of foot-binding but it was practiced even by peasant families in some regions. Among the Hakka of South China, "women did not have bound feet and normally worked in the fields" (Davin 1975:250) but elsewhere even the need to do hard outdoor work was no deterrent. Opposition to foot-binding was an important goal of modernist movements in the late nineteenth century when women's associations founded girls' schools and formed anti–foot-binding groups (Rankin 1975:39). In most parts of China the practice ended in the period between the two world wars, but in some remote areas "even in 1945 young girls with crippled feet could still be found" (Hinton 1966:24).

In short, this was a practice of imposing an almost unparalleled form of inequality on women: years of pain to achieve a modification of the body which not only had clearly erotic implications for men but was also a measure of how well a girl had been prepared to be a desirable marriage partner. The gardener's daughter made this clear when she remembered the saying "A plain face is given by heaven but poorly bound feet are a sign of laziness" (Pruitt 1967:22). Nothing could more clearly express the role of adult women in successfully socializing their daughters to accept inequality.

The mothers who bound their daughters' feet day after day and night after night could not have forgotten their own pain, as we can see from the story told by the gardener's daughter in her old age. How was it for them to start the cycle over again with their own daughters? Why did they not revolt? This is the crux of the matter in the perpetuation of inequalities.

In looking at mother–daughter relations using the foot-binding paradigm, two distinct forms of socialization are happening simultaneously, that of the child and that of the adult. For the child, this is her introduction to a future that contains many inequalities and often pain, especially during childbirth. For the adult, usually the mother, the imposition of remembered pain marks a "secondary socialization" from which there is no retreat, for her complicity in inequality has been made plain. This secondary phase is a severe test of women's successful internalization of the social norms of inequality: by going through with it, they show acceptance of their own inability to resist, even if they wanted to.

In the case of extreme practices, such as foot-binding and genital mutilation, the social norms of inequality require women to "produce" — through physical alterations of the female body — a daughter who can make a good marriage. The physical alterations are a sign of psychological changes that have also been achieved and that are, in the long run, even more significant. They show that women have accepted inferiority. In physically less extreme but psychologically equally stringent practices — such as purdah or veiling — the goal of producing a marriageable daughter also requires many years of care and control.

In all these cases, it takes a great deal of effort to teach a young woman her future place in society but, in my view, the adult women who do the teaching are at the same time learning their own place all over again. The anthropologist Lila Abu-Lughod said of the Bedouins, whom she studied in northern Egypt, that "separate paths to honor exist, appropriate to the socially and economically independent on the one hand, and to the dependent on the other. . . . The honor of voluntary deference [is] the moral virtue of dependents in Bedouin society" (Abu-Lughod 1986:165; see also Papanek 1988:67–70).

Another crucial psychological aspect suggested by the foot-binding paradigm requires empirical verification. Those who have struggled hard to reach a certain place, a certain security, will often insist that others must undergo the same struggle. This is typical of initiation practices in many societies, even in the process of "hazing" still common on university campuses in some societies. But this insistence requires an internal reversal, an acceptance of the justice and morality of a process against which one may have struggled earlier. Having done so, adult women confirm their complicity with a way of life marked by inequality. It is this complicity that is the sign of successful "secondary socialization," for it also marks the adult woman's acceptance of the fact that she sees no alternatives. She settles for "the honor of voluntary deference" as the only "path to honor" open to her.

Life histories that have already been collected in many countries in burgeoning women's studies research programs may provide some of the empirical evidence that could support or deny the validity of the foot-binding paradigm. These life histories may also reveal how, why, and when some women rebel. But it already seems clear that the point at which changes must occur in women's and men's lives to prevent the perpetuation of inequalities must come early enough to prevent adult complicity, because it will be much harder to retreat thereafter.

The Compulsory Emotions

Learning and teaching inequality also depends on teaching and learning what I call "the compulsory emotions": how one is supposed to feel toward specific others in a given situation. They become powerful tools to ensure conformity to group norms and are often invoked during the process of socialization. For example, the question "Don't you love your mother?" not only conveys the expectation that one *should* love one's mother but may also become an instrument to exact obedience.

Some of the compulsory emotions have acquired generic names, such as "filial respect" or "motherly love," but the use of generic terms without specific content obscures the large differences of meaning found in various settings. These differences may be emphasized or obscured, depending on the perspective of the observer, making research even more complex. For example, a North American observer of family life in Bangladesh may well be struck by the extent to which "filial respect" colors interactions. But a Japanese anthropologist, studying Bangladeshi families from the Japanese perspective, could easily find parents "too permissive" and children lacking in proper respect for elders. Obviously, generic terms for the compulsory emotions are not enough to describe a specific situation.

The compulsory emotions may be especially important in socializing women to accept inequalities. Given the absence of alternatives for women in many societies, the pressure of conformity to social norms is strongly conveyed through the compulsory emotions. This may, in turn, lead to tendencies to hide real feelings behind the screen of ostensible conformity, a point that needs further empirical study. For example, devices like "spirit possession" or episodes of clinical depression among women may well be the only available means of expressing rebellious and hostile feelings in environments where pressures to conform are very strong.

Compensatory justifications offered during socialization for inequality, such as women's superior spiritual qualities (mentioned earlier), are also part of the socialization process. In these cases, women are taught to express compulsory emotions that are consistent with the idea of their superior spiritual or religious status, helping them to accept tangible inequalities in resource allocation.

More generally, it is possible that material inequalities also imply less tangible inequalities in terms of the emotions. Women may be expected to carry heavier burdens of those compulsory emotions that assure conformity to group norms because the constraints placed on women's behavior in some societies are more stringent than those placed on men. For example, in highly sex-segregated societies—such as those where seclusion or veiling is practiced—women are responsible for keeping their distance from men. They have been taught that men are unable to control their emotions and sexual appetites and therefore represent a threat to women's virtue. The burden of fear is thus placed on women, indicating the inequality of conformity pressures and emotional stress.

Researchers who want to emphasize the psychological dimensions of socialization for inequality could begin by focusing on situations that are particularly stressful for women. In parts of South Asia, a crucial life crisis occurs when young women first leave their natal homes and move to the households of their new husbands. Pressures are severe at this time for women not to bring disgrace on their families of origin, yet new brides face special problems of adjustment, especially if the marital household is multigenerational, patrilocal, and patrilineal. Among South Asian Hindus, the situation is often made even more difficult for new brides by customs of marrying women into villages at some distance from their natal village. They enter the new household as strangers, on the lowest step of the household hierarchy. In this new and stressful environment, they come to rely heavily on the compulsory emotions inculcated in them from childhood to conform to social norms and control their feelings of hostility.

Another important area for research on inequality could be the study of ways by which women express negative feelings overtly or covertly and how they are able to get their way, again either by open or hidden means. An emphasis on the compulsory emotions and conformity to social norms does not, of course, mean that socialization for inequality is always effective. But because it often works quite well — as is shown by the persistence of inequalities — it is crucial to study both socialization and rebellion.

FINAL REFLECTIONS

Persistent inequalities based on gender differences have been well documented in many societies and this effort continues. Beyond documenting inequalities, researchers have joined activists in trying to bring about change toward equality. Strategies of change vary, ranging from efforts to influence governments to working through collective action to encourage women to feel more powerful and act more effectively in their own interests. All these strategies require a clear vision of how and why inequalities persist.

This chapter is part of a broader agenda to encourage a consciousness of inequalities by offering some new perspectives on old problems. The approaches I have used focus on the social learning of ideas about the value and place of women in their societies. These ideas are conveyed in concrete form through differences in entitlements to resource shares, experienced from childhood and reinforced as adults teach their children the old norms. Differences in entitlements have been studied in terms of their ultimate consequences for health, well-being, and survival; a focus on how these entitlements are communicated may suggest ways of unlearning as well as learning. The seeds of inequality are planted deep in the consciousness of women and men, often by other women who perceive their self-interests to lie in the hands of men rather than other women. But since inequality depends on social learning in the first place, it can also be unlearned.

It may be that this unlearning and relearning can occur best under circumstances of broader changes in societies, but ideas and practices can also be changed right now, without waiting for larger dislocations to make learning easier.

The bitterest task is to acknowledge the complicity of adult women in socialization for inequality. As I have tried to show through the foot-binding paradigm, the complicity of adult women in imposing remembered pain on younger women is crucial to the perpetuation of many inequalities. A precondition for understanding this complicity is an understanding of the circumstances that bring it about. Women, like men, learn to accept their life circumstances by means of the norms and expectations of the group to which they belong. Where women perceive no alternatives to living by these norms, they may see no other way to assure a good life for their children than by continuing to enforce inequality. Breaking the cycle of complicity then requires a change in the circumstances of adult women as well as a change in their ideas. As long as it is in the self-interest of older women to assert control over resource allocations for younger women, to limit their life options by restricting schooling, it will be hard to persuade them that other ways are better.

Inequalities in resource allocations hit poor women hardest, adding burdens to their powerlessness, but also affect women of other classes. It is already clear to activists and many scholars that strategies of change differ for the poor and the not-so-poor. But an exclusive focus on the poor obscures a clearer understanding of the inequalities that affect women because we are women, inequalities that often cross the barriers of class, race, ethnicity, religion, and nationality. Recognizing these commonalities is crucial not only to clear-headed research but also to effective action.

The research agenda that emerges from this first attempt to formulate an analytical framework suggests a focus on the social learning of differential entitlements to resource shares. This can begin with a careful look at outcomes but needs also to include the ways that justifications for inequalities are learned and taught. These justifications serve a clear didactic function, for they teach people how they stand with respect to others. If this standing is low, ideas and feelings of self-worth may also be low. This makes it easy to see one's self-interest only in deference to the more powerful. When one's situation changes, deference may be a poor tool for dealing with difficulties.

Underlying these issues for further research is the question of how self-interests are now perceived and how these perceptions might change toward equality. Examples of women's collective action and their effects on women's perception of self-interest are beginning to accumulate in the experiences and records of nongovernmental grassroots organizations. These are prime sources for scholars interested in the question of how self-interests are perceived, especially in those "traditional" societies where, it is thought, women have no self-interests other than the collective interest of the domestic group.

III
CHALLENGING PATRIARCHY

11

Sexual Division of Labor and the Subordination of Women: A Reappraisal from India

VINA MAZUMDAR AND KUMUD SHARMA

The search for the origins of women's subordination has led many to examine the historical context of sexual inequality and the relationship between the sexual division of labor and women's subordination. The sexual division of labor has been considered a key variable in the analysis of women's subordination, although the conceptual relationship between the two remains a source of contention. Are the roots of the sexual division of labor and the subordination of women located in the sphere of production, in religious and cultural institutions, or in familial structures and the unequal distribution of household labor? Do they reflect unequal distribution of resources, income, and power between women and men or a mutually supportive and interrelated system of institutions that perpetuate the subordination of women? Does the sexual division of labor form the basis of women's subordination, or is the sexual division of labor only a manifestation of women's subordination?

Scholars differ widely on the origins of the male-favored sexual division of labor. Some claim that its origins are biologically based and rooted in prehistoric cultures; but the heterogeneity of the sexual division of labor across time and space, cultures, regions, and classes within the same society refutes the case for biological determinism. Others argue that the subordination of women by men is the basis on which early civilization was formed and that the sexual division of labor has maintained a reciprocal state of dependency between the sexes (Levi-Strauss 1969). Marxists, as well as two Indian historians discussed later, attribute the origins of women's subordination to the emergence of social differentiation and patriarchy caused by shifts in models of production.

185

Eleanor Leacock and Mona Etienne (1980) contend that posing an inextricable link between socioeconomic and gender hierarchies results from a male-centered bias, and they warn that gender inequality does not necessarily follow class inequality. Rather, they hold that an increased need for trade, subsequent functional specialization, and the reorganization of production relations led to new patterns of dependence that have affected groups in general and gender relations specifically. The hierarchy between market and subsistence production and the concentration of women in subsistence production where their labor is invisible emerge as the key variables in this approach.

The important issue is not at what point of human history sexual division of labor emerged; the issue is how unequal relationships between men and women have been historically generated. Therefore, this chapter will examine the dynamics of the sexual division of labor and the subordination of women with specific reference to India. It begins with an overview of the literature on women's work, women's returns from their work, and women's contribution to economic change. The chapter then proceeds to investigate the historical dynamics that contributed to women's loss of status as evidenced by recent research in India.

THEORETICAL OVERVIEW

Sociological and economic research have generally presented a biased view of women's status and women's work. Research on the ideological bases of women's unequal status has tended to focus on women's role socialization, class and caste determinants, and the effect of these on women's aspirations, achievements, and commitments to the labor market. Scholars have examined the effect of women's employment status on the socialization of children, the division of labor within homes, and traditional norms related to gender-based behavior and sex role ideology. In contrast, they have been only minimally concerned with the power dimension of household structures that affected the allocation of labor, time, and other resources within the family and so have yielded limited insights into the lives of peasant or working-class women (CWDS 1983; Desai 1983). Further, there has been a tendency to assume that the majority of women are engaged in unpaid and "unproductive" domestic labor, which has led to consistent neglect of women's considerable economic contribution in the nonmonetized sectors and their unrecorded employment in the informal sectors.

As women move into employment in the formal sector, they encounter sex stereotyping. The human capital approach argues that the unique characteristics of women's educational background, skill development, and mobility patterns join the imperfections of the labor market and lead to the patterned hiring and subsequent overcrowding in stereotyped gender-specific occupations. Economists in this tradition attribute the root cause of such differential hiring to the differential investment in men's and women's education and training rather than addressing the structural reasons for women's concentration in low-skilled, low-paying, low-status jobs. Indeed, mounting evidence indicates that the requirements of profit maximization manipulate the sexual division of labor to exert pressure on the labor force itself, particularly where cheap labor is available and adaptable (Mitra 1980).

Conceptual dichotomies such as production versus reproduction or public versus private spheres have helped to obscure women's economic role. For example, in agrarian economies, and particularly among the rural poor, the division between productive and reproductive functions of the family is conceptually artificial and operationally impractical (Mitra 1980). In addition, Marxist feminists have held that domestic labor helps the capitalist to accrue surplus by not having to pay for the reproduction and maintenance of labor power. Women's domestic work, according to this argument, is an integral component of the process of capitalist development and though formally outside the capitalist mode of production could therefore be regarded as productive labor (Dalla Costa & James 1972; Menon 1982; Secombe 1974).

Research in the field of women in development has not only provided evidence that economic development has proven deleterious to women; it has also provided new insights into the interrelationships between the gender-based division of labor and the subordination of women under capitalism. This research can conveniently be grouped into three types of studies: women's actual economic activities; the extent to which women receive benefits from their work; and women's contribution to change.

Women's Economic Activity

Ester Boserup's (1970) pioneering analysis of women's agricultural roles and the impact of economic development on these roles challenged the centuries-old perception of the sexual division of labor between men as breadwinners and women as homemakers. Research since then has documented women's actual work in agriculture and manufacturing industries and services, both outside and within the household. This documentation has graphically illustrated women's pivotal agricultural involvement in most of the developing world. Rural women work in "all capacities, in growing food, post-harvest operations, marketing, animal husbandry, and related activities. In several cases, they also work as wage labor on farms" (ICPEDC 1986). Recent figures published by the Food and Agriculture Organization (FAO) show that women form 46 percent of the agricultural labor force in Sub-Saharan Africa, 45 percent in Asia, 40 percent in the Caribbean, and 31 percent in North Africa and the Middle East (1983).

Other studies have demonstrated how women's roles as economic producers are undermined or affected, first, by distortions and biases in information gathering that project women as mainly consumers and nonworkers dependent on men for their subsistence and, second, by the process of socioeconomic transformation, institutional and legal change, population dynamics, and ideological biases. The roots of such changes lie both within and outside national boundaries (ICPEDC 1986).

The transformation of agrarian structures that has accompanied the process of land commercialization and the proletarianization of the landless peasantry has eroded women's customary rights to land and other productive resources and sometimes destroyed social institutions that balanced the needs of gender-related occupations and the survival strategies of households (ILO 1984). For example, land alienation and deforestation precipitated large-scale migration of peasant women to become plantation labor in tea, coffee, and rubber estates, as sweat labor in mines, unprotected agricultural labor in seasonal migration, and unskilled labor in construction (Sharma, Pandey, & Nautiyal 1987; Sharma 1988). The erosion of customary rights has accelerated the decline in women's status as workers, producers, and supporters of families (Banerjee, Ray, & Sengupta 1987; Burman 1967). Prosperity resulting from agricultural development, on the other hand, brings about withdrawal of women from the labor process. This has accelerated subordination in other ways, changing marriage and ritual practices, rules of residence, lineage patterns, and the like, as well as the division of labor (Srinivas 1984).

The penetration of capital leading to the incorporation of local economies into wider national or international markets creates unequal opportunities for men and women and fosters new forms of women's oppression. For example, in a study of lacemakers in Narsapur, India, Maria Mies (1982b) argues that the impact of market forces, class polarization, and pauperization of the peasantry and petty commodity producers has polarized gender inequality and redefined the sexual division of labor. Women's responsibility for subsistence and biological reproduction provides the economic base that allows males to generate surplus value through productive labor. She argues that the social labeling of women as housewives plays a vital role in this process and is often supplanted by practices of social seclusion.

At another end, in Southeast and South Asia the growth of labor-intensive multinational industries, which draw a large proportion of young rural women into electronics and semiconductor industries, combines with the migration of the rural poor to urban centers to affect household structures and the nature of the sexual division of labor. Studies have shown that in industries that are highly susceptible to market fluctuations (such as electronics, garments, food processing, and leather goods) women migrants who have been inducted into the semiskilled urban work force form a characteristically malleable labor force (Heyzer 1982; Phongpaichit 1982; Trikla 1985). Such new opportunities for women's employment tied to the process of rural pauperization may provide relative freedom from the traditional forms of patriarchial control in the village. However, they create new forms of control that build on women's already subordinate position. Sometimes these two forms of control can combine: multinationals confronted by articulate women workers pressing for better wages and working conditions sometimes use the authority of the family or local government bodies to put down such simmerings of rebellion.

Women's Returns for Their Labor

Research in developing countries has used certain measurable standards in nutrition, education, health care, and employment to assess women's access to social goods and services. Impressive documentation has confirmed that women, as a subordinated category, have enjoyed comparatively few of the benefits of development. Women and children, especially in the developing world, constitute the overwhelming majority of the malnourished, illiterate or undereducated, overworked but unemployed (in terms of remunerative employment), and deprived of easy access to health care (ICPEDC 1986).

A new awareness coming out of this body of research is that gender differentials, or asymmetries, instead of decreasing with economic growth as predicted by earlier theories, tend to widen with increasing penetration of "modern," or capitalist, forms of production and organization of distributive services. Male–female disparities in access to economic and social services and resources appear to increase in some countries as the level of such services improves. Demographic indicators point to a rising proportion of women among illiterates and girls out of school against a backdrop of improving literacy and educational opportunities. The gender gap widens in the context of higher life expectancy rates and reduced mortality (Government of India 1974, 1985).

Attempts at explaining these trends have not yet gone beyond such external variables as population pressure, inadequate investment in social services or economic infrastructure, neglect of the rural areas, and increased class inequality. None of these, individually or taken together, can sufficiently explain the widening gender gap. We are thus back to where we started from—the reality of women's subordination, which imposes barriers on their access to vital services and resources, even where they exist.

Studies evaluating programs for women's education, health care, or income generation identify structural obstacles that resist policy attempts to equalize men's and women's opportunities. Official replies to the United Nations on the achievements of the Decade may still explain away failures by the convenient devices of social attitudes, lack of motivation, or nonresponse from women, but ground-level studies have identified resistances of a more tangible nature. The extension of women's work burden and their reduced ability to provide food to their family—often the direct consequence of economic development—is now recognized as a major cause of their inability to reach for services (Sharma, Hussain, & Saharya 1984; Sharma, Pandey, & Nautiyal 1987).

Most such studies and the experience of social action groups have also identified the apathy or resistance of local and national political elites as well as new forms of religious and cultural revivalism with their institutional manifestations as reasons for women's inability to benefit from development. These "structures of subordination" reinforce each other and draw renewed strength from certain forces of modernization, such as stereotyped images of women projected by the media and the educational process (Mazumdar 1985b).

Apart from the Marxist school, most earlier theories treated women's status and roles in the economy as essentially manifestations of local cultures and religious teachings.[1] Research since the early 1970s has swung the other way to identify linkages between changes in women's lives and the activities of large economic concerns — national and multinational — reflecting international economic relations. Set against the development crisis of the seventies and the emerging debates on the New International Economic Order, this preoccupation in Third World research is understandable. It moved inquiries into women's position from the limited, somewhat static perspectives of cultural anthropology into the more complex and fluid arena of development studies and legitimized such inquiries by demonstrating links with issues of national concern like poverty, unemployment, inequality, and exploitation from within and outside national boundaries. Access to similar evidence from different parts of the world also helped validate the results of such research into internationally accepted issues in development.

A limitation of such research, however, was the neglect of the political and historical dimensions of women's subordination. It is not enough to prove that multinational corporations use Third World women as cheap labor and throw them out when they are sucked dry. Powerful organizations would do that with any labor if they could get away with it. The question is — why women? And how do the multinationals get away with it? Why is there no protest?

"Sex tourism," or the growing international traffic in women, presents a particularly compelling picture of the gender implications of development. A few studies established links between the growth of such traffic and patterns of development in rural and urban areas (Phongpaichit 1982; Sharma & Sarkar 1986). Still fewer have looked for connections between trends in such practices and the "structures of subordination" within the community, the social system, and the historical position of the community itself within the political system.

Theories about the historical origin of patriarchy and of social stratification do not clearly demonstrate the nature of the relationship between the two. Recent studies across different regions, however, indicate a consistent alliance between patriarchy and social hierarchy, with one drawing strength from the other. When the hierarchical order is threatened by macro changes in the socioeconomic system and by the emergence of new political forces competing for power, it tries to reassert its strength through patriarchal controls over gender and age groups (Mazumdar 1985a). Patriarchal institu-

---

[1]The dominance of this theory can be gauged from the classification of women only under culture and religion in most of the internationally accepted library classification systems.

tions and values, often left untouched by the radical movements that challenge class or ethnic hierarchies, reappear through new class formations. The basic hierarchical order remains virtually unchanged. Only the incumbents of positions at different levels are different.

Another pattern reported by many studies is of an early alliance of the dominant class, or its closest competitor, with the exogenous forces of change leading to a virtual monopoly of all benefits that result from such change: access to education or jobs in new sectors or political offices. The dominant class is even willing to push aside, for a time, the patriarchal institution of confining its women to the home, in order to grab all the opportunities for its own benefit. A minority of women thus become the beneficiaries of these changes. But both class interests and small numbers stand in the way of such developments' making any real dent in the power of patriarchy, though the contradictions become apparent. These are noticed in increasing and new forms of violence against women within and outside domestic boundaries, disappearance of certain traditional norms that protected women from some forms of sexual aggression, rising divorce rates, and the appearance of new, public methods to push women back to their confined, subordinate position. Religious revivalism, cultural or ethnic nationalism, or various brands of esoteric cynicism can, and often have, become the tools for this brand of reaction, which manipulates peoples' faiths and sense of cultural or intellectual identities to restore the powers of patriarchy and hierarchy in new forms.

This hypothesis has been repeatedly validated in recent movements that attempt to assert a community-based identity against the forces of secularism, workers' rights, peasants' rights, and women's rights. Recent controversies have amply demonstrated this trend: the introduction of the Muslim Women's (Protection of Rights on Divorce) Act of 1986; the attempt to enact a separate personal law for Sikhs; the assertion in 1987 by the leaders of one caste group in Rajasthan that the practice of widow burning (*sati*) should be considered a customary right; the efforts by community and religious leaders in the Bohra, Satnami, and other communities, to restrict women's freedom to work, to study, and to marry according to their choice (Engineer 1987; Mishra 1987).

Women's Contribution to Change

Women's contribution to change has received only minimal attention from researchers in the Third World. A few case studies have documented women's successful economic ventures, entrepreneurial capacities, and collective organizations devoted to changing women's marginal position in the economy (e.g., Jain 1980; Singh & Kelles-Viitanen 1987; also forthcoming CWDS studies on the Self-Employed Women's Association, Ahmedabad and the Working Women's Forum, Madras). Concentration of research on women's role in agriculture has also led to the accidental discovery of women's active role in peasant movements during the colonial period. These examples challenge the myth that women have no interest in politics. Unfortunately they also illustrate how patriarchy manipulates traditional institutions both for and against women.

The real history of women's roles in the generation and transformation of economic activity remains to be discovered. This will not be an easy task, because data are rare and may even have been destroyed. An attempt is made in the following section at some speculative reconstruction, drawing on stray evidence from Indian history.

THE INDIAN EXPERIENCE

Indian scholars have observed some of the rituals and social institutions that exist in India's rural areas in order to glean knowledge of women's economic role in prehistoric and ancient times. One of the most outstanding scholars, D. D. Kosambi (1970), combined such study with a creative use of Marxist concepts and approaches to speculate on the early life of the common people as opposed to the elite. Without explicitly emphasizing gender issues, he drew several important conclusions about women's early economic roles. Based on empirical observation of primitive communities that continue to survive on food gathering, he concluded that women were not only food gatherers but the first managers of the "negligible surplus." Only much later was this managerial role transferred to the patriarch, tribal chief, and head of clan—often through family units. Even today gathering food or fodder and fuel from the forest is primarily women's work in different parts of India. This fact became visible for the first time with the eruption of the Chipko Movement, a classic protest by peasant women against deforestation, in the early seventies. The awareness of the close and distinct connection between peasant women and forests has increased since then (Sharma et al. 1987).

Kosambi also maintained that women were the first agriculturalists, a hypothesis offered by Gordon Childe as a general possibility. According to Irfan Habib (1988), Childe's hypothesis has not been disproved. The folklore and temple murals of some of the primitive tribes on the Indian subcontinent suggest women's early agricultural preeminence. Agriculture still remains the "monopoly of women" in some communities practicing *jhum*, a form of shifting cultivation. M. S. Swaminathan (1985) attributes the continuation of some highly specialized skills among certain groups of tribal women, such as fertilizing plants through hand pollination, to generations of female agricultural specialization. He further supports the theory that the cultivation of rice was discovered by women in South and Southeast Asia.

Kosambi also attributed the first pottery-making to women. He compared the prehistoric pottery found in South India with pots now made by the slow turning of a disk (*sevta*) or without any disk at all. While the "fast potters wheel" appears to have always been handled by men, pottery made without a wheel or with the *sevta* has been an exclusively female art from the earliest historical periods. Kosambi further acknowledged women as the first textile producers. All evidence, ancient or contemporary, records spinning as women's activity; Kosambi cites the Rig Veda, the oldest text in Sanskrit dating from 1500 to 1200 B.C., which refers to weaving also as a specialty of women. Among some contemporary communities — albeit a minority — particularly in the North Eastern Region of India, this continues to be an exclusively female activity.

The traditional textile industry in India provides an interesting case study of historical patterns within the sexual division of labor in India. The first industry to develop into commodity production, the textile trade has a long history of both domestic and export production, and this combination has caused economic historians a great deal of confusion. Some peasant women undoubtedly spun and wove cloth exclusively for family use. However, textile production has extended beyond the subsistence sector since before the beginning of the Christian era, when Indian textiles were the rage of the Roman Empire. Were women involved in early textile commodity production, or did they remain confined to the subsistence sector? The *Arthasastra* (circa fourth century B.C.) prescribed equal wages for men and women artisans producing silk in worksheds. It also laid down measures to protect women artisans from sexual harassment by the male supervisors (Dasgupta 1987). There are sufficient records to indicate large numbers of independent and highly skilled women professionals in the spinning industry at the beginning of the colonial period.[2] The rapid disappearance of these women beginning in the second half of the nineteenth century coincides with the colonial period of deindustrialization, the flooding of Indian markets with Lancashire textiles and eventually by the textiles produced by Indian mills.

It should be noted that the spinning of cotton, wool, flax, and silk has continued throughout India's history as a primary occupation of women. One of the reasons for the overwhelming response of rural and peasant women to Mahatma Gandhi's call for a mass movement against colonial rule in the early 1900s was his revival of *khadi*, or handspun and handwoven cloth, as the symbol of freedom from colonial rule. Even today women constitute the majority of hand spinners and practice it as their livelihood, although production takes place within the "interstices of the household routine" (Mitra 1980:44). In many poor, landless households, women's income from hand spinning is the primary household income, however small.

The history of women's participation in the textile trade is currently being researched and quantified with the aid of the decennial census data that exists from 1872. Two tentative hypotheses have emerged from these investigations. One argues that the steady reduction of women's role in this industry can be explained by the retention of outdated, unproductive, and traditional technology. It is a fact that female spinners are concentrated in the sector using the oldest technology, requiring virtually no investment. One

[2]See, for example, Nirmala Banerjee's ongoing research on women in the textile industry in Bengal from the eighteenth to the twentieth century.

scholar argued that even when new technology becomes available and new forms of production organization emerge, women retain the older, domestic, and low-cost technology. The new technology involves both investment, for which women do not have the capital, and higher risk, which women cannot afford, because the survival of the family depends on their earnings (Banerjee et al. 1987).

A study investigating women in the Bengali khadi silk industry gathered oral evidence suggesting that although women previously had been involved in silkworm rearing (sericulture), spinning, and weaving, they now serve merely as unpaid helpers in the weavers' and worm-rearers' households. A tentative hypothesis holds that in peasant households, sericulture originally represented a supplementary source of income to agriculture. However, when landholdings shrank in size and the share of income from sericulture increased, men tended to assume control and women's roles became secondary (Dasgupta 1987).

With the emergence of the modern textile industry during the late nineteenth century, a large number of women were employed in cotton and jute mills. Over the last six decades their numbers have dwindled. One reason for this trend may be that legal restrictions on the employment of women and children were imposed by the colonial government in 1912 under pressure from Lancashire. These and subsequent protective labor laws modeled on ILO conventions appear to have had a depressive effect on women's employment. In addition, rationalization of the industry, technological change, and the adoption of a three-shift production system have consistently tended to displace women (Government of India 1974).

A recent study on the Bombay textile industry indicates the expansion of an urbanized male labor pool and a decrease in women's textile employment. In earlier periods, male workers tended to be seasonal migrants from rural areas, whereas a large number of women were from the urban working class; thus employers' preference for male workers was encouraged by some middle-class women's organizations that disapproved of factory work by women as bad for children and family life (Savara 1981).

Women's role in agriculture remains an unbroken tradition among peasant communities, but the status of this role appears to have declined as communal ownership of land gradually gave way to individual ownership by kings, priests, and feudal functionaries. Peasant women and men alike were subjected to forced labor by feudal chiefs in agriculture, spinning, weaving, and household tasks (R. S. Sharma 1965). Acquisition of control over productive resources by some and development of ranking and specialization of functions between groups led to a reorganization of production relations and to forms of dependence that did not exist before. Sexual division of labor in this process was a tool rather than an explanation for the nature of social hierarchy and patterns of dominance and dependence which emerged.

One can speculate that increasing class differentiation with both upward and downward mobility of the peasantry and artisan groups contributed to the increasing penetration of the patriarchal norms and values of the dominant class. This penetration was not uniform and did not occur everywhere at the same time. Among the peasantry today, one may find groups for whom patriarchal norms provide only a veneer beneath which one can still discover the contours and spirit of free women who have never really experienced dependence on their men for their own upkeep. Instead, the subjection of these women, like that of their men, by a locally dominant group represented by landowners and moneylenders—that is, the people controlling the raw materials and the product markets—is due to poverty, vocational insecurity, indebtedness, and lack of assets. In addition to these disadvantages, women are also vulnerable to sexual exploitation by their employers.

The theory of "sanskritization" (Srinivas 1984) interprets a widely prevalent pattern of change, that of emulating higher castes in order to acquire greater social prestige. Among the peasantry, mechanisms to control women's behavior are tightened as the community or social group acquires an economically ascendant position relative to another community, caste, or class. Following Engels's thesis that women forced the transition to monogamy, one may even hypothesize that, faced with the possibility of sexual aggression from economically dominant males, women may have preferred a form of patriarchal family because it offered a modicum of protection. Even today, in rural India, married women enjoy relatively greater security from sexual attacks than do single women. Contemporary evidence from several studies on violence against women agricultural laborers corroborates these assumptions. One study of Calcutta jute workers at the turn of this century offers evidence that single female migrant workers entered into common law marriages with fellow male workers to avoid being reduced to the status of prostitutes. In return for the minimal protection offered by such marriages, these women undertook to maintain their "husbands," leaving the latter free to send back to their village families the bulk of their earnings (Bhattacharya n.d.).

India's rich and complex historical record illustrates the gradual process of class, caste, and gender differentiation and the emergence of hierarchical formations within society. Not enough work has been done to date the different stages of this process or to document fully the protests that were expressed by those experiencing an erosion of earlier status, real or imagined. Some explorations in cultural myths and folklore suggest a gradual submergence of matrilineal traditions by patrilineal and patriarchal beliefs.

Attributing the wide prevalence of female deities and cults in rural India to the predominance of matriarchal communities in various regions in the distant past, Kosambi links the triumph of the patriarchal form to the arrival and increasing dominance of the Aryans over the original peoples of the subcontinent. His reconstruction of this process, however, is not one of a violent overthrow of "mother-right" as described by Engels, but one of gradual assimilation through human and divine marriages:

> Matriarchal elements had been won over by identifying the mother goddess with the wife of some male god. The complex divine household carried on the process

of syncretism. . . . The marriages of the Gods imply human marriages as a recognized institution, and would be impossible without a social fusion of their formerly separate and even inimical devotees. . . . The resultant social combination was more productive, with a better mastery of the environment. (1970:11)

The process of assimilation made room for cultural myths and their ideological implications to continue side by side, often expressing contradictory ideological superstructures. The influences of earlier matriarchal traditions continued virtually unbroken through various cultural symbols that identified female deities with important aspects of social life such as knowledge, wealth, energy, change, or humanity's quest for survival against destructive forces emanating from the underworld. At the same time, alternative male principles emanating from patriarchal traditions emerged and were assimilated through the process of divine marriages and adoption of familial relations between different deities. As a result, Indian mythology encompasses a bisexual concept of reality (*ardhanariswar*).

Examining women's position in ancient India from documentary sources, A. S. Altekar (1938) argues that the emergence of a helot class, the Sudras, to take over all manual labor resulted in the withdrawal of women from the process of production in which they had been involved until then. The next step was to push women out of the educational process. In the third stage, the absence of "mental cultivation" was offered as a rationale to justify keeping women under the "control of their fathers, husbands, and sons from childhood to old age."

Although Altekar's analysis was confined to the high castes or women of Aryan origin, who were subjected to an increasing degree of social seclusion and subordination, it does relate the decline of women's economic roles and general status to the emergence of a social hierarchy. Jyoti Phule, a social reformer in Maharashtra, argued as early as the end of the last century that the subordination of women was an instrument for maintaining Brahmanical dominance in Hindu society (Vera 1975). This view is echoed by Srinivas, who noted that the pressure to withdraw women from active, visible economic roles as families increase their prosperity was gradually extended down through the caste hierarchy as lower classes imitated the behavior of the Sanskrit reading priests or Brahmans. The convergence of these views from different perspectives, regions, and historic periods, and their similarity to Engels's analysis, is significant. Together they suggest that the increasing subordination of India's matriarchal tradition reflected the increasing subordination of social groups which followed those traditions. This complex process must be attributed to more than simply changes in the forces or relations of production. Cultural factors, such as the dynamics of the Indian caste system, as illustrated by continued resistance to intercaste marriage even today, coupled with the emergence of political domination of certain groups, are also significant (Ghurye 1961).

At the same time, the importance of control over the means of production in influencing the direction of this process of emerging patriarchy should

not be underestimated. The increasing tension between communal ownership of land and other basic resources and claims of private ownership
adversely affected women's economic position. Contemporary analysis of
communities where communal ownership survives demonstrates that emerging politically dominant groups who want to maintain and conserve their
economic resources against the encroachments of the mainstream economy
will adopt political ideologies that reject those elements in their culture that
guarantee women's rights to these resources (Naik 1978). Culture thus becomes reinterpreted according to the economic interests of the emerging
political elite: even as they proclaim their desire to revive the cultural heritage of communal landholding, there appears to be an innate compulsion to
retain private ownership of basic resources.

The process of change thus reflects a competition between group interests
and group traditions. Politically dominant groups, with their command over
knowledge, political power, and literary traditions, are uniquely positioned
to reinterpret myths and ideologies to their own advantage. It is the combination of the monopolies of economic, political, and intellectual power that
has provided tremendous stability and resilience to the hierarchic structure
of Indian society. In this process, patriarchal forms have triumphed over
matriarchal ones, but the remnants of matriarchal myths and symbols are
still there to be used as allies in women's struggles for equality and justice.

12

Changing Patterns of Gender Stratification in West Africa

SIMI AFONJA

Writers on African women have been so beclouded by the "autonomy" of the African woman that they failed to appreciate the impact of old and new patterns of social stratification on the position of women in these societies and on their quality of life today. The celebrated autonomous African woman was attractive to women in other parts of the world because of the amount of control she appeared to exercise in both the domestic and public domains. Although there were undoubtedly case studies from different parts of the region providing the baseline data for this assessment of the position of African women, new sets of data based on new theoretical orientations show that the autonomy thesis blurred reality about gender stratification and left some crucial factors in gender relations and the structural placement of women in these societies untouched.

EARLY APPROACHES TO WOMEN'S ROLES

The early works of Mary Smith (1954) on the position of women in Hausa-Fulani society and Leith-Ross (1939) on the sociopolitical activities of Igbo women during the colonial era as well as the volume edited by Paulme (1963) on various dimensions of women's status in precolonial African societies changed the image of African women as "beasts of burden" and laid the foundation for the autonomy thesis. Detailed studies by social scientists in the 1960s and 1970s reinforced this conceptual reorientation. Books such as *Women in Africa* (Hafkin & Bay 1976), *Woman and World Development* (Tinker & Bo Bramsen 1976), and *Sexual Stratification* (Schlegel 1977) contained or were wholly devoted to empirical studies of women's role in the economy, politics, religion, and the domestic sphere. They illustrated the amount of control and power women wielded in these spheres in precolonial society. Yoruba and Igbo women became known for their political and economic independence. Ethnographies on various other societies and biographies of powerful women in these societies reinforced the same set of ideas.

Yet the persistent low status of women in the domestic domain and the disadvantaged position of all categories of women in spite of development pointed to weakness of the autonomy thesis. Literature about African women's autonomy emphasized their role in the public domain only. It overlooked the division of labor in biological and social reproduction and the resulting sexual stratification.

My earlier writings pointed out the problems engendered in modernization theory on which the autonomy thesis was fashioned (Afonja 1980, 1981). The basic limitation of modernization theory is that as a functionalist theory it cannot articulate all the main issues relevant to sexual stratification in Africa for three reasons. First, it neglects history, that is, the continuous interaction of social processes through different historical periods; second, it is unable to deal with various external phenomena which interact with the internal historical process; and third, it ignores the structural conditions created by the position of societies in the international economic system. Perhaps in recognition of some of these problems, Pala (1977) and Caulfield (1974) called for a perspective that will take cognizance of African culture and historical experience in analyzing the issue of sexual inequality in Africa.

Nonetheless, the autonomy thesis has been valuable because it altered the idea that African women were complete subordinates. It added strong support to prevailing arguments about the egalitarianism of preclass society and showed alarmingly the negative impact of development on women. The issues raised in later writings, however, show that there are other neglected dimensions of social stratification, rooted in the past and in the present, which make the issue of gender stratification a highly complex and enduring feature of modern industrial society.

Causes of gender stratification have been widely debated. In 1949 Margaret Mead presented empirical data from New Guinea to challenge widespread stereotypes that female subordination was caused solely by nature, that is, the biological differences between men and women. To Mead, the critical factor in the generation of emotional or intellectual differences was the psychological conditioning that starts very early in childhood. Two decades later Simone de Beauvoir (1953) juxtaposed biological factors and culture. The differences between men and women, she argued, arise from the fact that they are placed differentially to nature and culture. In the complex ordering of these two phenomena, women are placed nearer to nature and men nearer to culture. In this ordering, culture is superior to nature and thus, Beauvoir argues, women because of their reproductive role are considered inferior to men, who are creators of technology. These interpretations of gender inequality have made a mark on women's studies and demonstrated the explanatory value of concepts like the social structure, the economy, the polity, religion, and the norms and values of societies at different stages of development.

In the 1970s Ester Boserup (1970) gained wide publicity for collating a large volume of ethnographic and historical data for the comparative analysis of women's role in the development process. Her main thesis was that the level of female participation in agricultural production varied with population size and technology, where technology reflected the level of socioeconomic development. Boserup argued that women's role in agricultural production increased although the new farming systems eroded their traditional autonomy, subordinated women to men, and increased stratification between the sexes. In her recent writings Boserup (1985) reaffirmed this assessment: although Africa's population continues to grow rapidly, women have not been able to improve their status because of the low level of agricultural modernization.

In spite of the wide acclaim Boserup's work has received, it has been criticized as an incomplete representation of the gender-inequality issue. Beneria and Sen (1979; 1981) argued that Boserup concentrated on the inequalities generated in the sphere of production outside the home and failed to examine those generated in the sphere of reproduction. Closely related to this is the fact that Boserup did not distinguish between the sexual division of labor as the cause of female subordination and the sexual division of labor as the effect of female subordination. Boserup's work was limited to the former, whereas much recent literature closely associates the growing gender inequality in human societies with the sexual division of labor arising from the interaction between preexisting and new forms in production and reproduction.

In broadening the earlier explanations summarized above, recent writings adopt concepts that trace the negative impact of various cultures, situational factors, and symbolizations to the division of labor and the control of resources. Aside from cataloguing and documenting the contributions of women to economic development, these works also examine the inequality in different systems of production and the interaction between different historical epochs, which ensure the continuous reproduction of the norms and patterns of inequality in subsequent epochs. They suggest that the continuous reproduction of old values and structural arrangements make the gender-inequality issue an interminable problem.

REEXAMINING ROLES OF YORUBA WOMEN

This discussion of the changing gender inequality among the Yoruba is influenced by this recent orientation. The discussion rejects single causal explanations and searches through different categories of factors which interact in a complex fashion to ensure women's subordination to men. Specifically, this chapter will first show how social factors reinforce and exacerbate the basic biological differences between men and women and how the nature–culture dichotomy serves as an ideological tool to achieve ambiguous results. In particular, it will demonstrate that contradictory attitudes toward women exist in Yoruba society, a society whose women's autonomy has been a favorite theme in the literature. The next section will show that the concept of gender equality is distinct from the concept of female autonomy but that the two are related to each other. The example of Yoruba society will be used to demonstrate that even in preclass situations and precolonial times women known in the literature for their high autonomy lived under a system of gender inequality. These reformulations assist in achieving the main objective of the chapter, which is to locate social factors that generate gender differentiation over time and the structures that create these factors in modern African societies.

The social factors that generate gender differentiation are more pronounced in modern than in premodern societies. African societies today can be placed at different points along the egalitarian–inegalitarian continuum. This variation precludes generalizations about gender stratification in Africa as a whole. The example of the Yoruba will be used to stimulate comparisons between societies with similar structures and patterns of change and development and to generate further discussion of the causes and consequences of gender inequality in modern society.

Contradictions in the Nature–Culture Hypothesis

The argument that men are creators of culture and women are closer to nature by virtue of their biological reproduction roles is often used to suggest that the subordination of women to men is a universal phenomenon. Men's superiority over women is assumed to be inherent in the superiority of culture over nature. This nature–culture model has been publicized by feminist writers, but the same idea circulates widely in many cultures and may be difficult to erase from nonacademic discussions in spite of mounting evidence to the contrary. Historical and ethnographic data on non-European cultures, for instance, show that biological reproduction confers on mothers respect and honor transcending that accorded fathers. Women appear in folklore, poetry, art, religion, and so on, as symbols of fertility, love, peace, and stability. They are admired for their feminine personality and revered for the power believed to have been conferred on them by the biological reproduction function.

African art, religion, poetry, and other cultural symbolizations embody the cultures' love and respect for mother (Odugbesan 1979). Yoruba women feature prominently in rituals as a symbol of fertility. The inclusion of female forms in rituals is also connected to women's beauty and the symbolic meaning attached to being female in different ritual contexts (Ojo 1979). Thus in the context of Ifa rituals, for instance, feminine figures are believed to facilitate favorable consulting; in Eshu rituals the female figure helps to pacify the deity since females are perceived as cool headed; and in the

Shango cult the female figure is believed to ease a tense atmosphere.[1] These interpretations are extended to the art forms of the Yoruba. The Gelede Masquerade[2] headpiece represents *The Great Mother* (Iyanla), who is concerned with the most sacred and the most secret aspect of Gelede ceremonies. As explained by Ojo (1979), a female headpiece is used because women are believed to be able to keep secrets. In other forms of Yoruba art women symbolize protection, benevolence, and peace.

Women are most celebrated in Ifa divination poetry, a central body of writing which is believed to be the source of knowledge and the guardian of good behavior for the Yoruba.[3] Ifa poetry represents women as the first guardians of secret cults — bodies which are significant in the spiritual and political life of the Yoruba. Ifa poetry is replete with positive images of women, of their valor and courage, their contributions to the success of their husbands, the virtue of joint decision making in the household, and the consequences of undermining women. Ifa poetry recognizes sexual asymmetry and therefore the existence of purely female spheres and their autonomy. Although further research is needed to determine how widespread the values expressed in the verses are, it is certain that they are chanted to a large clientele who consult the Ifa priest before betrothal ceremonies or divorce, or when they are in search of better fortunes. Each time, the client's attention is drawn to a set of female personality traits, particularly their invisible power in ensuring success for the homestead.

In contemporary society, this ideology of Ifa poetry coexists with very negative and ambivalent attitudes toward women. For example, it is the pervasive assumption that the woman's place is in the home and that political office is primarily for men. Also, to spite women, trivial matters are termed matters for women, and women are portrayed as being more emotional than rational. The image of women as witches who have destructive tendencies, drawn from Ifa poetry as well and a necessary element in protecting the household, is often given only a negative interpretation. This ambiguity pervades women's perceptions of their own positions and how they are perceived by men.

The contradiction in Yoruba attitudes toward women points to an asymmetrical pattern, which might be universal in culture evaluations of women. Many writers adopted this idea to reconcile the contradictions they observed about the position of women in society. In a theoretical overview of analytical concepts of women's roles, Rosaldo (1974) noted that although women

[1]Ifa is a major divinity which is closely identified with Yoruba history, mythology, religion, and folk medicine and is a repository of Yoruba beliefs and moral values. Eshu (the devil) and Shango (thunder) are both deities worshiped by the Yoruba.

[2]Masquerades are earthly representations of Yoruba deities.

[3]Ninety verses on women and their position in society were analyzed for a study on perceptions of gender inequality in Yoruba society. The project was carried out by this author with a grant from the Ford Foundation.

may be powerful and influential, they generally lack authority relative to men of their age and status; biological and cultural factors alone cannot explain this. Therefore she opted for a structural model which related aspects of psychology and cultural and social organization to the dichotomy between the domestic orientation of women and the extradomestic ties that in most societies are available primarily to men. This explanation can be applied to the contradiction between the respect engendered by biological reproduction and the low status expressed in Yoruba cultural values. In this model the autonomy of women in a stratified status system therefore ceases to be tenuous. It becomes an aspect of social reality that is conditioned by the social structure rather than by biological differentiation.

Female Autonomy in a Precolonial Status System

Equating autonomy with equality of the sexes in much of the earlier literature obscured the various ways in which women were exploited in hierarchically organized preclass societies. According to Engels, social hierarchy developed with the domestication of animals and the breeding of herds, which invariably became the property of the family chiefs. In egalitarian societies, on the other hand, everybody had equal access to resources and surplus production for capital accumulation was unknown. Each sex carried out its own activities without meddling in those of the other. To emphasize the independence of women in such egalitarian societies, Leacock (1980:140) argued that there were no economic and social liabilities that bound women to be more sensitive to men's needs and feelings and vice versa.

It is clear from Engels's work that inequality existed before the evolution of class society. In feudal structures the wealth produced ended up in the hands of the ruling elite. This kind of inequality could be observed in European as well as some precolonial African societies. Yoruba society with its semifeudal patriarchal structure is a good example, as the Hausa-Fulani, Ankole, and Bugandan kingdoms, which are strictly patrilineal. In segmentary societies such as the Tiv, the Tallensi, and the Ibo, women controlled domesticated animals and rights to crops but were nevertheless subordinate to men. In Guro society, a society with complementary division of labor, Meillassoux (1964, 1975a, 1975b) observed that women were controlled by men—namely the elders of the lineage—through bridewealth and property rules. Double descent systems such as that of the Bakweri allowed for some female autonomy through the matrilineage, but the patrilineage controlled residence, the inheritance of land and cattle, and succession to political office. In spite of the structure of inequality created in these societies, women still exercised considerable control over their own lives, hence the suggestion that African women were autonomous within a status structure (Afonja 1986b).

Precolonial Yoruba society was not a class society, but centralized government, an exchange economy, and a tradition of urbanism encouraged the hierarchical ordering of positions. Status was based more on prestige and power than on economic criteria (Lloyd 1974; Tuden & Plotnicov 1970). In precolonial Yoruba society sex, age, descent, and political role determined social rank. According to Lloyd, power among the Yoruba was located in specific offices conferring political or economic authority, in other modes of control of scarce resources, and in the ability to apply sanctions and influence others without recourse to sanctions. But political roles were the most important predictor of power. An individual's power at the center of government and at the lower levels of the political administration affected how much wealth and status he or she could command. Women definitely ranked lower than men, but if they had political power, they could use it to attain status in other social realms.

There were fewer positions in the center for Yoruba women than there were for men. However, Bolanle Awe (1977) showed in her discussion of the position and role of the Iyalode in some Yoruba towns that the politically powerful women could gain economic power and high status. She discussed the examples of women who achieved their positions of power through hard work and who were successful entrepreneurs in their own right when trade with Europe expanded. Such positions, however, were few and were recognized within patrilineally hereditary structures for a short time only. There was a high degree of tokenism attached to high-level political roles of women, and some writers interpreted the phenomenon as an expression of inequality rather than equality (Mba 1983).

Other aspects of Yoruba culture exhibited inequality in spite of the autonomy of Yoruba women. The best recognized in the literature is their subordinate position in the domestic domain. This is apparent in the rules and rights established in marriage, the property distribution laws, and the relations of production. Boserup (1970) recognized that societies with such structural characteristics utilize female labor in farmwork, but she used this insight merely to confirm women's contribution to development. The contradiction between the high labor input and the principles of homogeneous inheritance, that is, the transmission of a man's property solely to members of his own clan, is evidence of the subordination of women to men in such strictly patrilineal systems (Goody 1976). In Yoruba society, the critical factor was land which was transferred patrilineally, and, as argued earlier (Afonja 1980), the continuity of male control was guaranteed by the imperviousness of kinship ideologies to change. The adoption of ideologies of kinship and marriage to the disadvantage of women was not restricted to the Yoruba. Similar ideologies supported men's control over livestock, the critical resource in East Africa (Schneider 1979).

Societies with cognatic descent present a contrast.[4] In such societies women's access to critical resources imposes a different pattern of social relations of production, one that encourages a complementary approach rather than competition in the division of labor and in family entrepreneurial activities.

---

[4]Descent in cognatic kin groups can be traced through *either* or sometimes through *both* males and females. Cognatic descent groups have also been referred to as "ambilineal" or "non-unilineal" descent groups.

Some subethnic groups among the Yoruba—the Ijebus, Eghas, and On-dos—historically operated on such egalitarian principles, but the best documented in the literature is the case of Sherbro women, who have been studied extensively by Carol MacCormack (1982). Sherbro women have been compound heads and continue to have access to land and labor. According to MacCormack these women still have potential investment assets and also markets in which to realize these assets; hence "it is difficult for men as a social category to appropriate the product of women's labor" (MacCormack 1982:50). For this reason, the capitalist penetration of Sherbro society did not have the same effect on women as it did in areas where coffee and cocoa were planted and so represents an exception to the pattern elsewhere in Africa. In most areas gender inequality was intensified through increased male control over critical resources and through the erosion of the traditional autonomy of the women, as shown below.

Female Autonomy Within a Class Structure

Class analysts are, in the traditional Marxist fashion, interested in a social hierarchy based on differentiation among the bourgeoisie, the proletariat, and the peasantry. The position of a woman in this structure is believed to be determined by her membership in these economic classes. Yet it is apparent that men and women in the same class position are exposed to different types of opportunities, are subjected to different life experiences, and are expected to possess different aspirations. To explain gender inequality, recent Marxist perspectives on women and development examined the interaction between class and gender. Robertson and Berger (1986) found "access to critical resources" had more explanatory power in a class–gender analysis of the inequality problem than did the concept of "access to means of production." According to these writers, "We remove ourselves from a mechanistic concern with occupation and can devote more attention to all forms of access to critical resources." This approach was a departure from earlier critical approaches, in which women's position in the stratification structure was explained only by the level of *participation* in social and economic processes. Robertson and Berger's approach put more emphasis on the gender differentials associated with the pattern of *distribution* and *control of resources*.

Precolonial trade with Europe and export commodity production helped increase male control over critical resources in Yoruba society. The new pattern of social differentiation during this period was consolidated by colonialism, the incoming religion, and new capitalist institutions that emerged. Slave trade, for instance, was male controlled and male directed and helped men acquire material gains and entrepreneurial skills. Thus men could attain a position of superiority in the emerging transatlantic trade after the abolition of the slave trade. But for the trading activities of a few women like Madame Tinubu and Madame Efunsetan, the coastal trade was a male monopoly. If women were involved, they were retailers at the local level, sometimes acting for their male kinfolk, just as in the traditional economy in which food crops were marketed on behalf of the household. The proceeds of the new trade were not distributed with the same kind of egalitarian ideology that bound members of the indigenous households together into a cooperative unit. The proceeds were controlled by the men and were disbursed toward other profitable ventures without reference to the wives. For instance, urban entrepreneurs who maintained sharecroppers or wage labor on the farms invested their surplus in cocoa production. The new cocoa magnates in turn invested in commercial property and trade in urban centers. Only a few women had acquired capital for such business ventures (Afonja 1980, 1985). Through these dynamics inherent in the capitalist system resources which could have helped women generate capital for their own investments became increasingly inaccessible to them.

The slave trade and legitimate trade in consumer items increased the volume of trade and the number of items traded; but the differential value placed on locally produced and foreign products was instrumental to the restructuring of the positions of men and women in trade. In the new order, local subsistence goods (usually controlled by women) were pushed into a secondary position while the position of men was enhanced by their control of the luxury imported goods and exports. Gender differentials were an inherent factor in the changing structure of early trade and continued to be crucial as trade and export commodity production expanded in the twentieth century. The ensuing inequality was obscured by the high degree of female participation in trade, which left the impression that trade and commerce are controlled by women in most African societies and that therein lies their autonomy. Recent writings on the structure of African labor markets, however, have drawn attention to the stratified structure of that sector and to the relatively disadvantaged position of trading women (Afonja 1985; Fapohunda 1983; Pearce 1984).

The best illustrations of gender inequality come from the literature on women in agricultural production. Data from this sector in the 1980s have in fact created more awareness about the hidden exploitations in the other sectors and justified the need to modify earlier conceptualizations of the women and development issue.[5]

Since land and the capital required for export commodity production were unavailable to women in most parts of Africa, they became an easy target for "peasantization" and "proletarianization." Where the household unit was organized into the production unit, women's primary obligations were to that production unit over which they had no control. As observed for Zambia by Muntemba (1982:85), "Male household heads mobilized the labor of their women so that women's labor productivity did in fact increase," and, as in Yoruba society, men used precapitalist systems of control to

[5]The data presented here and the works cited on rural women in Yoruba society correct the earlier impression that Yoruba women did very little farmwork. That error originated from the lack of attention to the rural sector in the majority of earlier studies.

monopolize the technology, the new knowledge, and the products. Studies on women in agricultural production along the Ile–Ife–Ondo cocoa-producing belt by Berry (1974), Aina (1984) and Afonja (1986a) show the inequities in this type of structure. The women studied were mainly landless rural residents who spent more time on their husbands' farms, with little or no remuneration, than on their own independent businesses. The few who owned cocoa farms were mostly widows or had inherited the farms directly from their fathers. The landless women farmers worked harder than men during the peak of cocoa production and still combined farming with standard reproduction functions, domestic chores, and the management of an independent income-generating activity. Women provided the labor but lacked control of the crop, the production process, the sale, or the disbursement of earnings. They controlled only the proceeds of their own independent economic activities.

Data on the Ile–Ife–Ondo farming communities (Afonja 1986a) show that all the women interviewed worked regularly on the husband's farm planting, weeding, harvesting, and carrying the harvests during the peak of production. Less than 1 percent had personal access to land, but the majority did not classify themselves as farmers, in spite of their heavy labor input. The women were mostly petty traders. The low capital input and the low income from the trade showed that very little surplus could be generated from their investments compared to those of men. In effect these landless women formed the lowest substratum of the peasantry.

A later study comparing women's work in two communities in the rural hinterland between Ilesha and Akure confirmed this pattern (Afonja 1986a). All women in the study worked a full day in some combination of farming, trading, food processing, or craft production. In the first community most of the women were full-time farmers, whereas in the second community one-fourth of the women farmed full time. However, 58 percent in the first community and 46 percent in the second generated income from their other activities, which was used in their farm operations. These women farmers generally grew food crops while their husbands grew primarily export crops; of course the women worked on both farms. Women's lack of access to agricultural extension meant that they continued to use low-technology farming techniques for food production. In both communities the time and labor input of women farmers was disproportionate to their income. Yet the study showed that female farmers suffered more from a shortage of labor than a shortage of capital. Traditionally, the whole family was available to work in agriculture. However, with the men pursuing their independent activities and children going to school, women were left alone with the farmwork.

The contemporary structure of agricultural production is used here to point out the gender differentials in Yoruba society today. The emphasis so far is on the inequality of access to resources needed for capital accumulation. Because of the persistence of the patriarchal ideology carried over from a preclass society, women are denied access to these resources. The entry of women into farming as a full-time occupation does not seem to break this tradition. Rather, it increases women's dependence on their husbands for labor, cash, technology, and administrative know-how in agricultural production.

Women's lack of access to critical resources is apparent in the other sectors of the economy as well, but unfortunately this has not been well documented. It can be suggested, however, that women's low level of entrepreneurial activities in the development of large- and small-scale industries is directly related to their low level of surplus creation and to the utilization of their small incomes to subsidize their husbands' earnings. Women in the rural studies mentioned earlier controlled their own earnings but gave their husbands money for a wide variety of purposes: house building, festivals, children's education, and household expenditure. The rubric of a joint decision-making process in the allocation of household resources is thus superimposed on a structure that denies women control of the most critical resources in modern capitalist society.

Poor access to critical resources is generating very rapid proletarianization among Yoruba women, as it has among women in most Third World countries. The labor of women has been proletarianized in three ways: as part of the family labor for export commodity production, as evident in the cocoa-growing regions of Yoruba and Ashanti societies; as part of the labor for (home-based) factor production; and as the predominant labor force mobilized in the export-processing zones. Women's proletarianization is facilitated by family ideologies that define production in new capitalist structures as an extension of their reproductive roles and by the ideology of exploitation of the landless, unskilled, and semiskilled in national and international labor markets.

Labor proletarianization proceeded fastest when the colonialists dispossessed Africans of their land and utilized their labor for export commodity production. But lately the literature on the Latin American countries has opened up a new pattern of labor proletarianization—that generated by the penetration of Third World economies by manufacturing complexes from the industrialized societies. This new pattern is predicated on a new economic order that involves a shift "from a base relying exclusively on the exploitation of primary resources and labor to one in which manufactures have gained preponderance" (Nash & Fernandez-Kelly 1983; viii). Accompanying this shift is the proliferation of export-processing zones in the Third World countries where women are attracted to the unskilled and low-skilled occupations that pay low wages and offer poor conditions. Such enclaves are still very few in the African region, but their effects on gender stratification are comparable to those of peasantization and proletarianization for export commodity production. Structural changes in the rural and urban economies throughout the region thus make gender inequality a persistent problem of development. The majority of women continue to be on the lowest rung of each substratum in the present class structure.

CONCLUSION

The emphasis in the preceding analysis of the changing patterns of gender inequalities in Africa is on the distinction between the concepts of autonomy and inequality. The central argument is that structures which encourage the autonomy of women can still be infused with inequality between men and women. Since it is now evident that development is intensifying the subordination of women to men, it becomes imperative to locate the causes of this subordination in the structures that created modern industrial development and in development itself. This calls for a detailed historical analysis of the process and of its content in each region. In the African region, one would be investigating the initial historical processes which transformed the household economy into a competitive one, bound by a set of values that encourage men to exploit women for profit and implant in women the need to fulfill a set of obligations defined by their reproductive roles. In this kind of analysis, biological factors are not completely irrelevant; they are in fact an important dimension of the gender-inequality problem. Yet the more interesting causal variables are those internal and international structures that interact with biological factors. To this extent, sociopolitical processes internal to a society are as important as the international processes that continue to restructure these societies: religious conversion, colonialism, racism, merchant capitalism, export commodity production, and the creation of the export-processing zones. Each time one of these factors generates social differentiation, women are moved further down the social hierarchy and gender inequality persists.

13

East African Women, Work, and the Articulation of Dominance

CHRISTINE OBBO

The family is the basic unit of peasant ownership, production, consumption, and social life. The individual, the family, and the farm are an indivisible whole. (Shanin 1971:241)

So long as gender is an important indicator of economic, social, and political roles there will be a need for special policies targeted to rural women [for education and training, technology transfer, credit]. (Loutfi 1980:51)

The persistent gender inequalities in Africa cannot be adequately explained by documenting women's assertions of their subjective experiences or by pointing to the privileges and influence historically and currently enjoyed by a minority of women. Rather, it is important to analyze how changes in different communities are experienced by women on a subjective level and to examine the insights provided by the empirical realities at the objective level. In other words, the personal interpretations and cultural meanings of events within a social setting must be juxtaposed against the economic, political, and cultural realities of women's lives. Anthropologist Roger Keesing is right in cautioning against universals and in insisting that the subjective (insider) and objective (outsider) views should both be evaluated with self-critical awareness.

It is perhaps true that women have been subordinate in some sense in all tradition-al [and modern?] societies. But there have been enormous differences in the status of women, their economic position in relation to the means of production, and their power in domestic and public realms. To understand the subordination of women, one must look at these variations and have a keen sense of *history* and *process* — a sense which is chilled if one emphasizes universals. (Keesing 1981:310)

This chapter examines African women and their work in an attempt to unravel the factors that have hindered their progress. It argues that the situation of African women cannot be understood in isolation from the power and control they have over their labor and persons. Power and control determine how resources are distributed among societal members. The main purpose of this chapter is to examine where power and control are located, how they are exercised and reproduced, and the extent of their impact on women's activities and consciousness. The main argument here is that the essence of women's work can be located in women's identification with, and perception of, certain tasks and the proper way to accomplish them. In other words, the sanctioning system that accords positive and negative rewards ensures that women understand the extent to which the work they do and how they do it actually defines them both for themselves and for the society at large.

IDEOLOGICAL, SYMBOLIC, AND PRAGMATIC SOCIALIZATION

Through the process of socialization, individuals are trained to be successful members of their societies. People learn the appropriate expectations linked with their sex roles. In other words, values are mediated and reproduced through socialization. The following example shows how women are constantly learning and reproducing sex roles in everyday social interactions.

> A lazy youth is rebuked,
> A lazy girl is slapped,
> A lazy wife is beaten,
> A lazy man is laughed at
> Not because they waste time
> But because they only destroy
> and do not produce.
>   (p'Bitek 1967:69)

The heroine of this p'Bitek study, Lawino, is disgusted that her Western-educated husband sees life in terms of Western notions of commoditized, linear, and compartmentalized clock time. She asserts that what matters to the Acholi of northern Uganda is the product of a person's labor and not how long the person spends on a task. In East Africa everyone is expected to give his or her very best to the task at hand. Boys and girls are taught to be clean and meticulous in their work and personal habits. However, an untidy home and unkempt children, a badly depressed husband, or poorly managed gardens producing poor food have serious social consequences for women, but not for men. It is therefore not surprising that in the socialization process mothers whine when sons are inattentive or lazy, but they scold daughters for the same tendencies. The notable thing about Lawino's statement is that lazy females suffer heavier penalties than lazy males.

During field work in eastern and southern Uganda, I collected many similar statements. "Lazy" daughters were often admonished by their mothers and other females in the household:

Don't work like a man! Bend down and collect all the weeds in a heap so that the land remains neat.

Unless you want to be a prostitute, a woman's lot is to work.

Kneel down. A woman does not bend or stand like that when working.

Only herdsmen squat while attending fires, women do not.

You hate working. But every woman has to be neat, clean, and cook well. Otherwise she cannot stay long in a marriage.

These quotes show some aspects of gender role socialization in Uganda. Women are socialized to be skillful and productive. Women and men are expected to fulfill gender-specific duties in a certain way. To understand the subtle and blatant aspects of the ideological, symbolic, and pragmatic socialization, it is important to understand the ethnographic context of work.

Ethnographic Context of Work

At this point let us examine *how* and *when* women work. Two case studies will serve as illustrations.

Case Study 1: How Women Work

A couple had to clear a two-acre piece of land that was partly in forest and partly in fallow under elephant grass. The elephant grass is the most common fallow plant because it has many uses. The green leaves provide fodder for calves and cows; the dried leaves can be used as house thatch; the mature leaves mulch banana gardens; the reeds are used to build houses or as firewood for quick cooking. In the past, the reeds were sharpened and used as spears.

The man and his son cut down the reeds with large knives and dug up the grass root clumps with large hoes. The wife and her sister collected the reeds and clumps and piled them neatly at the edge of the garden. They then shook the root clumps with their small hoes and piled them with small trees for a bonfire. Next they carefully prepared the soil before planting sweet potatoes, beans, yams, or groundnuts.

Later, the couple was observed weeding in the coffee trees. The men worked so fast with their long-handled hoes that they were always far ahead of the women. In contrast, the women used their smaller short-handled hoes to dig up the weeds by the roots; some they collected to burn but others they buried. In two hours the men had finished their work and returned home; the women took five hours. A week later the noxious weeds had, with the help of the rain, easily reestablished themselves back where the men had weeded, but the women's section was relatively weedless.

The last task for the season was to weed the sweet potatoes, groundnuts, and bean gardens. The men seemed to accomplish their tasks very readily. The women seemed to go on forever pulling long rhizomerous (lumbugo) roots from underground. At harvest time, smaller stunted potato tubers and groundnuts were harvested where the men had weeded because the weeds had choked the plants with their fast-spreading roots.

Case Study 2: When Women Work

Women work all the time, juggling several tasks. Gardening is constantly interrupted by guests or children needing attention. Nursing a baby is usually welcomed by women who need a break, but it can also be resented because the constant interruptions prolong the workday. A baby may refuse to sleep or to stay with the babysitter. A mother has to carry it on her back, which slows her down. The women say that "no woman wants to hear her child cry." However, very often if a woman is hoeing, chopping firewood, or sitting in a very hot kitchen preparing the midday meal when the child begins to cry, she may not respond immediately. Often the husband can be heard saying "take that child to its mother" or "what are you really doing that justifies the child crying so much?" Basically men will not help much with the children, nor will they tolerate their wailing.

As one woman put it, "I sometimes wonder if this man sees what I do. I have just returned from the garden, and I am having a cup of tea while the baby suckles and I prepare food. He wants me to cut his hair right away. After that he will want to bathe but I have not fetched the water."

The successful African woman is one who gets things done. The roles of wife, mother, and citizen require producing for family subsistence and reproducing (bearing and rearing children) the family. There are folk tales and riddles that further reinforce what society feels about lazy women, poor mothers, and bad wives. The distinction made between public and private in much of the feminist literature is blurred when the experiences of African women are examined.

The work of African women is domestically limited to the private nuclear family. Women's work is public and neighbors and relatives are free to criticize what women do. For example, women should work hard to produce enough for the consumption of their families and also enough for hospitality services. Women must therefore manage both production and storage skillfully. Women are also charged with the civic responsibilities of fellowship. When neighbors or relatives are ill, women are expected to visit or nurse as well as offer them food. Again, when a death occurs in the family or neighborhood, not only are women expected to suspend farmwork for a few days, but they are expected to make gifts of food. When one adds up the amount of time women spend on food processing, caring for the sick within and without their families, and providing fellowship in times of death, it is a miracle that they have time to be wives, mothers, and producers of food and cash crops. Chambers (1982) argued that the hardships women face are especially acute during the wet seasons when health problems seem to increase and transportation to hospitals and clinics becomes impossible.

Women's work is never done because they are expected to perform many functions meticulously. In order to fit as many activities as possible into a day, women carry out certain tasks simultaneously. Nursing mothers are also wives who cultivate and produce food at every meal. Social relations with relatives and neighbors are maintained through entertaining with food, visiting, and providing moral or professional support when birthing, illness, and deaths occur. Women are important as ritual performers during important occasions such as marriages and the opening or closing of agricultural seasons. This is most dramatically shown in societies with masking and masquerade traditions. The use of female masks underscores the importance of motherhood. The recurring themes are generosity (represented by the nurturing breasts milk-full), dignity and "coolness" (indicated by the composed aloof expressions), and ritual purity (represented variously by full breasts, pubic aprons, or both).

Most rituals require individuals, particularly women, to observe certain taboos to ensure that all goes well. Sometimes women may sponsor or host an important curative or mortuary ritual. Most often women and children are the focus of ritual. Women who have never menstruated or have reached menopause may participate directly or indirectly in rituals because they are perceived as free from menstruation, childbirth, or adultery,[1] all of which are potentially polluting. Activities associated with women's reproductive powers are so mysterious that often they require antipollution measures. Barren women or those past childbearing become honorary men, and they can be ritual experts as women with experience or supernatural powers. Diviners, curers, and midwives are usually from this class of women.

The picture that emerges is that of African women juggling economic (productive), domestic (reproductive), and civil (communal) duties and concerns. A good woman is a good wife, mother, and citizen. Women in households may see themselves as equal partners enjoying different rights and privileges, or they may see themselves as exploited workers. The former are likely to be older women and the latter young women. Women must be understood in context of the broad societal ideology, just as their economic decisions must be viewed in contexts of multiple and inseparable roles. Women are, in addition, societal actors with ambitions and desires. The differing consciousness of women is due to how they perceive and interpret their experiences in relation to their social positions, age, and share in power and resources.

In a classical study of the Guro of the Ivory Coast, Meillassoux (1964) argued that the elders dominated the young men through the control of resources and of women. Furthermore, the elders controlled the labor of young men and women (Meillassoux 1975a, 1975b; see also Rey 1975:29, 53–54). Studies of the Kpelle of Liberia (Bledsoe 1976) and Mende of Sierra Leone (MacCormack 1982) show that older women compete with older men over control of the labor, affection, and eventual political support of young people. The point is that women fare differently, depending on age and life

---

[1]Adultery is polluting because another man's semen is dangerous to the husband and infant.

circumstances. Older women who participate in rituals, or feel they have paid their dues to society, may emphasize the virtue and duty of serving the prestige of men. Younger women may be aware and resentful of the inequity and inequality that make them exploitable, but they often become resigned to it in the absence of apparent means of amelioration. Women need to control resources before they can at the pragmatic level effectively challenge the dominant ideologies and symbolic elaborations that reinforce them. As long as the household and kinship structures are seen as basic to economic, social, and individual survival, the power of the elders remains unassailable.

Women Are What They Do: Subjective Reality

Women's activities determine their consciousness. In Africa women's roles in the family define them as daughters, sisters, wives, and mothers. Kinship and marriage structures are concerned with property and sexual right and control. Fathers and brothers are expected to guard the virginity of daughters and sisters; husbands should insist on the chastity of their wives. A great majority of women lack formal, socially sanctioned power over other adults and have no legal rights themselves. This explains why older women are such staunch supporters of marriage. It is an institution that affords them access to rights in young people (Bledsoe 1976:377). Women's labor and sexuality are controlled by men because these activities are central to production and reproduction. These restrictions over women remain even when the nature, scope, and location of women's labor change.

What are the manifestations of domination and control? Domination over women is articulated in three ways: (1) in everyday personal and mundane circumstances, (2) in family relationships, and (3) in women's perceptions and interpretations of their experiences and circumstances.

Everyday Personal and Mundane Circumstances

During an international academic seminar, a male university professor interrupted a female colleague while she was making a point. He jumped up and shouted at her to go and cook for her children, or if she had none, to go and please her boyfriend. Participants were shocked at these personal and irrelevant remarks. But the professor tried to explain his rude behavior to several of the Western women participants by accusing them of misunderstanding the nature of domination between the sexes. "I shouted at her because she was wrong. That does not mean that we dominate our women," he insisted.

Apparently, a few months earlier he had tried to get her to lecture free of charge and she had refused, knowing that a man had given a similar lecture for a fee. The professor's anger was rooted in her refusal to respect his male power. He held to the basic assumption that women's raison d'être and social identity are inseparable from being serviceable to men and children, that they are lucky and privileged if they get paid for the labors.

Family Labor and Expectations

A Rwandan woman put it this way: "My husband feels cheated when he does *not* get paid for a gardening job. My husband also feels cheated when I *do* get paid for a gardening job. Yet I do this in addition to all my household chores and home gardening duties. It is my energy and my time that I use to earn money to buy decent clothes for myself and my children. It cannot be a crime."

A study of a Tanzanian village development scheme reported similar attitudes toward women's paid labor. Women had been contributing heavy labor for a successful income-generating brickmaking project. Since the project was injuring their health and they were not being compensated, they decided to withdraw. The response of the male village leadership was to levy a collective fee on the women for withdrawing their labor! They then turned around and hired men to do the work for a daily wage.

What then makes men's labor, but not that of women, worth compensating? Why did the women have to pay a penalty for withdrawing their labor? Once again the answer is that women's work is perceived as labor for subsistence. When women refuse to work or demand remuneration, they are stepping outside their social roles as providers of subsistence. Even when women are paid, it is seen as an extension of domestic work (Bryceson 1980), which raises the issue of control over earnings as illustrated by the foregoing Rwanda example. The fact that the village scheme was a cooperative effort did not ensure democracy and justice for women. The discrimination against them persisted, even though the circumstances had technically changed. The women in this Ujaama village were fined because they withdrew from unpaid labor to devote more time and energy to activities for which they could earn money. Yet when they managed to talk publicly about their unfair treatment they were criticized for their boldness by both men and women (Fortmann 1982).

Sometimes women's labor is not appropriated but excluded. The Ankole of Uganda are pastoralists; their women are barred from tending or milking the cattle. The women do look after the calves, but they get milk through their husbands, who in turn get it from their fathers. This practice seems to be an ingenious way of restricting women's claims to valuable resources. Further, Ankole husbands have the power to offer their wives' sexual services to entertain close friends who assist with the herding (Elam 1973). This is a good example of how women's work can be circumscribed and their bodies appropriated beyond conjugal expectations.

What Shapes Women's Experiences?

The analysis by Brittan and Maynard (1984) of how women's oppression in the Western nuclear family is articulated through familiar relationships is useful for understanding the situation of African women. These authors rightly warn against generalizations based on projections of Western scientific discourse or not based on empirical evidence (p. 147). Essentially they argue that there are four sites of female activity in the family that correspond to female consciousness or the way they perceive themselves. The social label *mother* encompasses the bearing and raising of children and allows women to see themselves as "caregivers," who anticipate and cater to the material and emotional need of other family members. The social label *wife* calls for women to provide sexual services to the men to whom they are married; this leads to the self-perception and acknowledgment by women that they are "sexual beings" concerned primarily with providing such pleasure to their husbands. The social label *love* includes all those activities that provide emotional comfort to family members; it leads women to see themselves as "succorers," who provide sympathy and emotionally cushion everyone. The social label *housewife* incorporates all the domestic chores vital to the smooth functioning of a home; through this term women see themselves as persons who can "cope," who successfully fulfill family obligations both on a day-to-day and on a long-term basis (p. 143).

Women are blamed for not living up to a social label. An untidy house is not an inviting place for a husband who has been working all day; deviant children are assumed to have been brought up badly. Thus women's consciousness is modeled as they learn to be successful female members of their society as specified by the prevailing gender system.

While the social labels may differ, African women are expected to care, cope, service their husbands' sexual needs, and bring up decent children in decent homes. But whereas in the West, in accordance with the ideals of privacy, the nuclear family is in theory seen as the locus of these activities and the resulting consciousness, African women have to contend with dominant ideologies that sometimes seem to extend right into their sleeping quarters. These ideologies are expressed through the public admonitions of women who have failed to fulfill their own socially allocated roles' activities. Telling the admonitors to mind their own business simply has the effect of provoking mocking laughter. The asymmetrical power relationships women have with men are therefore reinforced (Brittan & Maynard 1984:144).

In sum, women in Africa are controlled labor because the socialization and sanctioning systems ensure that women's consciousness is intricately focused in what they do. Failure to comply with the social activities of work chores, mothering, and sexual and emotional servicing can result in physical, financial, and social difficulties.

NEGOTIATING FOR CHANGE

In Africa, as apparently everywhere, the majority of women are coerced to marry in order to escape the material difficulties and ideological harassment of remaining as a dependent in their parents' home. In this manner are gender and sex roles reproduced at the pragmatic level through successful socialization into ideological and symbolic systems. However, personal relationships can be manipulated and negotiated to produce change even within the predominant mode of production and under the prevailing system of patriarchy, particularly in a time of economic crisis.

Urban Women

It is in the urban areas that African women seem to be most actively involved in negotiating, restructuring, and reestablishing relative positions with respect to benefits and power. However, the women who migrate to the towns or cities are those who have already caused their rural communities to change their perceptions of the nature of women's activities. They may be rural women who have been forced to sell their labor as seasonal agricultural workers in order to provide their families with adequate subsistence. Whereas men may find time to engage in additional income-generating activities by neglecting their off-farm activities (like repairing the house or draining the well), women tend to sacrifice their leisure time, if any, because their responsibilities to the household are so critical. Time constraints and lack of wage-earning opportunities may encourage them to seek refuge in an urban center.

Other migrants may be women who have defied custom to remain single in order to escape an increased workload and men's domination. Or they may be vulnerable widows or divorcees trying to support themselves and their children. Or they may be young women with a modicum of education who are seeking white-collar jobs. A few will be well-educated women, who constitute part of the national elite.

These city women can be divided into three categories: elite, incipient elite, and unskilled workers. Elite women work in well-paying and often professional jobs; incipient elite women work in offices, but mainly in the service sector; the unskilled workers earn wages by performing menial jobs or create their own employment opportunities by being resourceful and creative. The negotiation for changing women's roles also varies by these categories, influenced by the work the women perform.

Elite Women

Elite are by definition a minority, and in Africa they are even more so. Elite women have received educational training, which gives them access to well-paying jobs that provide economic security. They live in style in high-income neighborhoods, educate their children in good schools, and invest their money in business or real estate. Most women do not pool incomes or savings with their husbands; in this manner they ensure that there will be no ambiguity about resource ownership and control (Obbo 1980; Oppong 1974). This is a salient commentary on the legal and social controls that women see as biased in favor of men. The modern African state is based in the city and is patriarchal: women from all socioeconomic classes are cognizant of this reality.

Some elite women are quite articulate about their option for single motherhood. The lack of "desirable" or "enlightened" marriageable men is often discussed. While it is possible for these elite women to marry and have children with non-African men, many express a preference for African children. This preference has often led to short-lived second-wife arrangements or to long-term consensual relationships.

Incipient Elite Women

Incipient elite women are those who have had some secondary education and work in the white-collar service sector as typists, bank clerks, receptionists, and the like. Some of the jobs they do are at the lower echelons of elite women's professions. For example, lower grade teachers, nurses, and secretaries work below highly paid professionals. Incipient elite women often struggle to make ends meet. Their incomes go for subsistence—to pay for rent, clothing, public transportation, and beauty products. It is possible for some to climb the professional ladder through hard work, but the majority find their efforts frustrated by competition from men and by employers with chauvinistic attitudes toward working women.

Sometimes it seems as if the only way to be promoted is for these women to give in to the sexual advances of their married male bosses. This is a critical point because the affair can result in a tarnished reputation, which reduces a woman's chances of attracting an elite husband. However, it appears that most women submit to "sex on the job" only as a last resort when they have failed to locate alternative decent jobs or to attract eligible elite men. Occasionally such an affair may result in the boss divorcing his current wife so the lovers can marry; wealthy men may set up their mistresses in high style. More often, these women become unmarried mothers, unable to live on their small wages without seeking additional income through continual affairs. It is these "good time" women that pose the greatest threat to married elite women.

For some incipient elite women whose targets are elite or working men earning decent wages, shopping around for a husband may involve cohabitation or proof of fertility. If things do not go well, the women end up as single mothers. A few "lucky" ones can send their children back to their mothers in the rural areas. Others send for a poor relative to come and babysit. For the majority, life becomes a struggle to support themselves and their children. The literature leaves no doubt about the need for legislation to protect incipient elite women by ensuring equality and equity at least in conditions of employment and possible channels for support of their children. As long as the situation of these women is ignored, they will continue to live a hand-to-mouth life-style or prey on elite men to supplement their incomes or possibly form a liaison and so move up the socioeconomic ladder.

Unskilled Women

This last category is divided into semiliterate and illiterate women. The semiliterate may have had some elementary schooling, but they do not possess sufficient skills to work in offices. Work in light industries is highly competitive with men of similar qualifications, so many semiliterate women seek employment as domestic servants. Because they have had some education, these semiliterate women are often able to negotiate for reasonable hours and regular pay. However, these school dropouts are so numerous that some have begun working for the municipality in such menial jobs as sweeping streets or cleaning buildings. Curiously, men who used to do these jobs have been given uniforms and promoted to office errand boys who carry files about or serve tea and coffee to the bureaucrats. Shop clerks and bar waitresses are other jobs open to these semiliterate women. Because all these jobs are poorly paid, some women supplement their incomes by servicing the sexual needs of urban men of all income levels.

These women live in low-income areas where they share accommodations and eating arrangements with friends or relatives. If they enter into consensual union or marriage, they live in a one-room accommodation. Their men, like those of the incipient elite who have abandoned their ambitions of marrying up, are usually low-echelon civil servants or small entrepreneurs. Often these men are ambivalent about their wives working: they may boast that a working woman is the most desirable spouse, yet paradoxically they may order their wives to stop working. Women who stop working devote their energies to keeping themselves beautiful and preparing good food. However, the consumer goods and gifts that were lavished on them during courtship can no longer be afforded, and the woman has no money to buy the clothes and beauty items she craves. The resultant tension over money and dependency can easily dissolve the union if the man's pride and middle-class aspirations make him adamant. A typical compromise is for the woman to start an income-earning activity at home, such as braiding hair, selling snacks, weaving mats, or sewing. But many women find that they must return to domestic service or wage work in schools and hospitals in order to earn sufficient income for their needs. Due to the continual negotiations they conduct with the men with whom they live, these women move in and out of both wage labor and self-employment. And many also move in and out of their relationships with men.

Illiterate women most often utilize their domestic skills to work in the informal sector brewing beer, trading vegetables in the markets, or selling prepared foods along the streets. A few such women find wage employment as cooks for hospitals or schools. The dominant sentiment regarding these activities is that since women do not have to learn new skills to earn money, they are "coping without effort." Such attitudes mask the poverty of the urban poor and encourage official neglect of their plight.

Since a woman working at such jobs is perceived as merely carrying out traditional obligations in a new way, her income is regarded by her husband as part of the family coffer over which he can assert control. In areas where separate budgets are typical, a man may simply reduce his contribution to family support in direct proportion to his wife's earnings. Nonetheless, when women commoditize their everyday domestic work, they transform it into employment. Men who have hitherto taken for granted women's tasks of growing, preparing, and cooking food, constructing houses, or weaving or sewing articles are frequently threatened when women earn money from such activities and begin to challenge men's authority over their time and their spending.[2]

Planned Change

The erosion of traditional patterns of work and of sexual relationships in Africa has produced an uneasy transitional period requiring individual women and men to negotiate their relationships. These changes have not been incorporated into the design of most development programs. Rather, the emphasis has been on programs designed to raise the general standard of the community. These programs often fail because they continue to assume that the total family labor pool will be available at all times despite the changes in social relationships noted above. Increasingly, women must cope alone, yet they are hindered in their progress by lack of access and control over resources such as land, livestock (cattle and camels), information, and labor (Palmer 1977). These persistent inequalities in development projects have been attributed to prejudicial attitudes, women's invisibility, and administrative convenience (Staudt 1984). Changes in family relationships have also been ignored by family-planning projects. Some scholars argue that these projects will succeed only when the sexuality of women is addressed as a legal issue separate from the corporate rights of the kin group (MacFarlane 1978:118).

Attempts to integrate women into the development process have resulted in minimal success because little attention was paid to the way in which resources were allocated within the household or community. As a result of male control of these new resources, their dominance over women was further entrenched. The empowerment of women will come from their having access to and control over societal resources — land, livestock, and children — as well as information. As long as the equation of equality is missing, development projects will be unlikely to achieve their expected goals.

> Development never will be, and never can be, defined to universal satisfaction . . . development is more than passage from poor to rich, from a traditional rural economy to a sophisticated urban one. It carries with it not only the idea of economic betterment, but also of greater human dignity, security, justice, and equity. (North–South Institute, quoted in Loutfi 1980:1–2)

Development will occur when poverty is reduced, and the only way of reducing poverty is to reduce gender inequality.

---

[2]Discussions of women's domestic work in the Western nuclear family under capitalism are illuminating. Women's status is that of "unpaid workers" (Malos 1980) who are exploited (Delphy 1977; Eisenstein 1979) because men control their labor (Hartmann 1979). Furthermore, women are confined to the home because the outside world is dangerous to their sexuality (Poggi & Coomaert 1974).

CONCLUSION

It has been argued in this chapter that women are what they do, because work shapes their social identity and status. Women's consciousness is structured partly by the socialization process, which enculturates the gender ideals of the dominant ideology, and partly by women's pragmatic negotiation of their gender roles. The main thread running through this chapter is that persistent gender inqualities in Africa cannot be adequately explained away by referring to the prestigious roles of a few women or by taking refuge in women's subjective experiences. Rather, it is necessary to look closely at the symbolic system (issues of ritual and menstrual pollution and attitudes toward chastity) by which women's bodies are regulated for ideological reasons. This symbolic system rationalizes various institutions whose primary purposes are to control women's labor and sexuality because they are central to production and reproduction. Some may argue that women are not controlled labor because they are independent decision makers (due to age or the absence of their husbands) or because they participate fully in decisions regarding work. However, the point at issue is that women's unwitting interpretation of their own experiences and circumstances becomes an aspect of the articulation of dominance. Such internalization of dominance is less obvious than when male power is exerted in daily mundane circumstances. The preoccupation of men with appropriating women's labor or the resultant products (such as money or children) is legitimized by prevailing ideologies. Circumvention by some women is possible, particularly in the changing circumstances in urban areas, but the influence of this dominant ideology remains in important force affecting most women's pragmatic decisions.

What is at issue is the convenience with which women's work is appropriated, for the reality of women's work is widely appreciated. Politicians in public speeches and writers in poems and novels pay homage to their mothers, without whose hard work, determination, dedication, and courage they would not have achieved prestige, status, or power. It is public knowledge that the poorest man is one without a wife to work for him, since women's work is indispensable for producing both subsistence and wealth. However, such recognition and praise must be translated into concrete programs that assist women and give them access to valued societal resources. Gender inequality, fostered by development programs, is obscuring the multifaceted competence of African women.

14

Defining Women's Work in the Commonwealth Caribbean

JOYCELIN MASSIAH

One of the major achievements of the U.N. Decade for Women is the impetus it gave to research activity identifying the links between women's productive and reproductive levels and emphasizing women's contribution to economic development. That same research activity has been able to demonstrate that despite the activities of the Decade, significant and unacceptable gender differences continue to exist in the area of economic activity. Information flowing from the Commonwealth Caribbean[1] indicates that despite increases in female participation rates in some territories and the entry of women into male-dominated occupations in others, gender differences in levels and patterns of economic activity persist in the region.

This chapter argues that more refined techniques of researching women's work in this region have provided not only a more precise picture of women's activities but also an understanding of why gender differences in economic activity have persisted and are likely to persist in the future. Material is drawn from the multidisciplinary Women in the Caribbean Project (WICP), which was undertaken over the period 1979–82. The particular subset of data used originated from that phase of the project which was conducted in three territories — Barbados, Antigua, and St. Vincent — which were selected as indicative of a continuum of development levels in the region with Barbados at the highest level, St. Vincent at the lowest, and Antigua at an interme-

---

[1]This term refers to the English-speaking territories of the region, in particular those members of the Caribbean Community, which include Antigua, Barbados, Belize, British Virgin Islands, Dominica, Grenada, Guyana, Jamaica, Montserrat, St. Kitts–Nevis, St. Lucia, St. Vincent, and Trinidad and Tobago.

diary point.[2] Originally monocrop agriculture economies based on sugar plantations dating from the seventeenth century, these three territories illustrate economic changes that have occurred in the region. Barbados is an example of an economy that has moved away from exclusive reliance on plantation agriculture toward a diversified structure based on sugar, tourism, and light manufacturing. Antigua illustrates an economy that has abandoned sugar production and concentrated on tourism. The agricultural base of the St. Vincent economy continues, but the emphasis has moved away from sugar to crops such as bananas and arrowroot. Prevailing indicators such as per capita Gross Domestic Product (GDP) and the Physical Quality of Life Index place Barbados in the upper middle-income range of developing countries and Antigua and St. Vincent among the lower middle-income group.

HISTORICAL BACKGROUND

Historical documents and census data indicate that women in the Caribbean were engaged in economic activity from the time of slavery. Female slaves functioned as laborers in the sugar cane fields, as domestic laborers in the plantation houses, as primary food producers and distributors in the slave community. After emancipation, women engaged in wage labor on the plantations and in establishments in the urban areas; they also continued to produce and sell food. Toward the end of the nineteenth century, when educational opportunities began to open up, women used them to enter the teaching and nursing professions and to establish small business operations. Census figures from 1891 show that between 57 and 78 percent of Caribbean women were gainfully employed in the various territories and constituted 41 to 57 percent of the total of gainfully employed.[3]

In the early twentieth century, the heavy involvement of women in economic activity began to decline. The 1921 census shows a range of 14 to 67 percent of women employed in the different territories. Male emigration, changes in the structure of the labor market, and the emergence of the principle of collective bargaining were some of the factors affecting the participation of women in the labor market.[4]

---

[2]The WICP was conducted under the auspices of the Institute of Social and Economic Research (Eastern Caribbean), University of the West Indies, Barbados, with funding from a variety of international donor agencies. Data were collected during a documentary first phase at the regional level and a fieldwork second phase at the territorial level. This latter phase consisted of a multilevel interviewing process involving a questionnaire survey of a random sample of 1600 women aged 20 to 64 in the three territories cited; life history interviews of a subsample of 38 women from the original sample; and sector studies using a variety of techniques to explore specific issues in Barbados, Guyana, Jamaica, and the eastern Caribbean. For further details see Massiah 1986b. This chapter represents a distillation of the articles in that publication.

[3]Simultaneous censuses have been taken since 1844 in the region, but the questionable reliability of those early undertakings weakens the case for interterritorial comparison prior to 1891.

[4]Differences between individual territories and ethnic differences within territories also affect

By the mid-twentieth century, the region had experienced the closure of traditional emigration outlets to Panama, Cuba, Costa Rica, and the United States; the international economic recession of the 1930s; the labor riots of 1937; the opening of a new emigration outlet—the United Kingdom—following World War II; and the emergence of the five-year development plan as the major instrument of policymaking. Development planners—a new breed—began to explore sectors other than agriculture as engines of economic growth and to draw on funding from international sources for large-scale development projects. One result of these various developments has been a steady decline in the proportion of the working population engaged in agriculture and increases in areas such as tourism, manufacturing, and government services. Another has been a widening gap between male and female participation rates, which began to appear in 1946, reaching an apparent zenith in 1970 and showing imminent signs of narrowing by 1980. Whereas the proportion of women in the working population ranged between 14 and 51 percent in 1946, it dropped to 19 to 39 percent in 1970 and increased to 20 to 43 percent in 1980.[5]

The data clearly illustrate that female involvement in economic activity has been a longstanding feature of Caribbean society and that the level of that involvement had been declining steadily up to 1970. Since 1970, every territory, with the exception of Dominica and St. Vincent, has shown signs of increases in female labor force participation. But the proportions obtaining in 1980 were considerably lower than those one hundred years earlier.

ECONOMIC BACKGROUND

Economic thought in the Commonwealth Caribbean has focused on macroeconomic issues related to the causes of underdevelopment in the region, the reasons for its persistence, and possible strategies for transforming the structure of production. Most writers have argued for regional cooperation to counter the weaknesses of small economies. In this framework, women have been treated implicitly as a constituent of labor, hence as a factor of production.

Although economists have dealt with general issues of importance to women, specific problems relating to the utilization of female labor and the welfare of women have not been addressed directly. For example, economists expressed concern about persistently high rates of unemployment even after industrialization and about the dysfunctional effects of capital-intensive strategies (Beckford 1972; Brewster & Thomas 1967; Demas 1965; Girvan &

this general picture. Indications of these differences may be found in Mair 1974; Massiah 1984; Reddock 1984.

[5]Some of the differences over time may be attributed to changes in definition. Prior to 1946 the working population can be identified from the listings of the occupational distribution of the population. In 1946 the gainfully occupied approach was adopted, and in 1960 the labor force approach was introduced.

Jefferson 1971; McIntyre 1966). But none of them confronted the issues of appropriate strategies to increase female productive activity, nor did they address the question of differential employment opportunities for men and women, the problems related to the utilization of female labor, the reasons for and the implications of higher levels of unemployment prevalent among women than among men, and the implications of women's predominance in the disadvantaged sectors of the economy. In fairness it must be recognized that similar issues relating to men, young persons, or any other subgroup within the labor market are not discussed either. It is nevertheless remarkable that after 30 odd years of theoretical writings, not a single published article by an economist can be found on economic issues related to women in this region, particularly when the statistical evidence showed stark differences in male and female labor force participation and occupational categories.[6]

Sir Arthur Lewis was the only economist who addressed changes in women's labor force participation in the Caribbean throughout his writings. Lewis argued that the agricultural sector was unable to support the rapidly growing population in the region and that the substitution of capital for labor in agriculture had resulted in a reduction of employment opportunities. Men could take advantage of existing opportunities whereas significant numbers of women were forced to enter domestic service, engage in unproductive petty trading, or remain unemployed. To counteract this tendency, Lewis proposed the establishment of specialized labor-intensive manufacturing industries that would not only provide productive employment for the surplus labor, including women, but would also accord with the tenets of prevailing economic theory of comparative advantage (see Lewis 1949, 1950).

The Lewis strategy advocated export-oriented industrialization based on specialization in labor-intensive manufactures. This translated into government policy measures which became pejoratively branded as "Industrialization by Invitation," but they did result in increased employment for men — although for women the picture was varied. In some territories worker rates for women rose, but in most they fell. Further available employment opportunities for women forced a shift away from agriculture and into manufacturing, commerce, and the hospitality industry. Most importantly, significant unemployment coexisted with shortages of unskilled labor while underemployment, especially in rural areas, assumed increasing importance.

These processes have intensified over the years as territorial governments have experimented with various strategies to diversify their economies, to cooperate at the regional level, or, in some cases, even to transform their economies. The extent to which these strategies have been influenced by prevailing economic thought is debatable. But it is clear that attracting foreign investors continues to be the mainspring of their efforts. Thus the

[6]An attempt to rectify this has been made by the First Conference of Caribbean Economists held in Jamaica in July 1987, when a session "Gender Implications of the Development Crisis" was included in the program.

1980s have witnessed growing efforts to establish free trade zones to accommodate foreign investors, particularly in the apparel and electronic industries, both of which employ substantial numbers of women. In Jamaica, for example, employment in the garment industry in free trade zones rose from 200 in 1976 to 7000 in 1986 (Dunn 1987). Despite the many problems associated with creating this form of employment, governments in the region find it a ready palliative for the high levels of female unemployment.

THE WOMEN IN THE CARIBBEAN PROJECT

It is against this background that the WICP sought to include in its design techniques for researching women's work. The absence of economic analysis on the differential labor force participation of men and women signaled a gap not only in theory but also in methodological techniques. The project therefore sought to address three questions as prerequisites to a theoretical understanding of the wider question why do male and female worker rates differ so markedly[7]: What is women's work? How is women's work measured? Why do women work? The first of these questions was dealt with by asking the 1600 respondents in the first level of interviewing to itemize their activities in the 24 hours prior to the interview, then to identify which of these activities they consider to be work and why. The second question was addressed by using the women's definition of work to devise "activity status" categories, which were not only comparable to conventional categories but also more precise about what women were actually doing. The third question was addressed in the second (life-history) and third (sector study) levels of interviewing when fuller discussion with the women was possible. The remainder of this chapter reviews the findings of these questions in the three project territories, relating them where possible to relevant literature.

What Is Women's Work?

Conventional data-collection systems devised to identify those performing an economic role equate economic activity with work, distinguishing between paid and unpaid work on the basis of the receipt of a wage, salary, or profits over a specified time period. This approach adequately captures the volume and contribution of male and female wage/salary earners, but it fails to reflect the range of necessary noneconomic activities in which women engage in order to maintain their households and the economic product of the nation. The literature on industrialized countries appears to equate unpaid work with housework, seeing housewives as unpaid domestic workers. Such work is deemed to be concerned with elementary biological, psychological, and social needs, to be concerned with other people's welfare, to be

---

[7]Women's work was only one issue among the wide range covered by the project, thus only the methodology connected with that issue is presented here. For further details please refer to the references cited in footnote 2.

motivated by feelings of duty and love, to consist of tasks requiring high frequency and involving low visibility, and to be generated by feelings of economic dependency (Waerness 1978).

In the case of developing countries, the women in development literature identifies women's unpaid work as housework, unpaid work in a family business, and subsistence work on a farm. The latter activities are particularly important where the business or farm is run by members of the household and only one member, usually the male head of household, is counted as economically active—even though he may have a job away from the business or farm—and his wife maintains it singlehandedly. Equally important is the subsistence work done by women around the home, which is also not included in the count of the economically active. But the returns from both these types of activity are critical for the maintenance of the households and to the economic product of the nation.

In an attempt to expand the notion of unpaid work, Papanek (1979) suggested a third category, family status-production work, which is concerned with maintaining and enhancing the family's social standing, though not necessarily the women's status within the family unit. Such work includes activities concerned with "support work generated by the demands of income earning activities of other family or household members"; the socialization of children into the values of the class grouping to which the family belongs; and the establishment and maintenance of linkages with other families and the wider community. Increasing evidence from around the world indicates that women of all class groupings are involved in such activities in addition to their household chores and child socialization responsibilities, since it represents an important strategy for household survival as well as individual status of the woman herself.

Both the developing country literature defining unpaid work and the Papanek model have the merit of going beyond viewing unpaid work only as housework; they identify a range of women's activities which are recognized as culturally valuable and which involve time, energy, and organizational skills of women. But in both cases, the starting point is the identification of a range of activities which could be described as women's work on the basis of what women are seen to be doing. By contrast, the WICP attempted to describe women's work on the basis of the definitions of work provided by the women themselves. When women were asked to identify which of yesterday's activities they considered work, about 60 percent of the responses mentioned housework while just under 30 percent cite work for wages (see Table 14.1). Another 12 percent of the responses classify other types of income-earning activities as work, including regular self-employment and occasional sale of handicrafts and agricultural products.[8] A striking feature

----

[8]About 40 percent of the women in each sample cited housework alone, about 20 percent cited jobs and other income-earning activity alone, and about 25 percent of the women cited income-earning activity (including job) and housework jointly. About 10 percent of the sample in each territory offered no response.

Table 14.1. Activities Considered Work in WICP Project Territories

Activity	Barbados (%)	Antigua (%)	St. Vincent (%)
None[a]	1.5	3.0	3.4
Housework[b]	58.3	51.4	57.3
Work for wages[c]	30.9	31.1	22.6
Other income earning[d]	8.2	12.3	15.6
Other[e]	0.1	0.3	0.8
Not stated	1.0	0.9	0.2
Total responses	(818)	(701)	(640)

[a]None of the activities listed were considered work.
[b]Home services: domestic chores, child care, care of the aged and infirm, care of domestic pets, subsistence agriculture for use in the home.
[c]Jobs.
[d]Regular self-employment or home production for occasional scale.
[e]Community activities, personal care, leisure activities, unpaid family labor.

of the table is the convergence of opinion of the women in the three territories despite their different levels of economic development.

This pattern demonstrates the predominance of housework and income-earning activities in the women's perception of work. Content analysis of the detailed responses permit the identification of four main criteria by which the women in this study seem to define their work:

Income: "All (housework) would be work because you get tired just as if you are working for money. Is the same thing."

Time: "From the time I wake up and start washing down the pig pen, I am working. Everything is work."

Necessity: "Washing and cooking—you have to get clothes and food for the children so these jobs are the most important."

Energy: "You're tired when you're finished. So that is work."

In sum, conventional definitions that limit women's "work" to paid employment (including self-employment) represent only a partial aspect of work as perceived by women themselves. At its most rudimentary level, women in the WICP consider work to be anything that is functionally necessary to maintain themselves and their households. *Housework* is work since it involves the rearing of and caring for children, household chores, and related activity, activities that would be remunerative if done as a job. Further, it involves the expenditure of time and energy and it has to be done. A *job* is work since it too involves the expenditure of time and energy, but it also has the particular attraction of affording women an independent income. *Moneymaking activities* are also work since a woman must be able to "turn her hand to anything" that can bring in some "cash money" to help in the conduct of her household affairs. *Helping out in a family business* is work since it indirectly generates income for the benefit of the household. *Maintaining a kitchen garden* is work since it involves the use of time, effort, and energy for the production of food for household consumption. This all-embracing perception of work implies that, except for leisure, which itself requires definition, not merely those activities that are linked to a particular form of economic accounting but all women's activities that contribute to human welfare are work. In effect, Caribbean women in this study hold a broadly based perception of their work which implies that all women are, in fact, workers.

How Is Women's Work Measured?

This question has been debated in the literature largely in terms of the inability of conventional data-collection concepts and techniques to present a true picture of the extent of women's productive involvement. There is general consensus that the basic difficulty centers around the inapplicability of the labor force concept to developing countries in general and to women in those countries in particular.[9] In the first instance, there tends to be a high degree of seasonality of labor, a high degree of intermittent labor, and a high degree of underutilization of labor. Thus the notion of sustained economic activity over a specified period, which is central to the labor force approach, may not be relevant. Second, where unemployment is endemic, it is only a small proportion of the adult population which actively seeks employment, an activity the majority consider a waste of time since they perceive no employment to be available. Further, the processes of seeking work through formal channels such as submitting applications or registering with unemployment agencies are neither widespread nor necessarily used. Thus the simple equation of the unemployed with those seeking paid employment considerably understates numbers who are not engaged in productive activity during the specified period. In these circumstances conventional dichotomization into labor and nonlabor force, employed and unemployed is of limited utility.

When applied to women in developing countries, these arguments hold with even greater force. It has been argued that the activities of women, though constituting work in the literal sense of the word, are not considered work in the labor force sense for several reasons. First, since women's do-

---

[9]Many comments in the debate on these issues tend to overlook two fundamental points. First, purely from the point of view of logistics, it is unrealistic to expect an undertaking of the scale and magnitude of a decennial census to focus on the minutiae of any of the wide and varied topics it covers. Second, labor force methodology was not designed to address the kinds of issues with which contemporary inquiries into women's work, particularly in nonindustrialized countries, are concerned. More recent entrants into the discussion have begun to offer practical suggestions on how to deal with this very real problem (Anker, Buvinic, & Youssef 1982; Massiah 1986a; Mueller, Clark, & Kossoudji 1978; United Nations 1984).

mestic activities do not produce a marketable commodity, they do not quali-
fy as work. Second, women's subsistence activities tend to be inconspicuous
partly because they are often undertaken intermittently in the informal sector, partly because the income generated is so meager that the women prefer
not to discuss it, and partly because much of the activity is undertaken in
and around the house for household maintenance purposes (Boserup 1970;
Fong 1982). Third, some cultures prohibit women from participating in
income-earning activity, thus it is expedient for respondents, whether male
or female, to avoid admitting that their women may, in fact, be involved in
such culturally circumscribed behavior (Beneria 1982b). Because these activities — domestic, subsistence, and socially sanctioned income earning —
tend to be invisible, they are deemed to be impervious to measurement.

Taking its cue from the respondents, WICP opted to include in its measurement of women's work all activities that were so defined by the women
themselves: housework, the job, and other forms of income-earning activity.
Such measurement it was felt could take three forms:

1. An estimate of the volume of work activity of women. This could be
   simply expressed in terms of the number of women involved in different types of work activity and provides an indication of the gross order
   of magnitude of women's work.
2. An estimate of the amount of time women spend in different types of
   work activity. This provides an estimate of the value of women's work
   inputs in terms of hours.
3. An estimate of the monetary value of the different types of work
   activity in which women engage.

Because no income data were collected, WICP attempted to compile only
the first two of these types of measures. The categories selected to depict the
current status of work activities were as follows:

Not employed:	For those indicating no income-earning activity and no participation in home service activities.
Home service:	For those engaged solely in homemaking and childcare activities, care of the aged and infirm, and subsistence production for home use.
Home production:	For those who supplemented their home service activi-ties by the *production and occasional sale* of handi-craft, agricultural produce, and the like.
Self-employed:	For those operating their own business or farm, with or without paid help, *on a regular and continuous basis*.
Employed by family:	For those receiving wage/salary from family enter-prise.
Employed by others:	For those working for wage/salary from persons other than family members.

These categories were determined on the basis of a general question "How

Table 14.2. Current Activity Status of WICP Samples

Current activity status	Barbados (%)	Antigua (%)	St. Vincent (%)
Not employed	11.8	10.8	9.7
Home services[a]	34.1	26.5	40.0
Home production[b]	3.9	2.2	6.3
Own business[b]	5.7	12.0	9.5
Employed by family member[c]	0.3	1.0	0.4
Employed by others[c]	43.4	47.1	31.7
Total responses	(586)	(489)	(457)

Note: Overall totals exclude not stated.
[a]As defined in Table 14.1, note *b*.
[b]As defined in Table 14.1, note *d*.
[c]As defined in Table 14.1, note *c*.

do you make a living?" supplemented by appropriate probing questions. Further questions on the duration of the current status permit the introduction of time periods into the analysis.[10]

Using this classification, Table 14.2 illustrates how heavily women in the WICP study rely on employment by others, especially in Barbados and Antigua, the two territories that are moving away from agriculture. Sizable numbers were engaged solely in the provision of home services, particularly in St. Vincent. Self-employment accounts for about 10 percent, but home production is not as widespread as had been anticipated, amounting to only 5 percent in each of the samples. This pattern is retained when the data are controlled for each of the factors age, education, household headship, type of family union, motherhood status, and residential location.

The relatively low proportions found in the categories self-employed and home production raise the question of the possibility of occupational multiplicity among women.[11] WICP explored this by asking the respondents to identify those of their daily activities that bring in money. Only small numbers of women were found to be engaged in multiple moneymaking activities. Amounts vary from 4 percent of the sample in Barbados to 6 percent in Antigua, the most frequent combination being job with home agriculture, home handicraft, or own business.[12]

It is clear that for women who must add housework to whatever form

[10]This was the approach used in the first level of interviewing. Life-history data on the second level permit a detailed chronological analysis of work activities of a small group (38) of women. That material is not presented here.

[11]It should be noted that low proportions of self-employed are also recorded in the economically active population at both the 1970 and 1980 censuses of Barbados and St. Vincent. No census has been taken in Antigua since 1960.

[12]Proportions resemble those reported in another Institute-based survey in which 7 percent of the Barbados sample and 3 percent of the St. Vincent sample were identified as having multiple occupations (ISER 1981).

their economic life takes, simultaneous occupational multiplicity on an on-going basis may not be as readily manageable as it is for men, but consecutive occupational multiplicity may often be possible. The life-history data suggest that many women in the study maintain one activity status (e.g., employed by others), even though actual occupation might change over time, supplement that with other forms of activity (e.g., self-employment, home production) only when circumstances dictate, and look elsewhere for a steady inflow of supplementary cash (e.g., husband/partner, children).

If the women's definition of their work is taken into account, then almost 90 percent of the women in these samples can be described as workers. Two-thirds of that number are engaged in work activities that yield a monetary income, the remaining third being work without monetary reward. To translate this into conventional terminology, when home production activities are taken into account, general worker rates in these samples increase from 44.2 to 53.9 in Barbados, 48.3 to 62.6 in Antigua, and 32.6 to 48.6 in St. Vincent. The inclusion of home service activities increases the rates still further.

The second measure of women's work adopted by WICP is the amount of time spent in various work activities. Time is the one commodity women respondents do not have to spare. Decisions about the choice of techniques should therefore be based on achieving a balance between data reliability and genuine concern for the time constraints of respondents. The WICP opted to rely heavily on the interviewers' ability to obtain reasonable responses and their ability to record an assessment of the reliability of the response. This was supplemented by similar inputs from project researchers on the second round of interviews, and from one particular sector study, that of unemployed women, where participation observation techniques over a series of interviews were used to match data given in the first round of interviews (Barrow 1986b). The aim was to pursue two questions: "Which of your activities would you describe as work?" and "Which of these activities bring in money for you?"

The activity schedules of the women in this study reflect the considerable portion of their daily waking hours spent in activities they describe as work.[13] In an average 16-hour day, women who have a job are away from home for at least eight hours in connection with that activity. A further two to four hours are spent on household chores and related activity. Those who combine their job with home handicraft or agriculture are likely to spend another two hours on that activity. Little time is available for personal care or leisure activity. In the case of the latter group, however, there appears to be greater flexibility in organizing schedules in order to devote more time to home service activities. The women who are solely engaged in home service spend about eight hours in those activities. Where an infant or very young child is present, this increases home service activities to almost 12 hours, with another hour or two added if the woman engages in home production.

---

[13]The discussion on time use is based solely on the data from the 38 life histories. No tabular presentation is offered on account of the small numbers involved.

The day of these women is considerably fractionated, with frequent shifts from one activity to another, each one taking relatively short periods of time. However, this process permits a type of task allocation which ensures opportunity for rest and relaxation that is unattainable for the other women. But this advantage is offset by the extent to which these women are dependent on someone else — usually the husband/partner — for the economic livelihood of themselves and their children, a point that will be pursued later.

Given the women's definition of what constitutes work, it is evident that approximately three-quarters of their daily waking hours are devoted to work activities.[14] The remaining hours are devoted to personal care and leisure activities. Among the latter are included such activities as maintaining contact with friends and relatives, participating in community activities, including activities which Papanek has labeled family status-production work. If the time spent on these activities is also included in the accounting, then the proportion of the woman's daily time spent in work activities increases further. An initial approximation of the daily workload of the women in this study would suggest that 80 percent of their daily lives is spent in work activities.

Why Do Women Work?

When this question is raised, it is usually in the context of work for pay in the formal labor force. In many industrialized countries, where female economic activity rates have increased markedly since the 1950s, increasing levels of educational attainment, increasing use of sophisticated contraceptive techniques, rising costs of living, growing numbers of female-headed households, and increasing self-awareness are some of the reasons advanced. All of these factors operate to varying degrees in developing countries and influence the participation of women in the formal sector of the labor force.

But there are other factors to be considered. In the Caribbean, where female labor force participation rates tend to be relatively high compared to those prevailing in other parts of the developing world, an important consideration relates to the family structure. Unlike many societies, marriage is not the only type of family union in the Caribbean, and it does not necessarily denote the initiation of childbearing. At least three types of family union may be identified: marriage, which involves legal sanction and coresidence; common law, in which the partners share a common household but the union is not legally sanctioned[15]; and visiting, in which there is a regular sexual relationship but neither coresidence nor legal sanction. The latter

[14]Variables such as number of children, age of youngest child, and woman's employment status exert minimal influence on averages.

[15]Some territories, notably Jamaica and Barbados, have been moving in the direction of legalizing common law unions by protecting the inheritance rights of children born to those unions and of women who have been in such a union for a specified period prior to the death of the male partner.

must be distinguished from casual unions in which there is no steady relationship. Childbearing takes place in any of the union types.

Over a woman's life span she may move from one type of union to another, changing or not changing partners as she wishes, always in quest of a more permanent and secure status. Invariably, her children move with her. Because of the informality and fluidity of these procedures, Caribbean women are compelled to seek out sources of livelihood other than exclusive reliance on the male partner. Often he may not be resident; often his household contribution, if available, may be insufficient; often he may be unemployed; very often he is unwilling to contribute. The women's strategies therefore must be sufficiently flexible to allow them to fulfill their domestic and maternal roles while at the same time being firm enough to ensure some level of reliability and continuity. Reciprocal kinship and neighborhood arrangements support such a strategy but do not substitute for a steady source of income when monetary contributions from male partners are erratic, inadequate, or nonexistent.

Where such women have capitalized on the advantages provided by improved education and the increasing availability of occupational opportunities, they have been able to enter and remain in the formal sector of the labor force in relatively high numbers. Both census and WICP data indicate female worker rates of over 40 percent, which is relatively high compared with rates prevailing elsewhere in the developing world. Among women in the WICP samples who are wage/salary earners, over 30 percent held their present job for periods ranging between one year and five years, another 20 percent for periods of five to nine years, and a further 25 percent for periods of ten years and over. This indicates a high level of job stability and presumably a regular source of income. Both census and WICP data demonstrate that worker rates for women in visiting unions and women no longer in a family union are consistently higher than those obtaining for women in residential unions. For these women a steady job is a necessity. In the words of one respondent, "That idea [that a woman's place is in the home] was all right in the days when the man brought in enough to feed the family. But that is no longer possible—not if you want to educate your children and provide what we call the basic necessities for them."

However, a considerable number, indeed the majority of women, are either not engaged in any form of economic activity or are restricted to small-scale, low-status moneymaking activities with limited rates of return and no provision for social security, pension, and other benefits enjoyed by those in paid employment. In the WICP samples, the number of such women ranged from 40 percent in Antigua to 56 percent in St. Vincent. These women's ability to achieve paid employment, though highly valued, is constrained by their lack of time—partly because of childcare responsibilities, by their perceptions of the costs and benefits of home-based moneymaking activities, and by the attitudes of their male partners. However, because their financial contribution is necessary, whether as the primary or a supplementary source of household support, they do find some form of economic activity. But as soon as sufficient and reasonably reliable support becomes available from other sources, they cease that activity (Barrow 1986b). As the children leave school, find their own employment, and begin contributing to the household, the woman can devote herself more systematically to the matter of economic activity.

A second major reason why Caribbean women work for pay relates to the high valuation they attach to their independence (Barrow 1986a, 1986b; Brodber 1986). As used by the respondents in the study, this term implies economic or financial independence derived from having their own source of income in order to avoid dependence for support on others, particularly male partners—"me want me own money."[16] Women see an independent income as a means of avoiding, or at least reducing their vulnerability to their menfolk and of lessening the need to indulge in submissiveness as a strategy to achieve their own goals.

To obtain a regular and adequate flow of income women adopt a range of strategies in which paid employment, small business operations, and money-making activities play a leading, but not singular role. Other sources include the current partner, past partners who fathered children, older children, remittances from relatives overseas, gifts from local relatives, and, if all else fails, welfare payments and unemployment benefits. Most of the money is spent on food, clothing, and utilities, while any savings are used in household emergencies. Considerable pride is expressed in the woman's capacity to support herself and contribute financially to the upkeep of the household.

The nonremunerative aspects of women's work, child care, and household chores are regarded by both sexes as squarely within the province of female familial responsibility. Assistance with these tasks is neither readily forthcoming nor readily requested from male partners, many of whom are not even resident in the same household.[17] Household management which requires the harnessing and redistribution of available resources to meet familial and personal needs is also perceived to be the ultimate responsibility of the woman, both by the men—"My work is to bring the money, and she must hurt she [sic] head to decide how to make ends meet"—and by women—"You know you have to do it, so you do it."

WICP data indicate that decisions about questions related to childbearing, child rearing, and financial transactions outside the household are generally made on an egalitarian basis in married unions and are woman-

16Economic independence is to be distinguished from personal autonomy, a term that may be used to describe the ability to make and act on one's own decisions and generally to control one's own life. In contrast to the term "independence," which was constantly used by respondents, the term "personal autonomy" was coined to paraphrase a range of qualities which the women describe as being contingent on the much desired independence. A fundamental prerequisite to such autonomy is having one's own income.

17About one-fifth of the samples claimed to have no help with household tasks. Another fifth claimed help from their partners either singly or together with other persons. Most help came from children, especially girls, and from mothers.

dominated in other types of union (Powell 1986). Decisions about the collection and disbursement of money and other resources, about the use of kinship and friendship networks, and about the satisfaction of household needs are the women's area of authority. Thus even in the context of a patriarchal value system, women acquire a measure of power and influence that assures them of their own self-worth — "I do what I want."

CONCLUSION

The WICP argues that female familial responsibility rests not only on the ability of women to earn a living but also on their ability to exploit available social opportunities to maintain their households (Barrow 1986b; Durant-Gonzalez 1982). This involves the utilization of kin and friendship networks (Powell 1986; Barrow 1986b; Brodber 1986) institutional mechanisms (Jackson 1982); organizational and group membership (Clarke 1986); and partner relationships (Barrow 1986b; Brodber 1986; Powell 1986). The aim is to draw on these sources for goods, services, knowledge and money, either singly or in different combinations, in order to enhance their ability to meet their daily commitments. In the process women are involved in a range of activities which they describe as work and which go unmeasured in conventional statistics but which are an integral aspect of the social reality of Caribbean life.

Evidence from the vast literature on women's work around the world suggests that the statistical discounting of all aspects of women's work is not unique to the Caribbean. However, the context is different in that the gender-relations system in which it functions reflects relative autonomy between the sexes and a fair amount of interdependence while at the same time embodying areas of conflict between the two groups. It is a system based on what has been described as "inconsistencies and contradictions" (LeFranc 1983) which reflect an interplay between Euro-centrered and Afro-centered influences acted out in varying contexts.

A major conclusion of the WICP study is that the interaction between varying contextual factors and the two value systems of Europe and Africa has engendered both direct and indirect effects on the prevailing gender ideology in the Caribbean (Anderson 1986). The direct effect of the norm of male dominance is to increase female dependence. The indirect effect, mediated by the differing family structures, is to reinforce a gender-based division of labor. But in order to maintain its validity, the model must assume not only that the male is perceived as the economic provider, but also that he is able to discharge that role. The history of the Caribbean provides compelling evidence that the majority of men are seldom able to do this effectively because of the inherent fragility and instability of Caribbean economies. To offset this women have been, and are, compelled to exercise a much greater economic role than the classic patriarchal prescriptions confining women to the household would allow. They do this using the range of strategies described earlier in which work activities represent a continuum along which they move, adopting those activities, or combinations thereof, to the exigencies of their situation at particular times. Shifts from one point to the other on the continuum may be due to changes in the general economy or in the household or personal circumstances of the woman. But the nature of those shifts, the timing, and whether to shift at all are the sole decision of the woman herself.

WICP material suggests that the distinction between the public and private spheres is neither as rigid nor as pervasive as the literature might suggest. Several women in the study who described themselves as household workers were found to be engaged in moneymaking activities to supplement the household income, even if only on a temporary and intermittent basis. So too were others who described themselves as being "at home doing nothing." Yet theories would relegate those moneymaking activities to the "private," nonproductive and hence nonwork, sphere, even though they contribute to the economic sustenance of the woman and her household.

Women in the Caribbean have been balancing their domestic and job-related responsibilities for centuries. This has been documented with respect to the period of slavery (Mair 1974; Massiah 1981) as well as for contemporary times (Massiah 1986a; Powell 1986) and suggests that for Caribbean women the two roles are not inherently contradictory. Perhaps the most insightful contribution of the WICP data to this issue is the women's perception of these two roles. For them there is no real distinction. Mothering is important as an indicator of true womanhood. Earning one's own money is important as a source of household support—including the support of one's children—in addition to its importance as an indicator of a woman's independence. Thus for these women the question is not whether, or how, to combine their maternal and economic roles, since there is no real distinction between the two. For them the question is how to manipulate available circumstances to ensure economic support for themselves and their dependents for whom they assume ultimate responsibility. This may or may not include actual involvement in moneymaking activities; it certainly involves changing strategies and sources of support as alternatives expand or contract. But, most importantly, these strategies demonstrate the critical role economic uncertainty plays in determining how women are able to perform two of the critical functions society expects of them.

15

The Imminent Demise of Patriarchy

KEN KUSTERER

In 1972 Dalla Costa and James published an influential piece that asserted among other things that what housewives did was productive work, necessary to the reproduction of capitalism. By implication, housewives were central to women's struggles, part of the working class, wielders of the power to strike and deserving of wages for their work. The theoretical and strategic implications of this position were drawn out by Federici (1973) and others of the "wages for housework" school. Their work was for a time highly influential, a high-water mark in the elaboration of Marxist feminist theory.

But over the next decade, Marxist political economists heavily criticized the idea that housework was productive work in a capitalist social formation. A series of articles dealing with the issue appeared in the *New Left Review* (Gardiner 1975; Secombe 1974) and in the special women's issues of the *Review of Radical Political Economics* (Fee 1976; Nazzari 1980; Quick 1977). By the 1980s a consensus had emerged among these writers that housework was not productive work in the technical sense, that housewives were not part of the working class in the technical sense, and that their work, although necessary for capitalism, was not technically within the capitalist mode of production. Though Hartmann (1979) and others whose first allegiance was to feminist rather than Marxist theory objected, by the 1980s most Marxist political economists were satisfied that their understanding of housewives and housework within a capitalist social formation was now technically correct and theoretically sophisticated.

I agree. They were technically correct and theoretically sophisticated — and also essentially incorrect and fundamentally irrelevant. The basic challenge of feminists to Marxist theory — to explain the subjugation of women as a necessary step toward ending it — had been ignored, at the same time as the errors in Marxist interpretation by those who took up the challenge had been corrected. Though most of the guardians of Marxist theoretical purity on this issue were in fact women, a paternalist image nevertheless comes to mind in which the feminists' challenge is ignored while they are sent to read ever more esoteric passages of Marx's posthumously published work (*Theories of Surplus Value*, mainly) until they get their theoretical language straight.

Not surprisingly, by the late 1980s Marxist theory is widely considered to be in crisis. Rigorous concepts and precise language are important to theory, but so is the imagination and innovation necessary to address fundamental issues. Central to the crisis of Marxist theory today is its inability to say much of theoretical or strategic significance to the struggles of women. But, as most Marxist intellectuals realize, Marxist theory must explain the subjugation of women, for unless it does so, it can no longer claim to be either a theory or a practice of *human* liberation.

Phase one of any reconstruction of a Marxist theory of women's liberation must be a recognition of some basics that feminist theory since Mitchell (1971) and our own experience tell us. Women's subjugation is rooted not in capitalism, which it long predates, but in patriarchy; not in the wage relations between capitalist and worker, to which gender is essentially irrelevant, but in the domestic relations between men and women; not in the workplace, where sexism is but one of many forms of division and discrimination, but in the patriarchal household where gender roles are the essence of the division of labor. Nevertheless, the theory must also avoid the dualistic division between capitalism on the one hand and patriarchy on the other that feminist theorists have been decrying since the early 1980s (Young 1981).

This chapter outlines such a reconstruction of Marxist theory. It is divided into two parts. There is first a theoretical explanation of a domestic mode of production and its articulation with capitalism. This theory, a third-generation attempt to create a Marxist theory of women's oppression, is centered in the concept of a domestic mode of production. It could be called "domestic-mode-of-production" theory, but the name is long and awkward. It will be called *demop theory* instead, as an abbreviation that works as a slogan as well. Second, there is an overview of some key implications of the theory for the Marxist, feminist, and women in development practice of those who seek to build justice. The *imminent demise* of the title is foreseen in the theory but will happen later rather than sooner without more conscious practice.

AN OUTLINE OF DEMOP THEORY

The central idea that lifts Marxist theory up to a new plateau of conceptualizing women's subjugation, that puts patriarchy into a central position while avoiding dualism, is the idea developed to understand capitalist social formations in the Third World, the articulation of modes of production. As a response to dependency theory that avoids the old Marxist error of dualism between capitalism and "precapitalist remnants," articulation theory has sought to understand Third World social formations as articulations of a dominant capitalist mode of production and subordinant precapitalist modes. Feudalism and the Asiatic mode of production are those most often described, but less orthodox modes have also been described, including the petty commodity mode, the peasant mode, and the kinship mode (deJanvry 1981; Rey 1973; Taylor 1979).

The difference between older dualistic Marxist views and the new articulationist perspective, first voiced by Laclau (1971), is that earlier theorists saw capitalism as temporarily coexisting with precapitalist modes in the Third World. There was no real connection between the two. The precapitalist mode would struggle but eventually disappear as capitalism inevitably expanded. Articulationists noted that in many Third World societies, precapitalist modes were not disappearing and were sometimes even being strengthened by the growth of capitalism. These "social formations" consisted of two or more modes of production, each with their own "base" of economic organization but supporting one more-or-less coherent "superstructure" of legal and ideological institutions. Far from being distinct and antagonistic modes, capitalism and its articulated modes formed one whole socioeconomic system, functional for the capitalist mode at its present level but potentially hindering its further development.

Curiously and dishearteningly, the most widespread subordinate mode of production in the Third World—as also in the First and the Second—has been overlooked in the articulationist literature. This is household production of use values for consumption or accumulation within the household, the domestic, or the patriarchal mode of production. The reason for this oversight is in most cases probably simple sexist domain assumptions, but there is also the mainstream Marxist tradition that makes it hard to see social formations as made up of more than one mode of production, unless a society is clearly in a transitional phase from the dominance of one mode to the dominance of another (Taylor 1979). This emphasis on articulation as a transitory phase is one of the reasons that the most sophisticated review of the development-oriented mode of production literature (Booth 1985) ends up dismissing its utility, as does the Marxist feminist theorist, who most carefully reviews the idea of a domestic mode of production in advanced capitalist social formations (Vogel 1983).

Looking at housework as part of a subordinate mode of production gives us a new angle of vision that transforms that old debate about its productive or class character. Looked at this way, the "politics of housework" (Mainardi 1970) will come to be seen not as the peripheral and semiamusing side issue that most Marxists have presumed it to be, but as the central arena of an important class struggle that some feminist theorists and many feminist women have known it to be. But here the conclusion anticipates the argument. First, what are the contents of domestic production, and what are the production relations involved?

Domestic production has been called invisible work primarily because its products are not priced and traded in the public arena. But it has remained invisible to mainstream, Marxist, and even many feminist social scientists, too, because of two ideologically contaminated concepts too often used to analyze domestic activity. These two ideological veils, so thick as to be virtual blindfolds, that have prevented social scientists from seeing domestic production are the categories of consumption and reproduction.

Production and Consumption

Mainstream economists as well as Marxists have failed to see that both production and consumption are moments of a continuous process from extraction of the raw materials of nature to their final human use and return to nature. We decide where on the continuum to think of production having ended and consumption having begun only by social convention.

The convention among economists is to draw the line in the marketplace, where the product is transferred to the "final consumer," who does not intend to process it further and return it to the market for another resale. This convention, like most of those of neoclassic economists and too many of those of Marxist economists, is based on the workings of the capitalist mode of production. It assumes both that any further processing outside of capitalist relations of production is not significant and also that any further nonmarket transfers are not significant. These assumptions, to say the least, are not helpful to the analyses of people's production and consumption within the domestic mode of production or to the social relations of production within it.

But these economists' assumptions are understandable, as they are only direct extensions of a common attitude that I view as a central support to the ideological superstructure of the patriarchal mode of production, a falsely placed and falsely rigid separation between production and consumption. All extradomestic economic activity is seen as production, work, serving, social contribution; all domestic activity is seen as consumption, leisure, using, private appropriation. Extradomestic production adds use values to society; domestic consumption takes them away again. It takes almost a paradigm shift to recognize that all production is also consumption — and that, as Marx says, all consumption is also production (of labor power), but that is an issue best held for later.

If for purposes of analysis we must distinguish production from consumption, the only possible dividing line is after the last activity that added more utility to the product than it consumed and before the first activity that consumed more value than it added. Where is that? Perhaps an example will help.

Take a chicken egg, always a favorite example when a discourse threatens to get too abstract. It is apparently a natural food, yet it takes the work of many to get it from its hen to its consumer. Where does this productive work end and consumption begin? When the last wage worker checked it out of the supermarket into the hands of the domestic worker? But what use value does it have there in the supermarket? It must be transported home, an

activity no different from the productive work of others who had transported it along the earlier stages of its journey. It has more use value at home
than it did in the supermarket, so hauling it home is productive work. Once
home, someone unpacks the groceries and stores the egg into the refrigerator. Work? It was when the egg was put into cold storage two or three times
before, so it must be now. After all, if it adds use value to the egg to
transport it to where it is needed, it also adds value to preserve it until when
it is needed.

A few days later someone takes the egg out of the refrigerator and makes
herself an omelet. Is that production or consumption? What if a wife who
doesn't even like omelets makes it for her husband? In both cases, it's still
processing, still adding use value, still production. Sometimes, of course,
people use the egg as a raw ingredient for much more complex foods.
Sometimes these are consumed at once, sometimes frozen for use much
later. No matter—all of this activity is still production, still work. Once
finally readied to eat, the food must be served, whether onto plates for a
meal "at home" or into bags for a meal "at work." Still more use value
added, more production, more work. Even when food is set on the plate in
front of their faces, some members of the household—the infant and the
infirm—need more use value added to it, more work from someone, before
they can consume it.

The division between production and consumption is a matter of arbitrary convention. Different conventions will serve different ideological purposes. Whoever's ideological interest is served by drawing that line between
the capitalist and the domestic economy, it is obviously not the household
workers'. If we want to understand the nature of production and the relations of production within the household, it is obvious that the line must be
drawn much further along the chain of production–consumption. Why not
place it where logic would seem to require? As long as an activity adds rather
than subtracts use value, I am going to call that activity production and the
social relations involved in that activity, relations of production.

Production and Reproduction

Such multiple and overlapping confusions surround Marxist and feminist
uses of the term reproduction that one despairs of ever cutting through. But
one must, for it is the false distinction between production and reproduction
that has fogged even the most serious feminist analyses of the domestic
mode of production (Gardiner 1975; Sokoloff 1980; Vogel 1983).

Reproduction is one of the central concepts of Marx's political economy.
He devotes several chapters of Volumes 1 and 2 of *Capital* to an analysis of
its various forms. It is worth noting that he is discussing something that
takes place in all modes of production, and that the bulk of his analysis is
devoted to understanding how it happens in the capitalist mode of production specifically. In general he means by reproduction an ongoing process of
production by which a society each day simultaneously (1) replaces the
material goods which it has consumed; (2) puts back into its stock of pro-

ductive capital ("means of production") at least as much as has been depreciated; and (3) reinforces or recreates the institutional structure ("relations of production") by once again perpetuating the work role experiences of the past into the present.

Working in this tradition, the modern Marxist writer Pearlman can write his brilliant essay, "The Reproduction of Daily Life," without ever referring to any modern economic activity outside of capitalist relations of production (1969). For Marxist political economy before it began to address the question of household work, all social production was at the same time social reproduction — of the material necessities of life, of the means of production, and of the relations of production.

Feminist theorists, on the other hand, have a less abstract idea in mind when they refer to reproduction. At root they mean the literal reproduction of humans as individuals and as a species. Marxist feminists do not stray far from that root idea when they talk about women reproducing the labor force from generation to generation. When they talk of reproducing the labor force from day to day, however, they come closer to the traditional Marxist usage. But they think of it as something that happens exclusively in households, no less than Pearlman thinks of it as something that happens exclusively in plants and offices.

Marx's original understanding, that every act of production is necessarily at the same time an act of social and economic reproduction, is one of the three roads out of this mess. The relation of patriarchal household to capitalist firm is not that reproduction takes place in the former and production in the latter. Both are at the same time productive and reproductive organizations. The social and economic reproduction that takes place in the household could not happen without the production that takes place there also. Likewise, capitalist production would be impossible without capitalist reproduction. Whatever the articulation between these two modes of production, it is nothing so simple as the traditional idea that households do the reproduction for capitalism.

The second and third roads are the elimination from Marxism of two peculiarly male misunderstandings of the nature of production. One is the Victorian, antiecological distinction between productive work, which adds new use values by creating new things, and reproductive work, which merely maintains the use value of already existing things. If Marx and other Marxist men had done more of the latter kind of work, they might have realized that there really is such a thing as entropy. Things once separated from nature by human labor require constant continuing inputs of human labor to keep them from returning to nature. There is no physical, metaphysical, or economic difference between the two kinds of work. Both use up labor power to add use value to their product. Workers who make new bottles from sand and workers who clean and recycle old bottles are both productive workers. Similarly, factory workers who make new chairs and household workers who clean, refinish, and repair old chairs are both productive workers. The Victorian view has contributed enough to the devastation of the world's resources; there is no need for Marxist feminists to concur in it at this late date.

In a similar and related way, many Marxists have had a vulgar materialist perspective that denied the productive nature of much service work. The idea here is a radical distinction between the assumed durability of labor power embodied in material products and the assumed nondurability of labor power embodied in enhanced human beings or social organizations. While useful for limited purposes, the distinction is basically false, dependent on the denial of entropy on the one hand and on the denial of the importance of human and organizational "forces of production" on the other. This was another sexist assumption that consigned much of women's work to a secondary role of "reproductive" activities, because women do a disproportionate share of the work of maintaining and enhancing the capacities of workers and work organizations. Overcoming it is the third road to clear understanding of productive work and the social and economic reproduction it performs.

Relations of Production in the Domestic Mode

Thus housework is production, not reproduction or consumption. In fact, it has been argued that even in an advanced capitalist economy like the United States, "The household sector consumes roughly the same number of work hours as the market sector, and . . . produces an income in kind estimated somewhere between 25% and 50% of the GNP" (Goldschmidt-Clermont 1983:109). I will return to the implications of all this work later, but first it is useful to describe the relations of production within which it takes place, to see who produces these use values and who receives them as "income," in Goldschmidt-Clermont's terminology.

The central relations of production in any mode of production, and the ones that need to be analyzed first, are those between the class of direct producers and nonproducers in that mode. Here the emphasis must be on the mechanisms of expropriation that channel the surplus labor products of the producers into the hands of the nonproducers (Laclau 1971). In analyzing feudalism, we focus on the relations of exploitation between lords and serfs; in capitalism, between capitalists and workers. Though it is evident that in the domestic mode of production the producers are women and the nonproducers men, as housework surveys have shown us ad nauseam (e.g., Berk & Berk 1979), we lack a more precise vocabulary for describing the working and leisure classes of the domestic mode of production.

We need one, since we are talking here not about biological sexes or gender roles of all men or all women but about class positions some men and some women hold in the domestic mode of production. I propose to call those in the working class of the domestic mode of production "dependents" and those in the leisure class "heads of households." In doing so, I am using the terms commonly and legally applied to these roles before the women's movement began to call into question the legal and ideological superstructure that once supported this mode of production. In using the terms, I am

not implying that household subordinates are "really" or normatively dependent on their household heads, any more than an analyst of feudalism or
slavery is implying that serfs or slaves are "really" or normatively unfree
and dependent on their lords or masters. In a sense, of course, the relations of dependence are actually the reverse, since leisure classes are always
more dependent for their survival on the cooperation of producing classes
than vice versa.

The domestic or patriarchal mode of production is defined, then, as that
system of household labor in which household members produce use values
for direct consumption or accumulation within the household. It is an exploitative mode of production because the labor is almost wholly produced
by the female dependents within the household and because the male head
of household is therefore expropriating surplus labor when he consumes the
use values produced by his dependents. He benefits from this relation of
exploitation both in the use values he appropriates and in the leisure time
resulting from the necessary labor time he forgoes. As for any other mode,
the domestic mode of production should be understood to include not only
the direct relations of production and expropriation but also other social
and ideological activities necessary to sustain and reproduce the domestic
mode of production. As we shall see, these include most sexist attitudes and
actions that have the effect of keeping women in their place — as dependents
in a male-headed household.

Why Do Women Stay Home and Do Men's Housework?

A summary description of the economic "base" of the domestic mode of
production is this: women dependents produce most of the goods and services their household heads demand, even though they receive little or nothing in return. Why? What compels them to do this? A "superstructure" of
the same forms of power that generally force subordinates to forgo their
own self-interest for the benefit of their superiors: economic, legal, and
ideological sanctions backed by the threat of force. Let's examine these.

The principal economic force that has compelled women to work as
household dependents has been the denial to women of access to ownership
of their own means of domestic production, a physical residence outfitted
with the necessary household tools and furnishings. Before the full subordination of the domestic to the capitalist mode of production, this denial was
accomplished by legal and ideological norms that prevented all women (with
the exception of some widows) from establishing themselves as independent
heads of their own households. As is the general tendency within capitalism,
these extraeconomic norms have been replaced to some extent by economic
mechanisms: the denial to household dependents of access to cash or credit
necessary to rent or purchase the means of domestic production. It is therefore indispensable to the reproduction of the domestic mode of production
and to the continued extraction of surplus labor from dependents that wom-
en be permitted access to sufficient cash or credit to rent or buy a house or
apartment only in conjunction with their household heads. In my opinion,

this requirement of the domestic mode, and not any necessity internal to capitalism, is the principal basis for the persistence of sexist practices denying to women equal employment, comparable pay, or equal small business credit.

Preventing women from establishing themselves as their own heads of households is the most fundamental means to reproduce the domestic mode of production. It is analogous to the necessity for capitalism that laborers be free from owning their own means of production, thereby forcing them to become and remain proletarians. Once women can acquire households of their own — and capitalism combined with the women's movement has gone far in the United States toward making this possible — the domestic mode of production is threatened. Women, choosing poverty over patriarchy, begin to establish their own headless households.

But if this is why women live in households with men, why do they take on the role of dependents whose surplus labor provides for the consumption needs of a man, making him into a nonproducing household head? This is the area where most of the sociology of gender roles is applicable. Gender role norms, once embodied in law but now largely legitimized only by ideology, lead women to believe that the performance of this surplus labor is a "natural" and inevitable aspect of their gender roles as women, or of their family roles as wives and mothers, or of their roles as partners in a heterosexual love relationship. These ideologies constitute the norm of what Nazzari (1980) called the support/service marriage, and I agree that they are seriously undermined only when the household dependents join their household heads in "supporting" the household by entering the work force of the capitalist labor market, something which they are now doing in unprecedented proportions.

So potent are these ideologies that even the most liberated woman must make a conscious effort not to feel shame or guilt when the household head's human needs are not met after she ceases to perform this surplus labor, and he prefers dirt and deprivation to doing laundry. Yet even so, the United States is ahead of less developed countries in the delegitimization of these ideologies. I have frequently had the opportunity to lecture on American family life to visiting groups of professional men and women from Asia, Africa, and Latin America. Members of these groups, whether male or female, seem unable to comprehend that man's human needs are not "by nature" woman's responsibility to fulfill any more than her needs are his responsibility.

This is the arena for the politics of housework (Mainardi 1970), the class struggle between household heads and dependents in the domestic mode of production. Labor is necessary to sustain and reproduce males and females. Contrary to most Marxist feminist theory so far, the necessity for household dependents to perform this labor for household heads no longer stems from any requirement of the capitalist mode of production to reproduce its labor force. At the present stage of development of domestic technology, female proletarians reproduce themselves perfectly well without the benefits of domestic exploitation. No, this exploitation stems from the requirement of the domestic mode of production to reproduce its production relations at the same time as it reproduces its material conditions.

As important as the economic and ideological levels are for the extraction of this forced household surplus labor from women, however, they should not lead us to neglect the most primitive means of compulsion, violence and the threat of violence. Feminist work in family and criminal research has helped us to understand the extent of day-to-day violence to which men subject women within the household and without. Wifebeating permeated the society, was until very recently permitted by law, and for a very large but not yet estimable proportion of household dependents is the source of the fear that is part of the bond tying women to their household heads. Generalized male violence against women, where women are victimized by men outside of their own households, lends ideological and material support to the domestic mode of production by making women unsafe unless "protected" by the presence of their own household head.

Under these conditions, men can exchange protection for exploitation, an exchange that has formed part of the ideological justification for most precapitalist systems of class relations, especially including feudalism. Simple horticultural societies, with their division of labor between warrior men and farmer/worker women, were explicitly organized on this basis worldwide. These societies—which Marx and Engels ironically thought of as primitive communism—were probably the original historical form of the patriarchal mode of production. Organized male violence against women and the necessity for women to live under the domain of one male household head to protect them against random acts of violence of other men have been central to the patriarchal mode of production since its beginnings.

IMPLICATIONS FOR ANTIPATRIARCHAL PRACTICE

Demop theory implies shifts in consciousness and shifts in strategy for Marxists, feminists, and women in development advocates. It is possible to hope for more than we have sometimes dared—the demise of patriarchy, at least in advanced capitalist countries; at the same time it is necessary to reorient our understanding of what hurts and what helps women most. Discussion of some of the more important implications follows.

Implications for Marxist Theory and Practice

One of the signal failings of Marxist theory has been its prediction that the development of capitalism would result in a two-class society of bourgeoisie and proletariat. This was to be the material precondition for a growing solidarity and class consciousness among the working class, the ideological precondition in turn for any transition from capitalism to socialism. This has seldom happened at the national level, let alone the international level, and many plausible explanations have been offered for this. But one of the most plausible explanations has rarely been offered: the effect of multiple modes of production on a society's class structure.

Until now, almost all proletarians have had a substantial portion of their subsistance needs met through the domestic mode of production. Proletarians have in fact almost always occupied simultaneous class positions in two modes of production. For proletarian heads of households, this has meant a leisure-class position in one mode and a working-class position in the other; for proletarian dependents, a working-class position in both. Bourgeois household heads and bourgeois dependents are likewise differentiated. No wonder class solidarity, whether among dependents or among proletarians, has been hard to obtain.

Writing just before the U.S. Civil War, Marx (1860/1974) was of the opinion that the working class in the United States had no possibility of successful organization until slavery was overthrown. I would make the same argument about patriarchy, and I would add that the era in which Marx wrote and this are analagous. Slavery, which had been a functional subordinate mode in capitalism for a hundred years, was no longer needed by a more mature U.S. capitalism looking for an internal labor and wage goods market; abolitionism could finally triumph. Sharecropping feudalism similarly disappeared a century later, accompanied by an outburst of black liberation activity. And now the articulation between capitalism and patriarchy, the oldest and deepest rooted of the archaic modes, is likewise breaking.

On the one hand, capitalism has exported its manufacturing jobs, now needs almost all dependents in its service sector labor force, and seeks to sell the services (like child care, elder care, and household maintenance) the domestic economy has traditionally provided. On the other hand, the utilities and the pharmaceutical industry (Cowan 1983) have so increased the productivity of domestic labor that it is possible for every proletarian to also do his or her own domestic production. This is the material condition that has made possible the dramatic increase of single-adult households (Kusterer 1987b). It is now possible, in the most advanced capitalist countries of the world, to eliminate the domestic mode of production without at the same time having to eliminate the whole capitalist economic formation.

In a famous passage, Marx wrote that each generation takes up the historical task that is available to it (1859/1971). The end of patriarchy is ours. Despite a century of hopeful predictions, capitalism has not yet begun to peak. Patriarchy peaked long ago, and feminists are finishing it off.

Implications for Feminist Theory and Practice

Feminists have often objected to a Marxist theory of female subjugation such as this, disliking both dualism and economism. The articulation concept goes far toward answering the dualism objection, but the essential economism remains. The theory acknowledges the importance of male-to-female violence but conceives it as part of a superstructure supporting patriarchal relations of domestic production. The dimension of feminist theory and female experience that puts males' hostile sexuality at the biopsychological core of men's subjugation of women (Dworkin 1987; Hartsock 1983) will always be deemphasized in Marxist feminism. To many feminists, the Marxist assumption of the centrality of production relations instead of sexual relations seems a case of displaced essence. To any Marxist not fortified with the false concept of false consciousness, this lack of resonance with the material experience of so many women must be troubling. There is still theoretical work to be done.

But there is a striking resonance between feminist practice in the United States and the theory of an articulation of capitalism with a domestic mode of production. From the Fair Credit Act to no-fault divorce to "take back the night,"[1] feminists have fought to remove the obstacles that have made it hard for women to live in households without male heads. From affirmative action to comparable worth, they have fought for more equitable and more complete inclusion into the capitalist mode of production. This disbands the old articulation between capitalism and patriarchy. Women no longer have the need for a household head to gain access to income or the time to perform all the old dependent household services. It is as if the feminist movement had set its priorities according to demop theory. Of course it did not, having neither the theory nor an organizational mechanism for setting priorities. But the resonance with actual feminist practice is reassuring to any Marxist trying to build a feminist theory.

The main contribution of demop theory to future feminist practice must be the explicit disentanglement of the domestic mode of production from parenting and family life (however organized). The domestic mode of production is a historical form; parenting and intimacy are eternal human requirements. A genuine confusion among feminists about what aspects of domestic living we support and what aspects we reject has forced us onto the defensive about family life. The task before us at this juncture is precisely to distinguish life-enhancing love between partners and between parents and their children from soul-deadening domestic servitude. Precisely because it is antipatriarchy, feminism is profamily. Only by eliminating patriarchal exploitation can society preserve a family institution that serves its adult and child members at the same time as it serves society.

Antifeminists will always conflate intimate love and healthy parenting with the patriarchal mode of production. But there is no need for feminists to do so as well. In fact, there is an urgent need for feminists not to do so. Feminists are the ones who are trying to "save" the family by separating it from patriarchy, so that our children may finally have noncoercive and nonviolent homes in which to grow. We cannot convince anyone else of that until we really understand it ourselves.

---

[1]The movement to "take back the night" was an effort in urban centers in many parts of the world to have private households turn on outdoor lights and to bring massive numbers of women out into the streets as a means of publicizing the right of women to use public walkways after dark without fear of violence.

Implications for Women in Development Theory and Practice

The central conundrum of women in development thinking is whether economic development helps or harms the lot of women in developing countries. There is plenty of case study evidence that sometimes it does one and sometimes the other. How can we plan and predict to help women more and harm them less as development proceeds? Feminist arguments so far have concentrated on the necessity of building women's participation into the development-planning process. But articulation theory allows a more analytic approach to the problem as well.

Development harms women when it "domesticates" them, forces them back into the household from economic roles they played outside. This frequently happens as the "unintended" consequence of development projects that provide men employment that displaces informal sector work formerly done by women. Development helps women when it draws them partway out of the domestic economy, providing them an income and an economic life independent of their household patriarch. This, too, frequently happens as the unintended consequence of economic development activities (and too frequently is not an intention of specially designed women in development projects).

To see how and why women are sometimes drawn out of and sometimes pushed back into domestic work by economic development, there must be mention of the modes of production present in most less developed countries' economies. Besides the basic patriarchal mode, much more important in less developed societies where subsistence farming is still the dominant form of food production, there are the capitalist and statist modes contesting for dominance, and two smaller modes, petty commodity and coop socialism. The patriarchal mode has been defined before, and the capitalist mode is generally known. The statist mode refers to goods and services produced by government entities for distribution as they choose. The petty commodity mode involves production for the market, but by microenterprises without nonfamily wage labor. It is more or less synonymous with the informal sector of a country's economy. Coop socialism is production by church-based or community nonprofit organizations or cooperatives, more or less participatively managed.

The status quo ante of economic development today is that most domestic work is done by women, that most petty commodity microenterprises are run by women (Liedholm & Meed 1987; Tinker 1987), that the statist and coop modes overwhelmingly employ men unless an extraordinary conscious effort has been made to employ women, and that the capitalist mode has a noncompetitive state-regulated import-substitution sector that employs males at high wages and a competitive (often export-oriented) sector that employs women at low wages. In other words, "unplanned" work in the informal sector of domestic and petty commodity modes and in the competitive sector of the capitalist mode is done mostly by unpaid or low-paid women. "Planned" work in the state, coop, and noncompetitive capitalist modes is done mostly by high-paid men. This is not a coincidence.

State and Coop/Socialist Modes

Though there is no reason state agencies and nonprofits should not hire women, the people running them are part of the local culture based on patriarchy. Usually these cultures have ethical hooks on which feminists can hang their equity arguments; but these seldom influence people who are unconvinced that it is good for either society or women themselves to work outside the home. Development projects that expand either statist or coop modes may well do so at the expense of informal sector women who used to provide these goods and services. For example, government food distribution shops hire men and displace ten times their number in market women. Even PVO (Private Voluntary Organization) food distribution organizations usually have the same effect.

Women in development practitioners have countered this tendency by demanding female employment on individual projects, by arguing that only female employees can be effective when the agency provides services to women, and by encouraging the creation of parallel women's nonprofit organizations. There are many case studies where these efforts have succeeded well. But it's a slow, project-by-project progression upstream against the undiverted current of patriarchy.

Many U.S. women in development practitioners have strong ideological commitments to the coop/socialist mode of production, just as many of their counterparts in developing countries have strong ideological commitments to the statist mode. Often these practitioners see themselves as building socialism. Even if the socialism built seldom lives up to expectations, much can be done within these modes, usually from a base in parallel women's organizations or in "women-oriented" state agencies, to directly assist women in breaking out of their patriarchal household economies. Most frequently this has involved helping women develop strong self-esteem, literacy/numeracy, health/nutrition, birth planning, and other human capacities necessary to shift labor time out of the domestic economy.

The demop perspective, though, would insist that women in development practitioners working in these modes should recognize two things. One, all this work is effective only insofar as it actually helps women break out of patriarchy. None of it, even basic health care and birth control information, will do as much good if it remains an end in itself. Two, the modes in which they are working are, at least so far, part of the problem, not part of the solution. Building the state or building a community organization has no necessary connection whatsoever with ending patriarchy. An important part of their work must be the constant battle, within and among organizations and agencies, to neutralize their legal and ideological support for the maintenance of the patriarchal mode of production.

The Petty Commodity Mode

A second approach has been to go to the one mode where women predominate and where poor women obtain most of whatever cash income they do earn, the petty commodity mode. The idea here is to identify and eliminate the obstacles to microenterprise expansion to increase the income of female microentrepreneurs. The basic idea is sound, and the potential exists to help many women move from barely productive and poorly compensated work in this mode to a more substantial and economically independent role.

But who is going to provide the credits or training deemed necessary? Private markets have thus far failed to do this anywhere, so the answer will be either the state or nonprofit mode. The chances are slim to none that these modes will not treat preferentially the largest (mostly male) level of microentrepreneurs, who are the most visible and easiest to serve. Either strict quota systems or parallel female organizations will be necessary to ensure women equal access to these resources; neither approach has been an unproblematic solution to similar problems in the developed world. The essential difficulty here is trying to design a planned intervention into a heretofore unplanned sector, and having it actually serve women, when the track record shows that planned sectors have always been the more economically discriminatory environments for women.

A newer idea, based on deSoto's work in Peru (1989), would help microentrepreneurs primarily by removing licensing and regulatory obstacles that prevent them from growing organically into larger capitalist firms. At least this gives no state or nonprofit agency the ability to skew distribution of resources away from women, but it does mean that according to its own neoclassical economic theory, the microenterprises entering the new competition with more assets (i.e., male microenterprises) will be advantaged to expand at the expense of those with fewer assets (i.e., female microenterprises). Yet this approach has much promise for women, because many female microenterprises will thrive and because many times more women will have new employment opportunities as microenterprises emerge to become competitive sector capitalist firms.

The Domestic Mode

"WID ghetto" projects started out in the early 1970s working with women as domestic dependents. Then they shifted to income-generating projects, a good direction to move, but unfortunately most did not generate much income (Buvinic 1986). There is important work to be done with women in their capacities as dependents in the patriarchal mode, but the goal of this work has not been well conceptualized. One of the material preconditions for the withdrawal of women's labor from the domestic mode of production is a dramatic increase in the productivity of their household labor. This has been thought to have been accomplished by two principal mechanisms, "labor-saving" household machinery and export of tasks into the monetary economy (milling, soapmaking, etc.). But Cowan (1983) showed in the U.S.

case that the first mechanism raises household standards more than it reduces labor time and the second merely shifts labor time from household
manufacturing to shopping and transport. Both tend to improve the quality
of life of the household and make the household work slightly less physically
demanding, but neither actually reduces labor time much or raises its productivity.

So what does raise housework productivity? Cowan points out two factors. The first and most important is "utilization." No single act so reduces
household labor time as the bringing of water and fuel to the household.
Carrying water and gathering fuel are two of the most labor-intensive and
time-consuming tasks in the domestic economy. Utilization not only saves
this labor but saves labor in myriad other household tasks where a more
generous use of water or heat can clean or process things faster with less
work. The second factor, surprisingly, is simple pharmaceutical drugs. Some
of the time aspirin saves lives, but all of the time it greatly reduces the actual
time needed to care for the feverishly ill to bring their temperature down. In
poverty environments, caring for the sick can take a very high proportion of
a household's available dependent labor power.

At least as important as these productivity enhancers are improvements in
household human capital. Literacy, numeracy, and access to home economics information also lead to increased labor productivity as they build self-
esteem and broaden access to extrahousehold income opportunities. These
basic women in development project activities are no less important from
the articulationist perspective than they are from any other. What this perspective adds to traditional WID thought is insight into the importance of
potable water, new fuels, and electrification as crucial WID activities. Wom-
en cannot move out of the patriarchal economy until investments in physical
and human infrastructure have increased the productivity of their domestic
labor.

The Capitalist Mode

The fact that women are concentrated disproportionately in the low-wage
competitive sector of the capitalist mode has sparked a debate. Should this
sector be regulated also to raise women's wages to levels near men's? To do
so would make the sector internationally noncompetitive, as the regulated-
and-protected import-substitution sector already is. The dynamism and
growth of the sector would die, and the present articulation of capitalism
with the state and domestic modes would be frozen for as long as the state
subsidies could sustain it.

The possibilities for decoupling capitalism from the patriarchal mode in
developing countries can grow only with a long-term expansion of capitalist
employment and production. For countries with internal markets smaller
than China or India, this almost certainly requires that capitalist production
remain internationally competitive and therefore no more regulated than the
international norm. But what kind of so-called Marxist feminism is this?
Women's pay and working conditions in the world's clothing, electronic

assembly, and agribusiness factories are awful by any civilized standard. The only proposal here is expansion of these kinds of factories and this kind of work.

The standard needed to assess women's work in these plants is not any civilized standard but the one the women themselves apply, comparison to work in the patriarchal mode (Kusterer, Xuya Cuxil, & Estrada de Batres 1981). This is the concrete application of the theoretical argument a few pages back that the patriarchal mode may be overcome in our lifetimes and that the capitalist mode will not. Further, eliminating patriarchy requires that capitalist growth not be held back to stagnate its present articulation with patriarchy in the developing world. Fortunately for women, capitalism prefers cheap, productively disciplined workers. And in the developing world, the patriarchal mode is a much more reliable source of this kind of worker than any mode in which men have been engaged. Competitive sector capitalist firms hire women preferentially without feminists even having to make an argument, and without regard for the damage done to local, patriarchy-supporting cultural traditions.

Let these firms do their historical work. Their employees see working there as a step up, not a step down. Third World feminists are right when they ask their First World sisters why the jobs are bad for Third World women and yet so good for First World women that protectionist legislation is urged to keep remaining jobs from going overseas. Even if they are bad jobs by the most humane standards, a generation or even a century of capitalist work is a small price for humanity to pay if it rids us of a violent and inhuman mode, patriarchy, that has oppressed women for millennia.

CONCLUSION

This articulationist version of Marxist feminism puts a different perspective on traditional Marxist, feminist, and women in development thought. It endorses much of what women in development practitioners have done but rearranges the priorities to put more emphasis on human resource and infrastructure activities. It directly confronts much feminist theory but curiously resonates with most feminist practice. It less directly confronts most modern Marxist theory but finds misdirected much of modern Marxist practice, which seeks to overcome capitalism at a stage when it is still more a part of the solution than of the problem. With slavery and feudalism almost finished, patriarchy's time has passed. The material conditions for eliminating it have been created already in the developed world and can be created quickly with capitalist growth in the developing world. Ending patriarchy is the most important task facing not only feminism, but Marxism or any other humanism as well.

Bibliography

Abdullah, Mohammad, & Wheeler, Erica F. 1985. "Seasonal Variations and the Intra-household Distribution of Food in a Bangladeshi Village," *American Journal of Clinical Nutrition 41*: 1305–13.

Abu-Lughod, Lila. 1986. *Veiled Sentiments: Honor and Poetry in a Bedouin Society*. Berkeley: University of California Press.

Addison, Tony, & Lionel Demery. 1987. "Wages and Labour Conditions in the Newly Industrialising Countries of Asia." London: Overseas Development Institute, Working Paper.

Afonja, Simi. 1980. "Current Explanations of Sex-Inequality: A Reconsideration," *Nigerian Journal of Economic and Social Studies 21*(2).

_____. 1981. "Changing Modes of Production and the Sexual Division of Labor Among the Yoruba," *Signs 7*(2): 299–313.

_____. 1985. "The Emergence of a Competitive Sex Roles Structure in Yoruba Society." UNESCO SHS-85/CONF.803/17.

_____. 1986a. "Land Control: A Critical Factor in Yoruba Gender Stratification Structure," in Claire Robertson & Iris Berger, eds., *Women and Class in Africa*. New York: Holmes and Meier, pp. 71–89.

_____. 1986b. "Women's Power, Authority and Influence in Precolonial Yoruba Society," in Leela Dube, Eleanor Leacock, & Shirley Ardener, eds., *Visibility and Power: Essays on Women in Society and Development*. New York: Oxford University Press.

Agarwal, Bina. 1981. "Agricultural Modernization and Third World Women: Pointers from the Literature and an Empirical Analysis," ILO Working Paper.

_____. 1985. "Women and Technological Change in Agriculture: The Asian and African Experience," in Iftikhar Ahmed, ed., *Technology and Rural Women: Conceptual and Empirical Issues*. London: George Allen and Unwin, pp. 67–114.

_____. 1986. "Women, Poverty and Agricultural Growth in India," *Journal of Peasant Studies 13*: 165–220.

Ahmed, Iftikhar. 1978. "Technological Change and the Condition of Rural Women: A Preliminary Assessment," ILO Working Paper, Geneva.

_____. 1983. "Technological and Rural Women in the Third World," *International Labour Review 122*.

_____. ed. 1985. *Technology and Rural Women: Conceptual and Empirical Issues*. London: George Allen and Unwin.

Ahmed, Zubeida M., & Loutfi, Martha. 1982. "Women Workers in Rural Development: A Programme of the ILO," ILO Working Paper, Geneva.

Ahooja-Patel, Krishna. 1979. "Women, Technology and Development," *Economic and Political Weekly 14*(36): 1549–54.

———. 1986. "Economic and Social Status of Women in Asia Today," INSTRAW Working Paper 101. Santo Domingo: UN/INSTRAW.

———. ed. 1980. *Women at Work*, Nos. 1 and 2. Geneva: ILO.

Aina, Olabisis. 1984. "Relative Time Allocation between Women's Multiple Roles: A Case Study of Women in Cocoa Production," Masters dis. University of Ife, Ile-Ife, Nigeria.

Alamgir, Mohiuddin. 1980. *Famine in South Asia: Political Economy of Mass Starvation in Bangladesh*. Cambridge, Mass.: Oelgeschlager, Gunn and Hain.

Altekar, Angat Sadashiv. 1938. *The Position of Women in Hindu Civilisation*. Benares: Benares Hindu University.

Amsden, Alice Hoffenberg. ed. 1980. *The Economics of Women and Work*. Harmondsworth: Penguin.

Anderson, Mary B. 1985. "Technology Transfer: Implications for Women," in Catherine Overholt, Mary B. Anderson, Kathleen Cloud, & James E. Austin, eds. *Gender Roles in Development Projects*. West Hartford, Conn.: Kumarian Press.

Anderson, Mary B., & Chen, Marty A. 1988. "Integrating WID or Restructuring Development?," paper presented for the AWID Conference, Washington D.C., April.

Anderson, Patricia. 1986. "Conclusion: Women in the Caribbean." *Social & Economic Studies 35*(2): 291–324.

Anker, Richard, Buvinic, Mayra, & Youssef, Nadia, eds. 1982. *Women's Roles and Population Trends in the Third World*. London: Croom Helm.

Antrobus, Peggy. 1985. "Caribbean Women and Development: A Reassessment of Concepts, Perspectives and Issues," WAND (Women and Development) occasional paper, Women and Development Unit Extra Mural Department, University of the West Indies, Barbados, January.

———. 1987. "A Journey in the Shaping: A Journey Without Maps," Bunting Institute, Radcliffe College. (unpublished paper)

APCWD (Asian and Pacific Centre for Women and Development). 1979. "Feminist Ideology and Structures in the First Half of the Decade for Women." Report of a workshop held in Bangkok, June 23–30. Republished in IWTC, 1980, *Developing Strategies for the Future*.

Appadurai, Arjun 1984. "How Moral Is South Asia's Economy: A Review Article," *Journal of Asian Studies 43*(3): 481–97.

———. 1985. "Dietary Improvisation in an Agricultural Economy," Dept. of Anthropology, University of Pennsylvania, Philadelphia. (mimeographed)

Apps, Patricia. 1981. *A Theory of Inequality and Taxation*. Cambridge: Cambridge University Press.

Apter, David. 1987. *Rethinking Development*. Beverly Hills, Calif.: Sage Publications.

Arizpe, Lourdes, & Aranda, Josefina. 1981. "The 'Comparative Advantages' of Women's Disadvantages: Women Workers in the Strawberry Export Agribusiness in Mexico," *Signs 7*: 453–73.

Arnold, Erik, Birke, Lunda, & Faulkner, Wendy. 1982. "Women and Microelectronics: The Case of Word Processors," in Joan Rothschild, ed., *Women, Technology and Innovation*. New York: Pergamon Press.

Arrow, Kenneth J. 1982. "Why People Go Hungry," *New York Review of Books*, 15 July.

Ashley, Richard. 1986. "The Poverty of Neorealism," in Robert Keohane, ed., *Neorealism and Its Critics*. New York: Columbia University Press.

Asian Women Workers Newsletter. n.d. Hong Kong: Committee for Asian Women, Urban-Rural Mission of the Christian Conference of Asia.

Aslanbeigui, Nahid, & Summerfield, Gale. 1989. "The Impact of the Responsibility System on Women in Rural China: A Theoretical Application of Sen's Theory of Entitlement," *World Development 17*.

Atiya, Nayra. 1982. *Khul-Khaal: Five Egyptian Women Tell Their Stories*. Syracuse, N.Y.: Syracuse University Press.

Austin, James E. 1980. *Confronting Urban Malnutrition: The Design of Nutrition Programs*, World Bank Staff Occasional Paper No. 28. Baltimore, Md.: Johns Hopkins University Press.

Awe, Bolanle. 1977. "The Iyalode in the Traditional Yoruba Political System," in Alice Schlegel, ed., *Sexual Stratification: A Cross-Cultural View*. New York: Columbia University Press.

Banerjee, Narayan, with Lokenath Ram & Barati Sengupta. 1987. *Women's Work and Family Strategies: A Case Study from West Bengal*. New Delhi: Centre for Women's Development Studies.

Banerjee, Nirmala. 1979. "Women in the Urban Labour Market," *Labour, Capital and Society 12*.

———. 1982. *Unorganized Women Workers: The Calcutta Experience*. Calcutta: Centre for Studies in Social Sciences.

———. 1983. "Indian Women and the Urban Labour Market," Centre for Studies in Social Sciences, Calcutta. (mimeographed).

———. 1985. "Women's Work and Discrimination," in Devaki Jain & Nirmala Banerjee, eds. *Tyranny of the Household: Investigative Essays on Women's Work*. New Delhi: Vikas.

Banister, Judith. 1987. *China's Changing Population*. Stanford: Stanford University Press.

Bardhan, Kalpana. 1985. "Women's Work, Welfare and Status," *Economic and Political Weekly 20* (December 21–28).

———. 1986. "Stratification of Women's Work in Rural India: Determinants, Effects, and Strategies," in Dilip K. Basu & Richard Sisson, eds., *Social and Economic Development in India: A Reassessment*. New Delhi: Sage Publications, pp. 89–105.

———. 1987. "Gender and Class in the Economic Growth Process in South Asia," *Committee on South Asian Women Bulletin 5*(3–4): 3–14.

Bardhan, Pranab. 1974. "On Life and Death Questions," *Economic and Political Weekly 9* (special number), August: 1293–1304.

———. 1982. "Little Girls and Death in India," *Economic and Political Weekly*, September, pp. 1448–50.

———. 1984. *Land, Labour and Rural Poverty: Essays in Development Economics*. New York: Columbia University Press.

———. 1987. "On the Economic Geography of Sex Disparity in Child Survival in India: A Note," University of California, Berkeley. (mimeographed)

Barrios de Chungara, Domitila, with Viezzer, Moema. 1978. *Let Me Speak! Testimony of Domitila, A Woman of the Bolivian Mines*. New York: Monthly Review Press.

Barrow, Christine. 1986a. "Autonomy, Equality and Women in Barbados," paper prepared for XI Annual Caribbean Studies Conference, Caracas, Venezuela, May.

_____. 1986b. "Finding the Support: A Study of Sources of Livelihood and Strategies for Survival Among Poor Women in Barbados," *Social and Economic Studies 35*(2): 131–76.

Barry, Brian. 1973. *The Liberal Theory of Justice: A Critical Examination of the Principal Doctrines in "A Theory of Justice" by John Rawls*. Oxford: Oxford University Press.

Basu, Alaka. 1987. "Is Discrimination in Food Really Necessary for Explaining Sex Differential in Childhood Mortality?," National Council of Applied Economic Research. (mimeographed)

_____. 1988. *Culture, the Status of Women and Demographic Behaviour.* New Delhi: National Council of Applied Economic Research.

Basu, Amitabha, Ray, Sabrata K., Mukhopadhyay, Barum, Bharati, Premananda, Gupta, Ranjan, & Majumder, Partha P. 1986. "Sex Bias in Intrahousehold Food Distribution: Roles of Ethnic and Socioeconomic Characteristics," *Current Anthropology 27*(5): 536–39.

Batliwala, Srilatha. 1985. "Women in Poverty: The Energy, Health and Nutrition Syndrome," in Devaki Jain & Nirmala Banerjee, eds., *Tyranny of the Household: Investigative Essay on Women's Work*. New Delhi: Vikas.

Becker, Gary S. 1965. "A Theory of the Allocation of Time," *Economic Journal 75*: 493–517.

_____. 1973–74. "A Theory of Marriage," *Journal of Political Economy*. Part I, *81*: 813–46 and Part II, *82*: 511–26.

_____. 1981. *A Treatise on the Family*. Cambridge, Mass.: Harvard University Press.

Becker, Gary S., Landes, Elizabeth M., & Michael, Robert T. 1977. "An Economic Analysis of Marital Instability," *Journal of Political Economy 85*: 1141–87.

Beckford, George. 1972. *Persistent Poverty: Underdevelopment in Plantation Economies of the Third World*. New York: Oxford University Press.

Behrman, Jere. 1986. "Intrahousehold Allocation of Nutrients in Rural India: Are Boys Favored? Do Parents Exhibit Inequality Aversion?," mimeographed, forthcoming in Oxford Economic Papers.

_____. 1987. "Intrahousehold Allocation of Nutrients and Other Gender Effects," WIDER (World Institute for Development Economics Research). Helsinki. (mimeographed)

Behrman, Jere, Pollak, Robert, & Taubman, Paul. 1982. "Parental Preferences and Provisions for Progeny," *Journal of Political Economy 90*: 52–73.

Behrman, Jere R., & Wolfe, Barbara L. 1984. "More Evidence of Nutrition Demand: Income Seems Overrated and Women's Schooling Under-emphasized," *Journal of Development Economics 14*(1): 105–28.

Beneria, Lourdes, ed. 1982a. *Women and Development: The Sexual Division of Labour in Rural Societies*. New York: Praeger.

_____. 1982b. "Accounting for Women's Work," in Lourdes Beneria, ed., *Women and Development: The Sexual Division of Labour in Rural Societies*. New York: Praeger.

Beneria, Lourdes, & Roldan, Martha. 1987. *The Crossroads of Class and Gender: Industrial Homework, Subcontracting, and Household Dynamics in Mexico City*. Chicago: University of Chicago Press.

Beneria, Lourdes, & Sen, Gita. 1979. "Reproduction, Production and the Sexual Division of Labor," *Cambridge Journal of Economics 3*: 203–25.

———. 1981. "Accumulation, Reproduction, and Women's Role in Economic Development: Boserup Revisited," *Signs 7*(2): 279–98. Reprinted in Eleanor Leacock & Helen I. Safa, eds., 1986, *Womens Work: Development and the Division of Labor by Gender*. South Hadley, Mass.: Bergin and Garvey, pp. 141–57.

———. 1982. "Class and Gender Inequalities and Women's Role in Economic Development: Theoretical and Practical Implications," *Feminist Studies 8*(1).

Benhabib, Seyla. 1987. "The Generalized and the Concrete Other," in Seyla Benhabib & Drucila Cornell, eds., *Feminism as Critique*. Minneapolis: University of Minnesota Press.

Bennett, Lynn. 1983. *Dangerous Wives and Sacred Sisters: Social and Symbolic Roles of High-Caste Women in Nepal*. New York: Columbia University Press.

Benston, M. 1969. "The Political Economy of Women's Liberation," *Monthly Review 21*(4): 13–27.

Bergom-Larsson, Maria. 1982. "Women and Technology in the Industrialized Countries," in Pamela M. D'Onofrio-Flores & Sheila M. Pfafflin, eds. *Scientific-Technological Change and the Role of Women in Development*. Boulder, Colo.: Westview Press.

Berk, Richard A., & Berk, Sarah Fenstermaker. 1978. "A Simultaneous Equation Model for the Division of Household Labour," *Sociological Methods and Research 6*(4): 431–66.

———. 1979. *Labor and Leisure at Home: Control and Organization of the Household Day*. Beverly Hills, Calif.: Sage Publications.

Berry, Sarah. 1975. *Cocoa, Custom and Socio-Economic Change in Rural Western Nigeria*. Oxford: Clarendon Press.

Bhalla, Ajit. ed. 1975. *Technology and Employment in Industry: A Case Study Approach*. Geneva: ILO.

Bhatt, Ela. 1987. "The Invisibility of Home-Based Work: The Case of Piece Rate Workers in India," in Andrea Menefee Singh & Anita Kelles-Viitanen, eds., *Invisible Hands: Women in Home-Based Production*. New Delhi: Sage, pp. 29–33.

Bhattacharya, Diptesh. n.d. *Growth of Class Consciousness Among Jute Workers in Early 20th Century in Bengal*. Australian National University, doctoral dis.

Bhatty, Zarina. 1980. "Economic Role and Status of Women: A Case Study of Women in the Beedi Industry in Allahabad," ILO Working Paper, Geneva.

Bhuiya, A., et al. 1986. "Socioeconomic Determinants of Child's Nutritional Status: Boys Versus Girls," *Food and Nutrition Bulletin 8*.

Binmore, Ken. 1980. "Nash Bargaining Theory," London School of Economics (mimeographed). Revised version in K. Binmore & P. Dasgupta, eds. 1987. *The Economics of Bargaining*. Oxford: Blackwell,

Binmore, Ken, & Dasgupta, P., eds. 1987. *The Economics of Bargaining*. Oxford: Blackwell.

Blair, Patricia. 1980. *Health Needs of the World's Poor Women*. Washington, D.C.: Equity Policy Center.

———. 1983. *Women's Issues in US Aid Administration: Implementation of the Percy Amendment*. Washington, D.C.: Equity Policy Center.

Bledsoe, Caroline H. 1976. "Women's Marital Strategies Among the Kpelle of Liberia," *Journal of Anthropological Research 32*: 372–89.

Bleier, Ruth. 1984. *Science and Gender: A Critique of Biology and Its Theories on Women*. New York: Pergamon.

———. 1986. *Feminist Approaches to Science*. New York: Pergamon Press.

Blumberg, Rae Lesser. 1988. "Gender Stratification and Economic Development: Paradigm and Praxis at the Intersection of Social Structure, Human Lives, and the African Food Crisis," in Matilda White Riley, Beth Hess, & Bettina Huber, eds., *Social Structures and Human Lives*. Beverly Hills, Calif.: Sage Publications.

Blumberg, Rae Lesser, & Hinderstein, Cara. 1982. "At the End of the Line: Women and United States Foreign Aid in Asia, 1978–80," *Women and Politics 2*(4): 43–66.

Bolles, A. Lynn. 1983. "IMF Destabilization: The Impact on Working Class Jamaican Women," *Trans Africa Forum 2*(1): 63–75.

Booth, David. 1985. "Marxism and Development Sociology: Interpreting the Impasse," in Martin Shaw, ed., *Marxist Sociology Revisited*, London: Macmillan.

Boserup, Ester. 1965. *The Conditions of Agricultural Growth*. London: George Allen and Unwin.

———. 1970/1986. *Women's Role in Economic Development*. New York: St. Martin's Press. 2nd ed. Aldershot, England: Gower Publishing.

———. 1981. *Population and Technological Change*. Chicago: University of Chicago Press.

———. 1985. "Economic and Demographic Interrelationships in Sub-Saharan Africa," *Population and Development Review 11*(3): 383–97.

———. 1986. "Shifts in the Determinants of Fertility in the Developing World." In D. Coleman & R. Schofield, eds., *Forward from Malthus: The State of Population Theory*. New York: Oxford University Press.

Boulding, Elise. 1976. *The Underside of History: A View of Women Through Time*. Boulder, Colo.: Westview Press.

———. 1977. *Women in the Twentieth Century World*. New York: Halstead Press.

———. 1980. *Women: The Fifth World*. New York: Foreign Policy Association.

———. 1981. "Integration into What? Reflections on Development Planning for Women," in Roslyn Dauber & Melinda L. Cain, eds., *Women and Technological Change in Developing Countries*. Boulder, Colo.: Westview Press, pp. 9–30.

———. 1988. "Women's Movements and Social Transformations in the Twentieth Century," in Yoshikazu Sakamoto, ed., *The Changing Structure of World Politics*. Tokyo: Iwanami Shoten. (In Japanese.)

Bourque, Susan C. 1985. "Experiments with Equality: Complexities in Peruvian Public Policy," *Journal of Asian and African Studies 20*(3–4): 156–68.

Bourque, Susan C., & Warren, Kay B. 1981a. *Women of the Andes: Patriarchy and Social Change in Rural Peru*. Ann Arbor: University of Michigan Press.

———. 1981b. "Rural Women and Development Planning in Peru," in Naomi Black & Ann Baker Cottrell, eds., *Women and World Change: Equity Issues in Development*. Beverly Hills, Calif.: Sage Publications, pp. 183–97.

———. 1987. "Technology, Gender, and Development," *Learning About Women: Gender, Power and Politics,* Daedalus (special issue) *116*(4): 173–97.

Bowman, Mary, and Anderson, C. Arnold. 1980. "The Participation of Women in Education in the Third World," *Comparative Education Review 24*(2): 13–32.

Brandt, Willi. *North–South: A Program for Survival*, Report of the Independent Commission on International Development Issues. London: Pan Books.

Braithwaite, Richard Bevan. 1955. *Theory of Games as a Tool for the Moral Philosopher*. Cambridge: Cambridge University Press.

Brewster, H., & Thomas, Clive Y. 1967. *The Dynamics of West Indian Economic Interaction*. Kingston: ISER.

Briscoe, Anne, & Pfafflin, Sheila. eds. 1979. *Expanding the Role of Women in the Sciences*. New York: Annals of the New York Academy of Sciences, Vol. 323.

Brittan, Arthur, & Maynard, Mary. 1984. *Sexism, Racism and Oppression*. New York: Blackwell.

Brodber, Erna. 1975. "A Study of Yards in the City of Kingston." Jamaica: ISER. Working Paper No. 9.

_____. 1986. "Afro-Jamaican Women and Their Men in the Late Nineteenth and Early Twentieth Century," *Social and Economic Studies 35*(3): 23–50.

Brown, M., & Chuang, C. F. 1980. "Intrahousehold Power and Demand for Shared Goods," SUNY, Buffalo. (mimeographed)

Bruegel, Irene. 1978. "What Keeps the Family Going?," *International Socialism 2*:(1).

Bryceson, Deborah. 1980. "The Proletarization of Women in Tanzania," *Review of African Political Economy 17*, (January/April): 4–27.

_____. 1985. *Women and Technology in Developing Countries: Technological Change and Women's Capabilities and Bargaining Positions*. Santo Domingo: UN/INSTRAW.

Bunch, Charlotte. 1987. *Passionate Politics: Feminist Theory in Action*. New York: St. Martin's Press.

Bunster, Ximena, & Chaney, Elsa. 1985. *Sellers and Servants: Working Women in Lima, Peru*. New York: Praeger.

Burman, B. K. Roy. 1967. "Problem of Codification of Personal Laws of Tribal Communities," *Journal of the Tribal Research Institute 4*(2).

Burman, Sandra, ed. 1979. *Fit Work for Women*. London: Croom Helm.

Buvinic, Mayra. 1983. "Women's Issues in Third World Poverty: A Policy Analysis," in Mayra Buvinic, Margaret Lycette, & William P. McGreevey, eds., *Women and Poverty in the Third World*. Baltimore: Johns Hopkins University Press, pp. 14–31.

_____. 1986. "Projects for Women in the Third World: Explaining Their Misbehavior," *World Development 14*(5): 653–64.

Buvinic, Mayra, Lycette, Margaret, & McGreevey, William P. eds. 1983. *Women and Poverty in the Third World*. Baltimore: Johns Hopkins University Press.

Buvinic, Mayra, & Youssef, Nadia with Von Elm, B. 1978. "Women-Headed Households: The Ignored Factor in Development Planning," Washington, D.C.: International Center for Research on Women.

Carloni, Alice Stewart. 1981. "Sex Disparities in the Distribution of Food within Rural Households," *Food and Nutrition 7*(1): 3–12.

_____. 1987. *Women in Development: AID's Experience, 1973–1985*, Vol. 1. Synthesis Paper. Washington, D.C.: USAID.

Carr, Marilyn. 1978. *Appropriate Technology for African Women*. Addis Ababa: Economic Commission for Africa, United Nations.

_____. 1981. "Technologies Appropriate for Women: Theory, Practice and Policy," in Roslyn Dauber & Melinda L. Cain, eds., *Women and Technological Change in Developing Countries*. Boulder, Colo.: Westview Press, pp. 193–203.

————. 1984. *Blacksmith, Baker, Roofing-Sheetmaker*. London: Intermediate Technology Publications.

Carter, Susan, & Carter, Michael. 1981. "Women's Recent Progress in the Professions or Women Get a Ticket to Ride After the Gravy Train Has Left the Station," *Feminist Studies 7*(3): 477–504.

Caulfield, Mina Davis. 1974. "Imperialism, the Family and Cultures of Resistance," *Socialist Revolution 4*(20): 67–85.

CCIC (Canadian Consortium for International Cooperation). 1987. "Feminist Perspectives on Development," discussion paper of the CCIC Inter-Agency Working Group on Women and Development.

Cecelski, Elizabeth. 1984. *The Rural Energy Crisis, Women's Work and Family Welfare: Perspectives and Approaches to Action*. Geneva: ILO.

CEPAL (Economic Commission for Latin America). 1983. *Five Studies on the Situation of Women in Latin America*. Santiago: UN/ECLA.

Chakravarty, Lalita. 1986. "Poverty Studies in the Context of Agricultural Growth and Demographic Pressure: Case of Post-Independent India," Indraprastha College, Delhi University, Delhi. (mimeographed)

Chambers, Robert. 1982. "Health, Agriculture and Rural Poverty: Why Seasons Matter," *Journal of Development Studies 18*(2): 217–38.

Chaney, Elsa M. & Schmink, Marianne. 1976. "Women and Modernization: Access to Tools," in June C. Nash & Helen Safa, eds., *Sex and Class in Latin America*. New York: Praeger, pp. 160–82.

Chapkis, Wendy, & Enloe, Cynthia. 1983. *Of Common Cloth: Women in the Global Textile Industry*. Washington, D.C.: Transnational Institute.

Charlton, Sue Ellen. 1984. *Women in Third World Development*. Boulder, Colo.: Westview Press.

Chaudhury, Rafiqul Huda. 1983. "Determinants of Intrafamilial Distribution of Food and Nutrient Intake in a Rural Area of Bangladesh," Bangladesh Institute of Development Economics, Dacca. (mimeographed)

————. 1986. "Determinants of Nutrient Adequacy in a Rural Area of Bangladesh," *Food and Nutrition Bulletin 8*(4): 24–31.

————. 1987. "Dietary Adequacy and Sex Bias: Pre-School Children in Rural Bangladesh," *Social Action 37* (April–June): 107–25.

Chen, Lincoln C. 1982. "Where Have the Women Gone?," *Economic and Political Weekly 17* (March).

Chen, Lincoln C., Haq, Emdadul, & D'Souza, Stan. 1981. "Sex Bias in the Family Allocation of Food and Health Care in Rural Bangladesh," *Population and Development Review 7*(1).

Chen, Martha. 1983. *A Quiet Revolution: Women in Transition in Rural Bangladesh*. Cambridge, Mass.: Schenkman Publishing.

Chincilla, Norma S. 1977. "Industrialization, Monopoly Capitalism, and Women's Work in Guatemala," *Signs 3*(1): 38–56.

Chodorow, Nancy. 1978. *The Reproduction of Mothering*. Berkeley: University of California Press.

Christian Conference of Asia. 1981a. *In Clenched Fists of Struggle*, Report of the Workshop on the Impact of Transnational Corporations in Asia. Hong Kong: Urban–Rural Mission of the Christian Conference of Asia.

————. 1981b. *Struggling to Survive: Women Workers in Asia*. Hong Kong: Urban–Rural Mission of the Christian Conference of Asia.

_____. 1982. *The Plight of Asian Workers in Electronics*. Hong Kong: Urban–Rural Mission of the Christian Conference of Asia.

_____. 1984. *Our Rightful Share*. Hong Kong: Urban–Rural Mission of the Christian Conference of Asia.

CIMMYT (International Maize and Wheat Improvement Center). 1983. *An Analysis of Rapidly Rising Third World Consumption and Imports of Wheat*, in 1983 World Wheat Facts and Trends, Report 2. London.

Clark, Alice W. 1987. "Social Demography of Excess Female Mortality in India," *Economic and Political Weekly*, Special issue entitled "Review of Women Studies," *22*/17(/): WS12–21.

Clarke, Roberta. 1986. "Women's Organization, Women's Interests," *Social and Economic Studies 35*(3): 107–55.

Claudio, Virginia S., DeGuzman, Patrocenio E., Oliveros, Moninia S., & Dimaamo, Gemma P. 1982. *Basic Nutrition for Filipinos*. Manila: Merriam Corporation.

Clemhout, A. 1979. "A Life-Cycle Theory of Marriage and Divorce: A Pareto-Optimal Differential Game Model," in P. Liu & J. F. Sutinen, eds., *Control Theory in Mathematical Economics*. New York: Marcel Dekker.

Clemhout, A., & Wan, H. Y., Jr. 1977. "Symmetric Marriage, Household Decision Making and Impact on Fertility," Working Paper 152, Cornell University.

Cohen, Ronald L. 1986. "Introduction," in R. L. Cohen, ed., *Justice: Views from the Social Sciences*. New York: Plenum Press, pp. 1–10.

Cohen, Yolanda. 1984. "Women's Strategies: Le pourvoir derive du contre pourvoir" paper presented at the American Political Science Association Annual Meeting, Washington, D.C., August 30–September 2.

Columbia Human Rights Law Review. 1977. "Symposium on Law and the Status of Women" *8*(1): 1–371.

Committee on Foreign Affairs. 1974. "The Status of Women" hearings October 24, 1973; published in *International Protection of Human Rights: The Work of International Organizations and the Role of US Foreign Policy*. Washington, D.C.: U.S. Government Printing Office for the House of Representatives, 93rd Congress, pp. 439–78.

Conway, Jill. 1982. *The Female Experience in Eighteenth- and Nineteenth-Century America*. New York: Garland.

Conway, Jill, Bourque, Susan C., & Scott, Joan W. 1987. "The Concept of Gender." *Daedalus 116*(4): xxi–xxix.

Cowan, Ruth Schwartz. 1983. *More Work for Mother: The Ironies of Household Technology from the Open Hearth to the Microwave*. New York: Basic Books.

Crandon, Libbet. 1985. *Women, Enterprise and Development*. Chestnut Hill, Mass.: Pathfinder Fund.

Croll, Elisabeth. 1979. *Women in Rural Development: The People's Republic of China*. Geneva: ILO.

_____. 1986. "Rural Production and Reproduction: Socialist Development Experiences," in Eleanor Leacock & Helen I. Safa, eds., *Women's Work: Development and the Division of Labor by Gender*. South Hadley, Mass.: Bergin and Garvey.

CWDS (Center for Women's Development Studies). 1983. *Review of Research on the Family*. New Delhi.

Dalla Costa, Marirosa, & James, Selma. 1972. *The Power of Women and the Sub-version of the Community*. Bristol: Falling Wall Press.

Das, T. 1949. *Bengal Famine (1943)*. Calcutta: University of Calcutta.

Das, V., & Nicholas, R. 1981. "'Welfare' and 'Well-being' in South Asian Societies," ACLS (American Council of Learned Science)-SSRC Joint Committee on South Asia. New York: Social Science Research Council.

Dasgupta, A. 1987. *Women and Silk Industry in Bengal—18th-20th Century*. New Delhi: Centre for Women's Development Studies.

Dasgupta, Biplab. 1977. *Village Society and Labour Use*. Delhi: Oxford University Press.

Das Gupta, Monica. 1987. "Selective Discrimination Against Female Children in Rural Punjab, India," *Population and Development Review 13*(1): 77–100.

Dasgupta, Partha. 1987. "Trust as a Commodity," in Diego Gambetta, ed., *Trust and Agency*. Oxford: Blackwell.

Date-Bah, Eugenia, & Stevens, Yvette. 1981. "Rural Women in Africa and Techno-logical Change: Some Issues," *Labour and Society 6*: 149–62.

Dauber, Roslyn, & Cain, Melinda L., eds. 1981. *Women and Technological Change in Developing Countries*. Boulder, Colo.: Westview Press.

Davin, Delia. 1975. "Women in the Countryside of China," in Margery Wolf & Roxane Witke, eds., *Women in Chinese Society*. Stanford: Stanford Universi-ty Press, pp. 243–73.

Deaton Angus. 1987. "The Allocation of Goods Within the Household: Adults, Children and Gender," Princeton University, Princeton, N.J. (mimeographed)

Deaton, Angus, & Muellbauer, John. 1980. *Economics and Consumer Behavior*. Cambridge: Cambridge University Press.

de Beauvoir, Simone. 1953. *The Second Sex*. New York: Alfred A. Knopf; Har-mondsworth: Penguin.

Deere, Carmen D., & Leon de Leal, Magdalena. 1980. *Women in Agriculture: Peasant Production and Proletarianization in Three Andean Regions*. Gene-va: ILO.

———. 1982. *Women in Andean Agriculture*. Geneva: ILO.

———. 1987. *Rural Women and State Policy: Feminist Perspectives on Latin Ameri-can Agricultural Development*. Boulder, Colo.: Westview Press.

de Janvry, Alain. 1981. *The Agrarian Question and Reformism in Latin America*. Baltimore: Johns Hopkins University Press.

Delphy, Christine. 1977. *The Main Enemy*. London: Women's Research and Re-source Centre Publications.

Demas, William. 1965. *The Economics of Development in Small Countries*. Montre-al: McGill University Press.

Den Hartog, A. P. 1973. "Unequal Distribution of Food Within the Household," *FAO Newsletter 10*(4).

Desai, Meghnad J. 1984. "A General Theory of Poverty," *Indian Economic Review*.

Desai, Neera. 1983. Paper presented at "Women, Work and Society" seminar, Indian Statistical Institute, New Delhi.

de Soto, Hernando. 1989. *"The Other Path."* New York: Harper and Row.

de Treville, Diana. 1987. *Fuelwood-Based Small-Scale Enterprise Assessment: An Analysis of Renewable Energy Users and the Informal Sector*. Chevy Chase, Md.: Equity Policy Center for FAO.

Development Dialogue. 1982. "The Dakar Declaration on Another Development with Women," passed in a conference co-sponsored by the Association of

African Women for Research and Development and the Dag Hammarskjold Foundation, pp. 1–2.

Devereux, S., & Hay, R. 1986. "The Origins of Famine," Queen Elizabeth House, Oxford. (mimeographed)

di Leonardo, Micaela. 1985. "Women, High Technology, and Society Conference." *International Labor and Working Class History*, *28* (Fall): 100–102.

————. n.d. "Clericals, Computers and Culture: Two Discourses in Search of a Subject." In *Women's Work and High Technology*. Silicon Valley Research Group manuscript.

Dinnerstein, Dorothy. 1977. *The Mermaid and the Minotaur*. New York: Harper and Row.

Dixon, Ruth. 1978. *Rural Women at Work*. Baltimore: Johns Hopkins University Press.

————. 1982. "Mobilizing Women for Rural Employment in South Asia: Issues of Class, Caste, and Patronage," *Economic Development and Cultural Change* 30(2): 373–90.

————. 1983. "Land, Labour and the Sex Composition of the Agricultural Labour Force: An International Comparison," *Development and Change 14*(3): 347–72.

Dixon-Mueller, Ruth. 1985. *Women's Work in Third World Agriculture*. Geneva: ILO.

D'Onofrio-Flores, Pamela. 1982. "Technology, Economic Development, and the Division of Labor by Sex," in P. D'Onofrio-Flores and Sheila M. Pfafflin, eds, *Scientific-Technological Change and the Role of Women in Development*. Boulder, Colo.: Westview Press, pp. 13–28.

Drèze, Jean, & Sen, Amartya. 1989. *Hunger and Public Action*. Oxford: Clarendon Press.

————. eds. 1990. *The Political Economy of Hunger*. Oxford: Clarendon Press.

Dunn, Leith. 1987. "The Free Zone and Caribbean Women: Employment or Exploitation," paper presented at Symposium on Issues Concerning Women. Department of Economics, University of the West Indies at Kingston, Jamaica, March.

Durant-Gonzalez, Victoria. 1982. "The Realm of Female Familial Responsibility" in Joycelin Massiah, ed., *Women in the Family*. WICP Research Papers, Vol 35(2). Institute of Social and Economic Research (Eastern Carribean). University of the West Indies, Barbados.

Dworkin, Andrea. 1987. *Intercourse*. New York: Free Press.

Dworkin, Ronald. 1981. "What Is Equality? Part 1: Equality of Welfare," *Philosophy and Public Affairs 10*.

Dwyer, Daisy, & Bruce, Judith, eds., 1988. *A Home Divided: Women and Income in the Third World*. Stanford: Stanford University Press.

Dyson, T. 1982. "India's Regional Demography," London School of Economics. (mimeographed)

————. 1987. "Excess Female Mortality in India: Uncertain Evidence on a Narrowing Differential," London School of Economics. (mimeographed)

Dyson, T., & Moore, M. 1983. "On Kinship Structure, Female Autonomy, and Demographic Behavior," *Population and Development Review 9*(1): 35–60.

Eisenstein, Zillah R. 1979. "Developing a Theory of Capitalist Patriarchy and the Case for Socialist Feminism," in Zillah Eisenstein, ed., *Capitalist Patriarchy and the Case for Socialist Feminism*. New York: Monthly Review Press.

Elam, Y. 1972. *Employment, Incomes and Equality: A Strategy for Increasing Productive Employment in Kenya.* Geneva: ILO.

————. 1973. *The Social and Sexual Roles of Hima Women.* Manchester: Manchester University Press.

Elliot, Carolyn, & Kelly, Gail P. 1982. "New Directions for Research," in Gail P. Kelly & Carolyn Elliott, eds., *Women's Education in the Third World: Comparative Perspectives.* Albany: SUNY Press, pp. 331–43.

Elshtain, Jean B. 1983. "Antigone's Daughters: Reflections on Female Identity and the State," in Irene Diamond, ed., *Families, Politics and Public Policy.* New York: Longman.

Elson, Diane, & Pearson, Ruth. 1981a. "Nimble Fingers Make Cheap Workers: An Analysis of Women's Employment in Third World Export Manufacturing," *Feminist Review* (Spring): 87–107.

————. 1981b. "The Subordination of Women and the Internationalisation of Factory Production," in Kate Young, Carol Wolkowitz, & Roslyn McCullagh, eds. *On Marriage and the Market: Women's Subordination in International Perspective.* London: CSE Books, pp. 144–66.

Engels, Friedrich. 1884. *The Origin of the Family, Private Property and the State.* Moscow. Rpt. Moscow: Foreign Language Publishing House, 1969; New York: Pathfinder, 1972.

Engineer, Asghar Ali, ed. 1987. *Status of Women in Islam.* New Delhi: Ajanta.

Etienne, Mona, & Leacock, Eleanor, eds. 1980. *Women and Colonialization.* New York: Praeger.

Evans, Judith, with Meyers, Robert G. 1985. "Improving Program Actions to Meet the Intersecting Needs of Women and Children in Developing Countries: A Policy and Program Review." The Consultative Group on Early Childhood Care and Development. High/Scope Educational Research Foundation. Ypsilenti, Michigan.

Evans, M., ed. 1982. *The Women Question: Readings on the Subordination of Women.* London: Fontana.

Evenson, Robert E. 1976. "On the New Household Economics," *Journal of Agricultural Economics and Development* 6(1): 87–107.

Evenson, Robert E., Popkin, Barry M., & Quizon, Elizabeth K. 1980. "Nutrition, Work, and Demographic Behavior in Rural Philippine Households," in Hans P. Binswanger, Robert E. Evenson, Cecilia A. Florencio, & Benjamin N. F. White, eds., *Rural Household Studies in Asia.* Singapore: Singapore University Press, pp. 289–364.

Fabella, Raul Villasenor. 1982. "Economics of Scale in the Household Production Model and Intra-family Allocation of Resources," doctoral diss. Yale University.

FAO. 1983. *The Role of Women in Agriculture Production, Expert Consultation on Women and Food Production.* Rome: FAO.

Fapohunda, Eleanor. 1983. "Female and Male Work Profiles," in Christine Oppong, ed., *Female and Male in West Africa.* London: George Allen and Unwin.

Fausto-Sterling, Anne. 1985. *Myths of Gender: Biological Theories About Men and Women.* New York: Basic Books.

Fawcett, James T., Khoo, Siew-Ean, & Smith, Peter C. eds. 1984. *Women in the Cities of Asia, Migration and Urban Adaptation.* Boulder, Colo.: Westview Press.

Federici, Sylvia. 1973. *Wages Against Housework.* Bristol: Falling Wall.

Fee, Terry. 1976. "Domestic Labor: An Analysis of Housework and Its Relation to the Production Process," *Review of Radical Political Economics 8*(1): 1–8.

Ferguson, Kathy. 1984. *The Feminist Case Against Bureaucracy*. Philadelphia, Pa.: Temple University Press.

Fernandez-Kelly, Maria Patricia. 1983a. "Gender and Industry on Mexico's New Frontier," in Jan Zimmerman, ed., *The Technological Woman: Interfacing with Tomorrow*. New York: Praeger, pp. 18–29.

_____. 1983b. *For We Are Sold, I and My People: Women and Industry in Mexico's Frontier*. Albany: SUNY Press.

_____. 1983c. "Mexican Border Industrialization, Female Labor Force Participation, and Migration," in June Nash & Patricia Fernandez-Kelly, eds., *Women, Men, and the International Division of Labor*. Albany: SUNY Press, pp. 205–23.

_____. 1983d. "Contemporary Production: Seven Features and One Puzzle," paper presented at the Conference on Microelectronics in Transition: Industrial Transformation and Social Change, Silicon Valley Research Project, University of California-Santa Cruz, May.

Finn, Jeremy, Reis, Janet, & Dulberg, Loretta. 1982. "Sex Differences in Educational Attainment: The Process," in Gail P. Kelly & Carolyn Elliott, eds., *Women's Education in the Third World: Comparative Perspectives*. Albany: SUNY Press, pp. 107–26.

Fletcher, Stanley M. 1981. "Economic Implications of Changing Household Away-from-Home and At-Home Food Expenditure Patterns," doctoral diss. North Carolina State University.

Folbre, Nancy. 1984a. "Cleaning House: New Perspectives on Household and Economic Development," New School for Social Research. (mimeographed)

_____. 1984b. "Household Production in the Philippines: A Non-neoclassical Approach," *Economic Development and Cultural Change 32*(2): 303–30.

Fong, Monica. 1982. "Designing a Methodology for Measuring Women's Work in Agriculture," paper read at the Technical Seminar on Women's Work and Employment, Thirteenth International Conference of Labor Statisticians, Delhi, April 9–11, in *Report of Conference*, ICLS/13/D.11.

Foo, Gillian H. C. 1987. "Work and Marriage: Attitudes of Single Women Factory Workers in Malaysia," doctoral diss. University of Michigan.

Foo, Gillian H. C., & Lim, Linda Y. C. 1987. "Poverty, Ideology and Women Export Factory Workers in Asia," in Haleh Afshar & Bina Agarwal, eds., *Women and Poverty*. London: Macmillan.

Foreman, Ann. 1977. *Femininity as Alienation*. London: Pluto Press.

Fortmann, Louise. 1982. "Women's Work in Communal Setting: The Tanzanian Policy of Ujaama," in Edna G. Bay, ed., *Women and Work in Africa*. Boulder, Colo.: Westview Press.

Fortmann, Louise, & Rocheleau, Dianne. 1985. "Women and Agroforestry: Four Myths and Three Case Studies," *Agroforestry Systems 2*: 253–72.

Fraser, Arvonne. 1987. *The UN Decade for Women: Documents and Dialogue*. Boulder, Colo.: Westview Press.

Fraser, Nancy. "What's Critical About Critical Theory?," in Seyla Benhabib & Drucila Cornell, eds., *Feminism as Critique*. Minneapolis: University of Minnesota Press.

Friedan, Betty. 1986. *The Second Sex*. New York: Summit Books.

Frobel, Folker, Heinrichs, Jurgen, & Kreye, Otto. 1977–80. *The New International Division of Labour*. Cambridge: Cambridge University Press.

Fuchs, Victor Robert. 1983. *How We Live*. Cambridge, Mass.: Harvard University Press.

Fuentes, Annette, & Ehrenreich, Barbara. 1983. *Women in the Global Factory* (Institute for New Communications Pamphlet No.3). Boston: South End Press.

Gambetta, Diego, ed. 1987. *Trust and Agency*. Oxford: Blackwell.

Ganesh, Kamala. 1985. "State of the Art in Women's Studies," *Economic and Political Weekly*, April 20, pp. 683–89.

Gardiner, Jean. 1975. "Women's Domestic Labour," *New Left Review 89*: 47–58.

Gearhart, Sally M. 1983. "An End to Technology: A Modest Proposal," in Joan Rothschild, ed., *Machina Ex Dea*. New York. Pergamon Press, pp. 171–82.

Germaine, Adrienne. 1987. *Reproductive Health and Dignity: Choices by Third World Women*. New York: International Women's Health Coalition.

Ghosh, A. 1979. "Short-Term Changes in Income Distribution in Poor Agrarian Economies: A Study of Famines with Reference to the Indian Subcontinent," ILO Working Paper, Geneva.

Ghurye, Govind Sadashiv. 1961. *Caste, Class, and Occupation*. Bombay: Popular Book Depot.

Giele, Janet, & Smock, Audrey C., eds. 1976. *Women and Society in International and Comparative Perspective*. New York: Wiley-Interscience.

Gilligan, Carol. 1982. *In a Different Voice*. Cambridge: Cambridge University Press.

Girvan, Norman, & Jefferson, O., eds. 1971. *Readings in the Political Economy of the Caribbean*. Kingston: New World Group.

Goldschmidt-Clermont, Luisella. 1982. *Unpaid Work in the Household*, Geneva: ILO.

_____. 1983. "Does Housework Pay?," *Signs 9*(1): 108–24.

Goody, John R. 1976. *Production and Reproduction*. Cambridge: Cambridge University Press.

Gosling, J. C. B. 1969. *Pleasure and Desire*. Oxford: Clarendon Press.

Government of India. 1974. *Towards Equality: Report of the Committee on the Status of Women in India*. New Delhi: Ministry of Education and Social Welfare, Department of Social Welfare.

_____. 1985. *Women in India: A Country Paper*. New Delhi: Ministry of Education and Social Welfare, Department of Social Welfare.

Greenough, Paul R. 1982. *Prosperity and Misery in Modern Bengal: The Famine of 1943–44*. New York: Oxford University Press.

Greer, Germaine. 1984. *Sex and Destiny: The Politics of Human Fertility*. New York: Harper and Row.

Griffin, James. 1987. *Well-Being*. Oxford: Clarendon Press.

Griffin, Keith. 1978. *International Inequality and National Poverty*. London: Macmillan.

Grindle, Merilee S. 1986. *State and Countryside: Development Policy and Agrarian Politics in Latin America*. Baltimore: Johns Hopkins University Press.

Gronau, Robert. 1974. "The Effect of Children on the Housewife's Value of Time," in T. W. Schultz, ed., *Economics of the Family*. Chicago: University of Chicago Press.

_____. 1977. "Leisure, Home Production, and Work: The Theory of the Allocation of Time Revisited," *Journal of Political Economy 8*(6): 1099–1123.

Grossman, Rachael. 1978/79. "Women's Place in the Integrated Circuit," Joint issue of *Southeast Asia Chronicle*, No. 66, and *Pacific Research 9*(5–6): 2–16.

Gulati, Leela. 1981. "Women and Technological Change: A Case Study of Three Fishing Villages," Trivandrum, India: Centre for Development Studies, Working Paper.

Haaga, John G., & Mason, John B. 1987. "Food Distribution Within the Family: Evidence and Implications for Research and Programmes," *Food Policy 12*(2): 146–60.

Habib, Irfan. 1988. Inaugural Address, National Seminar on Women's Access to Land and Other Productive Resources. Delhi University, January.

Hacker, Andrew. 1986 "Women and Work," *New York Review of Books 33* (August 14).

Hafkin, Nancy J. & Bay, Edna, eds. 1976. *Women in Africa: Studies in Socio-Economic Change*. Stanford: Stanford University Press.

Hall, Diana Long. 1979. "Academics, Bluestockings, and Biologists: Women at the University of Chicago, 1892–1932," in Anne Briscoe & Sheila Pfafflin, eds., *Expanding the Role of Women in the Sciences*. New York: Annals of the New York Academy of Sciences, Vol. 323, pp. 300–20.

Hansen, Karen Tranberg. 1987. "Urban Women and Work in Africa: A Zambian Case," *Trans Africa Forum 4*(3): 9–24.

Hare, Richard Mervyn. 1981. *Moral Thinking*. Oxford: Clarendon Press.

Harrison, J. 1974. "Political Economy of Housework," *Bulletin of the Conference of Socialist Economist 3*.

Harriss, Barbara. 1977. "Paddy Milling: Problems in Policy and Choice of Technology," in B. F. Farmer, ed., *The Green Revolution*. London: Billing.

————. 1987. "Intrafamily Distribution of Hunger in South Asia," WIDER Conference paper. To be published in Drèze and Sen, 1990, *The Political Economy of Hunger*. Oxford: Clarendon Press.

Harriss, B., & Watson E. 1984. "The Sex Ratio in South Asia," London School of Hygiene and Tropical Medicine. (mimeographed)

Harsanyi, John. 1976. *Essays on Ethics, Social Behavior*, and *Scientific Explanation*. Dordrecht: Reidel.

————. 1977. *Rational Behaviour and Bargaining Equilibrium in Games and Social Situations*. Cambridge: Cambridge University Press.

Hartmann, Heidi. 1979. "The Unhappy Marriage of Marxism and Feminism: Toward a More Progressive Union," *Capital and Class 8*: 1–33.

————. 1981. "The Unhappy Marriage of Marxism and Feminism," in L. Sargent, ed., *Women and Revolution*. Boston: South End Press.

Hartsock, Nancy C. M. 1983. *Money, Sex, and Power: Toward a Feminist Historical Materialism*. Boston: Northeastern University Press.

Hassan, Nazmul, & Ahmad, Kamaluddin. 1984. "Intrafamilial Distribution of Food in Rural Bangladesh," *Food and Nutrition Bulletin 6*(4): 34–42.

Heckman, James J. 1974. "Shadow Prices, Market Wages, and Labor Supply," *Econometrica 42*(4): 679–94.

————. 1979. "Sample Selection Bias as Specification Error," *Econometrica 47*(1): 153–61.

Heyzer, Noleen. 1982. "From Rural Subsistence to an Industrial Peripheral Work Force: An Examination of Female Malaysian Migrants and Capital Accumulation in Singapore," in Lourdes Beneria, ed., *Women and Development*. New York: Praeger, pp. 179–202.

_____. 1986. *Working Women in South-East Asia: Development, Subordination and Emancipation*. Milton Keynes, England: Open University Press.

Himmelstrand, Karen, & Bickham, Noella, eds. 1985. *The Peripheral Center: Swedish Assistance to Africa in Relation to Women: An Assessment*. Stockholm: Swedish International Development Agency (SIDA).

Himmelweit, Susan, & Mohun, S. 1977. "Domestic Labour and Capital," *Cambridge Journal of Economics 1*.

Hinton, William. 1966. *Fanshen: A Documentary of Revolution in a Chinese Village*. New York: Vintage Books.

Hochschild, Jennifer L. 1981. *What's Fair? American Beliefs About Distributive Justice*. Cambridge: Harvard University Press.

Hoskins, Marilyn, 1983. *Rural Women, Forest Outputs, and Forestry Projects*. Rome: FAO.

Humphries, Jane. 1977. "Class Struggle and the Persistence of the Working-Class Family," *Cambridge Journal of Economics 1*. Reprinted in Alice Hoffenberg Amsden, ed., 1980, *The Economics of Women and Work*. Harmondsworth: Penguin.

Huntington, Suellen. 1975. "Issues in Woman's Role in Economic Development: Critique and Alternatives," *Journal of Marriage and the Family 37*(4): 1001–12.

ICPEDC (International Center for Public Enterprise in Developing Countries). 1986. *The Role of Women in Developing Countries: A Study*. Ljubljana, Yugoslavia: ICPEDC.

Illich, Ivan. 1982. *Gender.* New York: Pantheon Books.

ILO (International Labour Organization). 1972. *Employment, Incomes and Equality: A Strategy for Increasing Productive Employment in Kenya*. Geneva: ILO.

_____. 1982a. *Rural Development and Women in Asia*. Geneva: ILO.

_____. 1982b. *Rural Women Workers in Asia*. Geneva: ILO.

_____. 1984. "Report of African and Asian Interregional Workshop on Strategies for Improving Employment Conditions of Rural Women." Workshop held in Arusha, Tanzania, August 20–26, 1984. Geneva: Rural Women's Programme.

_____. 1985. *Women Workers in Multinational Enterprises in Developing Countries*. Geneva: ILO. Prepared by Linda Y. C. Lim.

_____. 1986. *Economically Active Population Estimates and Projections, 1950–2025*. Geneva: ILO.

ISER (Institute of Social and Economic Research [Eastern Caribbean]). 1981. Man and the Biosphere Project. "Four Country Questionnaire Survey, 1980: Preliminary Report," University of the West Indies, Barbados, February. (mimeographed)

ISIS International. 1985. "Industrial Women Workers in Asia," *ISIS International Women's Journal*, No. 4. Published with the Committee for Asian Women of the Urban–Industrial Mission of the Christian Conference of Asia.

_____. 1986. "The Latin American Women's Movement: Reflections and Actions," *ISIS International Women's Journal*, No. 5.

ISIS International Women's Information and Communication Service. 1983. *Women in Development: A Resource Guide for Organization and Action*. Geneva: ISIS.

Islam, M. Nurul, Morse, Richard, & Soesastro, M. Hadi, eds. 1984. *Rural Energy to Meet Development Needs: Asian Village Approaches*. Boulder, Colo.: Westview Press.

IWTC (International Women's Tribune Centre). 1987. *It's Our Move Now: A Community Action Guide to the U.N. Nairobi Forward Looking Strategies for the Advancement of Women*. New York: IWTC.

———. 1980. *Developing Strategies for the Future: Feminist Perspectives*. Report of a workshop co-sponsored by APCWD and the Women and Development Unit (WAND) of the University of the West Indies, at Stony Point, N.Y., June.

Jackson, Jean. 1982. "Stresses Affecting Women and Their Families," Massiah, J., ed., *Women in the Family*, WICP Research Papers, Phase I. Barbados: ISER (EC), UWI.

Jacob, P. 1983. "The Activity Profile of Indian Women," National Sample Survey, Calcutta. (mimeographed)

Jahan, Rounaq. 1985. "Participation of Women Scientists and Engineers in Endogenous Research and Development," in Shirley Malcolm, Hiroko Morita-Lou, Patricia Boulware, & Sandra Burns, eds., *Science, Technology and Women: A World Perspective*. Washington, D.C.: AAAS and Centre for Science and Technology for Development, United Nations, pp. 44–52.

Jahan, Rounaq, & Papenek, Hanna, eds. 1979. *Women and Development: Perspectives from South and Southeast Asia*. Dhaka: Bangladesh Institute of Law and International Affairs.

Jain, Devaki. 1980a. *Women's Quest for Power*. New Delhi: Vikas.

———. 1980b. "Women's Employment: Possibilities of Relevant Research." (mimeographed) New Delhi: Institute of Social Studies Trust.

———. 1983. "Development as if Women Mattered or Can Women Build a New Paradigm?" New Delhi: Institute of Social Studies Trust.

———. 1985. "The Household Trap: Report on a Field Survey of Female Activity Patterns," in Devaki Jain & N. Banerjee, eds. *Tyranny of the Household: Investigative Essays on Women's Work*. New Delhi: Vikas.

Jain, Devaki, & Banerjee, N., eds. 1985. *Tyranny of the Household: Investigative Essays on Women's Work*. New Delhi: Vikas.

Jain, Devaki, & Chand, M. 1982. "Report on a Time Allocation Study: Its Methodological Implications." New Delhi: Institute of Social Studies Trust.

Jain, Devaki, Singh, Nalini, & Chand, Malini. 1979. "Women's Work: Methodological Issues," in Rounaq Jahan & Hanna Papanek, eds., *Women and Development: Perspectives from South and Southeast Asia*. Dhaka: Bangladesh Institute of Law and International Affairs.

James, Jeffrey. 1980. "Appropriate Technologies and Inappropriate Policy Instruments," *Development and Change 11*: 65–76.

Jaquette, Jane S. 1982. "Women and Modernization Theory." *World Politics 34*(2): 267–84.

———. 1985. "Female Political Participation in Latin America: Raising Feminist Issues," in Ruth Ross & Lynne Iglitzin, eds., *Women in the World: The Decade for Women 1976–85*. Santa Barbara: ABC/Clio.

Jaquette, Jane, & Staudt, Kathleen. 1985. "Women 'At Risk' Reproducers: Biology, Science, and Population in U.S. Foreign Policy," in Virginia Sapiro, ed, *Women, Biology, and Public Policy*. Beverly Hills, Calif.: Sage Publications.

———. 1988. "Gender and Politics in U.S. Population Policy," in Kathleen Jones & Anna Jonasdottir, eds., *The Political Interests of Gender*. London: Sage Publications.

Jayawardena, Kumari. 1986. *Feminism and Nationalism in the Third World*. London: Zed Press.

Jetley, Surinder. 1987. "Women's Work and Family Strategies." Draft Report for Discussion at the United Nations University International Workshop on Women's Work and Family Strategies in South and Southeast Asia. Kathmandu, December 16–21.

Jiggins, Janice. 1986. *Gender-Related Impacts and the Work of the International Agricultural Research Centers*. Washington, D.C.: World Bank. Study Paper 17.

Joekes, Susan. 1988. "Gender and Macro-Economic Policy," paper for the AWID Colloquium on Gender and Development, Washington, D.C. April 11–12.

Jones, Christine. 1983. "The Mobilization of Women's Labor for Cash Crop Production: A Game-Theoretic Approach," *American Journal of Agricultural Economics 65*(5): 1049–54.

Jones, Gavin W., ed. 1984. *Women in the Urban and Industrial Workforce: Southeast and East Asia*. Development Studies Centre Monograph No. 33, Australian National University, Canberra.

Kakwani, Nanak. 1986. "Is Sex Bias Significant?," World Institute for Development Economics Research (WIDER) Working Paper, Helsinki.

Kalai, E. 1977. "Nonsymmetric Nash Solutions and Replications of Two-Person Bargaining," *International Journal of Game Theory 6*.

Kalai, E., & Smordinsky, M. 1975. "Other Solutions to Nash's Bargaining Problem," *Econometrica 43*(3): 513–18.

Kamsler, V. 1986. "Distribution, Entitlement and the Family," Oxford University. (mimeographed)

Kandiyoti, Deniz. 1985. *Women in Rural Production Systems: Problems and Policies*. Paris: UNESCO.

Kaneko, M. 1980. "An Extension of the Nash Bargaining Problem and the Nash Social Welfare Function," *Theory and Decision 12*.

Kaneko, M., & Nakamura, K. 1979. "The Nash Social Welfare Function," *Econometrica 47*(2): 423–35.

Karim, Wazir-Jahan. 1987. "Report on Women's Work and Family Status Production Processes in Malaysia." For Discussion at United Nations University International Workshop on Women's Work and Family Strategies in South and Southeast Asia. December 16–21.

Karl, Marilee. 1983. "Women and Multinationals," in ISIS, *Women in Development: A Resource Guide for Organization and Action*. Geneva: ISIS International Women's Information and Communication Service.

Katz, Michael. 1968. *The Irony of Early School Reform: Educational Innovation in Mid-Nineteenth Century Massachusetts*. Cambridge, Mass.: Harvard University Press.

Keesing, Roger. 1981. *Introduction to Cultural Anthropology: A Contemporary Perspective*. New York: Holt, Rinehart and Winston.

Keller, Evelyn Fox. 1985. *Reflections on Gender and Science*. New Haven: Yale University Press.

Khan, Qaiser M. 1985. "A Model of Endowment-Constrained Demand for Food in an Agricultural Economy with Empirical Applications to Bangladesh," *World Development 13*(9): 1055–66.

Kinsey, Jean. 1983. "Working Wives and the Marginal Propensity to Consume Food

Away from Home," *American Journal of Agricultural Economics 65*(1): 10–19.

Kirp, David L., Yudof, Mark, & Franks, Marlene Strong. 1986. *Gender Justice.* Chicago: University of Chicago Press.

Kishwar, Madhu, & Vanita, Ruth, eds. 1984. *In Search of Answers: Indian Women's Voices from Manushi.* London: Zed Books.

Kleinig, John. 1978. "Human Rights, Legal Rights, and Social Change," in Eugene Kamenka & Ehr-Soon Tay, eds., *Human Rights.* New York: St. Martins Press.

Koentjaraningrat. 1985. *Javanese Culture.* Oxford University Press.

Kongstad, Per, & Monsted, Mette. 1980. *Family, Labour and Trade in Western Kenya.* Uppsala: Scandinavian Institute of African Studies.

Kosambi, Damodar, Dharmanand. 1970. *The Culture and Civilization of Ancient India in Historical Outline.* London: Routledge and Kegan Paul.

Krishnaswamy, Kadur Shamanna, & Rajgopal, S. 1985. "Women in Employment: A Micro Study in Kannataka," in D. Jain & N. Banerjee, eds., *Tyranny of the Household: Investigative Essays on Women's Work.* New Delhi: Vikas.

Kuhn, Annette, & Wolpe, Ann Marie, eds. 1978. *Feminism and Materialism.* London: Routledge and Kegan Paul.

Kurian, R. 1982. *Women Workers in the Sri Lanka Plantation Sector.* Geneva: ILO.

Kusterer, Ken. 1987a. "Nontraditional Agribusiness: Impacts on Women," paper presented at Association for Women in Development, Biannual Meeting, Washington, D.C., March.

_____. 1987b. "Post-Industrial Housework," paper presented at District of Columbia Sociological Society, Annual Meeting, George Mason University, Fairfax, Virg., May.

Kusterer, Ken, Xuya Cuxil, Josefina, & Estrada de Batres, Maria Regina. 1981. *The Social Impact of Agribusiness: The Case of ALCOSA in Guatemala.* Special Study 4, Agency for International Development, Washington, D.C.

Kynch, Jocelyn, & Sen, Amartya. 1983. "Indian Women: Well-Being and Survival," *Cambridge Journal of Economics 7*: 363–80.

Laclau, Ernesto. 1971. "Feudalism and Capitalism in Latin America," *New Left Review 67*: 19–38.

Lapidus, Gail. 1978. *Women in Soviet Society.* Berkeley: University of California Press.

Larwood, Laurie, Stromberg, A. H., & Gutek, Barbara, eds. 1986. *Women's Work: An Annual Review.* New York: Sage.

Laslett, Peter, with the assistance of Richard Wall. 1972. *Household and Family in Past Time.* Cambridge: Cambridge University Press.

Leacock, Eleanor, & Etienne, Mona, eds. 1980. *Women and Colonization: Anthropological Perspectives.* New York: Praeger.

Leacock, Eleanor, & Safa, Helen I., eds. 1986. *Women's Work: Development and the Division of Labor by Gender.* South Hadley, Mass.: Bergin and Garvey.

Lee, Eddy, ed. 1984. *Export Processing Zones and Industrial Development in Asia.* Bangkok: Asian Employment Program of ILO.

Leet, Mildred Robbins. 1981. "Roles of Women: UNCSTD Background Discussion Paper," in Roslyn Dauber & Melinda Cain, eds. *Women and Technological Change in Developing Countries.* Boulder, Colo.: Westview Press, pp. 229–36.

LeFranc, Elsie. 1983. "Overview and Conclusions," in Joycelin Massiah, ed., *Report of the Conference on the Role of Women in the Caribbean* (Barbados, September 12–16). Cave Hill, Barbados: ISER (EC), UWI.

Leith-Ross, Sylvia. 1939/1958. *African Women: A Study of the Ibo of Nigeria*. London: Faber & Faber.

Lele, Uma. 1975. *The Design of Rural Development: Lessons from Africa*. Baltimore: Johns Hopkins University Press.

_____. 1984. "Women and Structural Transformation," *Economic Development and Cultural Change 34*(2): 195–221.

Leslie, Joanne, Lycette, Margaret, & Buvinic, Mayra. 1986. *Weathering Economic Crises: The Crucial Role of Women in Health*. Washington, D.C.: International Center for Research on Women.

Levi-Strauss, Claude. 1969. *The Elementary Structures of Kinship*. Trans. J. H. Bell & J. R. von Sturmer; ed. R. Needham. Boston: Beacon Press.

Levy, Howard S. 1966. *Chinese Footbinding: The History of a Curious Erotic Custom*. New York: Walton Rawls.

Lewis, William Arthur. 1949. "Industrial Development in Puerto Rico," *Caribbean Economic Review 1*(1,2).

_____. 1950. "Industrialisation of the British West Indies," *Caribbean Economic Review 2*(1).

Liedholm, Carl, & Meed, Donald. 1987. *Small Scale Industries in Developing Countries*, Michigan State University International Paper No. 9.

Lim, Linda Y. C. 1978. *Women Workers in Multinational Corporations: The Case of the Electronics Industry in Malaysia and Singapore*. Michigan Occasional Papers No. 9, Women's Studies Program, University of Michigan.

_____. 1981. "Women's Work in Multinational Electronics Factories," in Roslyn Dauber & Melinda. L. Cain, eds., *Women in Technological Change in Developing Countries*. Boulder, Colo.: Westview Press, pp. 181–92.

_____. 1983. "Capitalism, Imperialism, and Patriarchy: The Dilemma of Third-World Women Workers in Multinational Factories," in June Nash & Maria Patricia Fernandez-Kelly, eds., *Women, Men and the International Division of Labor*. Albany: SUNY Press, pp. 70–91.

_____. 1987a. "Capital, Labor and the State in the Internationalization of High-Tech Industry," in Mike Douglas & John Friedman, eds., *Transnational Corporations and Urbanization in the Pacific Rim, Proceedings of a Conference*. Center for Pacific Rim Studies, University of California, Los Angeles. Summer.

_____. 1987b. "Export-Oriented Industrialization and Asian Labor," paper presented at the Conference on Origins and Consequences of National Development Strategies: Latin America and East Asia Compared. Duke University, March 31–April 1. In volume of conference proceedings edited by Gary Gereffi.

_____. 1987c. "Export-Led Industrialization, Labour Welfare, and International Labour Standards in Singapore," in Tony Addison & Lionel Demery, eds., *Wages and Labour Conditions in the Newly Industrializing Countries of Asia*. London: Overseas Development Institute.

_____. 1989a. "Women Industrial Workers: The Specificities of the Malaysian Case," in Jamilah Ariffin & Wendy Smith, eds., *Malaysian Women and the Urban and Industrial Labor Force*. Singapore: Institute of Southeast Asian Studies.

_____. 1989b. "The Impact of Changes in the World Economy on Developing Countries," in David Gordon & Robert Berg, eds., *Cooperation for Interna-*

tional Development: U.S. Policy and Programs for the 1990s. Boulder, Colo.: Lynne Rienner.

Lin, Vivian. 1986. "Health, Women's Work and Industrialization: Women Workers in the Semiconductor Industry in Singapore and Malaysia," Women in International Development Working Paper No. 130. Women in International Development Program, Michigan State University.

Lipton, Michael. 1983. *Poverty, Undernutrition and Hunger.* World Bank Staff Working Paper No. 597, Washington, D.C.

Lloyd, Cynthia E., & Niemi, Beth T. 1979. *The Economics of Sex Differentials.* New York: Columbia University Press.

Lloyd, Peter Cutt. 1974. *Power and Independence: Urban Africa's Perception of Social Inequality.* London: Routledge and Kegan Paul.

Loutfi, Martha F. 1980. *Rural Women: Unequal Partners in Development.* Geneva: ILO.

Loza-Soliman, Sarah. 1981. "Roles of Women and Their Impact on Fertility: An Egyptian Case Study," International Union for the Scientific Study of Population (IUSSP), International Population Conference, Manila, Solicited Papers.

Luce, Robert Duncan & Raiffa, Howard. 1957. *Games and Decisions.* New York: Wiley.

MacCormack, Carol. 1982. "Control of Land, Labor and Capital in Rural Southern Sierra Leone," in Edna G. Bay, ed., *Women and Work in Africa.* Boulder, Colo.: Westview Press.

MacCormack, Carol, & Strathern, Marilyn, eds. 1980. *Nature Culture and Gender.* Cambridge: Cambridge University Press.

MacFarlane, Alan. 1978. "Modes of Reproduction," *Journal of Development Studies 14*(40): 100–20.

Mackintosh, M. M. 1979. "Domestic Labour and the Household," in S. Burman, ed., *Fit Work for Women.* London: Croom Helm.

Madisen, Birgit. 1984. *Women's Mobilization and Integration in Development.* Copenhagen: CDR Research Report No. 3.

Maguire, Patricia. 1984. *Women in Development: An Alternative Analysis.* Amherst, Mass.: Center for International Education.

Mahmud, W. & Mahmud, S. 1985. "Age-Sex Aspects of the Food and Nutrition Problems in Rural Bangladesh," ILO Working Paper, Geneva.

Mainardi, Pat. 1970. "The Politics of Housework," in Robin Morgan, ed., *Sisterhood Is Powerful.* New York: Random House, pp. 447–54.

Mair, Lucille. 1974. "A Historical Study of Women in Jamaica, 1655–1844," doctoral diss. University of the West Indies.

———. 1986. "Women: A Decade Is Time Enough," *Third World Quarterly 8*(2): 583–93.

———. 1987. "Women in the World: The Challenge of the Nineties," WAND: Women and Development Unit Extra-Mural Department, University of the West Indies, Barbados, Occasional Paper.

Malcom, Shirley. 1985. "The Participation of Women in Policy and Decision-Making Regarding the Use and Development of Technologies," in Shirley Malcom, Hiroko Morita-Lou, Patricia Boulware, and Sandra Burns, eds., *Science, Technology and Women: A World Perspective.* Washington, D.C.: AAAS and Centre for Science and Technology for Development, United Nations, pp. 61–67.

Malcom, Shirley, Hiroko Morita-Lou, Patricia Boulware, & Sandra Burns, eds., 1985. *Science, Technology, and Women: A World Perspective.* Washington, D.C.: AAAS and Centre for Science and Technology for Development, United Nations.

Malos, Ellen. 1980. *Politics of Housework.* London: Allison and Busby.

Manser, Marilyn, & Brown, Murroy. 1980. "Marriage and Household Decision-Making: A Bargaining Analysis," *International Economic Review 21*(1): 31–44.

Martorell, Reynaldo. 1982. "Nutrition and Health Status Indicators: Suggestions for Surveys of the Standard of Living in Developing Countries," World Bank Living Standard Measurement Study, Working Paper No. 13.

Marx, Karl. 1859/1971. *A Contribution to the Critique of Political Economy.* New York: International.

_____. 1860/1974. *Political Writings: Volume 2, Surveys from Exile.* ed. David Fernbach. New York: Vintage.

_____. 1863/1969. *Theories of Surplus Value.* New York: International.

_____. 1867/1967, 1885/1985. *Capital*, Vols. 1 and 2. New York: International.

Mason, Karen Oppenheim. 1984. *The Status of Women: A Review of Its Relationships to Fertility and Mortality.* New York: Rockefeller Foundation.

Massiah, Joycelin. 1981. "The Population of Barbados: Demographic Development and Population Policy in a Small Island State," doctoral diss. University of the West Indies.

_____. 1984. *Employed Women in Barbados: A Demographic Profile.* Occasional Paper No. 8, ISER (EC), UWI.

_____. 1986a. "Work in the lives of Caribbean Women," *Social and Economic Studies 35*(2): 177–239.

_____, ed. 1986b. "Women in the Caribbean" (Special Issue). *Social and Economic Studies 35*(2,3).

Mattelart, Armand, 1983. *Transnationals and the Third World: The Struggle for Culture.* South Hadley, Mass.: Bergin and Garvey.

Mazumdar, Vina. 1985a. *Emergence of Women's Questions in India and the Role of Women's Studies.* New Delhi: Centre for Women's Development Studies.

_____. 1985b. "Introduction to Women and Cultural Values," in Vina Mazumbar, ed., *Education for Women's Equality.* New Delhi: Centre for Women's Development Studies (CWDS).

Mazumdar, Vina, & Kasturi, Leela. 1984. *Political Participation of Women in Developing Countries.* New Delhi: Centre for Women's Development Studies (CWDS).

Mba, Nina. 1983. *Nigerian Women Mobilized: Women's Political Activity in Southern Nigeria, 1960–65.* Berkeley: Institute of International Studies.

McCormack, Jeanne, Walsh, Martin, & Nelson, Candace. 1986. *Women's Group Enterprises: A Study of the Structure of Opportunity on the Kenay Coast.* Boston: World Education Inc.

McCormack, Thelma. 1981. "Development with Equity for Women," in Naomi Black & Ann Baker Cottrell, eds., *Women and World Change.* Beverly Hills, Calif.: Sage Publications, pp. 15–30.

McElroy, Marjorie B., & Horney, Mary Jean. 1981. "Nash-Bargained Household Decisions: Toward a Generalization of the Theory of Demand," *International Economics Review 22*(2): 333–50.

McIntosh, J., Nasim, A., & Satchell, S. 1981. "Differential Mortality in Rural Bangladesh." (mimeographed)

McIntosh, M. 1978. "The State and the Oppression of Women," in Annette Khun & Ann Marie Wolpe, eds., *Feminism and Materialism*. London: Routledge and Kegan Paul. Rpt. M. Evans, ed. 1982. *The Woman Question: Readings on the Subordination of Women*. London: Fontana.

McIntyre, A. 1966. "Some Issues of Trade Policy in the West Indies," *New World Quarterly 11*(2): 1–20.

McKee, Lauris. 1984. "Sex Differentials in Survivorship and the Customary Treatment of Infants and Children," *Medical Anthropology 8*(2): 91–108.

Mead, Margaret. 1949. *Male and Female*. New York: William Morrow.

Meillassoux, Claude. 1964. *Anthropologie economiques des Gouro de Cote d'Ivoire*. Paris: Mouton.

_____. 1972. "From Reproduction to Production," *Economy and Society 1*.

_____. 1975. *Femmes, greniers et capitaux*. Paris: F. Maspero. *Maidens, Meal and Money*. Cambridge: Cambridge University Press.

Mencher, Joan P. 1988. "Women's Work and Poverty: Women's Contribution to Household Maintenance in South India," in Daisy Dwyer & Judith Bruce, eds., *A Home Divided: Women and Income in the Third World*. Stanford: Stanford University Press, pp. 99–119.

Menon, Usha. 1982. "Women and Household Labour," *Social Scientist 110* (July).

Merchant, Carolyn, 1980. *The Death of Nature: Women, Ecology, and the Scientific Revolution*. San Francisco: Harper and Row.

Michael, Robert T., & Becker, Gary S. 1973. "On the New Theory of Consumer Behavior," *Swedish Journal of Economics 75*: 378–96.

Mies, Maria. 1980. *Indian Women and Patriarchy*. New Delhi: Concept Publishing Company.

_____. 1982a. "Rural Women and the World Market," in Lourdes Beneria, ed., *Women and Development: The Sexual Division of Labor in Rural Societies*. New York: Praeger, pp. 1–28.

_____. 1982b. *Lacemakers in Narsapur: Indian Housewives Produce for the World Market*. London: Zed Press.

_____. 1986. *Patriarchy and Accumulation on a World Scale: Women in the International Division of Labor*. London: Zed Press.

Milkman, Ruth. 1976. "Women's Work and the Economic Crisis: Some Lessons from the Great Depression," *Review of Radical Political Economics 8*.

Mill, John Stuart. 1980. "On the Connection Between Justice and Utility," in John Sterba, ed., *Justice: Alternative Political Perspectives*. Belmont, Calif.: Wadsworth.

Miller, Barbara D. 1981. *The Endangered Sex: Neglect of Female Children in Rural North India*. Ithaca, N.Y.: Cornell University Press.

_____. 1982. "Female Labor Participation and Female Seclusion in Rural India: A Regional View," *Economic Development and Cultural Change 30*: 777–94.

Mincer, J. 1962. "Labour Force Participation of Married Women," in H. G. Lewis, ed., *Aspects of Labour Economics*, Princeton: N.J. Princeton University Press. Reprinted in Alice Hoffenberg Amsden, ed., 1980, *The Economics of Women and Work*. Harmondsworth: Penguin.

Mincer, J., & Polachek, S. 1974. "Family Investments in Human Capital Earnings of Women," *Journal of Political Economy 82*(2): 576–5108. Reprinted in Alice

Haffenberg Amsden ed., 1980, *The Economics of Women and Work*. Harmondsworth: Penguin.

Minow, Martha. 1987. "Feminist Reason: Getting It and Losing It," paper presented at the American Political Science Annual Meeting. Chicago, Ill., September 3–6.

Mishra, Ish. 1987. "The Women's Question in Communal Ideologies," *Teaching Politics 13*(1).

Mitchell, Juliet. 1971. *Woman's Estate*. New York: Vintage.

Mitra, Asok. 1980. *Implications of Declining Sex Ratio in India's Population*. Bombay: Allied Publishers.

Mitra, Asok, Pathak, Lalit P., & Mukherjee, Shekhar. 1980. *The Status of Women, Shift in Occupational Participation, 1961-71*. New Delhi: Abhinav Publications.

Molyneux, Maxine D. 1979. "Beyond the Domestic Labour Debate," *New Left Review 116* (July–August): 3–27.

——. 1981. "Women's Emancipation Under Socialism: A Model for the Third World," *World Development 9*(9–10): 1019–37.

——. 1982. *State Policies and the Position of Women Workers in the People's Democratic Republic of Yemen, 1967-77*. Geneva: ILO.

——. 1985. "Mobilization Without Emancipation? Women's Interests, State, and Revolution in Nicaragua," *Feminist Studies 11*(2): 227–54.

Momsen, Janet Henshall, & Townsend, Janet. 1987. *Geography of Gender in the Third World*. Albany: SUNY Press.

Morgen, Sandra, & Bookman, Ann, eds. 1988. *Women and the Politics of Empowerment: Perspectives from Workplaces and Communities*. Philadelphia: Temple University Press.

Moser, Caroline O. N. 1980. "Why the Poor Remain Poor: The Experience of Bogota Market Traders in the 1970s," *Journal of Interamerican Studies and World Affairs 22*(3): 365–87.

——. 1987. "Women, Human Settlements, and Housing: A Conceptual Framework for Analysis and Policy-Making," in C. Moser & L. Peake, eds., *Women, Human Settlements, and Housing*. London: Tavistock.

Muellbauer, John. 1987. "Professor Sen on the Standard of Living," in Amartya Sen et al., *The Standard of Living,* ed. Geoffrey Hawthorn. Cambridge: Cambridge University Press.

Mueller, Eva, with Clark, Carol, & Kossoudji, Sherri. 1978. "The Design of Employment Surveys for Developing Countries," Population Studies Centre, University of Michigan. (mimeographed)

Mukherjee, M. 1985. "Contributions to and Use of Social Product of Women," in D. Jain & N. Banerjee, eds., *Tyranny of the Household: Investigative Essays on Women's Work*. New Delhi: Vikas.

Mukhopadhyay, S. 1982. "The Nature of Household Work," Delhi School of Economics. (mimeographed)

Muntemba, Maud Shimwaayi. 1982. "Women and Agricultural Change in the Railway Region of Zambia: Dispossession and Counterstrategies, 1930-70," in Edna Bay, ed., *Women and Work in Africa*. Boulder Colo.: Westview Press.

Muzaale, Patrick J., & Leonard, David K. 1985. "Kenya's Experience with Women's Groups in Agricultural Extension," *Agricultural Administration 19*: 13–28.

Naik, J. P. 1978. Pune University Convocation Address. Pune, India.

Namboze, Josephine. 1985. "Participation of Women in Education and Communications in the Fields of Science and Technology: A National Perspective," in Shirley Malcom, Hiroko Morita-Lou, Patricia Boulware, & Sandra Burns, eds., *Science, Technology and Women: A World Perspective*. Washington, D.C.: AAAS and Centre for Science and Technology for Development, United Nations, pp. 68–73.

Nash, John F. 1950. "The Bargaining Problem," *Econometrica 18*: 155–62.

_____. 1953. "Two-Person Cooperative Games," *Econometrica 21*(1): 128–40.

Nash, June. 1983. "The Impact of the Changing International Division of Labor on Different Sectors of the Labor Force," in June Nash & Maria Patricia Fernandez-Kelly, eds, *Women, Men, and the International Division of Labor*. Albany: SUNY Press, pp. 3–38.

Nash, June, & Fernandez-Kelly, Maria Patricia, eds. 1983. *Women, Men and the International Division of Labor*. Albany: SUNY Press.

Nash, June, & Safa, Helen, eds. 1985. *Women and Change in Latin America*. South Hadley, Mass.: Bergin and Garvey.

Natarajan, K. S. n.d. "Child Mortality: Rural–Urban and Sex Differentials: Further Analysis of 1972 Fertility Survey," Indian Institute of Technology, Bombay. (mimeographed)

Nazzari, Muriel. 1980. "The Significance of Present Day Changes in the Institution of Marriage," *Review of Radical Political Economics 12*(2): 63–75.

Nerlove, Marc. 1974. "Household and Economy: Toward a New Theory of Population and Economic Growth," *Journal of Political Economy 82*(2), part 2: 200–18.

North–South Institute. 1985. *Women in Industry, North–South Connections*. Ottawa, Canada: North–South Institute.

Nozick, Robert. 1974. *Anarchy, State, and Utopia*. Oxford: Blackwell.

Oaxaca, Ronald. 1973. "Male–Female Wage Differentials in Urban Labour Markets," *International Economic Review 14*(3): 693–709.

Obbo, Christine. 1980. *African Women*. London: Zed Press.

Odugbesan, Clara. 1969 "Femininity in Yoruba Religious Art," in Mary Douglas & Phyllis M. Kaberry, eds., *Man in Africa*. London: Tavistock.

Ojo, J. R. O. 1979. "Semiotic Elements in Yoruba Art and Ritual," *Semiotica, Journal of the International Association for Semiotic Studies 28*(314): 333–48.

Okeyo, Achola Pala. 1984. *Towards Strategies for Strengthening the Position of Women in Food Production*. Nairobi: Institute of Development Studies.

Olsen, Frances. 1983. "The Family and the Market," *Harvard Law Review 96*: 1497.

Ong, Aihwa. 1983. "Global Industries and Malay Peasants in Peninsular Malaysia," in June Nash, & Maria Patricia Fernandez-Kelly, eds., *Women, Men and the International Division of Labor*. Albany: SUNY Press, pp. 426–41.

Oppong, Christine. 1974. *Marriage Among the Matrilineal Elite*. London: Cambridge University Press.

_____., ed. 1983. *Female and Male in West Africa*. London: George Allen and Unwin.

Ortner, Sherry B., & Whitehead, Harriet, eds. 1981. *Sexual Meanings: The Cultural Construction of Gender and Sexuality*. Cambridge: Cambridge University Press.

Oughton, E. 1982. "The Maharashtra Drought of 1970–73: An Analysis of Scarcity," *Oxford Bulletin of Economics and Statistics 44*.

Overholt, Catherine, Anderson, Mary B., Cloud, Kathleen, & Austin, James E., eds. 1985. *Gender Roles in Development Projects*. West Hartford, Conn.: Kumarian Press.

Padmanabha, P. 1982. "Trends in Mortality," *Economic and Political Weekly 17*(32): 1285–90.

Palmer, Ingrid. 1977. "Rural Women and the Basic Needs Approach to Development," *International Labor Review 115*(1): 97–107.

———. 1978. "Women and Green Revolution," ILO Working Paper. (mimeographed)

———. 1980. "Women in Rural Development," *International Development Review 22*: 39–45.

Pala (now Okeyo), Achola. 1977. "Definitions of Women and Development: An African Perspective," *Signs 3*(1): 9–13.

Papanek, Hanna. 1973. "Men, Women and Work: Reflections on the Two-Person Career," *American Journal of Sociology 78*(4): 852–72.

———. 1979. "The 'Work' and 'Non-Work' of Women," *Signs 4*(4): 775–81.

———. 1984. "False Specialization and the Purdah of Scholarship: A Review Article," *Journal of Asian Studies 44*(1): 127–48.

———. 1985a. "Class and Gender in Education–Employment Linkages," *Comparative Education Review 29*(3): 317–46.

———. 1985b. "Family Status-Production Work: Women's Contributions to Class Differentiation and Social Mobility," paper presented at Regional Conference on Women and the Household in Asia, New Delhi, January.

———. 1988. "Afterword: Caging the Lion: A Fable for Our Time," in Rokeya Sakhawat Hossain, *Sultana's Dream*. New York: Feminist Press, pp. 58–85.

———. Forthcoming. *The Escalator Hierarchy: Dynamics of Domestic Groups*.

Parfit, Derek. 1984. *Reasons and Persons*. Oxford: Clarendon Press.

Paulme, Denise, ed. 1960. *Femmes d'Afrique Noire*. Paris: Mouton.

———. ed. 1963. *Women in Tropical Africa*. Berkeley: University of California Press.

p'Bitek, Okot, 1967. *Song of Lawino*. Nairobi: East Africa Publishing House.

Pearce, Ibitola. 1984. "The Economics of Street Food Vending: A Case Study of Ile-Ife." Department of Sociology/Anthropology, University of Awolowo Obefemi, Ile-Ife, Nigeria.

Pearlman, Fred. 1969. *The Reproduction of Daily Life*. Detroit: Black and Red.

Pernia, Ernesto M. 1979. "The Economic Costs of Children in the Philippines: A Survey," School of Economics Discussion Paper No. 7911, University of the Philippines.

Phelps, Elizabeth. 1972. "The Statistical Theory of Racism and Sexism," *American Economic Review 62*. Reprinted in Alice Hoffenberg Amsden, ed., 1980, *The Economics of Women and Work*. Harmondsworth: Penguin.

Phongpaichit, Pasuk, 1982. *From Peasant Girls to Bangkok Masseuses*. Geneva: ILO.

Pitt, Mark, & Rosenzweig, Mark. 1985. "Health and Nutrient Consumption Across and Within Farm Households," *Review of Economics and Statistics 67*(2): 212–23.

———. 1986. "Agricultural Prices, Food Consumption and the Health and Productivity of Indonesian Farmers," in Inderjit Singh, Lyn Squire, & John Strauss, eds., *Agricultural Household Models: Extension, Applications and Policy*. Baltimore: Johns Hopkins University Press, pp. 153–82.

Piven, Frances, & Cloward, Richard. 1971. *Regulating the Poor*. New York: Pantheon Books.

Piwoz, Ellen Gail, & Viteri, Fernando E. 1984. *Understanding Health and Nutrition Behavior Through the Study of Household Decisionmaking and Intrahousehold Resource Distribution*. Washington, D.C.: Food and Nutrition Program, Pan American Health Organization (PAHO).

Poggi, Dominique, & Coormaert, Monique. 1974. "The City: Off Limits to Women," *Liberation*, July/August.

Pollak, Robert A. 1983. "A Transaction Cost Approach to Families and Households," University of Pennsylvania. (mimeographed)

Pollack, Robert A., & Wachter, Michael L. 1975. "The Relevance of the Household Production Function and Its Implications for the Allocation of Time," *Journal of Political Economics 83*(2): 255–77.

Powell, Dorian. 1986. "Caribbean Women and the Family: Their Response to Familial Experiences," *Social and Economic Studies 35*(2): 83–130.

Prochaska, Frederick J., & Schrimper, Ronald A. 1973. "Opportunity Cost of Time and Other Socioeconomic Effects on Away-from-Home Food Consumption," *American Journal of Agricultural Economics 55*(4): 595–603.

Pruitt, Ida. 1967. *A Daughter of Han: The Autobiography of a Chinese Working Woman*. Stanford: Stanford University Press.

Quick, Paddy. 1977. "The Class Nature of Women's Oppression," *Review of Radical Political Economics 9*(3): 42–53.

Rae, Douglas. 1981. *Equalities*. Cambridge, Mass.: Harvard University Press.

Rankin, Mary B. 1975. "The Emergence of Women at the End of the Ch'ing: The Case of Ch'iu Chin," in Margery Wolf and Roxane Witke, eds., *Women in Chinese Society*. Stanford: Stanford University Press, pp. 39–66.

Ravallion, Martin. 1985. "The Performance of Rice Markets in Bangladesh During the 1974 Famine," *Economic Journal 92*.

———. 1987. *Markets and Famines*. Oxford: Clarendon Press.

Rawls, John. 1971. *A Theory of Justice*. Oxford: Clarendon Press; Cambridge, Mass.: Harvard University Press.

Reddock, Rhoda. 1984. "Women Labour and Struggle in the Twentieth Century in Trinidad and Tobago: 1898–1960," doctoral diss. University of Amsterdam.

Reiter, Rayna, ed. 1975. *Toward an Anthropology of Women*. New York: Monthly Review Press.

Rey, Pierre Phillipe. 1973. *Les Alliance de Classes*. Paris: Maspero.

———. 1975. "The Lineage Mode of Production," *Critique of Anthropology 3*: 27–79.

Robertson, Claire, & Berger, Iris. 1986. *Women and Class in Africa*. New York: Africana Publishing Company.

Rochford, S. C. 1981. "Nash-Bargained Household Decision-Making in a Peasant Economy." (mimeographed)

———. 1982. "General Results for Stable Pairwise-Bargained Allocations in a Marriage Market." (mimeographed)

Rogers, Barbara. 1980. *The Domestication of Women: Discrimination in Developing Societies*. London: St. Martin's Press.

Rogers, Beatrice Lorge. 1983. "The Internal Dynamics of Households: A Critical Factor in Development Policy." School of Nutrition, Tufts University. (mimeographed)

Rosaldo, Michelle Zimbalist. 1974. "Women, Culture, and Society: A Theoretical

Overview," in Michelle Zimbalist Rosaldo and Louise Lamphere, eds., *Women, Culture, and Society*. Stanford: Stanford University Press.

Rosaldo, Michelle Zimbalist, & Lamphere, Louise, eds. 1974. *Women, Culture, and Society*. Stanford: Stanford University Press.

Rosenzweig, Mark Richard, & Schultz, T. Paul. 1982. "Market Opportunities, Genetic Endowments, and Intrafamily Resource Distribution: Child Survival in Rural India," *American Economic Review 72*(4): 803–15.

Rotberg, Robert I., & Rabb, Theodore K. 1985. *Hunger and History*. Cambridge: Cambridge University Press.

Roth, Alvin E. 1979. *Axiomatic Models of Bargaining*. Berlin: Springer-Verlag.

Rowbotham, Sheila. 1973. *Women's Consciousness, Man's World*. Harmondsworth: Penguin.

Rubin, Jeffrey Z., & Brown, Bert R. 1975. *The Social Psychology of Bargaining and Negotiation*. New York: Academic Press.

Ruddick, Sara. 1980. "Maternal Thinking," *Feminist Studies 6*(2): 342–67.

Rudolph, Hedwig. 1985. "Educating Women for the Engineering Profession," paper presented at the International Conference on Gender, Education and Technology, Rockefeller Center, Bellagio, Italy, October 7–11.

Sacks, Karen Brodkin. 1987. "A Two-Way Street: Gendering International Studies and Internationalizing Women's Studies," Working Paper 24, Southwest Institute for Research on Women, Tucson.

Safa, Helen I. 1987. "Women and Change in Latin America," in Jack Hopkins, ed., *Latin America: Perspectives on a Region*. New York: Holmes and Meier.

Safilios-Rothchild, Constantina. 1972. "Methodological Problems Involved in the Cross-Cultural Examination of Indicators Related to the Status of Women," Paper presented to the Population Association of America Meeting, Toronto, Canada, April 13–15.

Salaff, Janet. 1981. *Working Daughters of Hong Kong: Filial Piety or Power in the Family?* New York: Cambridge University Press.

Samuelson, Paul A. 1956. "Social Indifference Curves," *Quarterly Journal of Economics 70*(1): 1–22.

Sanday, Peggy Reeves. 1974. "Female Status in the Public Domain," in Michelle Zimbalist Rosaldo & Louise Lamphere, eds., *Women, Culture, and Society*. Stanford: Stanford University Press.

————. 1981. *Female Power and Male Dominance: On the Origins of Sexual Inequality*. Cambridge: Cambridge University Press.

Sandel, Michael J. 1982. *Liberalism and the Limits of Justice*. London: Cambridge University Press.

Sarvasy, Wendy. 1986. "Gender, Race, Class and the Contradictory Legacy of the Feminist Welfare State Founders," paper presented at the Western Political Science Association, Eugene, Oregon, March.

Savane, Marie-Angelique. 1984. "Feminizing Development: A Perspective," *Development 4*.

Savara, Mira. 1981. "Women in the Bombay Textile Industry," doctoral diss. Bombay University.

Scanlon, Thomas. 1975. "Preference and Urgency," *Journal of Philosophy 72*.

Scanzoni, John H. 1970. *Opportunity and the Family*. New York: Free Press.

Schelling, Thomas C. 1960. *The Strategy of Conflict*. Oxford: Clarendon Press.

Schlegel, Alice, ed. 1977. *Sexual Stratification: A Cross-Cultural View*. New York: Columbia University Press.

Schmink, Marianne, Bruce, Judith, & Kohn, Marilyn, eds. 1986. *Learning About Women and Urban Services in Latin America and the Caribbean*. New York: Population Council.

Schneider, Harold K. 1979. *Livestock and Equality in East Africa: The Economic Basis for Social Structure*. Bloomington: Indiana University Press.

Schofield, S. 1975. *Village Nutrition Studies: An Annotated Bibliography*. Brighton, Sussex: Institute of Development Studies.

Schuler, Margaret. 1986. *Empowerment and the Law: Strategies of Third World Women*. Washington, D.C.: OEF International.

Schuster, Ilsa. 1979. *New Women of Lusaka*. Palo Alto, Calif.: Mayfield.

Schutjer, Wayne, & Stokes, Shannon, eds. 1984. *Rural Development and Human Fertility*. New York: Macmillan.

Schwartz, Vanessa. 1985. "Gender and Technology: Women, the International Division of Labor, and High-Tech Production. A Selected and Annotated Bibliography." Princeton University Program in Women's Studies Bibliography No. 3.

Scott, Hilda. 1974. *Does Socialism Liberate Women?* Boston: Beacon.

———. 1984. *Working Your Way to the Bottom: The Feminization of Poverty*. Boston: Pandora Press.

Scott, Joan. 1982. "The Mechanization of Women's Work," *Scientific American*, July *247*(3): 167–87.

Seager, Joni, & Olson, Ann. 1986. *Women in the World. An International Atlas*. New York: Simon and Schuster.

Sebstad, Jennefer. 1982. *Struggle and Development Among Self Employed Women: A Report on the Self Employed Women's Association, Ahmedabad, India*. Washington D.C.: United States Agency for International Development, Bureau for Science and Technology.

Secombe, Wally. 1974. "The Housewife and Her Labour Under Capitalism," *New Left Review 83*: 3–24.

Sen, Amartya. 1970. *Collective Choice and Social Welfare*. San Francisco: Holden-Day; republished by North-Holland, Amsterdam, 1979.

———. 1975. *Employment, Technology and Development*. Oxford: Clarendon Press.

———. 1976. "Famines as Failures of Exchange Entitlements," *Economic and Political Weekly 11*.

———. 1977. "Starvation and Exchange Entitlement: A General Approach and Its Application to the Great Bengal Famine," *Cambridge Journal of Economics 1*.

———. 1981. *Poverty and Famines: An Essay on Entitlement and Deprivation*. Oxford: Clarendon Press.

———. 1982a. *Choice, Welfare and Measurement*. Oxford: Blackwell; Cambridge, Mass.: MIT Press.

———. 1982b. "Food Battles: Conflicts in the Access to Food," Coromandel Lecture, New Delhi, 13 December; rpt. *Mainstream*, January 8, 1983.

———. 1983a. "Carrots, Sticks and Economics: Perception Problems in Incentives," *Indian Economic Review 18*(1): 1–16.

———. 1983b. "Economics and the Family," *Asian Development Review 1*(2): 14–21.

———. 1984. *Resources, Values and Development*. Oxford: Blackwell; Cambridge: Harvard University Press.

————. 1985a. *Commodities and Capabilities*. Amsterdam: North-Holland.

————. 1985b. "Well-Being, Agency and Freedom: The Dewey Lectures 1984," *Journal of Philosophy 82*(4): 169–221.

————. 1985c. "Women, Technology and Sexual Divisions," *Trade and Development*. Study prepared for UNCTAD/INSTRAW. New York: United Nations.

————. 1986. "Food, Economics and Entitlements," *Lloyds Bank Review 160*.

————. 1987. *Hunger and Entitlements*. Helsinki: World Institute for Development Economics Research.

————. 1988. "Africa and India: What Do We Have to Learn from Each Other?," in K. J. Arrow, ed., *The Balance between Industry and Agriculture in Economic Development*. London: Macmillan.

————. 1989. "Women's Survival as a Development Problem," *American Academy of Arts and Sciences,* forthcoming.

Sen, Amartya K., & Sengupta, Sunil. 1983. "Malnutrition of Rural Children and the Sex Bias," *Economic and Political Weekly 18* (19–21): 855–63.

Sen, Amartya K., & Williams, Bernard, eds. 1982. *Utilitarianism and Beyond*. Cambridge: Cambridge University Press.

Sen, Gita. 1985. "Women Agricultural Labourers: Regional Variations in Traders and Employment," in D. Jain & N. Banerjee, eds., *Tyranny of the Household: Investigative Essays on Women's Work*. New Delhi: Vikas.

————. 1988. "Ethics in Third World Development: A Feminist Perspective," Rama Mehta Lecture, Radcliffe College, Harvard University, April 28.

Sen, Gita, & Grown, Caren. 1987. *Development, Crises, and Alternative Visions: Third World Women's Perspectives 2nd ed*. New York: Monthly Review Press. Written for the project Development Alternatives for Women in a New Era: DAWN. First edition without authors' names published by DAWN 1985.

Senauer, Benjamin, & Garcia, Marito. 1988. "The Determinants of Food Consumption and Nutritional Status Among Preschool Children: Evidence from the Rural Philippines," University of Minnesota, St. Paul. (mimeographed)

Senauer, Benjamin, Garcia, Marito, & Jacinto, Elizabeth. 1988. "Determinants of the Intrahousehold Allocation of Food in the Rural Philippines," *American Journal of Agricultural Economics 70*(1): 170–80.

Senauer, Benjamin, Sahn, David, & Alderman, Harold. 1986. "The Effect of the Value of Time on Food Consumption Patterns in Developing Countries: Evidence from Sri Lanka," *American Journal of Agricultural Economics 68*(4): 920–27.

Shanin, Teodor, ed. 1971. *Peasants and Peasant Societies*. London: Penguin.

Sharma, Kumud. 1988. "Macro Policies Relating to Natural Resource Management (land, water, forest): Marginalization of Poor Rural Women." New Delhi: Centre for Women's Development Studies (CWDS). (mimeographed)

Sharma, Kumud. n.d. *Women in Struggle: Role and Participation of Women in the Chipko Movement in Uttarakhand Region of Uttah Pradesh, India*. Geneva: ILO.

Sharma, Kumud, with Hussain, Sahba, & Saharya, Archana. 1984. *Women in Focus*. New Delhi: Sangam Books.

Sharma, Kumud, with Panday & Nautigal. 1987. *Social Forestry and Women's Development*. New Delhi: Centre for Women's Development Studies (CWDS).

Sharma, Kumud, & Sarkar, Lotika. 1986. *Women, Media and Prostitution: A Com-*

parative Study in South and South East Asia. New Delhi: Centre for Women's Development Studies (CWDS).

Sharma, Ram Sharan. 1965. *Indian Feudalism, c.300–c.1200*. University of Calcutta: Centre of Advanced Study in Ancient Indian History and Culture.

Sharma, Ursula. 1980. *Women, Work and Property in North-West India*. London: Tavistock.

———. 1986. *Women's Work, Class, and the Urban Household: A Study of Shimla, North India*. London: Tavistock.

Sheshinski, E., & Weiss, Y. 1982. "Inequality Within and Between Families," *Journal of Political Economy 90*.

Shklar, Judith N. 1986. "Injustice, Injury and Inequality: An Introduction," in Frank S. Lucash, ed., *Justice and Equality Here and Now*. Ithaca, N.Y.: Cornell University Press, 13–33.

Shubik, Martin. 1983. *Game Theory in the Social Sciences: Concepts and Solutions*. Cambridge, Mass.: MIT Press.

Singer, H. 1977. *Technologies for Basic Needs*. Geneva: ILO.

Singh, Andrea Menefee, & Kelles-Viitanen, Anita, eds. 1987. *Invisible Hands: Women in Home-Based Production*. New Delhi: Sage Publications.

Slocum, S. 1975. "Women the Gatherer: Male Bias in Anthropology," in Rayna Reiter, ed., *Toward an Anthropology of Women*. New York: Monthly Review Press. Rpt. M. Evans, ed. 1982. *The Woman Question: Readings on the Subordination of Women*. London: Fontana.

Smith, James P., ed. 1980. *Female Labor Supply: Theory and Practice*. Princeton, N.J.: Princeton University Press.

Smith, Mary. 1954. *Baba of Kano*. London: Faber & Faber.

Smock, Audrey. 1981. *Women's Education in Developing Countries*. New York: Praeger.

Snowdon, B. 1985. "The Political Economy of the Ethiopian Famine," *National Westminster Bank Quarterly Review*.

Sokoloff, Natalie J. 1980. *Between Money and Love: The Dialectics of Women's Home and Market Work*. New York: Praeger.

Solow, Robert M. 1984. "Relative Deprivation?," *Partisan Review 51*.

Sopher, David Edward. 1980. *An Exploration of India: Geographical Perspective on Society and Culture*. London: Longman.

Souza-Lobo, Elizabeth. 1986. "The Sexual Division of Labour in Brazilian Industry," in IDRC Manuscript Report Women in Development: Perspectives from the Nairobi Conference. Ottawa: International Development Research Centre.

Srinivas, Mysore Narasemhashar. 1974. Foreword, in A. M. Shah, *The Household Dimension of the Family in India*. Berkeley: University of California Press.

———. 1984. *Social Change in India and Changing Position of Women in Developing Countries*. New Delhi: Centre for Women's Development Studies (CWDS).

Srinivasan, Mangalam. 1982. *Technology Assessment and Development*. New York: Praeger.

———. 1982. "The Impact of Science and Technology and the Role of Women in Science in Mexico," in Pamela M. D'Onofrio-Flores and Sheila M. Pfafflin, eds., *Scientific-Technological Change and the Role of Women in Development*. Boulder, Colo.: Westview Press. pp. 113–48.

Standing, G., & Sheehan, G. eds. 1978. *Labour Force Participation in Low-Income Countries*. Geneva: ILO.

Staudt, Kathleen. 1982. "Bureaucratic Resistance to Women's Programs: The Case of Women in Development," in Ellen Boneparth, ed., *Women, Power, and Policy*. New York: Pergamon Press.

———. 1984. *Agricultural Policy Implementation: A Case Study from Western Kenya*. West Hartford, Conn.: Kumarian Press.

Staudt, Kathleen, & Jaquette, Jane, eds. 1983. *Women in Developing Countries: A Policy Focus*. New York: Haworth Press.

———. 1987. "Women's Programs, Bureaucratic Resistance and Feminist Organizations," in Ellen Boneparth and Emily Stoper, eds. *Women, Power and Policy*. New York: Pergamon Press.

Stewart, Frances. 1977. *Technology and Underdevelopment*. New York: Macmillan.

Stolcke, Verena. 1981. "Women's Labours: The Naturalisation of Social Inequality and Women's Subordination," in Kate Young, C. Wolkowitz, & R. McCullagh, eds., *On Marriage and the Market: Women's Subordination in International Perspective*. London: CSE Books, pp. 30–48.

Stone, Lawrence. 1977. *The Family, Sex, and Marriage in England, 1500–1800*. London: Weidenfeld.

Strauss, John. 1986. "Does Better Nutrition Raise Farm Productivity?," *Journal of Political Economy 94*(2): 297–320.

———. 1987. "Households, Communities, and Preschool Children's Nutrition Outcomes: Evidence from the Rural Cote d'Ivoire," Economics Department, Yale University. (mimeographed)

Stromquist, Nelly. 1985. "Empowering Women Through Knowledge: Politics and Practices in International Cooperation in Basic Education." Manuscript submitted to UNICEF.

Sultana, Monawar. 1988. "Participation, Empowerment, and Variation in Development Projects for Rural Bangladeshi Women," doctoral diss. Northeastern University.

Swaminathan, M. S. 1985. "The Role of Education and Research in Enhancing Rural Women's Income and Household Happiness," first J. P. Naik Memorial Lecture, Centre for Women's Development Studies, New Delhi.

Tadesse, Zenebeworke. 1982. "Women and Technology in Peripheral Countries: An Overview," in Pamela M. D'Onofrio-Flores & Sheila M. Pfafflin, eds., *Scientific-Technological Change and the Role of Women in Development*. Boulder, Colo.: Westview Press. pp. 77–111.

Taylor, Charles. 1986. "The Nature and Scope of Distributive Justice," in Frank S. Lucash, ed., *Justice and Equality Here and Now*. Ithaca: Cornell University Press, pp. 34–67.

Taylor, Debbie, ed. 1985. *Women: A World Report. A New Internationalist Book*. London: Oxford University Press.

Taylor, John G. 1979. *From Modernization to Modes of Production*. London: Macmillan.

Tendler, Judith. 1987. *What Happened to Poverty Alleviation?* New York: Ford Foundation.

Tilly, Louise A. 1985. "Food Entitlement, Famine and Conflict," in R. I. Rotberg & T. K. Rabb, eds., *Hunger and History*. Cambridge: Cambridge University Press.

———. 1986. "Sex and Occupation in Comparative Perspectives," New School for Social Research, New York. (mimeographed)

Tilly, Louise, & Scott, Joan. 1978. *Women, Work and Family*. New York and London: Holt, Rinehart and Winston.

Tinker, Irene. 1976a. "The Adverse Impact of Development on Women," in Irene Tinker & Michelle Bo Bramsen, eds., *Women and World Development*. New York: Praeger.

_____. 1976b. "Women in Developing Societies: Economic Independence Is Not Enough," in Jane Roberts Chapman, ed., *Economic Independence for Women: The Foundation for Equal Rights*. Beverly Hills, Calif.: Sage Publications, pp. 113-35.

_____. 1981. "New Technologies for Food-Related Activities: An Equity Strategy," in Roslyn Dauber & Melinda L. Cain, eds., *Women and Technological Change in Developing Countries*. Boulder, Colo.: Westview Press, pp. 51-88.

_____. 1983. "Women in Development," in Irene Tinker, ed., *Women in Washington: Advocates for Public Policy*. Beverly Hills, Calif.: Sage Publications, pp. 227-38.

_____. 1984. "The Percy Amendment Promoting Women in Development: Its Origin, Meaning, and Impact." Washington, D.C.: Equity Policy Center.

_____. 1985. "Feminist Values: Ethnocentric or Universal?," in M. J. Goodman, ed., *Women in Asia and the Pacific: Towards an East–West Dialogue*. Published for University of Hawaii Women's Studies Program by University of Hawaii Press.

_____. 1987a. "The Real Rural Energy Crisis: Women's Time," *Energy Journal 8*: 125-46.

_____. 1987b. *Street Foods: Testing Assumptions About Informal Sector Activity by Women and Men. Current Sociology 35*(3). Total issue. Issue reprinted as a book.

_____. 1987c. "The Human Economy of Micro-entrepreneurs," address to the International Seminar on Women in Micro- and Small-scale Enterprise Development, convened by the Canadian International Development Agency, October 26, 1987.

_____. 1989. "Credit for Poor Women: Necessary but Not Always Sufficient for Change," *Journal of the Marga Institute*, Colombo, Sri Lanka, special issue on women.

Tinker, Irene, & Bo Bramsen, Michelle, eds. 1976. *Women and World Development*. New York: Praeger.

Tinker, Irene, & Jaquette, Jane. 1987. "UN Decade for Women: Its Impact and Legacy," *World Development 15*(3): 419-27.

Tinker, Irene, & Cho, Hyoung. 1981. "Women's Participation in Community Development in Korea," in Man-Gap Lee, ed., *Toward a New Community Life: Reports of International Research Seminar on the Saemaul Movement*. Seoul: Seoul National University.

Trikla, Sushil K. 1985. *Women Workers in Kandla Free Trade Zone*. Bombay: Tata Institute of Social Sciences.

Tuden, Arthur, & Plotnicov, Leonard. 1970. *Social Stratification in Africa*. New York: Free Press.

United Nations. 1984. Department of International Economic and Social Affairs. *Improving Concepts and Methods for Statistics and Indicators on the Situation of Women*. New York: United Nations.

USDA (U.S. Department of Agriculture, Nutrition Economics Group, Office of International Cooperation and Development). 1983. *Intra-Family Food Dis-*

tribution: Review of the Literature and Policy Implications. Washington, D.C.

Vaughan, Megan. 1985. "Famine Analysis and Family Relations," *Past and Present 108* (August): 177–205.

———. 1987. *The Story of an African Famine: Gender and Famine in Twentieth-Century Malawi.* Cambridge: Cambridge University Press.

Venkatramani, S. H. 1986. "Female Infanticide: Born to Die," *India Today*, June 15, pp. 10–17.

Ventura-Dias, V. 1982. "Technological Change, Production Organization and Rural Women in Kenya," ILO Working Paper, Geneva.

Visaria, P. 1961. *The Sex Ratio of the Population of India*, Monograph 10, Census of India 1961. New Delhi: Office of the Registrar General.

Visaria, P., & Visaria, L. 1985. "Indian Households with Female Heads," in D. Jain & N. Banerjee, eds., *Tyranny of the Household: Investigative Essays on Women's Work.* New Delhi: Vikas.

Vogel, Lise. 1983. *Marxism and the Oppression of Women.* New Brunswick, N.J.: Rutgers University Press.

Vora, D. N. 1975. *Liberal Thought in Maharashtra.* University of Pune, unpublished doctoral diss.

Waerness, Kari. 1978. "The Invisible Welfare State: Women's Work at Home," *Acta Sociologica 21* (Supplement): 193–207.

Waldron, I. 1976. "Why Do Women Live Longer Than Men?," *Social Science Medicine.*

Walker, S. Tjip. 1987. *Making Agricultural Extension Work with Women: The Efforts of MIDENO in Cameroon.* Chevy Chase, Md.: Equity Policy Center.

Walzer, Michael. 1983. *Spheres of Justice: A Defense of Pluralism and Equality.* New York: Basic Books.

Ward, Barbara E., ed. 1963. *Women in the New Asia: Changing Social Roles of Men and Women in South and Southeast Asia.* Paris: UNESCO.

Ward, Kathryn B. 1986. "Women and Transnational Corporation Employment: A World-System and Feminist Analysis," Women in International Development Working Paper No. 120, Michigan State University.

Warren, Kay B. 1986. "Capitalist Expansion and the Moral Order: Anthropological Perspectives," in David Krueger & Bruce Gruelle, eds., *Christianity and Capitalism: Perspectives on Religion, Liberalism and the Economy.* Chicago: Center for the Scientific Study of Religion.

Warren, Kay B., & Bourque, Susan C. 1985. "Gender, Power, and Communication: Women's Responses to Political Muting in the Andes," in Susan C. Bourque & Donna Robinson Divine, eds., *Women Living Change.* Philadelphia: Temple University Press, 355–86.

Wasserstrom, Robert. 1985. *Grassroots Development in Latin America.* New York: Praeger.

Weitzman, Lengre J. 1981. *The Marriage Contract.* New York: Free Press.

Werneke, Diane. 1983. *Micro-electronics and Office Jobs: The Impact of the Chip on Women's Employment.* Geneva: ILO.

Wheeler, E. F. 1984. "Intrahousehold Food Allocation: A Review of Evidence," London School of Hygiene and Tropical Medicine. (mimeographed)

Whitehead, Ann. 1981. "A Conceptual Framework for the Analysis of the Effects of Technological Change on Rural Women," ILO Working Paper, Geneva.

———. 1984. "Women's Solidarity—and Divisions Among Women," *Institute of Development Studies, University of Sussex, Bulletin 15*(1): 6–11.

_____. 1985. "Effects of Technological Change on Rural Women: A Review of Analysis and Concepts," in Iftikhar Ahmed, ed., *Technology and Rural Women: Conceptual and Empirical Issues*. London: George Allen and Unwin, pp. 27–64.

_____. In press. "Gender and Famine in West Africa," *Review of African Political Economy*, forthcoming.

Williams, Bernard Arthur Owen. 1973. "A Critique of Utilitarianism," in B. Williams & J. J. C. Smart, eds., *Utilitarianism For and Against*. Cambridge: Cambridge University Press.

Williamson, Oliver E. 1979. "Transaction-Cost Economics: The Governance of Contractual Relations," *Journal of Law and Economics 22*(2): 233–61.

Wilson, Gail. 1987. *Money in the Family*. Aldershot: Avesbury.

Wolf, Margery. 1985. *Revolution Postponed: Women in Contemporary China*. Stanford: Stanford University Press.

Wolff, Robert Paul. 1977. *Understanding Rawls: A Reconstruction and a Critique of "A Theory of Justice."* Princeton: Princeton University Press.

Wolgast, Elizabeth. 1980. *Equality and the Rights of Women*. Ithaca, N.Y.: Cornell University Press.

Worland, Stephen T. 1986. "Economics and Justice," in Ronald L. Cohen, ed., *Justice: Views from the Social Sciences*. New York: Plenum, pp. 47–84.

World Development Report 1986. Published for the World Bank by Oxford University Press.

Wyon, John B., & Gordon, John E. 1971. *The Khanna Study*. Cambridge: Harvard University Press.

Young, Iris. 1981. "Beyond the Unhappy Marriage: A Critique of Dual Systems Theory," in Lydia Sargent, ed., *Women and Revolution*. Boston: South End Press, pp. 43–70.

Young, Kate. 1978. "Modes of Appropriation and the Sexual Division of Labour: A Case Study of Oaxaca, Mexico," in Annette Kuhn & Ann Marie Wolpe, eds., *Feminism and Imperialism*. London: Routledge and Kegan Paul.

_____. 1984. "Future Rapid Appraisal Work of the IDS Women's Cluster," *Institute of Development Studies, University of Sussex Bulletin 15*(1): 62–63.

Young, Kate, & Moser, Caroline, eds., 1981. "Women and the Informal Sector," *Institute of Development Studies, University of Sussex Bulletin 12*(3).

Young, Kate, Wolkowitz, C., & McCullagh, R., eds. 1981. *On Marriage and the Market: Women's Subordination in International Perspective*. London: CSE Books.

Youssef, Nadia H., & Hetler, Carol. 1983., "Rural Households Headed by Women: A Priority Concern for Development," ILO World Employment Programme Working Paper, Geneva.

Youssef, Nadia H., Nieves, Isabel, & Sebstad, Jennefer. 1980. *Keeping Women Out: A Structural Analysis of Women's Employment in Developing Countries*. Washington, D.C.: International Center for Research on Women.

Yudelman, Sally. 1987. *Hopeful Openings: A Study of Five Women's Development Organizations in Latin America and the Caribbean*. West Hartford, Conn.: Kumarian Press.

Zeuthen, Frederik. 1930. *Problems of Monopoly and Economic Welfare*. London: Routledge and Kegan Paul.

Zimmerman, Jan. 1982. "Technology and the Future of Women: Haven't We Met Somewhere Before?," in Joan Rothschild, ed., *Women, Technology and Innovation*. New York: Pergamon Press, pp. 355–67.

Index